Roberts R.A.

THE LEVANT

THE LEVANT

History and Archaeology
in the Eastern Mediterranean

EDITOR

Olivier Binst

PHOTOGRAPHY

Robert Polidori

AUTHORS

Pierre-Louis Gatier

Eric Gubel

Philippe Marquis

Laïla Nehmé

Marie-Odile Rousset

Jean-Baptiste Yon

KÖNEMANN

Preface

Western culture today is considered to be the result of traditions and intellectual achievements rooted in the ancient east. Archaeology (etymologically derived from *archaios*, old, and *logos*, science) gives substance to this knowledge of ancient cultures by showing us their monuments and tangible traces. The very term *monument* evokes this aspect of archaeology very strikingly. It conjures up the work of human hand, in a form that aims to perpetuate the memory of the past.

Every country has its cultural legacy that needs preserving and from which all humanity and future generations can profit. It is a legacy that is handed on from each generation to the next, in order to build the future.

Few relics of our past survive. Once they are destroyed, we can never bring them back. Although the Greeks elevated some outstanding structures to the status of the seven wonders of the world, usually the only value of an abandoned monument was to serve as a quarry for the next generation. Only in the 19th century, with the emergence of national consciousness, did the concept of mankind's cultural heritage develop in contemporary thinking, and along with that awareness, the obligation to protect this heritage.

The result was that Western travelers packed their bags and ventured eastwards to admire ruins overgrown with weeds or buried under the sand. However, it is only in our day that the remnants of ancient cities have drawn thousands of sightseers year after year. Is this enthusiasm based only on curiosity and the desire of people to gaze in wonder at the "exotic" with their own eyes? My view is that, in a society where so many basic values are under threat, men and women sense a need to return to those values, on which time has conferred great importance and a reassuring aura. The visible traces of cultures, such as the evidence of their faiths, rites, and customs, constitute the common, irreplaceable legacy of everyone on this planet. The value of these testimonials of the past knows no frontiers. They are an inalienable component of the collective heritage and remembrance of all mankind.

The present volume draws our attention to the masterpieces that were created in the cradle of humanity, making them accessible to a broad public and reminding us all of our global responsibility towards the present and all following generations.

Mounir Bouchenaki
Director, Cultural Department, UNESCO

Crusader castle, Byblos
The history of the Phoenician port and trading city of Byblos goes back 7,000 years. In the foreground the last ruins of antiquity that served the Crusaders as a quarry still stand. The Crusader castle in the background consists of a square keep and its surrounding walls.

Foreword

It is surprising that a book about the archaeology of the Levant, which here means more specifically the region east of the Mediterranean between Turkey in the north and Egypt in the west, should appear only now. This is after all the very region which has always acted as a natural intermediary between Europe and the East. Not only writers, painters and scholars of past centuries succumbed to the magic of what is the Levant's familiarity and yet at the same time its otherness. In the first lines of his *Histories*, the "father of history" himself, Herodotus of Halicarnassus (d. c. 430 B.C.), assumes a causal connection between the Phoenicians – the inhabitants of the Levant – and the contrast and interaction between Orient and Occident.

The present volume sums up the results of research in various disciplines. During the period of the French mandate in Syria and Lebanon, it was largely French scholars who substantially advanced the state of our knowledge. They were the first to investigate thoroughly the three great Phoenician cities of Byblos, Sidon (Saida) and Tyre. To them we are also indebted for work at Mari on the Euphrates, an important link between the Levant and Mesopotamia, and Ugarit (Ras Shamra) on the Syrian coast of the Mediterranean, where historically important religious texts in an alphabetic script (in contrast with ancient oriental syllabic scripts) were discovered. French scholars were likewise to the fore in the thorough study of early Christian architecture and the art of Syria, and indeed in investigating the art and architecture of the Islamic and Crusader periods.

At the beginning of the 20th century, German and British archaeologists were active in the region for reasons not entirely unconnected with politics and strategy. Since World War II, scholarship has become increasingly international. Nowadays Japanese excavation teams work alongside Dutch, Polish, and American teams, or Germans alongside British or French. In fact, beside the national projects, teams of international composition are increasingly common. New finds are made almost every day, and new links are discovered that convey a perceptibly more and more differentiated and variegated picture of the area known as the Levant.

The concept of the Levant – the historical and once greater Syria which Arabs of the medieval period justly saw as a region of culture and called "*Bilad el-Sham*" or "The Syrian lands" or "Lands of Syria" – has almost vanished from common parlance in recent times. The reason for this is to be sought in the developments during the period since 1918.

The end of World War I also terminated a fascinating state entity, the Turkish Ottoman Empire, which since the early 16th century had encompassed within its frontiers the Levant in a wider sense, from Greece via the coast of Asia Minor down to Egypt. It was in many respects a modern state and not just the oriental despotism that it is often blithely said to have been. The Ottoman empire was modern in that it had found a form of statehood that allowed a wide range of ethnic groups and religions to coexist peacefully and with dignity for lengthy periods. Under its umbrella, the concept of the Levantine developed in European language usage as a type of human being whose sophistication, complicated genealogy and polyglotism linked Orient and Occident via the Mediterranean for centuries, thus bestowing on him the mantle of the Phoenicians.

After World War I, "Levantines" saw themselves increasingly as belonging to individual states. Today, these states are Syria, Lebanon, the autonomous area of Palestine, Jordan and Israel. That their peoples – Jordanians, Palestinians, Lebanese and Syrians – are inhabitants of a culturally unified region, linked moreover by a common language,

Bronze statuettes, Byblos
18th cent. B.C., bronze, partially gilt; height c. 15 cm. Archaeological Museum, Beirut
These deity figurines were found hidden in a barrel in the obelisk temple of Byblos.
It has yet to be established to which deity the temple was dedicated.

history, and close family ties, is easily forgotten. Mutual enmities, and since the foundation of Israel in 1948, ongoing conflict between the new state and its neighbors, have distorted the view of the Levant as a unity of culture and history.

This culture not only linked Europe with the Orient, but in the same degree the Orient with Europe. It is here that we should seek the roots of the Levant's importance for human history. The reason for this is the Levant's geographical location: it lies between Mesopotamia and Egypt, twin centers of highly developed ancient eastern cultures, between the Mediterranean and deposit-rich mountain ranges that slope down to it, between the agricultural belt east of these mountain ranges and the desert plains that mark its frontier with the Arabian peninsula. We do not need to be prophets to predict that the importance of the region will continue to lie in this unique and favorable situation in the not too distant future. It is the predestined intermediary, the intermediary it has often been in history and will be again in the future.

The present volume will surely encourage travel to this cradle of western civilization, the area whence the "western" God and "western" alphabet came, where the roots of "western" art lie, not just early Greek art but also early Christian art. A region that to a considerable extent determined what we mean by theology and philosophy, and that fashioned the forms of our language, historical perception and statehood. We need to understand the region over and above its current frontiers and appreciate the unity of a unique cultural area, whether we call it "Levant" or "Bilad el-Sham."

Heinz Gaube
Oriental Seminar, Tübingen

The Levant

Artists and literary figures of the 19th century painted a mainly Romantic picture of the Levant, as the watercolors of the Scottish painter David Roberts (1796–1864) or *Travels in the Orient* by Alphonse de Lamartine (1790–1869) bear out. But it really does exist, this legendary region between sea, mountains and desert, characterized by specific landscapes, kinds of people, vegetation, and cultures.

The charms and characteristics of the Levant are nowadays probably valued most because of the constant presence of its glorious past. This is only partially familiar to us, for example when we consider the legend of Europa, the Phoenician princess who gave Europe its name. In fact the region still holds in reserve surprises, in the great archaeological discoveries such as those at Ebla. What was originally only known as a name in Mesopotamian texts was revealed as a city – indeed, more than that, a royal city whose history could be reconstructed through the discovery of thousands of inscribed tablets. The subjects of these inscriptions range from great events to the most trivial occurrences.

In the Levant, where writing was used very early on – indeed, where the alphabet was invented and where historians have been provided with an extraordinary tool for their work – written material is still not enough to investigate the past.

The buildings that successive civilizations have left behind are no longer considered just as typical features of the Levantine landscape. They are much more: they illustrate the legends, customs, and changing fortunes of the region. It is through them that we have any access at all to its history, or can extend our knowledge of it. To the traveler exploring the Levant for the first time, it appears as a cornucopia of archaeological sites, presenting scholars with an inexhaustible resource from all historical periods.

Some cultures have of course been better treated by time than others. Greco-Roman antiquity and its monumental buildings are more easily comprehensible to the eye of a modern archaeologist than much older brick walls standing half-ruined over the site of a tomb. The following chapters will reflect the differences in quality and quantity of the archaeological evidence and finds dating from different eras over the millennia.

Mountains on the road to the Dead Sea
The mountains with their dry climate form the eastern frontier of the Dead Sea rift. Although these heights did not constitute a real obstacle to settlement and communication, the natural balance is not at all stable, and the survival of people settling here is always at risk.

Dead Sea
Singular in every respect, the Dead Sea lies about 1,600 feet (500 m) below sea level in a trough that runs through the Levant from north to south. Despite an almost menacing landscape, people have settled in the vicinity since earliest times.

The geological formation

The countries of the Levant, lying between the landmasses of Eurasia and Africa, are a western continuation of the extensive geological formation that constitutes the Arabian peninsula, opening expansively seawards on to the Mediterranean basin.

The physical geography of the countries of the Levant is characterized by a number of large elements that for the most part cross political frontiers and are thus common to all countries. Nonetheless, there are differences in the character of the landscapes of Syria and Jordan, and the mountains in Lebanon are higher than those further south in the range and the foothills.

The coast – The eastern end of the Mediterranean forms the coast of the Levant; it is exposed to the prevailing east and north winds. As far south as Lake Tiberias it is largely rocky, but from the Gaza Strip on it is lower and sandier. Along the whole length of this coastal strip are a series of interlocking rocky foothills exposed by currents and local geology. These capes (*ras* in Arabic) were useful as anchorages or navigation points for the seamen of antiquity. When the modern ports came to be laid out, in most cases advantage was taken of these natural harbors, in use since time immemorial.

Between the coast proper and the first of the high ground we find a fertile coastal plain in the north of Syria, in northern Lebanon and at the mouths of the most important rivers that flow down from the mountains of Lebanon.

The Lebanon Mountains and their foothills – The most important mountain massif both in extent and height is the Lebanon Mountains, which reach a height of 10,131 feet (3,098 m) and constitute a real natural barrier within the country. Its northern extension is Jebel Ansariye (the Ansariye Range), in Syria, while the hills of Galilee lie to the south. This Tertiary-formation range contains a great wealth of minerals, especially metals (gold, copper, etc.). It is a major obstacle to communications, and can only be crossed via certain passes. For this reason it has also served as a refuge, and developed into a rich repository of cultures and traditions.

The Bekaa Valley – The Bekaa and its foothills (in the north forming the basin of the Ghab and the Gujor, and in the south the valley of the Jordan) represent an extremely uneven topography. The Bekaa is in fact a trough, caused by sinking, and is the northern extension of the Rift Valley in Africa. From a maximum height of 5,250 feet (1600 m) in the region of Baalbek it falls away toward the north and even more toward the south, where the Dead Sea lies at 1,286 feet (392 m) below sea level. This grouping forms an axis of easy communication from north to south.

The Anti-Lebanon Mountains – The Anti-Lebanon range, whose foothills are the Zawiye and Jebel Seman ranges in the north and Mount Hermon and the uplands of western Jordan in the south, is somewhat less of a barrier than the Lebanon Mountains, even though it reaches over 6,500 feet (2,000 m) in places (8,000 feet/2,464 m in Syria). Its windward side is steep in some areas, while the lee forms something of a plateau sloping east. The Anti-Lebanon range does not really present an obstacle to communication and trade, but is more of a natural frontier between two natural zones.

The steppe – Beyond the Anti-Lebanon Mountains is a steppe region with sparse vegetation, almost having the character of a desert. In this extensive area of rock massifs of volcanic origin, the most remarkable irregularities of terrain are the Jebel Druz, the Hauran and the Palmyrene hill chains (Jebel Sharqui, Jebel Abu Rumanieh).

Wadi Rum
The desert around Wadi Rum in Jordan displays all the classic features: sand dunes, hardly any vegetation, and cliffs scorched by the sun. Before tourist groups began to overrun the region, Wadi Rum was an important transit artery for the not always peaceful relations between the Levant and the nomads of the desert. The latter represented the essential link in maintaining contacts over the whole Arabian peninsula.

The hydrography of the region

In any explanation of the development of human settlements in the Levantine countries, the hydrography of the region must play a very important role. In districts where water is particularly valuable because agriculture depends on it, the distribution of the streams and rivers is often an essential precondition and indicator that human communities were able to occupy the area time and again.

Most of the streams spring from within Lebanon and irrigate the coastal plain of the Levant. They are very short water courses that carry irregular, though very considerable, volumes of water and are therefore prone to cause violent flooding in surrounding areas.

The Bekaa plain and its southern extension give rise to more substantial rivers – the Litani and Nahr el-Asi, once known as the Orontes – whose valley bottoms allow easy crossing of the coastal region, like the river Jordan in the south. The latter is fed by tributaries running off Mount Hermon or the uplands of western Jordan.

The Anti-Lebanon is the source of smaller water courses such as the Barada or Maraba. Despite their rather low water volumes, they are very important to a region whose agriculture is heavily dependent on irrigation.

The only major river of the Levant is the Euphrates (1,450 miles/2,330 km in length, of which about one fifth is in Syria), which with its major tributaries the Belikh and the Khabur not only form an inexhaustible water supply but also a transport and communications route, being all the more important for enabling access to lower Mesopotamia and the Persian Gulf.

Natural resources

Mineral resources are few in this region compared with what Cyprus and Anatolia, for example, can offer. Minor deposits of precious metals are indeed found in the Lebanon Mountains, but nothing that would justify substantial mining.

The forests, once so substantial, have been almost completely destroyed. Trees such as cedars, which provided excellent timber for buildings and ships, were plentifully available on the well-watered slopes of the Lebanon. But despite the favorable climatic conditions for the development of these tree species, predatory consumption of such natural resources by man, decimating the tree stocks very rapidly, dates back a long way.

Climatic conditions and the volume of rainfall in the coastal area encourage agriculture. Likewise, agriculture is possible in the central ranges, the Syrian rift, and in the steppe region and the oases. Although here even minimal variations in climate can make the efforts of their inhabitants a hazardous business.

For the remainder of the region, the paleoclimatic data do not indicate any great breaks in general climatic conditions since the Bronze Age. Of course, even minor variations in the volume of rainfall or temperature levels sometimes had a dramatic effect on vegetation stocks and the upper layers of sediment, which easily fell victim to erosion, particularly if they coincided with the periods of intensive timber-felling and settlement of the cultivable land.

Afqa

According to popular tradition, the springs of Nahr Ibrahim in the heart of the Lebanon Mountains have been a source of fertility since time immemorial. They are of the greatest importance today, as the reserves of the Lebanon range provide the whole region with water for agricultural purposes. According to legend, Adonis fell victim to his own foolhardiness at this spot.

Philippe Marquis

The Bronze Age
The Birth of a Civilization

3100–1200 B.C.

Palace G, Ebla

Ebla is one of the most important north Syrian
sites of the 3rd millennium. Palace G
constitutes its largest interconnected complex
of the period. In 1974 thousands of inscribed
tablets were found in the administrative
quarters of the palace, and these are what
made the site so special for scholars. This
picture shows the arrangement of the rooms in
the vicinity of the ceremonial staircase and
audience court. These were the rooms kept for
the archives.

Lake Tiberias

Lake Tiberias forms one of the biggest freshwater reservoirs in the region. The river Jordan flows down from the Lebanon Mountains into it and runs right through it. Its natural resources caught the attention of those passing through very early on, and today it still constitutes a focal point of agricultural activity, even if its fish stocks have been seriously depleted since ancient times and its eastern shore is less irrigated and less inviting than the western shore.

Illustration, pp. 16–17

Wadi Rum

Even if the desert constitutes a natural environment unsuited to permanent settlement, it is by no means devoid of humans. A few archaeological traces prove that small groups of people regularly passed through or visited Wadi Rum, which directly borders the Levant region. Nomadic shepherds, traders, and clerics were those who ventured into these magnificent landscapes.

The first cities

Archaeological work in the Levant has led to extensive discoveries of early urban cultures mentioned in biblical texts and reports by ancient classical authors, but of which no clear picture has emerged.

It took the pioneering work of the French archaeologist Ernest Renan, which began in 1860 after France intervened in the Lebanon, to bring us to a better understanding of the origins and development of the cities in the area.

Initially, the area had seemed less rich in important sites than the Nile Valley. However, French excavations in Byblos, initially by Renan, then from 1921 by Pierre Montet and later Maurice Dunand, in Mari (Tell Hariri), by André Parrot from 1933 and then by Jean Claude Margueron, and finally the discovery of the city of Ebla in 1979 by the Italian team led by Paolo Matthiae – just to name a few – quickly showed that the Levant was in no way lacking in archaeological riches compared to its neighbor, and that this region should be considered remarkable in its own right. There were of course territorial differences, but the Levant was certainly not to be thought of as just an extension of the New Assyrian, Late Babylonian or other empires.

The history of human habitation is evident in a network of settlements that exploited as far as possible the opportunities afforded by existing natural circumstances, and whose characteristics modern archaeology has endeavored to reconstruct. It is also traceable in new territories taken over which had hitherto been less intensively occupied. In the meantime we need to remember that while through scholarship we are beginning to understand the developmental processes of cities, very little is known about rural life and segments of population that lived on the edge of urban cultures.

Finally, it should also be remembered – with regard to this period perhaps more than with others – how fragile a basis underpins historical reconstructions using archaeological data. The wealth of the archaeological potential of the Levant should not allow us to overlook the fact that only a tiny fragment of the possible archaeological material evidence is available, and that the early history of these regions will constantly be rewritten, as every excavation site that is opened up brings new answers – as well as offering as many new questions.

The Early Bronze Age – The emergence of the first city-states

The countries of the Levant form part of the "fertile crescent" in which the "Neolithic revolution" of humanity began, as the Australian archaeologist Gordon Childe put it. The process began with the settlement there by hunter-gatherers, who at first lived mainly by foraging for the fruits of nature, and was further developed as the settlers acquired skills in arable farming and keeping livestock.

The latest research has shown how strong and enduring an influence this progress in the field of human husbandry had on the natural environment. In the millennia that followed the adoption of these new ways of life, the establishment of trade routes and the development of economic exchange that can be discerned went on to attain remarkable dimensions with the development of metal working. This was principally due to trade in copper and tin, which were indispensable for making bronze.

During these periods, people who associated in village communities used a defined area on which to grow grain and, above all, to rear sheep. The existence of nomadic populations who lived alongside these settled groups is on the other hand very difficult to prove archaeologically.

After several millennia of brilliant cultures, from the end of the 4th millennium B.C. onward, this region played a secondary role in comparison to the cultural centers of Mesopotamia and the Nile Valley as far as we are aware at present. Especially in Mesopotamia, a network of cities developed that was closely associated with the emergence of the first stable political structures.

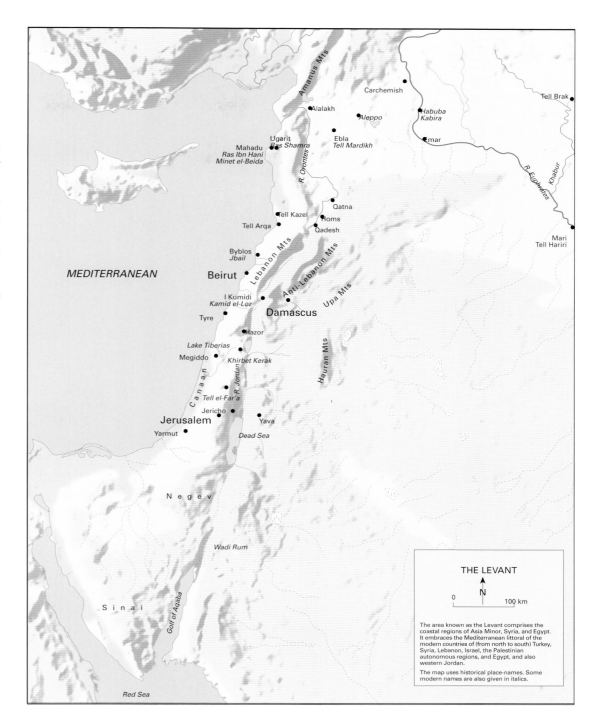

THE LEVANT

0   100 km

The area known as the Levant comprises the coastal regions of Asia Minor, Syria, and Egypt. It embraces the Mediterranean littoral of the modern countries of (from north to south) Turkey, Syria, Lebanon, Israel, the Palestinian autonomous regions, and Egypt, and also western Jordan.

The map uses historical place-names. Some modern names are also given in italics.

Tell Arqa

Probably inhabited since Neolithic times, Tell Arqa overlooks the fertile coastal plain of Akkar in northern Lebanon, where large olive tree plantations are still to be found. Excavations undertaken by the IFAPO (Institut Français d'Archéologie Proche-Orient) have reached the Early Bronze Age layers. This is probably the best-preserved site in northern Lebanon.

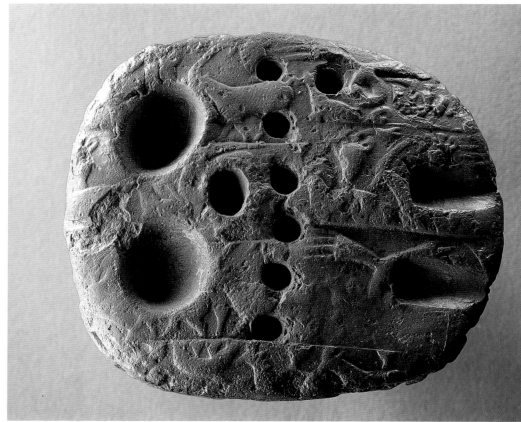

Clay foil with calculi (inside), Habuba Kabira

3200–3100 B.C.
Unfired clay; diam. 6.3 cm
National Museum, Aleppo

Calculi are small pieces of terracotta whose shape and number appear to give various clues as to their function. They are often found wrapped in clay containers impressed with a cylinder seal outside. The cylinder seal presumably gives information about its owner or the person who entrusted it to him. Objects of this kind allowed systematic bookkeeping.

Above, right

Counting tablet, Jebel Aruda

3200–3100 B.C.
Unfired clay; height 9.2 cm, width 8 cm, depth 2.8 cm
National Museum, Aleppo

Before there was a proper script, the tablets were an additional method of recording bookkeeping along with the calculi. In this case, the figures are combined with the impression of a cylinder seal showing a zoomorphic scene.

Habuba Kabira – The influence of powerful neighbors

The best information about the first cities of the Levant, which were established in Syria, is provided by the settlement on the western bank of the upper Euphrates of Habuba Kabira with its acropolis of Tell Qanna. It was excavated in connection with construction work on the Tabqa dam. Along with Tell Brak in the steppe desert of the Jezira, it is among the few excavation sites of the Levant that can be attributed to the Uruk culture (from c. 3000 B.C.). This was clearly the period when writing was invented in southern Mesopotamia, and when the first cities can be identified.

After a first phase of settlement on the west bank of the Euphrates, a rectangular urban area of over 25 acres (10 ha) was developed at Habuba Kabira and was gradually extended to cover around 49 acres (20 ha). Two gates provide access to the city, which was surrounded by a complex defense system comprising a rampart protected by towers and an outer wall. Inside this fortified area, houses with a ground plan roughly resembling a basilica have been excavated, with the network of streets running approximately parallel to the river.

Overall, the finds at Habuba Kabira give the impression that this was an Uruk colony, founded for reasons of trade. This would explain why the city was established so close to the Euphrates, despite the risk of flooding. It was abandoned in about 3100 B.C., bringing to an end this first attempt at an urban settlement in the Levant.

A local development

At the beginning of the 3rd millennium B.C. the urbanization process seems to start with a local development in Jordan and Palestine. The dense occupation of this area by man, and the continuity in the style of pottery production and burial customs, are very clear indications of a stable population between the pre-urban phases of the Early Bronze Age and the development of the first cities.

The choice of site for the cities was based in the first place on the need for security – which was generally guaranteed by fortifications – and a reliable water source. Mostly small cities were involved, with an extent of between 6 acres (2.5 ha) at Jericho and about 49 acres (20 ha) at Khirbet Kerak. In most cases, the defensive systems are the best-planned elements of the city, and, because of their massiveness, those most easily identified by archaeology. In every place investigated, it was established that the sites were repeatedly repaired in the Early Bronze Age periods II and III (2900–2650 B.C. and 2650–2400 B.C.). Originally quite simple walls 3–4 feet (1.5–2 m) thick could, as a result of repairs and gradual reinforcements, reach a considerable thickness (c. 100 feet/30 m in Jericho and 125 feet/38 m in Yarmut, this figure includes the foundations in all layers and the slope leading to the parapet). Ditches, towers, and outer walls completed these systems. Access to the city was through gateways that were sometimes protected by flanking towers such as in Tell el-Far'a, or guarded by pairs of projections (pincers) that narrowed the passageway, as in Yava.

The scale of the building schemes carried out shows clearly the existence of a strictly structured society with a central authority that was strong enough to implement such an investment in people and materials. However, the size of the cities shows that in every case they formed the focal point of a very small territory that was just adequate for the community's survival. Places that lie in the desert such as Yava, illustrate very clearly the processes involved in creating from nothing a city of this kind. Here too we can only regret that no information is available about the human settlements outside the city centers.

At the end of the Early Bronze Age period III (2650–2400 B.C.), these cities were abandoned. We have no really satisfying hypothesis as to why. Many consider it to have been the effect of invasions by Amorites, a tribe of Semitic semi-nomads, while others think that it was the result of damage to the natural environment by human exploitation. The fact is that the end of the 3rd millennium in Palestine was at the same time the end of these first attempts at urbanism.

The division of the Early Bronze Age into periods I–IV is adopted in this and the following chapters. This chronology is based on the development of metallurgy, that is, the skills used in and technical advantage taken of metal working. A more rigorous scholarly formula for subdividing the period has still to be devised.

Thus the advent of the Mesopotamian ruler Sargon of Akkad (2340–2284 B.C.) changed the situation in the Levant as well. He established a huge empire with its capital in Akkad, and thus united the whole of Mesopotamia under a single ruler for the first time. From Akkad, he undertook at least one great expedition westwards in the direction of the "cedar forests" and the "silver mountains" (the Amanus and Taurus ranges). Phases of destruction in the city of Ebla are dated to this period that can be verified archaeologically. Sargon's grandson Naramsin (2259–2223 B.C.) likewise undertook campaigns into the same areas and proclaimed in inscriptions that he had subjected Ebla. Whether the installation of a military governor in Mari, leading to the eventual subjugation of the city during his rule, dates from his time or his grandfather's has not been clarified.

After the collapse of the Akkadian empire, Lagash regained its independence and influence. During the time of Gudea of Lagash (2144–2124 B.C.) trade links between this city state and Ebla are mentioned. With the third dynasty of Ur and the union of southern Mesopotamia under the control of Ur, we find the sources mentioning the presence of a "governor" called Ibdati in Byblos and someone called Megum in Ebla. It is now agreed that these titles do not necessarily mean that the cities concerned did not in

Geographical list, Ebla
24th century B.C.
Clay; height 18 cm, width 18 cm, depth 2 cm
National Museum, Aleppo

This tablet, from Palace G in Ebla, is an Eblaite version of a list of place-names copied from an original of Mesopotamian origin. It mentions places in the regions of Mari, Diyala and the Kish area of central Mesopotamia. This kind of epigraphic text has to be treated with caution, because it is very difficult to establish a definite relationship between the names mentioned and the assumed sites.

The first historical evidence –
The relationship with the empires in the east

Scholars today have texts which date from the 3rd millenium B.C. and which can be used to reconstruct historical processes. With a slight time-lag compared with neighboring Mesopotamia, the use of writing begins to develop in The Levant.

We rely principally on tablets and inscriptions from the city of Ebla in order to reconstruct the history of empires that sprang up around the large city-states such as Ebla or Mari and the names of their kings. We know for example that both these capitals – about which we shall have more to say – controlled extensive territories in western Syria and the middle Euphrates. Inscriptions have provided proof that during the rule of King Iblul II of Mari (24th century B.C.), the Euphrates valley upstream of Mari to west of Carchemish was under his control and that Ebla was a dependency of his – as is demonstrated by the tribute the city paid to him.

The relationships, dependencies and overlord-ships between the cities and city-states of the entire Near Eastern area were nonetheless subject to permanent change, and often sources provide only an occasional glimpse of who was predominant at a given point in time. Great empires were formed and decayed, protagonists suddenly appeared on the political stage in dominant roles, only to disappear again just as rapidly.

fact lie under the control of the Mesopotamian kings. Mari was independent at this time: its rulers, the *shakkanaku*, not only left evidence of their work as great builders but also displayed talent as astute diplomats. Fragments of their correspondence mention the wedding of one of the royal daughters of Mari, Apil-kin, with a prince of Ur.

A densely populated settlement

Over and above the historical data, archaeology has discovered what was effectively a population explosion in northern Syria. The phenomenon is in total contrast to contemporary findings for historical Palestine. Even so, one would have to be able to explore not only the well-known cities but also excavate dozens of tells in order to get a clear picture of the population development of this area. It has been established that in the case of the northern Syrian cities the populated area of each was very large, comparable in size with the cities of southern Mesopotamia. The city of Ebla for example covers 125 acres (50 ha) and the main tell of Mari 110 acres (45 ha). Valleys such as those of the Nahr el-Balikh and Nahr el-Khabur rivers, like the Orontes plain, were densely inhabited and the countryside built on, with settlements radiating from a hierarchical network of more or less important urban centers. Apart from the remarkable exception of the city of Byblos, we have only fragmentary knowledge of how the coastal region was settled in this period.

Ebla – The rediscovery of a capital

Ebla occupies a special position within the study of urban development and the settlement history of this period, though for reasons different from those relating to Byblos or Mari. However the Italian team led by Paolo Matthiae had some grounds to suppose at the start of excavations in 1964 that in Ebla (Tell Mardikh) they had one of the most important sites in northern Syria awaiting them, at least in respect of size. No-one could know that it would be the source of fundamentally new discoveries about the cultures of the 3rd millennium in this region. The hill of Ebla lies 34 miles (55 km) south of Aleppo, on the fringe of the steppe belt, on the border between a region where agriculture is still possible and an area where livestock is the best form of husbandry. This ideal situation allowed the inhabitants both to improve the use of agricultural areas and keep an eye on the livestock-rearing nomads, who had become to some extent settled.

By the end of Early Bronze Age period IV (2400–2000 B.C.) the city had become fully developed. A palace (currently known as Palace G) constitutes the principal linked complex in Ebla from this period. It was still being excavated by the Italian team in the 1990s, but it is only a small part of the entire city of Bronze Age period IV.

The palace stood on an acropolis that loomed over the lower city. The most remarkable features in what has been excavated so far are, according to the archaeologists, the audience court and the administrative quarters. The audience court was a large, open courtyard estimated to be in excess of 115 x 200 feet (35 x 60 m). It was flanked on at least two sides by porticos, whose function among others, was to mark the transition from the districts of the lower city to the acropolis area. The concept and design of the complex look very much like a stage set forming a backdrop to the appearance of the king or the royal household. A huge flight of steps (a ceremonial staircase) from the acropolis allowed them access to the court. The administrative quarters were where the first of 17,000 script tablets and

Pieces from an inlaid plaque: warriors, Ebla

Around 2400 B.C.
Marble; height 14–15 cm, depth 5–7 cm
Idlib Museum

These pieces from a large inlaid plaque come from Palace G in Ebla. They show victorious Eblaite soldiers fighting their enemies. In this warlike iconography, it is easy to distinguish the vanquished, who are generally naked, and the victors, who wear a loincloth and many of them a helmet as well. The type of representation and the postures of victors and vanquished show conformity with a style found in other Ebla representations of the period.

fragments of tablets were uncovered in 1974, which lent this site immense importance for scholarship. This sector consisted of several rooms and possessed direct access to the audience court.

In the same part of the palace alabaster and diorite goblets made in Egypt and small blocks of lapis lazuli were found. These "exotic" objects indicate the existence of extensive trading links to both west and east, since lapis lazuli is found almost exclusively in Afghanistan.

Even more than the archaeological finds, a study of the archives permits us to sketch in a possible picture of Ebla society, and the activities and relationships that presumably connected it with other city-states of Mesopotamia or the Levant. The city was ruled by a king (*en* in Semitic, which means something like "priest king") who probably performed both political and religious functions. At his side were the royal family and some 15 dignitaries. In addition there were high officials, the "Ancients,"

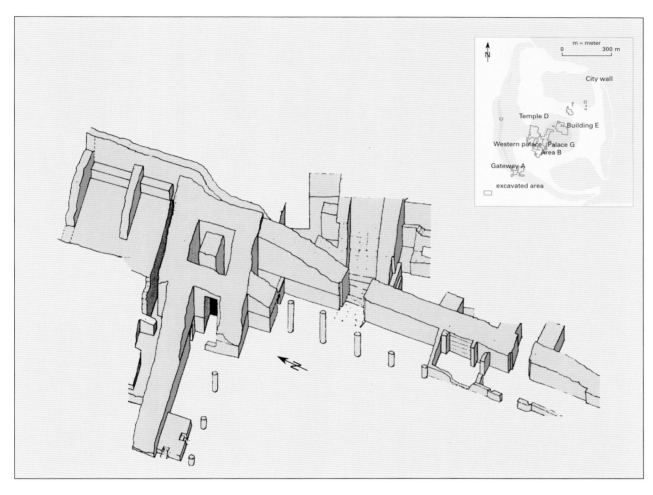

Drawing of Palace G and location plan, Ebla

The excavations by the Italian team have allowed a precise reconstruction of the topography of the city of Ebla. Thus the archaeologists were able to locate the upper city with its palaces, the areas where the temples were, the lower city and fortifications enclosing the city. The total area comprised about 135 acres (55 ha). The Early Bronze Age palace, the destruction of which is attributed to a king of Akkad, contained a store of cuneiform texts and numerous valuable objects that had to be left behind when the palace was stormed and today constitute valuable finds for scholars.

Gold figure of a bull man, Ebla

2300 B.C.
Gold, lapis lazuli and wood; length 5 cm
National Museum, Aleppo

This minotaur found in Palace G in Ebla depicts a divine being that served as an idol in the worship of the sun god Shamash. It is in addition an example of craftsmanship: gold, lapis lazuli and wood are splendidly combined. The simply-worked precious metal and lavishly detailed beard set each other off beautifully.

Wig from a female statue, Ebla

Around 2300 B.C.
Soapstone; height 30.3 cm, width 14.5 cm
National Museum, Aleppo

This female wig fashioned from steatite (soapstone) was presumably made in the royal workshops of Ebla, where indeed it was found. It probably belonged to a composite statue of which we may assume that the face was made of a light-colored material – marble or ivory – in order to make the work more realistic. The hair itself consists of several steatite plates, and we can appreciate the technical skills of the artisans who must have worked exclusively for the court.

who took part in decision-making. Most of the city's residents carried out activities that had something to do with the palace. The number of inhabitants in Ebla at this time is estimated at around 20,000.

The trade controlled by the palace seems indeed to have been a royal monopoly. Weaving was one of the specialties of Ebla, as was producing statues, statuettes and articles made of gilded wood. It also seems that the lapis lazuli was worked in Ebla, even if the discovery of blocks of rough stone would indicate that at least some of the stones were exported on further west; in other words Ebla was used as a commercial storehouse.

Finally, the inscribed tablets provide information about the religious life and pantheon of Ebla. Three gods – Dagan, Hadad, and the sun god – stand at the top of the hierarchy. Whereas Hadad counted as the great god of storms, the sun (represented by the Sumerogram *utu*) is the equivalent of the Akkadian sun god Shamash.

Mari – A city on the banks of the Euphrates

After an accidental discovery in December 1933, Parrot decided to undertake an excavation of Tell Hariri, which up to then had not particularly attracted the attention of the experts. The hill was explored by this famous scholar, with interruptions, until 1974, and then from 1979 by Margueron.

Though Mari has not borne as rich an epigraphic witness to the 3rd millennium as Ebla, the excavations have revealed the unusual nature of the foundation of this regional capital. Indeed, the question was long discussed, what could have led to the founding of a city in an almost desert-like steppe zone? With inadequate rainfall, agriculture could only have been possible with

the help of irrigation. A study which also involved geologists and geomorphologists showed that, to understand this phenomenon, the nature of the environment around the city must also be considered.

A complex system of canals has been discovered that gave the city remarkable opportunities for development. One of the canals was 75 miles (120 km) long and 36 feet (11 m) wide for the whole of its length, and established good connections between the Mesopotamian plain and the first foothills of the Taurus. Other less comprehensive works indicate systematic irrigation of the agricultural areas. This permitted the continued existence of the urban center that appears increasingly to have been an important base for river-borne trade on the Euphrates.

The city itself was linked with the Euphrates by a canal. Its site, at a certain distance from the river and the area at risk from flooding, was undoubtedly deliberately chosen to ensure the security and development of what was probably a new city foundation. Mari is characterized more by its architectural features than by the way in which it has improved the surrounding landscape. According to Margueron, the city had a circular plan with a diameter of 875 yards (800 m) to 1,095 yards (1,000 m). A dam protected it from serious floods, and the canal that linked it with the river ran diagonally through the city. The archaeologist presumes that the artisan district lay along its banks.

The center of the city was crossed by radiating streets, at the focal point of which were the palace and sundry temples. The houses uncovered were constructed to a classic ground plan: around a central space, in which a shrine was sometimes found, were other smaller rooms, one of which generally served as a kitchen. The palace was constructed of several large and independent units, one of which has been identified as being a religious sanctuary, and there were arrangements of large courts which it is thought, may have housed specialized artisans. In the Temple

Pieces of an inlay plaque: lion-headed eagles and human-headed bulls, Ebla
Around 2400 B.C.
Marble; height 16/18 cm, depth 5/7 cm
Idlib Museum

As is clear from Eblaite iconography, the lion-headed eagle symbolizes the presence of a deity of war, possibly Rasap, the god of war and death. That explains his representation on a panel on which battle scenes are also visible. These iconographical themes resemble what we are familiar with from southern Mesopotamia and Babylon, and illustrate well the common features of the various pantheons venerated in the kingdoms of the region.

Winged lion Imdugud, Mari
Around 2650 B.C.
Lapis lazuli, gold, bitumen and copper;
height 12.8 cm, width 11.8 cm
National Museum, Damascus

The winged lion Imdugud, presented as an apotropaic pendant, was found in a palace in Mari. It belongs to the "Ur treasure"; it is not clear if it is a royal gift or a piece of booty.

A letter from the archive in Mari

2nd millennium B.C.
Clay; height 7.1 cm, breadth 4.3 cm
Unité Propre de Recherche, Paris

This letter with the title "A dramatic night in Mari," which is dated to the 2nd millennium, illustrates the worries associated with maintaining the canals. The tablet describes the misadventures of a royal official who, despite being unwell, undertook emergency measures one night to staunch the flow of water from a hole in the dike.

of Ishtar to the west of the city archaeologists found many votive tablets as well as a statue of Ebih-il, a high official of the temple. In another place of worship dedicated to the Ninni-Zaza a betyl (sacred stone) was found, bearing witness to Syrian religious traditions in this region. These traditions were overlaid by the rise of Mesopotamian culture, of which the expeditions of Sargon of Akkad and his successors provided the clearest historical expression. A temple tower with a high terrace can also be seen in this context; it certainly seems to have dominated the city.

The wealth of artistic life of a capital city like Mari is most elegantly evident in the production of statues and inlaid plaques. These goods were probably exported from one capital to another or were exchanged, and presumably constituted an important part of diplomatic giving such as is mentioned in connection with political embassies, peace treaties, and marriage negotiations. The same applies to roll or cylinder seals, of which examples of local production and also pieces of foreign origin have been found in Mari.

Statue of Ebih-il, Mari

2500 B.C.
Alabaster, eyes made of mother-of-pearl and lapis lazuli in a slate setting; height 52.5 cm
Louvre, Paris

The statue of Ebih-il, an important official of the Temple of Ishtar, is typical of the sculpture of Early Bronze Age IV. The figure is seated, with his arms across his chest and is dressed in a *kaunake* or "rat's tail" skirt. The way this person is shown, the posture and the garment he is wearing are typical of the period. Apart from the undoubted art-historical interest of this piece, it provides iconographical evidence of a person mentioned in the archives of Ebla.

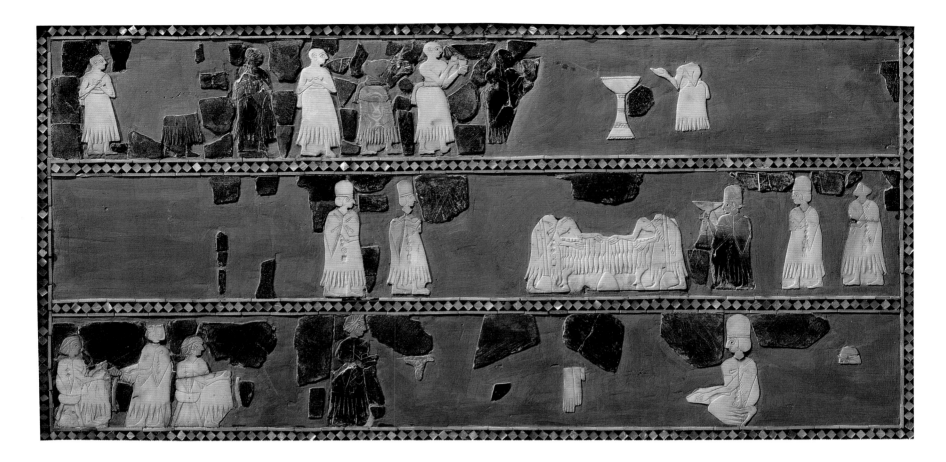

Above

Inlay plaque: religious scene, Mari
2600–2500 B.C.
Mother-of-pearl, ivory, slate, lapis lazuli;
height 25.9 cm, width 52.6 cm, depth 5 cm.
National Museum, Damascus

This inlaid panel, which probably came from a
workshop in the palace at Mari, shows us in a
particularly vivid manner a scene from the
religious life of this city on the banks of the
Euphrates. The choice of material and quality
of depiction make it an altogether unusual
piece that, apart from its artistic qualities, has
real narrative value. Priestesses, priests, and
servants are shown carrying out rites. Libations
can be discerned here.

Below

Cylinder seal with ship deities, Mari
2400 B.C.
Limestone; height 3.6 cm, diam. 1.9 cm
Louvre, Paris

Cylinder seals are excellent examples of
Mesopotamian stone carving. This item, found
in the Temple of Ishtar in Mari, displays, as so
often, a religious theme. The economy of
feature and narrative intent in the decoration
are remarkable. The elements, ship deities and
animals seem almost part of a picture puzzle.

Aerial view of Byblos

The tell of Byblos is surmounted by a Crusader castle. Seen from the town and the surrounding countryside – on which building activity has, unfortunately, not been controlled – it looks like a uniformly green island. The red spot in the lush vegetation is Dunand's excavation house. It reminds us that during the time of the pioneers of Levantine archaeology, this hill was still covered by houses, which had to be moved in order to carry out the excavations. The rocky promontory to which the ancient buildings cling commands the modern harbor, which was probably used from 7000 B.C. onward by Levantine and Egyptian merchants who came here looking for valuable cedarwood. The town itself was founded around 6000 B.C.

Byblos – Between Egypt and the Lebanon Mountains

A few miles north of Beirut is Byblos (Jbail), one of the best-explored sites on the Levantine coast. The first studies of the place were carried out by Renan as part of his work on the Phoenicians. He published the results, showing that the site had been settled very early on, in 1864. The first systematic excavations were done by the French Egyptologist Montet in 1921, and after him the archaeologist Dunand continued investigations in the city, in collaboration with the Department of Antiquities in Lebanon, up to the end of the 1970s.

The site of the settlement is a rocky outcrop in the foothills of the Lebanon Mountains running right to the seashore. The water supply was provided by an all-season spring in the middle of the settlement. The city commanded a small, natural anchorage which is excellently protected from wind and has served as a harbor into modern times. There are parallels in other coastal towns such as Beirut, where excavations in the inner city have shown that there too the settlement looked out over a natural harbor basin. Byblos lies on the edge of a fertile coastal plain that was probably used for agriculture. But it seems that proximity to the valley of the Nahr Ibrahim and the Lebanon Mountains was more important for the city's development, since their forests were exploited in ancient times for shipbuilding and the construction of monumental buildings.

The city had an almost circular layout, and was surrounded by a massive stone rampart reinforced several times over. By the end of the 3rd millennium it was about 100 feet (30 m) thick and protected an area of over 12 acres (5 ha). Two gateways have been discovered, one in the east, and another in the north-west giving access to the harbor.

Inside the city archaeologists have been able to explore temples and houses dating from the Early Bronze Age, while the necropolis which has been uncovered clearly belongs to the Middle Bronze Age.

North of the spring a temple of Baalat Gubla, the female ruler of Byblos, has been identified. According to Dunand, it was established in 2800 B.C. and reconstructed at regular intervals. It appears to have served as a religious site into Roman times. Northeast of the well was another L-shaped temple, which is described – presumably incorrectly – as the Temple of Reshef. An open space between the two shrines is interpreted by Dunand as a "sacred lake," such as was typical for Egyptian temples.

The houses uncovered in the western part of the city have almost rectangular ground plans. The walls were erected from sandstone blocks, but the roof was carried on wooden pillars. The houses described seem to have been the homes of aristocrats. No palace dating to this period has been found such as could have been expected in line with finds in other cities. The possibility that it was destroyed by more recent buildings cannot be ruled out.

The excavations have revealed a lot of evidence for links between the Levantine city and Egypt. The finds thus corroborate the texts and inscriptions found in the Nile valley referring to Byblos, and illustrate the political and commercial relationships linking the two. For example, excavations have brought to light fragments of alabaster vases bearing the names of the Egyptian kings Menkaure (4th dynasty), Wenis (5th dynasty), and Pepy I and Pepy II (6th dynasty). Relationships seem to have reached such a high point with this latter dynasty that the Egyptians equated Baalat Gubla with Hathor of Dendara, as a hieroglyphic inscription in the Baalat temple demonstrates.

The reason for the virtual integration of this city into the Egyptian world is given by the Egyptians themselves. An inscription from the reign of Snofru (4th dynasty) suggests that great quantities of cedarwood from Byblos were supplied to Egypt, which lacked timber resources. We now understand better the interest of the pharaohs in this coastal area of the Levant, which was both close to the source of the valuable timber and was in a strategically favorable position for a sea route – undoubtedly the most effective way to transport this heavy and awkward material.

Despite this, Byblos cannot be considered as a real Egyptian colony. We must imagine it as a place of exchange that was bound in to a functioning trading relationship and, under the guise of political subservience, hosted profitable business deals.

The goddess Hathor, Byblos
2000–1500 B.C.
Ivory; height 9.5 cm, width 5 cm, depth 2 cm
Department of Antiquities, Beirut

Here, the goddess Hathor was made of a material often used by craftsmen in the area. They were skilled masters in ivory carving (using hippopotamus teeth or elephant tusks), as the quality of the draftsmanship and fine rendering of the relief we can see on this piece shows.

Bull's head, Byblos
3100–2000 B.C.
Fired clay; height 17.3 cm, width 26.9 cm
Department of Antiquities, Beirut

This bull's head from Byblos is a unique testimonial to the work of the craftsmen there and a local variant of a theme frequently represented in the religious iconography of this region. Bulls feature in the art of the Middle East from the Stone Age on, and crop up in all mythologies right up to the Roman period (where they reappeared for example in the Mithraic cult). They are associated with such qualities as fertility and strength.

The Middle Bronze Age

The Levant of the Early Bronze Age was characterized by the emergence and development of relatively independent small city-states. They flourished in the Middle Bronze Age, but later gradually came under the control of the two large neighboring empires – Pharaonic Egypt and the kingdoms based in Mesopotamia. In the complex power games that developed in the encounters between these two great powers of the ancient world, there were nonetheless always other outside parties involved, such as the Amorites, Hittites, and Mitannians.

At the end of the 3rd millennium, invasions of Amorites – a semi-nomadic Semitic people – mark the end of a first stage of urban colonization. Identified by inscriptions and onomastics (the study of the origins and forms of words), such tribes are difficult to identify with a particular culture, and thus our study of them is hampered.

However, the new arrivals, who had initially settled in the foothills of the Arabian desert, were very quick to occupy the framework set up by the previous ruling classes, and from 1815 B.C. dynasties of Amorite origin were firmly established in control of cities such as Mari.

Thus no really profound changes took place. Instead, the larger settlements were taken over by sections of population that hitherto lived on the edge of the cities. New large cities such as Aleppo or Qatna in the vicinity of Homs crop up in the texts. At the site at Aleppo, it is difficult to discern how it was occupied because the ancient tell is covered by the historic part of the present city.

Above

Fragments of a mural, Mari
1850–1780 B.C.
Plaster; width 135 cm
Louvre, Paris

The painted fragments of fallen plaster were found by the southern wall of the west court of the palace at Mari. They show the ruler towering over his subjects in importance. The bulls are presumably sacrificial victims.

Excavations, Mari

Excavations of Tell Hariri began in 1933, and Parrot very soon identified it as Mari. Successive excavations since then have uncovered not only an entire palace complex that stood on top of the tell but also temples and significant parts of the residential areas.

In Qatna, on the other hand, the archaeological results threw up clear findings: in this case, the Middle Bronze Age defensive system of the city was rediscovered.

Urban living was resumed in Palestine at the beginning of the 2nd millennium B.C.. This is demonstrated by the repairs to fortifications at ancient sites where a large part of the population settled once again. The cities evidently took advantage of the contraction of Egypt's foreign policy to develop autonomously. The invasions of the Amorites seem only to have had a marginal influence on this phenomenon of the urban renewal of Palestine.

For this period the archives of Mari provide a valuable documentation of everyday life in the Amorite realm in northern Syria and its geopolitical surroundings. On the other side, the anathematizing texts of the Egyptians, depict the political situation on the Levantine coast from an Egyptian viewpoint. These documents are inscriptions on pots and terracotta figurines naming the tribes or cities to be destroyed. These objects were symbolically broken in ritual acts, in the hope this would achieve the same effect in battle. Because of their general focus on the Near East, these texts must of course be used with care as a historical source.

The construction of new city walls in Syria, as well as in Palestine, now with complex gateway systems and massive earth banks, probably the remnants of Bronze Age defenses, indicate very clearly the threats to which the region was exposed. The capture and destruction of Mari by the Babylonians under Hammurabi in 1757 B.C., followed by that of Ebla by the Hittites between 1625 and 1600 B.C., marks a long period of decline for northern Syria at the end of the Middle Bronze Age, for which the cities have thrown up little usable historic material.

Excavations, Tell Arqa

Excavations on the western edge of Tell Arqa, directed by Jean Paul Thalmann, have brought to light the remains of buildings that probably leaned against the rampart that enclosed the city in the Bronze Age. Archaeologists uncovered evidence of potters of the period at work in these buildings.

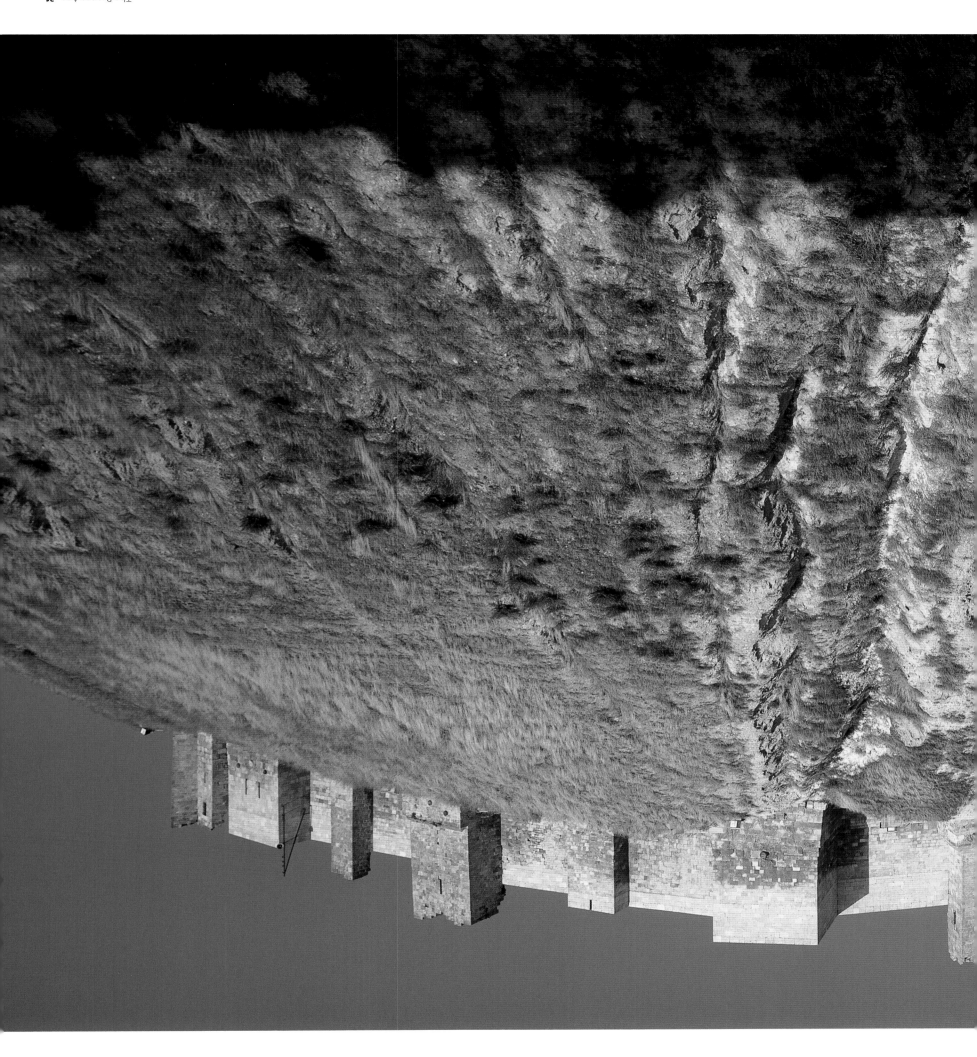

Pages 30–31

Citadel, Aleppo

Aleppo is a remarkable example of the continuity of settlement at urban sites in the Levant. Its citadel stands on the highest part of the tell. Excavations in 1997 and 1998 brought to light remains of a temple that confirm the previous assumption that this was the site of the remains of a capital of an empire known from texts from the 3rd century B.C. This is only one example of the difficulty of finding these ancient cities, whose remnants are overlaid by those of more recent settlements and constructions, as the excavations recently carried out in Beirut have also shown clearly.

Ground plan of an ancient Babylonian palace, Mari

Although excavation work has been going on in Mari for over 50 years, Tell Hariri, which overlies the ancient city of Mari, is by no means completely explored yet. Principally the upper city and palace have been uncovered. They form the central point of a circular area which is enclosed within a boundary wall. Traces of the latter are still visible in the topography.

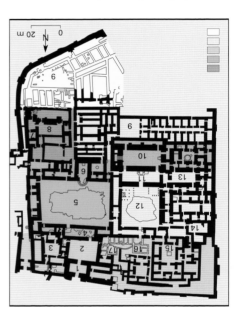

1 Gate hall, 2 Gate court, 3 Palace guard house and guest wing, 4 Connecting vestibule, 5 Large court, 6 Audience hall, 7 Temple, 8 Public reception rooms, 9 Service area and storerooms, 10 Banqueting hall, 11 Throne room, 12 Square court, 13 Administrative wing, 14 Scriptorium, 15 King's residential wing, 16 Palace chapel, 17 Service court

The life of a city seen through the archives of Mari

The city of Mari has furnished us with more than 20,000 tablets inscribed in a Semitic language, namely Babylonian. The evaluation of these texts is supplemented by the results of archaeological explorations, which for this period of the city relate particularly to the palace that is supposed to have been built by King Zimrilim (1775–1761 B.C.). It is thus possible to reconstruct completely the organization of the palace complex and the way of life of the city inhabitants who lived at the court of the Syrian king during the Bronze Age.

The palace, comprising more than 300 rooms and courts, covered an area of over 6 acres (2.5 ha) and seemed to contain all functional installations that can be imagined for this period (such as basins, cisterns, ovens, drains, and so on). Thanks to its excellent state of preservation, it represents one of the most complete testimonies we have of a palace of this period. That the palace is in such excellent condition for archaeological purposes is apparently due to the devastating suddenness of Mari's ruin and the abandonment of the city following Hammurabi's campaign against it in 1757 B.C.

It took at least 300 years to build the complex, with the palace of the 2nd millennium partly covering the preceding Early Bronze Age building. Many of its walls, which consisted of clay bricks, were several yards thick. The good state of preservation of the ruins permitted the reconstruction of one upper floor and even part of a second. The various rooms were grouped around open courts, but also around central, roofed halls. Remnants of painted plaster on the wall of the principal rooms allow us to assume they were decorated with murals (see p. 28 above).

Overall the palace consisted of five parts. The entrance was in the north of the building and led indirectly to a large court, which opened up to the other parts of the palace. The temple area was in the southeast, while in the south were the storage and provisions areas. The west part of the palace was accessed via a well-protected entrance, beyond which were the rooms that were reserved for the king and the harem.

The temple area suggests that connections between religious and political life were close. That this connection was so obvious is unusual, and Margueron's theory is that this represents the survival of an old practice, according to which religious authority would be predominantly united with political power.

The center of the complex includes the official area, which is organized in the form of courts and state rooms. The palm court, which owes its name to the artificial palm that presumably stood at the center, allowed access to a room that constituted the antechamber to the throne room. In its dimensions (82 ft/25 m long, 39 ft/12 m wide, and probably about 39 ft/12 m high) and its wall decorations, this room displayed all the required splendor to emphasize the monarchic role. The throne stood on a pedestal on the western side, while the statues of various kings must have stood on the raised gallery opposite. From the throne room entry could be gained to the private chambers of the king, which lay on the first floor on the east side of the palace. In the north there were administrative quarters, where documents with inscriptions concerning the administration of the palace were found.

In the northwestern part were the women's quarters. The whole southern part in contrast was devoted to storerooms and warehousing, which opened either directly from the great court or via a small entrance off the large corridor that ran through the palace from east to west. Control of the admission and release of goods and people was in the hands of the steward, who had his seat at the main entrance.

The everyday life of the palace and thereby of the city can also be traced through the archives. Best documented is the period of the reign of Zimrilim. The administrative texts enable us to reconstruct both the royal environment and the presence of a large group of women in the palace, which, beside the royal harem, included a host of servants and domestics. No less interesting is the scale of the provisions needed for all these people, which were clearly provided by the palace. The documents also mention valuable goods that were produced in the locality or reached the palace as gifts – these are indirect evidence of the intensive diplomatic and economic activity that was carried out here.

Even more than these often long-winded administrative documents, the royal correspondence presents a picture of the personality and concerns of a ruler in this period. There are, therefore, details of negotiations for the marriage of Zimrilim and one of the daughters of the king of Aleppo, the purpose of which was mainly political. We can also reconstruct one of the journeys that Zimrilim undertook to Ugarit (Ras Shamra) on the Mediterranean coast in 1765 B.C.

In this correspondence plans for treaties with other kings such as Hammurabi are similarly discussed. Along with the events of major historical significance we also find reports of the misfortunes that overtook a steward, depictions of nomadic life as the ideal of male existence, or the report of an accident on one of the dikes belonging to the network of waterways of Mari.

Inscribed tablet, Mari

2000 B.C.
Clay, height 10.5 cm, width 5.4 cm
Unité Propre de Recherche, Paris

From the descriptions preserved, we can conclude that the articles described as gal vases in the texts from Mari were among possible barter goods or gifts. According to the written testimony they were made, probably with the utmost care, from gold or silver. Unfortunately not a single example of a utensil of this kind has so far been found. The study of this unusual historical document contained in the archive of Mari provides us with a glimpse into a whole area of culture to which archaeology as such has no access.

Seated female clay figure, Mari

Around 1800 B.C.
Fired clay, height 23.4 cm, width 12.6 cm, depth 6.7 cm
National Museum, Aleppo

This clay piece, found in the vicinity of an oven, shows a seated female figure. It was probably intended as a cheap image of the deity for the minor palace employees, to allow everyday contact with the gods who were to be favorably disposed to them or protect them.

Torso from a basalt statue, Ebla
Beginning of 2nd millennium B.C.
Basalt; height 53 cm, width 46 cm, depth 24 cm
National Museum, Damascus

Thanks to the inscription on this fragment of a basalt statue representing a bearded, cloaked figure, it was possible to identify modern Tell Mardikh with the ancient Ebla. It is a gift that the ruler of Ebla, Ibbit Lim, has offered to the goddess Ishtar and must originally have been installed in her temple.

The reconstruction of Ebla

At the beginning of the 2nd millennium, after a phase of urban contraction, Ebla entered into a new phase of development. Though the inscription documentation is much less extensive than for the 3rd millennium, the Italian excavations have enabled us to understand the inner structure of the city better, as the archaeological material for this period was easily accessible.

The physical reconstruction of Ebla is particularly impressively demonstrated in the enormous city fortifications. First, massive earth ramparts were constructed with a base thickness of 65–100 feet (20–30 m). They reach a height of 72 feet (22 m) and enclose an area of 125 acres (50 ha). A layer of plaster protected the top of the wall, which supported projecting towers. Four gates allowed entry through the walls, in the southwest, southeast, northeast, and northwest. The southwest entrance was, remarkably, endowed with an additional outer gateway, that led first into a small gate court and from there into the inner gateway containing a passage 72 feet (22 m) long. Inside this was an inner ring of walls, which also served to protect the citadel. This defensive system contained a foundation structure of stone surmounted by an upper structure of earth and then topped by a brick wall.

The citadel contained the royal palace (Palace E) and a temple dedicated to the goddess Ishtar (Temple D). With its tripartite arrangement and rectangular ground plan, this shrine is reminiscent of the temple constructed by Solomon in Jerusalem and of others in northern Syria, such as at Alalakh. It was probably the main temple of the city. Ishtar was depicted on a stele found in Ebla, as ruler over nature both wild and tamed, and as protectress of the empire.

A further palace was found in the lower city, the ruins of which are recognizable as extending over 8,400 square yards (7,000 sq m). A small temple was also uncovered in this part of the city dedicated to Reshef, god of the underworld, war, and plague, as well as another temple which very probably served funerary purposes and served the cult of deceased kings.

This type of religious site is referred to as *rapi'uma* in Ugaritic texts, a term which is presumably connected with the Rephaim valley of the Bible (II Samuel, 5:18). Likewise in this part of the city a monument now known as P3 was also found, a huge stone terrace measuring 172 x 138 feet (52.5 x 42 m), which encloses an inner court three feet lower. This arrangement, which is unique of its kind, poses a number of questions. The possibility cannot be ruled out that the structure had some connection with the cult of Ishtar. In the northern part of the lower city is Temple N, which is dedicated to Shamash, the sun god, the protector of justice and law.

Building P3, Ebla

Only a stone plinth survives of what was probably a religious structure dedicated to the goddess Ishtar. This building is unusual for its size and layout. The Italian team under Paolo Matthiae assumes that it was a large terrace with a central internal court. On the basis of its distinguishing features and the special situation of the structure in an area where temples have been identified, it has been assumed that it is a religious site.

Obelisk temple, Byblos

The obelisk temple was excavated by Dunand, who dated it to the Middle Bronze Age. In order to uncover the older site that still lay beneath it, the archaeologist had the obelisk temple completely removed and reerected a few yards from its original site. The obelisks stood in a courtyard that formed the cella of the holy site on three sides. Dunand also found a stone anchor here and numerous offerings to the deity venerated at the site.

Byblos – Royal tombs and temples of the gods

At the beginning of the 2nd millennium, connections between the city of Byblos and Egypt seem to have acquired a new intensity. Most of the evidence for these links derive from the tombs in the royal necropolis, which lie on the topmost prominence of the tell. Their discovery, which proved important for our knowledge of the history of the region, came about through a trivial incident. On February 16 1922, one of the cloudbursts so common in this region caused an earthslip that exposed a subterranean burial site hewn 39 feet (12 m) deep in the rock. The excavations subsequently undertaken led to the discovery of nine tombs. They were square or rectangular shafts 26–40 feet (8–12 m) deep that had been opened out into a chamber on one side to accommodate the sarcophagus and grave goods.

Although they had been plundered, the tombs still contained plentiful burial gifts, including numerous objects of Egyptian origin. Their careful execution gives rise to the assumption, to be treated with great caution, that these were royal gifts.

The names of two people buried during this period are known from hieroglyphic inscriptions. They are the Gublitic prince Abishemu and his son Ipshemuabi, who, it seems, was his successor in office (see the illustration at the foot of p. 38). Both are accorded the Egyptian title *haty-a*, which corresponds to "count" or similar.

The second large building complex excavated in Byblos and dating from the same time as the royal necropolis is the obelisk temple, erected over the L-shaped temple of the Early Bronze Age. To facilitate excavations of the older layers it was moved by the archaeologists to another site, where it can now be visited. The obelisk temple was built on a terrace surrounded on three sides by an enclosed court. In this court, particularly in the southwestern part, small sandstone or limestone obelisks were set up, along with temple models and a stone anchor.

The sanctuary itself was rectangular and subdivided into the cella and a tripartite antechamber. Excavated in this part of the temple were coins and votive tablets of metal, pottery, and glazed earthenware that are certainly of Egyptian provenance. In the vicinity of the temple, in an area called the "sacrificial site" by the excavators, a series of depositories of weapons and bronze statues was uncovered.

Concealed in pottery and covered with a layer of lime, the finds are considered by Dunand to be offerings to the deity venerated in the temple by the Gublites. The Middle Bronze Age layers also yielded pottery of Cretan and Cypriot origin, suggesting that Byblos played a role in Mediterranean trade. At a time when new political links were being forged, strongly structured and in a position to organize large trading expeditions by sea routes, the purpose and nature of this trade underwent major changes.

Obsidian casket, Byblos

1797–1790 B.C.
Obsidian, gold leaf; height 9.8 cm,
width 15.2 cm, depth 9.5 cm
Department of Antiquities, Beirut

This casket made of obsidian and finished with gold leaf bears an inscription with the name of the pharaoh Amenemhet IV (1797–1790 B.C.) and comes from Tomb II of the royal necropolis. We may imagine that the pharaohs secured the loyalty of the petty princes of Byblos with gifts of this kind, which were held in such respect that they served as burial gifts.

Bronze figurine covered in gold leaf, Byblos

2000–1600 B.C.
Bronze, gold leaf; height 38 cm
Department of Antiquities, Beirut

This bronze figurine covered in gold leaf was found during Dunand's excavations in Byblos. It belonged to the layer with offerings discovered under the floor of the obelisk temple that are dated to the Middle Bronze period. The figurine is novel in that it is possibly not the representation of a deity and thus allows us to reconstruct typical items of male clothing, i.e. a tall cap.

A number of other excavations, which have been carried out in the center of Beirut since 1994, have shown the existence of a small city-state there too. As in the case with Byblos, the upper town was constructed on a rocky outcrop that commanded a well-protected natural anchorage. Here too, tombs containing objects of Egyptian origin were found in the center of the tell. The evaluation of the archaeological data will also show whether the fortification system can similarly be dated to the time of the Middle Bronze Age.

Below

Shell-shaped pendant bearing the name of Prince Ipshemuabi, Byblos

2000–1500 B.C.
Gold, semi-precious stone; height 7.5 cm,
width 7 cm, depth 1.5 cm
Department of Antiquities, Beirut

The name of Ipshemuabi, prince of Byblos, is inscribed on this shell-shaped pendant, which depicts a falcon with outstretched wings, a scarab, and two uræi (sacred asps), which were taken over directly from Egyptian iconography.

Various objects, probably from a religious site, Beirut

2000–1500 B.C.
Pottery, alabaster, bronze, ivory,
glazed earthenware
Department of Antiquities, Beirut

During excavations carried out since 1994 on the site of the old tell of Beirut, a small cache was found comprising alabaster vases, small earthenware animal figurines (including a sphinx), miniature objects (weapons, drinking and offering vessels, and so on) and also ivory disks. Similar stores were found in the obelisk temple in Byblos.

Ceremonial gold ax, Byblos

2000–1600 B.C.
Gold; height 7 cm, width 10 cm, depth 2 cm
Department of Antiquities, Beirut

The ceremonial ax is typical of the military weaponry in the Levant in the Bronze Age. The article shown here is, however, decorative and valuable rather than functional. The filigree decoration of the handle and the material highlight the wealth of the urban center that Byblos constituted and the skills of its craftsmen. Such an object also indicates the importance of religious life, since it was among the offerings found in the obelisk temple.

The Late Bronze Age – A period of change

Whereas in the Middle Bronze Age Egyptian influence in the region waned, the Late Bronze Age was marked by the pharaohs of the 13th dynasty reassuming effective control. Parallel to this, Mesopotamian influences declined. At this phase of expansion, the Egyptians had to fight the Hurrians (the Horites of the Old Testament) who had settled in the extensive region described in Assyrian texts as the Mitannian realm. At the beginning of the Late Bronze Age (c. 1500 B.C.), this new force in the local political structure controlled a territory probably centered on the upper valleys of the Euphrates and Khabur rivers and stretching as far the Mediterranean littoral so as to include the Orontes valley and at least the northern part of the Bekaa Valley. Our historical knowledge of this time rests principally on Egyptian sources. Numerous clay tablets bearing the diplomatic correspondence of Egyptian rulers have survived, particularly for the reigns of pharaohs Amenophis III (1388–1350 B.C.) and Amenophis IV/Akhenaten (1353–1335 B.C.). These documents were found in Tell el-Amarna (the Amarna letters), the new capital of the heretic pharaoh Akhenaten, and are exceptional in being written both in cuneiform and the Babylonian language, the diplomatic language of the time.

During the reign of Thutmosis I (1504–1492 B.C.) the Egyptians assumed control over the Levant and extended their sphere of influence up to the Euphrates. However, the power of this pharaoh seems to have been of a somewhat theoretical nature, because his son Thutmosis II had to wage war again in Palestine, and Thutmosis III (1479–1425 B.C.) also trekked north in the 22nd year of his reign. He challenged the king of Qadesh and his allies in

Duck-shaped cosmetics bowl, Kamid el-Loz

1500–1200 B.C.
Ivory; height 12 cm, width 24 cm, depth 6 cm
Department of Antiquities, Beirut

This ivory cosmetics bowl was found in a "royal" tomb discovered in Kamid el-Loz, in ancient times known as I Kumidi. Although it was probably made by a local craftsman, the subject chosen and the treatment of it reveal strong Egyptian influence.

Megiddo and conquered the city. In the 33rd year of his reign he crossed the Euphrates in the course of his eighth campaign. Inscriptions contain the names of more than 100 cities conquered by this pharaoh. This illustrates the political fragmentation of the area coveted by both the Egyptians and the Mitannians, which was consequently exposed to any surprise attack or political and diplomatic constellation. The subsequent pharaoh, Amenophis II (1428–1397 B.C.), continued the work of his father. In 1421 B.C. he again took his troops across the Orontes, which had come to represent the traditional frontier of pharaonic territory in the Levant. Three "provinces" constituted this Egyptian Levant: Canaan, which corresponds to modern Palestine; Upe further to the northeast, which included the Bekaa Valley and stretched as far as modern Damascus; and Amurru in the north, which lay between the Orontes and the sea. Indeed, the Egyptians seem to have constructed a network of strategically well-placed bases such as Simyra (which, it is supposed, could be Tell Kazel, which was by the sea and commanded the Homs rift), or I Kumidi (modern Kamid el-Loz) in the Bekaa Valley.

During the reign of Thutmosis IV (1401–1391 B.C.), the game of conflict between the Mitannians and Egypt entered a quiescent phase. We may assume a balance of power between the opponents and a measurement of agreement on their territorial claims. The period coincides with the growth of Hittite power, which constituted a major threat to the Mitannians. The diplomatic correspondence of pharaohs Amenophis III (1391–1353 B.C.) and Amenophis IV (1353–1335 B.C.) make reference to negotiations for the marriage of Amenophis III with Giluhepa, a daughter of the Mitannian king. By this marriage connection, the two rulers guaranteed the security of their joint frontier, which allowed them to square up to any other opponents who might turn up. During the reign of King Suppiluliuma I, however, the Hittites played a subtle game of intrigue combined with military maneuvers that drove the Mitannians from the political scene. Suppiluliuma I adopted the methods of his defeated opponent and concluded marriage alliances with the Egyptians, for example marrying one his daughters to a pharaoh (in all probability Tutenkhamun). Moreover, he ensured the loyalty of the various city-states, such as Ugarit, within his sphere of influence, by forcing treaties on them that demanded subservience in exchange for security and prosperity. His successors, who profited from a weakening of Egyptian power, extended their influence towards the south.

With the beginning of the 19th Egyptian dynasty, the pharaohs sought to regain control over their possessions in the Levant. Seth I went to war in Palestine and reasserted his power in Canaan. His son Rameses II (1279–1213 B.C.) embarked on an expedition to Lebanon in the first years of his reign. He crossed the Nahr el-Kelb near Beirut, where he had a memorial stele inscribed. The following year he

took on the Hittite army in Qadesh – a battle recorded in Egyptian history as a victory, even though the outcome appears to have favored the Hittites more. However, it marks a turning point in this long-running conflict. Possibly Egyptian pressure in the area was relaxed because neither party had really made headway, leading to a *modus vivendi* with the subjugated Hittites. The latter succumbed in fact to the ever greater threat from the Assyrians.

Fragment of a stele commemorating Pharaoh Rameses II, Tyre
1276-1275 B.C.
Basalt; height 67 cm, width 79 cm,
depth 29 cm
Department of Antiquities, Beirut

This stele found in Tyre is dated to year 4 of Rameses II's reign. The pharaoh is shown on it beating his enemy with his club. A stele from Nahr el-Kelb likewise mentions that this ruler passed along the Lebanese coast in the course of one of the "pacification" campaigns that he conducted in this area.

Ugarit – An independent kingdom

Like Byblos in Lebanon, the site of Ugarit (Ras Shamra) has been the object of very thorough excavations. Exploration of this tell was led both before and after World War II by Claude Schaeffer, then Henri de Contenson (1972–73), and subsequently Margueron (1975–76). Since 1978, the team led by Marguerite Yon has been at work here. Nearby, the site of Minet el-Beida, which was excavated by Claude Schaeffer, brought to light the remains of port installations from the time Ras Shamra was occupied, meanwhile 3 miles (5 km) away, excavations at Ras Ibn Hani by Adnan Bounni and Jacques Lagarce have uncovered an Ugaritic city that, according to Yon, should be considered as a newly created dependency of the capital. The main settlement period ended here at the beginning of the 13th century B.C., at the same time as in Ugarit. Although the large tract over which the city extended is by no means fully understood, we can get an overall impression as to how this city state fitted into its region. The discovery of tablets in Ras Shamra bearing cuneiform inscriptions written in the Semitic language Ugaritic has added to the special interest of the site.

Originally, at the beginning of the Late Bronze Age, a massive stone wall protected the city. In the west, a fort standing at the top of the glacis guarded the entrance to the palace area, thus also safeguarding one of the city's entrances, over which a square tower loomed. The royal palace occupied almost 2.5 acres (1 ha) and comprised at least 90 rooms, which were arranged around six large courts. Parts intended for the royal household have been identified, such as a throne room, administration areas and rooms reserved for the king and his family. The royal burial vaults were found under the floor of the palace. This area possessed a sewerage system and probably a temple reserved for royal use.

The two most important shrines were in the east of the city, on the acropolis; one of them was dedicated to Baal (probably in connection with the goddess Anath), while the other was dedicated to Dagan. They feature an almost identical floor plan. The temples were surrounded by an enclosed court. The building itself had a flight of steps and vestibule at the front. From the architectural and archaeological data it is inferred that the temples were tower-shaped structures.

A very dense network of narrow, tortuous streets on to which houses opened has been exposed at various points on the tell. The indications are of a very busy, picturesque city with houses of differing sizes that occasionally had terraces and more than one story. The former appear to have been the main residential parts, while the lower floors of the houses were reserved for storage and sanitary installations. Many houses also possessed subterranean tombs.

Since the tablets found both in the palace archives and the houses in the temple areas have

been deciphered, numerous details about life in the city and also the names of the kings of Ugarit have become known. Even though the city's principal source of income lay in exploiting its fertile soil, producing wheat, wine and olives, Ugarit was very willing to consider other opportunities. Thanks to the proximity of the harbor at Mahadu (Minet el-Beida) and the chain of harbors along the cost, Ugarit was able to take an active part in Mediterranean trade, which was in the process of being developed. The city also possessed excellent access to the interior, which made it a good starting or finishing point for large trade expeditions.

Parts of the correspondence found on the site mainly contain clues about what was exchanged: wheat, oil, wool, horses, metals, and slaves were the principal items. The discovery of Mycenean and Cypriot vases, Egyptian alabaster and even pieces of ivory of Indian or African origin enable us to guess at both the manner and the scale of the system of trade in which Ugarit participated.

Possibly this role of Ugarit as a trading center can explain why it was one of the first places in which the alphabetic system of writing was developed – the system that to this day has remained the most widespread among all peoples. The new script made do with far fewer symbols than had been customary up to then, and thanks to its simplifications was accessible to a far greater number of people than just the scribes. Although many of the texts found in Ugarit have a religious content, it was undoubtedly the merchants who profited most from this innovation, as it simplified correspondence and reduced the number of intermediaries, in the form of scribes, required for transactions.

Opposite

Stele of the god Baal, Ugarit

1500–1200 B.C.
Oolitic limestone; height 142 cm, width 50 cm,
depth 28 cm
Louvre, Paris

This stele depicting the god Baal was found in the acropolis in the west of the Baal temple. The god bears attributes (especially the spear) that emphasize his role as a fertility god. He is also guardian of order both in nature and in Ugaritic society, as indicated by the small figure at his feet, which is generally interpreted as the ruler of Ugarit.

Mycenaean krater, Ras Ibn Hani

1400-1300 B.C.
Mycenaean pottery; height 46.7 cm, diam. 36 cm
National Museum, Damascus

This Mycenaean krater was found in a tomb in Ras Ibn Hani. It reveals how important the existing links with the growing power in the eastern Mediterranean became, as the Mycenaean empire gradually developed.

Seated figure, Mari

2500 B.C.
Plaster; height 26 cm
National Museum, Damascus

This seated figure, which was found in the Temple of Ishtar in Mari, is identified in an inscription as "Ur Nanshe the singer." He was singer to Ebih-il and possibly a eunuch, as his feminine features suggest, despite the male name. He was employed in the temple.

Byblos and Beirut are threatened

Thanks to the excavations in Beirut, the evaluation of the archaeological data from Byblos, and the historical information emanating from the texts of Tell el-Amarna, life in these city-states can be reconstructed. Too small to be really independent, they were constantly suffering from the political vicissitudes of their neighbors.

The reestablishment of Egyptian control over the coastal strip of the Levant is evident from the growing plunder of the forest resources in the Lebanon. The sources available mention several expeditions whose purpose it was to provide the pharaohs with wood. Archaeologists have dated few buildings in Byblos to this period, although the site contained hieroglyphic inscriptions and cartouches bearing the name of Rameses II.

Excavations in the center of Beirut have proved much more fruitful in this respect. The main part of the Late Bronze Age city was built on top of the settlement of the Middle and Early Bronze periods. Even the fortifications sat on top of the remains of the older defenses, and were additionally protected by a layer of river stones massed at their base. The part lying opposite did not need reinforcing, as it stood on a cliff above the bank. The whole layout covered an area exactly the same size as that at Byblos. Beneath the tell and in the hollow of a natural route through a valley traces of a simple settlement were also found. But the most detailed information available about the two sites at this time is contained in the letters from Tell el-Amarna. They illustrate best of all the kind of relationship that the minor local kings had with their powerful protectors in the southwest. A total of 54 letters from the king of Byblos, Rib-Addi, have been preserved, written to pharaohs Amenophis III and Amenophis IV, and three letters from Ammunira, the king of Beirut, to Amenophis IV (Akhenaten). We learn there that the fortified city of Byblos was threatened by an Amorite prince, Aziru, who was secretly supported by the Hittites. Apart from the military danger that this represented for Egyptian dependencies, he is supposed to have stirred up rebellion in the rural population and even in Byblos itself. As the expected help or material help from the pharaoh or his representative on the spot failed to materialize, and his fate had been greeted with indifference, Rib-Addi decided to turn to his ally and neighbor, the king of Beirut, while the other cities in the area fell one after the other into the hands of Egypt's enemy. Fleeing to Beirut, Rib-Addi sent one last cry for help to the pharaoh. Meanwhile even Ammunira, the loyal ally, was ready to surrender to Aziru for want of the expected succor. The end of the story is unfortunately unknown. These final records ushered in a period of instability and the rebalancing of the political equilibrium.

Opposite

Palace G, Ebla

This ceremonial staircase is 72 feet (22 m) long, and is an essential feature of Palace G in Ebla. It led up to the audience court. Apart from its practical function, the monumental nature of the structure projected a strong image of king and city.

Eric Gubel

The Phoenicians
A Nation of Seafarers and Merchants

1200–330 B.C.

Anthropoid sarcophagi, Sidon
Mid to end 5th century B.C.
marble; length 203 cm, height 68 cm,
width 84 cm
Department of Antiquities, Beirut

As on the island of Arvad in Sidon, contact
between Phoenician and Greek artisans from
Ionia resulted in the production of a number of
anthropoid sarcophagi, many examples of
which are to be found in the Sidonian necropoli
of the 5th to 3rd century B.C.

Aerial View of Tripolis

In the foreground is el-Mina, where there was probably once a Phoenician harbor; it may be mentioned in an Assyrian text dating from the 7th century B.C. Beyond the periphery of the modern city, between the Lebanon Mountains and the Mediterranean, lies the Plain of Akkar, which continues northward into the Homs district of Syria.

Phoenicia facing the great powers

A number of city-states had developed since the 3rd millennium B.C. along the Mediterranean coast west of the Lebanon chain, between the Plain of Akkara in the north and Mount Carmel in the south. Despite the polycentrism that characterized this region until the 4th century B.C., these political units differed from their neighbors in a dynamic that found expression in both culture and trade. Later the Greeks called the seafaring descendants of the inhabitants of these city-states by the borrowed name of "Phoenicians," which they derived from the Greek word for "purple." It is unclear whether the term referred to the reddish skin color of the Phoenicians or their production of purple dye. The Phoenicians gave the Mediterranean world a rationalized alphabetical system of writing in the early first millennium as well as other techniques in which they were then ahead of their time. This may explain why the western continent is named after a princess of Tyre in Phoenicia – Europa.

The dynamic of Phoenician culture was already manifest in this period of economic mobility in the choice of papyrus instead of the traditional clay tablets to bear the alphabetical script that replaced the almost endless combinations of cuneiform. However, the tendency of papyrus to disintegrate in a damp climate has meant that only sparse remnants of the Phoenicians' own historical source material have survived, mostly in the form of inscriptions on monuments.

Although the direct and indirect sources do give us a basic outline of political and economic events, we know very little about material and cultural life in Phoenician cities during their "golden age." The political instability from which Lebanon, the modern descendant of Phoenician culture, has been suffering for all too long, and the uncontrolled growth of settlements – only one of the negative effects of the political situation – have been catastrophic for archaeology. Therefore a huge puzzle is only gradually being sorted into an overall impression – built up from isolated reports, widely scattered inscriptions and archaeological finds, the significance of which is often only apparent on closer study.

A lasting peace

The peace treaty concluded between the Hittites and the Egyptians in 1259 B.C., after the battle of Qadesh in 1275 B.C., held for nearly a century. It brought the transfer of technologies, knowledge and culture instead of warfare. Moreover, a well-considered marriage policy helped to seal the ties of friendship between the former enemies. As much of this exchange was along the Levantine coast, the coastal towns naturally benefited, regardless of whether they lay in the zone controlled by the Hittites or within the pharaohs' sphere of power.

Initially, these cities must be seen as individual seeds from which the Phoenician realm was developing. Only after about 1200 B.C. did they form a cultural unit. As historical sources for this period are particularly rare the cultural relations are deduced mainly from archaeological finds. However, it is becoming increasingly clear that the process of integration was also a process of continuous change. At first, the development of the trading centers was highly individual.

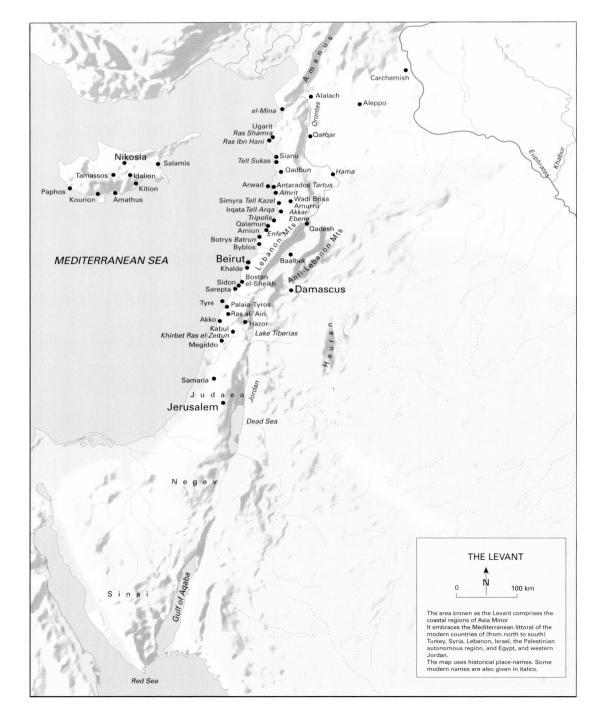

THE LEVANT

0   N   100 km

The area known as the Levant comprises the coastal regions of Asia Minor
It embraces the Mediterranean littoral of the modern countries of (from north to south) Turkey, Syria, Lebanon, Israel, the Palestinian autonomous region, and Egypt, and western Jordan.
The map uses historical place-names. Some modern names are also given in italics.

Ugarit – A paleo-Phoenician trading partner

The Bronze Age excavations in Ugarit (Ras Shamra) have not only yielded exemplary evidence of the magnificence of one of these trading centers, they have also clearly shown the transition from Bronze Age art to Phoenician art in the true sense – and that is concrete evidence of the cultural continuity in this region. The figures of gods that have survived on many columns and in sculptures in stone or gilded bronze are prototypes of the portraiture that developed later in archaic Phoenician art. Ugarit is also regarded as the bastion of Palestine's Canaan culture, which was spread through trade between Ugarit and the paleo-Phoenician centers such as Byblos, Beirut, Sidon and Tyre in the north. Numerous objects from this southern artistic tradition were found in Ugarit, and the tradition was taken up later by the Phoenician artists. Despite its geographical position, or its close connections with the Hittite government, Ugarit also demonstrates the revival of an Egyptian style, which is evident in artifacts such as the many seals, stamps, and rings.

However, Ugarit, where cuneiform remained the prescribed form for recording ancient Akkadian script, was also the home of the oldest known alphabet. Unlike the traditional cuneiform, which was highly complex, the two systems developed in Ugarit in the 14th to 13th centuries B.C. needed far fewer signs. The first, which was adapted to the Ugaritic language, used 30. Its "nails," which are cuneiform signs, point from left to right. The second system is known as the "short alphabet," and it requires only 22 signs; they point left (the "head" of the sign indicates the orientation). It is even closer to the next stage of development, the proto-Phoenician system, the course of whose development took place in the following centuries. The cuneiform signs were replaced by more linear signs, and they in turn are the basic types of the Greek alphabet.

In addition to using the two new systems that were developed in the 14th to 13th centuries B.C., the main benefit of which was to facilitate the recording of economic data, the scribes did occasionally prefer to use Egyptian hieroglyphs for the records of local members of the dynasty. In this they were following the example of the scribes of Byblos, who were then actually developing their own system of "pseudo-hieroglyphs."

If one follows the coast south one comes to several centers, each of which had different relations with the metropolis in Ugarit. In the early days of archaeological research only the place-names of these towns were known from archives in Ugarit, and their actual location could at best be only roughly determined.

More recent research has not only added greatly to geographical knowledge about the region, it has also increasingly shown that the culture that grew up in these places played a decisive part in the development of Phoenicia. Some of these towns, which are known to have been large centers in the later Phoenician period, show a cultural continuity from before 1200 B.C.

Table showing the development of scripts

Starting with the 22 letters of Ugaritic cuneiform, this table shows the development of the signs into the Latin alphabet. The letters that do not occur in the inscription on Ahirom's coffin are known from earlier documents. The Mobaitic inscription on the Mesha stele shows the similarity of the early Phoenician linear script to other Semitic forms of writing at this time, such as Aramaic, Hebrew, and so on.

The Development of the Alphabet	a	b	g	d	h	w	z	ḥ	ṭ	e	k	l	m	n	s	o	f	ṣ	q	r	ṡ	t
Ugarit 14th cent. B.C.	⟨cuneiform⟩	⟨cuneiform⟩	⟨cuneiform⟩	⟨cuneiform⟩	⟨cuneiform⟩	⟨cuneiform⟩	⟨cuneiform⟩	⟨cuneiform⟩	⟨cuneiform⟩	⟨cuneiform⟩	⟨cuneiform⟩	⟨cuneiform⟩	⟨cuneiform⟩	⟨cuneiform⟩	⟨cuneiform⟩	⟨cuneiform⟩	⟨cuneiform⟩	⟨cuneiform⟩	⟨cuneiform⟩	⟨cuneiform⟩	⟨cuneiform⟩	⟨cuneiform⟩
Ahirom c. 1000 B.C.	K	⟨glyph⟩	1	O	Ⅎ	Y		⧓	⊕	⟨glyph⟩	⟨glyph⟩	⟨glyph⟩	⟨glyph⟩	⟨glyph⟩	⧧	O	⟨glyph⟩			⟨glyph⟩	w	+
Mesha Late 9th cent. B.C.	⟨glyph⟩	⟨glyph⟩	1	Δ	⟨glyph⟩	Y	I	⟨glyph⟩	⊗	Z	y	L	⟨glyph⟩	⟨glyph⟩	⧧	O	⟨glyph⟩	⟨glyph⟩	φ	⟨glyph⟩	W	X
Eshmunazor 5th cent. B.C.	⟨glyph⟩	⟨glyph⟩	⟨glyph⟩	⟨glyph⟩	⟨glyph⟩	Y	⟨glyph⟩	⟨glyph⟩	⟨glyph⟩	⟨glyph⟩	⟨glyph⟩	L	⟨glyph⟩	⟨glyph⟩	⟨glyph⟩	O	⟨glyph⟩	⟨glyph⟩	φ	⟨glyph⟩	⟨glyph⟩	⟨glyph⟩
Greek 7th cent. B.C.	Δ		⟨glyph⟩	Δ	⟨glyph⟩	Y	I	θ	⊕	⟨glyph⟩	⟨glyph⟩	⟨glyph⟩	⟨glyph⟩	⟨glyph⟩		O	⟨glyph⟩			φ	⟨glyph⟩	⟨glyph⟩	Τ
Classical Greek	Α	Β	Γ	Δ		Γ	Z	H	Θ	E	K	Λ	M	N		O	Φ			P	Σ	T
Latin	A	B	G	D		V	Z	H		E	K	L	M	N		O	F			R	S	T

The island city of Arvad off the coast is also mentioned in the archives of Amarna and Ugarit, but its importance in regional policy is not clear from these. As the ancient city is completely covered by layers of medieval and modern dwellings, definite clarification cannot be expected from excavations in the foreseeable future.

Nearby, about 12 miles (20 km) north of Tripolis, the mighty Tell Arqa contains the ruins of the ancient city of Irqata, which does not appear to have played a very important part at this time. However, the excavations on this site that were resumed in 1992 could cause that picture to be revised shortly.

On a tablet made just before the destruction of Ugarit, Byblos (also called Jbail and Jublu) is described as a sea power. The tablet states that the king of Byblos had sent 14 items (presumably ships) to his "brother," Prince Hammurapi of Ugarit (1200–1185 B.C.). Except once in connection with trade in fabrics, there is only sparse mention of the port of Byblos in contemporary Ugaritic and Egyptian sources. That may be connected with the sudden cessation of building towards the end of the late Bronze Age. Only objects placed in subterranean tombs outside the city walls are known from Byblos at this time; the tombs contained either one or two chambers.

Opposite, above

Statuette of the god Baal, Ugarit
14th–13th century B.C.
Gilded bronze; height 12.2 cm
National Museum, Damascus

The motif of the male god (Baal) shooting lightning is to be found in Phoenician workshops until the 7th century B.C.

Left

Statuette of the god El, Ugarit
14th–13th century B.C.
Gold; height 13.5 cm
National Museum, Damascus

The image of the god on a throne (here the great god El) recurs until the Roman conquest. After that date it is replaced, like others, by the gods of the Roman Pantheon.

The other trading partners on the Syrian coast

Sianu, where the main office of the Syrian Antiquities Department started excavating in 1990, or Sukas, which is being researched by a Danish team, are now definitely known to have been part of the chain of coastal towns that were (relatively?) autonomous regarding international trade. Formerly, scholars believed that this was only the case with El Minar, a trading and financial center further north, at the mouth of the Orontes. The same applies to Simyra, the locality of which has not yet been definitively established. It was the capital of the kingdom of Amurru, which marked the border between the Hittite and Egyptian spheres of influence. Every year that the excavations by the American University in Beirut provide new evidence makes it more likely that the city stood on Tell Kazel. Simyra's history is described in detail in the archives of Amarna (known as the Amarna tablets). During the great age of Ugarit the kings of Simyra, who bore Hittite names, firmly established links with this metropolis, as the marriages of Princess Ahatmilki and the daughter of King Benteshina with kings of Ugarit show.

Lid of a pyxis:
goddess between rams, Ugarit
14th century B.C.
Ivory, height 13.7 cm
Louvre, Paris

As a result of international trading the art of the Late Bronze Age in Ugarit already points to the eclecticism of Phoenician iconography. Mycaenean influence predominates in this oriental composition.

The trading centers on the Phoenician coast

In the 13th century B.C. Beirut was engaged in a trade war with Ugarit, and it maintained direct or indirect contacts with Egypt, as excavations in the city center have shown. This was also the case with Sidon, where the dynasts Adummu and his son Annipi, who were contemporary with the Rameses rulers in Egypt, used cylinder seals whose decoration is a faithful copy of contemporary Egyptian iconography. The god Seth is prominent on both these seals; he was the Egyptian god of deserts and weather and the patron divinity of the Rameses, and he was equated with Baal, the Levantine god of the weather and fertility. These two cylinders prove that Seth and the gods Reshef and Re-Horachte had a status in Sidon – as they had once enjoyed in Byblos – comparable with

that in the then Egyptian capital Pi-Ramesse. Tyre evidently also played a part in Mediterranean trade at this time. Several containers found in the Nile delta in Egypt reveal the hand of Levantine artists, who were evidently working in this region. The stylistic features of their work are known not only from finds in Ugarit but also from a horse harness from Tyre. Like these two centers, the district around Tyre also has a high concentration of imported Cypriot and Mycenaean ceramics. These finds confirm the reports in the archives of Ugarit which also name Tyre as a trading center.

These texts also show that the mainland territories of the island city – it was only connected with the mainland by a dam under Alexander the Great – at least included the region known as the "Tyrian ladder" towards the end of the 13th century B.C. Silver, copper,

Two cylinder seals bearing the names of King Annipi (above) and his father Adummu, Sidon

13th century B.C.
Blue glass; height 2.7/2.6 cm
Louvre, Paris

The decorations on the two Sidonian seals prove that there was continuous contact between this coastal city and Egypt. Examinations under fluorescent microscopes have shown that the two cylinder seals were colored with cobalt. The unusual method could suggest that the workshops in Sidon had specialized in the production of an imitation lapis lazuli, for which there was keen demand at that time.

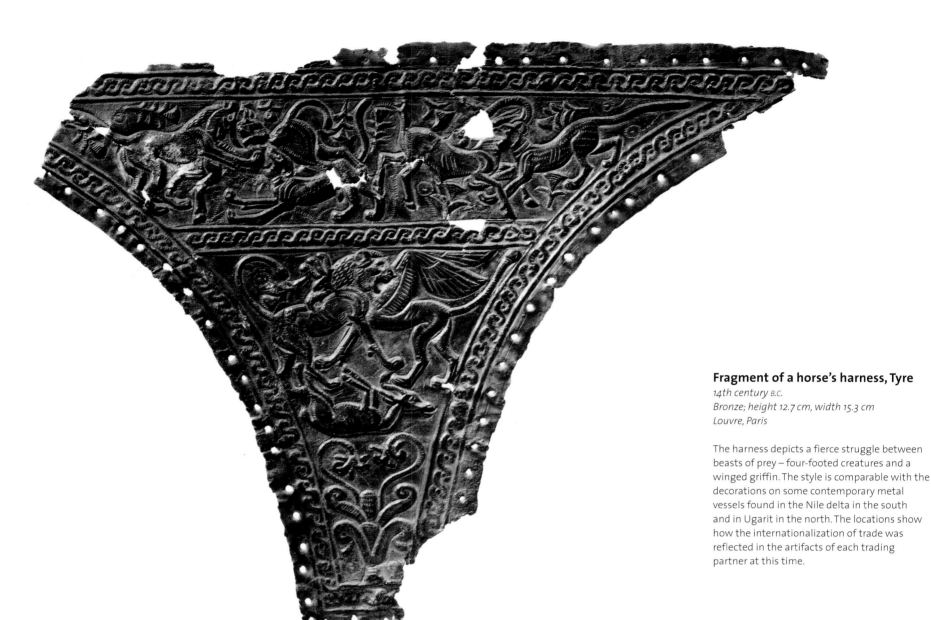

Fragment of a horse's harness, Tyre
14th century B.C.
Bronze; height 12.7 cm, width 15.3 cm
Louvre, Paris

The harness depicts a fierce struggle between beasts of prey – four-footed creatures and a winged griffin. The style is comparable with the decorations on some contemporary metal vessels found in the Nile delta in the south and in Ugarit in the north. The locations show how the internationalization of trade was reflected in the artifacts of each trading partner at this time.

multicolored woven fabrics, dried fish, and caraway are named as export goods. The Ugarit archives also give information about relations between Ugarit and Tyre. A king of Tyre, who is not named, demanded justice for one of his subjects in what is now Ras Ibn Hani. In a third document he takes on the role of supreme judge to arbitrate in a dispute over goods which his overseer had confiscated as stranded.

In conclusion it can be said that the cultural profile of Phoenicia at the end of the Bronze Age derives mainly from two types of source material that are not without their problems: first, external sources, mainly Ugaritic writings, and secondly, objects placed in tombs. These have been found in greater quantity than objects from settlements, so there are few sources from the daily lives of the people themselves. Nevertheless, a picture does emerge of a society that, despite the decline of the great palace culture in the late Bronze Age in the Levant, had control of international trade. Individual finds of art works in the paleo-Phoenician style of this time in the Mediterranean area are proof of this. However, the lack of evidence of the material culture prevents a more precise classification of a number of objects that have been found in Aegean sites and which are clearly of eastern provenance. They may be remnants of the export trade from the smaller paleo-Phoenician ports rather than examples of the influence of a trade center of the size of Ugarit.

Arrowheads, southern Lebanon

1200–110 B.C.
Copper alloy; lengths 6.6, 10.4, 7.8 cm
Department of Antiquities, Beirut

The inscriptions bear the names of Zakkurs, son of Binana, Zakarbaal, King of Amurru and Gerbaal, "of Sidon" (from top) and are among the oldest Phoenician inscriptions. The Phoenicians' neighbors used the 22 letters of the linear script on these arrowheads to write in Aramaic, Ammonitic, Moabitic, Edomitic, and Hebrew.

The "Dark Age"

Several written records speak of the devastating invasion by the "sea people," as they are called. They were an alliance of migratory peoples who attacked the eastern Mediterranean around 1185 B.C., whose appearance marked a break in the history of the entire region. The capital of the Hittite kingdom, Hattusa, was destroyed, as were Ugarit and numerous other cities. However, it is still not known exactly how much of many of the Phoenician coastal towns was destroyed. The invasion certainly caused changes in the region, and the invaders filled the political vacuum left by the collapse of Ugarit, the heart of international trade.

The kingdom of Amurru

Before drawing conclusions too hastily, we should examine the sparse evidence archaeology has produced. The invasion by the sea people cost the kingdom of Amurru in the north its trump card of a favorable position between the Hittite and Egyptian spheres of influence, as the hostile great powers were involved in sometimes desperate struggles with the invaders. The political instability that weakened the region in the phase before the invaders penetrated the Amurru kingdom is evident from how obviously dependent on Simyra (Tell Kazel) most of the centers on the Plain of Akkara (of those that have been researched) had become. Simyra is believed to have

been the capital of Amurru, and if one believes the annals of Pharaoh Rameses III in the temple of Medinet Habu, this bastion around the year 1186 B.C. also fell to attack by the sea people. According to these annals, tribes known as Peleset (Philistines), Tjeker (pirates), Shakalash (Sikilese), Danuna (Danoae), and Washash set up camp at Amor (Amurru), massacred the native population and transformed their ground into a land that, according to the record, never appeared to have existed before.

However, the report is in the style of Egyptian propaganda, and it was intended to glorify the victories of Rameses III over the invaders as compared with the defeats suffered by his rivals in the north. And although the excavations in Ugarit and Tell Kazel have produced powerful testimonies to widespread destruction at precisely this time, the effects cannot have been as lasting as the Egyptian document would have us believe. We have another source from barely two generations later that suggests that the kingdom soon revived. This information is from two arrowheads that are engraved with the name Zakarbaal, on one of which he is called "King of Amurru." Finally, on the threshold of the first millennium B.C., the city of Simyra (Tell Kazel) also regained its former dynamic.

This development evidently coincided with the establishment of a Phoenician trading post on Tell Kazel which soon resumed contact with Cyprus. Two other important sources, the so-called "Stele of Amrit," which is actually from the mouth of the nearby Nahr el-Abrach, and the stele found in 1988 in the northern part of the kingdom of Qadbun, both bear characteristic features of the art of the late Bronze Age in the form of the weather god. Each of these steles, however, also contains Phoenician elements, and so represent an important stage in this phase of Phoenician acculturation.

The island of Arvad

Arvad, although as an island less exposed to attacks – which usually came from the land side – seems to have suffered as well from the invasion by the sea people at the turn of the 2nd to the 1st millennium B.C. However, as many factors prevent this assumption from being tested archaeologically, it is based only on the mention of Arvad as one of the cities conquered by the invaders in the inscriptions of Rameses III. The Greek geographer Strabon, however, reports that people from Sidon quickly resettled Arvad; the extension of its power into the coastal region and later north Syria, and the presence of Phoenicians in neighboring Tell Kazel towards the end of the 2nd millennium B.C., suggest that Strabon's report is reliable.

However, subsequently the Levant came once more under the influence of the great powers. The Assyrians, who had been a major power in Mesopotamia since the 13th century B.C., intervened repeatedly in the power struggle in the Levant from the end of the 12th century B.C. An Assyrian report on the first "Syrian" campaign under Tiglathpileser I, around 1100 B.C., mentions tributes paid by Byblos, Sidon, and Arvad. The expedition was clearly aimed at Phoenician trading posts set up to protect the caravan trade up into the north of Syria, and it was obviously more of a commercial than a military nature. This may be assumed from the fact that Tiglathpileser I records receiving valuable Lebanese cedars. In addition, the Assyrian ruler took advantage of a voyage to Simyra to hunt at sea, killing a *nahiru*, that is, a hippopotamus or a young seal. Before 875 B.C., under Ashurnasirpal II, Arvad was again forced to pay tribute to the Assyrians. The first mention by name of a king of Arvad in Assyrian sources dates from 853 B.C. He was Matinuabali, and he was a member of a coalition which included the kings of Sianu, Simyra, and Irqata, rulers of "Greater Syria" and Phoenicia, who had formed an alliance against the Assyrians. However, according to Assyrian propaganda they were defeated by the troops of Shalmanesar III in the battle of Qarqar.

Who controlled the southern Plain of Akkara?

If one crosses the Nahr el-Kebir heading south and continues down the southern Plain of Akkar, which is marked by strangely formed tumuli along the coastal road in the Lebanon, one wonders which kingdom took this territory after the kingdom of Amurru had

The "Stele of Amrit," mouth of the Nahr el-Abrach in Sumur territory
850–750 B.C.
Limestone; height 178 cm
Louvre, Paris

The stele from the mouth of the Nahr el-Abrach in Sumur (Tell Kazel) shows a god of thunder standing on a lion. In one hand he holds a weapon and in the other the body of a lion. The style still bears strong Phoenician influence, but this was soon to be wiped out by the Assyrian rule in the region. In Persian times this stele was appropriated and dedicated to the god of healing, Shadrapa, one of the divinities worshipped in the sanctuary of Amrit.

had to accept defeat. The question is difficult to answer both as regards the late Bronze Age and the following period, long before Tripolis was established as the center of Phoenician power in southern Akkar.

A report by Wen-Amon on Egyptian papyrus may provide some information. Wen-Amon was the ambassador sent by the weakened pharaoh to Byblos around 1050 B.C., and he was instructed by Herihor, high priest of Amun in Thebes, to buy cedarwood in Lebanon. As the unfortunate ambassador had his gold and silver stolen at a stopover in Tyre he tried to invoke the dying power of Egypt and demanded the wood as tribute. His report recounts in satirical fashion how he found himself facing mighty power structures in his doomed undertaking – for instance, he was made to wait a long time for the audience usually granted by the city king of Byblos. Interestingly, this city king was called Zakarbaal, the name that is found as "King of Amurru" on the arrowhead mentioned above. Could this be one and the same person, rather than there being two with the same name? Had Byblos acquired a kind of hegemony through a concentration of power that included the region that had once been part of the kingdom of Amurru? That would be all the more remarkable as King Rib-Addi of Byblos had complained 300 years earlier in numerous letters to the pharaoh of the expansion of this kingdom. Some scholars interpret these sources as merely coincidence – two rulers with the same name, Zakarbaal – but was this really coincidence? The worthy Wen-Amon mentions another astonishing fact in his report, namely the presence of a man with the Egyptian name Pen-Amon at the court of the petty prince of Gubla. Of course he could be a local courtier who had assumed an Egyptian name. However, the same name occurs on another significant find. This is the fragment of an Egyptian

altar that was found in the Plain of Akkar, opposite Arvad – in other words, in an area that was then ruled by none other than Zakarbaal, King of Amurru (and Byblos?).

We shall not comment further on these speculations here, for the local conditions are such that it is not possible to clarify to which kingdom southern Akkar belonged after the sea people invaded the region. In towns such as Enfe, Batrun (Botrys), and Aminu that could perhaps provide information, it has not, unfortunately, been possible to undertake proper excavations yet. And many other ports such as Qalamun and smaller settlements were razed to the ground shortly before or during the civil war, before any archaeological examination to assess their age had been carried out.

Byblos – If I command with a loud voice in Lebanon ...

And how should we consider Byblos itself, the city that provides evidence of many epochs on Phoenician soil of which we otherwise have no testimony? The finds brought to light in situ so far are extremely rare. It is known that ambassador Wen-Amon was confronted with a political structure that was ruled by a tradition going back a thousand years. This appears to have been hardly touched by the destruction known or surmised to have been wrought elsewhere by the invaders from the sea. Moreover, Wen-Amon also learned to appreciate King Zakarbaal's authority, for he was given to understand that if the king commanded with a loud voice in Lebanon the heavens would open and the trees (which Wen-Amon wanted) would lie along the beach. In view of the importance of this ruler, whose name was famous enough to have entered Egyptian literature, perhaps the anonymous sarcophagus that was later usurped by King Ittobaal of Byblos to bury his father Ahirom was his, or at least intended for a member of his family.

A short time later the emergence of the new power of Assyria brought about a clear strengthening of relations between the Gublites and Egypt. Around 1100 B.C. Byblos was forced to pay tribute to Tiglathpileser I, and the city will certainly have been keen to revive its alliance with the Egyptian court, which was now in Tanis. Byblos thus secured a political and economic dynamic that could also explain the important contribution made by ancient Gublitic script in the development of the Phoenician alphabet. Until concrete evidence is available, however, other events suggest that this cultural renaissance should be dated about 150 years later, when Byblos was providing cedars and craftsmen for Solomon to build his temple in Jerusalem. Independent of whether these deliveries, as will become clear later, were through Tyre or the result of direct contact with the Israelite monarchy, the

The Sarcophagus of Ahirom, Byblos
Around 1300–1200 B.C.
Limestone with red paint;
length 297 cm, width 115 cm, height 140 cm
Department of Antiquities, Beirut

King Ethbaal, who had an inscription in honor of his father Ahirom, who died around 1000 B.C., engraved on the lid of this sarcophagus, was probably not the first Gublitic ruler to usurp the anonymous tomb. The decoration suggests the 12th, or even the 13th century B.C. The items of furniture depicted, the alternating garlands of lotus flowers and blossoms, and the lions at the foot are all features of Phoenician art of the first millennium.

transaction shows that Byblos had obviously regained its former importance by the beginning of the 1st millennium. Between 945 and 850 B.C. the pharaohs Sheshonk I, Osorkon I, and Osorkon II sent granite busts and statues as diplomatic gifts, and thus confirmed the privileged position of the city. The second inscriptions in Phoenician language added to the hieroglyphs record the succession of contemporary fellow rulers, Abibaal, Elibaal, and Shipitbaal.

It appears that at this time a kind of "joint venture" was formed between Byblos and Tyre with the intention of optimizing the yield from the cedar-wood trade. According to the historian Flavius Josephus ("Jewish Antiquities"), Ittobaal of Tyre succeeded shortly before 850 B.C. in turning Batrun, a town near Byblos, into a Tyrian trading center. As the Gublitic economy was still in full upswing at this time it is unlikely that the base was used to control the independent course taken by Byblos, and one must assume that there was cooperation between the towns. However, a short time later Byblos gradually began to lose its leading role.

The excavations that have been taking place since 1994 in the center of Beirut have spectacularly refuted the opinion held until now that the city lost all its importance after the invasion by the sea people. Even though most of the finds still need more detailed examination, it is already clear that the ceramics are very similar to those in southern Phoenicia, which was continuously inhabited. So Beirut may also be assumed to have been inhabited, and these settlements must have survived the

invasion. In Khalde the necropolis of the Hedlua settlement of the 10th to the early 7th century B.C., that had not until the excavations been located, has provided further examples of the bichrome (two-colored) ceramics that are typical of this period. Around 850 B.C. they were superseded by a highly polished ware with red slip. Terracotta objects, bronzes showing a goddess enthroned, and finally one of the oldest examples of Phoenician carving, give a good overview of the cultural profile.

Brilliant Sidon

Sidon shines in this tumultuous age like a beacon of Phoenician civilization. Traditionally it is regarded as having "refounded" the towns of Arvad and Tyre after their destruction by the sea people. Sidon's prominent position towards 1050 B.C. is also evident from Wen-Amon's report. According to the ambassador, 50 ships were then operating between Tanis and Sidon, whereas only about 20 vessels were operating the line to Byblos, a traditional ally of Egypt.

The tributes paid jointly by Sidon, Arvad, and Byblos to Tiglathpileser I date from the same period. However, Sidon's reemergence in history is also illustrated by archaeological finds. An arrowhead has been found bearing the name of Gerbaal, "of Sidon." It dates from this time and is one of a number of about 50 similar arrowheads that belonged to the *ash*, mercenaries in the pay of the *rabbif*, the commander of the Levantine petty princes. Another arrowhead

View of the southern hill of ruins, Byblos

It is striking that very few remnants of buildings from the Early Iron Age were found during the excavations on the Tell of Byblos, although it is known that local princes such as Yehawmilk (about 925 B.C.) and Shipitbaal I (about 850 B.C.) continued to furnish the temple of Baalat-Gebal, or at least had it renovated. Could this mean that the settlement of those times lies hidden under the foundations of the modern city at the foot of the acropolis?

Relief showing the transportation of wood in boats from the palace of Sargon, Khorsabad

7th century B.C.
Limestone, detail (total length 2.44 m)
Louvre, Paris

Cedarwood beams from the Lebanese Mountains were transported by sea to the banks of the Euphrates during Assyrian rule. The two fortresses depicted above are generally interpreted as Phoenician coastal towns (Tyre, Arvad, or Byblos)

found in el-Ruweise bears the name of a mercenary from Akko, who was buried near Sidon at the end of the 11th century B.C.

Sidon appears to have played a leading part in the exploration of the Mediterranean undertaken by the Phoenician cities from the end of the 2nd millennium. These trade explorations, which ultimately covered the entire Mediterranean, were first concentrated on the Aegean Sea. Sources from classical times name Sidon as the founder of several trading posts and this explains why the Phoenicians are called "Sidonians" by Homer. The name recurs several times in Assyrian and biblical sources, all of which praise the brilliance of the city. The use of this "pars pro toto" may perhaps be rooted in the coalition in the form of a dual kingdom formed by Sidon with Tyre; it was established towards 850 B.C. under Ittobaal. The "King of the Tyrians and the Sidonians" had until then held the office of high priest of Astarte, the goddess of love and war, in Sidon.

If there were a dual kingdom this would explain the lack of any dynastic names in Sidon before Luli, the last ruler of the dual monarchy, towards the end of the 8th century B.C.

Tyre crowned

The city of Tyre had been a royal seat since the late Bronze Age, and it appears to have been spared the destruction wrought by the sea people. Antique sources do mention the "refounding" of Tyre by Sidon, but many historians see this as meaning either the resettlement of the mainland part of the city (Palaia-Tyre) or the redesign of the island city. The latter certainly served the people of Tyre, and refugees from Sidon, as a last refuge from attacks from the mainland.

Sources of information on Tyre are rare. Towards 1050 B.C. the Egyptian ambassador Wen-Amon made a brief stop in the harbor of Tyre. A short time later a Tyrian warlord named Shafat had his name engraved on an arrowhead. A comparison with the arrowhead bearing the name of Gerbaal "of Sidon" leaves no doubt that at this time Tyre and Sidon were regarded as two individual political units of a common state. The lack of mention of Tyre in the list of Phoenician cities obliged to pay tribute to Tiglathpileser I in the list dating from around 1000 B.C. is not irrefutable proof that Tyre was subject to Sidon.

On the contrary, it may be assumed that Tyre felt safe enough from the Assyrians to win over a former invader to its side. The report by Wen-Amon, biblical sources (Judges 10:11–12; Psalms 83:3ff.), and Flavius Josephus all assume that Tyre was allied with the Philistines, one of the tribes invading from the sea who had now settled in Palestine. Tyre presumably formed this alliance in order to secure a trade route by sea to Palestine and Egypt – and it was obviously successful, since the city of Kition on Cyprus became a Tyrian colony toward the end of the 11th century B.C. However, on the mainland the defeat of the Philistines by David created new political realities, and Tyre was forced to abandon its policy of expansion.

Relations with Israel

Under King David Israel extended its borders down to the southern border of the Tyrian kingdom of Abibaal. Archaeologists are certainly right in assuming that the cedars supplied from the Lebanon for the building of the temple of Yahwe (Chronicles I, 22:4) were actually part of a large-scale diplomatic offensive to cement the good relations between the two new neighbors.

A generation later Hiram I of Tyre (970–936 B.C.) and Solomon of Jerusalem (969–930 B.C.) cemented these diplomatic ties. Solomon handed over a number of villages in the land of the Assers to Hiram, and the two rulers began trading. The details of this still need to be researched; however, it is clear that these diplomatic relations went far beyond a simple exchange of Lebanese cedarwood for grain and oil.

Moreover, the Old Testament records an expedition by sea to the distant land of Ophir (East Africa?) from which the Tyrian-Israeli fleet returned with gold and possibly ivory and precious stones.

Hiram again sent Solomon wood for his temple in Jerusalem, and his craftsmen worked under an overseer who was also called Hiram. Various sources confirm the assumption that the young state of Israel allowed itself to be guided by the more experienced men of Tyre in architecture and town planning.

In Tyre, Hiram the architect had created a new shrine to the gods Melkart and Astarte by connecting together some rocky cliffs. This was followed by another temple in the east of the island dedicated to a god who was the equivalent of Zeus of Olympus.

Unfortunately the few sources we have do not say whether the political and economic alliance between the two states was of long duration. Not only were the successors to the two partners confronted with dynastic disputes, around 930 B.C. Israel and Judaea actually had to suffer an Egyptian invasion under Pharaoh Shesehonk I. However, he did not advance his war chariots further north into Tyrian territory, as he could not estimate how well a city whose fleet controlled the sea would be able to defend itself. Had the pharaoh perhaps endowed Byblos with the privileges it enjoyed in order to break Tyre's monopoly of the sea?

Accession of the Priest-King

A *coup d'état* around 887 B.C. put a priest from Sidon on the throne of Tyre, as we have already mentioned. Ethbaal, "King of the Sidons" or "King of the Tyrians

View of the city of Jerusalem

Very little has survived of the magnificent buildings which David and his son Solomon commissioned early in the 1st millennium B.C. However, the biblical sources leave no doubt that the first rulers of the young state of Israel owed the realization of their ambitious projects to the knowledge and skill of the Phoenician experts sent to Jerusalem by their ally, Hiram I of Tyre. In Persian times it was again Sidonians and Tyrians who worked on the reconstruction of the temple of Yahwe.

and the Sidons," ruled for 32 years. He is said to have been responsible for founding Auza in north Africa and Batrum north of Byblos. In 879 B.C. he was received by Ashurnasipal II on the occasion of the dedication of his new palace in Nimrud, but he also had excellent relations with the Aramaic states. The influence of trade with Tyre in these states is clear from the use of Phoenician script there. It was made possible by a tribute paid to the Assyrians in 883 B.C. The Phoenician gods also had worshippers among the Aramaic people as a Melkart stele from the region around Aleppo shows. In 858 B.C. Tyre also had to pay tribute to Ashurnasipal's son Shalmanesar III, when he took up a position before the city. However, Ethbaal also maintained the good relations with Israel by giving his daughter Jezebel in marriage to King Ahab (871–852 B.C.).

Ethbaal died in his city shortly before the battle of Qarqar. The great age of Tyre is nowhere better described than in the book of Ezekiel (27:2–24). However, Isaiah bemoans its downfall: "Who hath taken this counsel against Tyre, the crowning city, whose merchants are princes, whose traffickers are the honorable of the earth?" (Isaiah, 23:8).

Statuette of a goddess making the gesture of dedication, location unknown

900–800 B.C.
Bronze, head covered with silver leaf; height 20.1 cm, width 4.8 cm
Louvre, Paris

The goddess's arm is raised and her hand is open, the palm facing the viewer. Her head is covered with silver leaf, using an old technique that the Phoenicians took to Egypt. Her ears are pierced and she once wore earrings that are now lost.

Opposite, below

Aerial view of the island of Arvad

According to Assyrian sources the island city of Arvad was ruled originally not by a king, but by a political alliance of the leading merchants. From the early 1st millennium kings with Phoenician names are also known on the island; they appear to have been relatively independent of the mainland, as the annals of the Assyrian rulers show. Thanks to its favorable position the island also remained untouched by the many wars that were fought on the mainland. The people of Arvad buried their dead on the mainland opposite the island, in the plain south of the city of Tartus, and evidence of the local arts and crafts has also been found there.

Fragment of the Balawat gateway, Balawat
9th century B.C.
Bronze, height 27 cm
British Museum, London

Shalmanesar III embarked upon campaigns in the west during his first year on the throne (858 B.C.), in the course of which he received tribute payments from the people of Sidon and Tyre. The Assyrian conquerors used the Phoenician fleet and boats to fetch the tribute from the island of Tyre to the mainland.

The "Golden Age"

The brief historical survey of the time known as the "dark age" has shown with what effort some cities slowly recovered from a serious crisis. Nevertheless, some classical writers date the foundation of the first Phoenician colonies as early as the start of this period. Cadiz in Spain, for example, Utica in Tunisia, and Lixus in Morocco are believed to have been founded at the end of the 12th century B.C., and to have served from that date as sources of supply for gold, raw materials, and other natural products from their hinterland. However, not only would this have been contrary to the political situation in Phoenicia itself, it is not confirmed by any inscription or other archaeological finds. The oldest of these go back just to the end of the 9th century B.C., that is, the time when Carthage was also founded. There are a few exceptions, but they at most show a simple use of sea routes, and the first sporadic trade of a pre-colonial phase to explore potential trading places. Early traces of commercial interaction with the Aegean, and a freight voyage by Phoenician vessels to Egypt mentioned in Wen-Amon's report suggest that the Phoenician expansion in the Mediterranean was not, as was frequently assumed by scholars earlier, a direct consequence of the Assyrian threat, but an intensification of Phoenician trading expeditions.

Imports dating from the early phase of expansion are more frequent in the eastern Mediterranean at the start of the 1st millennium B.C. The Syrian–Palestinian potentates of the Egyptian protectorate of the Levant mentioned in the Amarna tablets maintained jealously guarded relations with the Aegean world in the Late Bronze Age. Again and again archaeological research has encountered new traces of Phoenician presence. They mark the Phoenician sea routes, as their vessels penetrated the as yet unexploited markets of Crete, Cyprus, and the Greek mainland, and profited from the decline of the Mycenaean sea power. It cannot be said with certainty whether the metal beakers and items of jewelry found in Attica (Eleusis, Athens) and Lefkandi on Euboa were brought directly by the Phoenicians or via other traders; the finds rather suggest the latter. Euboic ceramics occur in the Levant from the second half of the 10th century B.C., but the characteristic Phoenician jugs with a rim were only exported to the Aegean (Crete, Kos) from the second half of the following century. So the start of Phoenician penetration into the eastern Mediterranean can be estimated at not long before 850 B.C., that is, towards the end of the "dark age."

There were Phoenician settlements on Cyprus even before 900 B.C., at the end of a transition period that was started by the waves of immigration due to the invasion by the sea people. In addition to the geographical proximity of Cyprus to the Levant these waves of immigration were a further reason why the Phoenicians were able to establish themselves here earlier than in other regions.

On the mainland the spread of bichrome ceramics (painted in two colors) and Phoenician script demonstrates the expansion of trade in the direction of the Aramaic states of northern Syria on the one hand, and towards Galilee in the south on the other. There are also some indications of a Phoenician diaspora in Palestine; they mark the stages of a caravan route that ran parallel to the coastal road, the "via maris," that had existed since the 3rd millennium B.C. It also ended in the Nile delta in Egypt. Here too, as in the Egyptian metropoles of Memphis, Heracleopolis, and possibly even Thebes, the imported ceramics show the presence of Phoenicians before the end of this period, around 900 B.C. Thus archaeology confirms Wen-Amon's account. According to him the Phoenician ship-owners maintained regular branch offices to guarantee sea routes to Byblos from as far away as the Egyptian capital Tanis, but apparently particularly to Sidon. Probably rightly, these trading communities are the first to be cited to explain the rapid spread of the metal industry in Egypt under the Libyan pharaohs (950–730 B.C.). This phenomenon of the transfer of technology can in turn be seen in

connection with the renaissance of an Egyptian style in contemporary Phoenician art. And finally it must be remembered that the tribute which the Phoenician cities offered to Tiglathpileser I also would include exotic animals, such as apes and crocodiles, imported from Egypt.

Amulet to hang from a chain, Carthage
4th–3rd century B.C.
Colored sand glass; c. 3 cm
Louvre, Paris

Phoenician mask beads have been found in the western Mediterranean, showing that the Phoenicians traded here from shortly before the turn of the millennium. In the early 1st millennium B.C. this evidence mainly consists of ceramic finds, bowls in precious metals, bronze jugs, jewelry, and seals.

Stele on a rock celebrating a victory of Rameses II, in the south of Nahr el-Kelb

The outcrop of rock in the south of Nahr el-Kelb (between Byblos and Beirut) has been a strategic military passage since history began. Numerous rulers from distant lands have aimed to secure political stability in the Levant, a buffer zone between the superpowers of that time, and have left their traces here. This stele records a victory of Pharaoh Rameses II (1279–1212 B.C.) that was dedicated to the supreme god of Thebes, Amun-Re. It is one of three steles that Rameses had made after his first Asia campaign in the fourth year of his reign. The two others were commissioned after the defeat at Wadesh and in the eighth or tenth year of his reign. On the left stele, which is framed by an arch, we see an Assyrian king with a beard, wearing a diadem and a long robe. His arms are raised in prayer, recalling the posture taken by Asarhaddon on a neighboring stele, possibly dating from 677 B.C. Unfortunately the inscription is too badly eroded for the name of the Assyrian king to be recognizable.

The threat from Assyria

"Thanks to the power of Assur, Sin, Shamash, Abu, Marduk, the Ishtar of Nineveh, and the Ishtar of Arbela I conquered all my arrogant foes; at their divine command the hostile princes swayed like the reeds before the storm.

The kings who inhabit the sea, whose walls are the sea itself and for whom the tide is the city wall, who steer a boat as if it were a warrior's chariot, and who harness oarsmen, not horses, live in growing fear; their hearts beat fast and they spit gall."

(Passage freely translated from Prisma A of the Asarhaddon: IV.78–V.25).

During the first Assyrian advance into northern Syria under Ashurnasipal II (866 B.C.) and later under Shalmanesar III (838 B.C.), Byblos, Sidon, and Tyre were able to retain some scope for action by paying tributes to the newcomers. The dynasts in the trading cities preferred to secure safe conduct for their caravans rather than incur the risk of political conflict, and certainly of military conflict, for which they were not in any way adequately equipped. Nevertheless, the pressure increased from the 8th century B.C. The kingdom of Amurru, that had once been ruled by the Phoenician dynasty of Zakarbaal, had apparently come under the control of the kings of Hama before the start of the 9th century B.C., before Tiglathpileser III turned it into an Assyrian province in 738 B.C.

The uprising of the "Aramaic" provinces of Syria was ruthlessly put down by Sargon in 720 B.C., as was the area around the town of Simyra, that was incorporated into the Assyrian kingdom as the province of Sumur around 738 B.C. If one remembers the long and close relations between these powers – they are proven for the Amarna period and under the government or reigns of Zakarbaal – there may be a possible connection between the slackening of the Gublitic economy and the loss of its trading partner. Certainly Assyrian policy caused a decline in Phoenician activities in northern Syria.

In the south, Assyrian pressure proved an increasingly destabilizing factor politically, forcing the following kings to look increasingly to the Aegean and the western Mediterranean for new markets. The legend of the founding of Carthage must also be seen in this context. The city that was later to replace its mother town as the leader of the western world is assumed to have been founded in 814 B.C. by Tyrian refugees. The events are recorded in the form of a legend by the Roman writer Justinus. Elissa-Dido, sister of King Pygmalion of Tyre (831–785 B.C.) fled from persecution by her brother and founded the city of Carthage with her followers. At the end of the story she throws herself on to a funeral pyre to avoid a hated marriage. The version in Virgil's "Aenead," in which Dido burns for love of Aeneas, is only a poetic adaptation.

Internal problems and the increases in the tithes demanded by the Assyrians shook the dual kingdom. In 727 B.C. Sidon, Akko, and Palaia-Tyros allied with Shalmanesar V against King Luli in Tyre. Luli, "King of the Sidonians," also had to organize a punitive expedition to Cyprus to put down a revolt there by the Tyrian colony Kition. (The date of this expedition cannot be accurately ascertained; some writers date it as occurring in 701 B.C.). Although he emerged victorious from the sea battle against the Phoenician allies of the Assyrian ruler, he had to withstand a blockade of Tyre on the mainland which was only withdrawn under Sargon II (721–705 B.C.).

The Tyrian fleet was of interest to Sargon for a number of reasons – to transport wood to his new capital of Chorsabad, north of Nineveh, or to combat the Greek pirates (717–716 B.C.). In 707 B.C. Sargon had a column of victory erected in Kition to proclaim Assyrian power over this Phoenician colonial territory as well.

The autonomy which the Phoenician cities regained after the death of Sargon was only of brief duration. In 701 B.C. Arvad, Sidon, and Byblos were forced to affirm loyalty to his son and successor Sennacherib (705–681 B.C.), while Luli had to flee from Tyre to Cyprus, where he died in exile. Sennacherib set a "puppet" king named Ethbaal on the throne of Sidon and so ended the existence of the dual kingdom of Tyre and Sidon; Tyre's territory was limited to the island city. The shift in power from Tyre to Sidon was, however, only temporary, as

Sennacherib's successor Asarhaddon (681–668 B.C.) razed Sidon to the ground in 675 B.C., since its prince Abdimilkutti showed little inclination to accept his authority. Despite the dramatic repercussions of this event, which was followed a short time later by the restriction of the power of the city of Tyre, ruled by Baal I, the conquest merely demilitarized the region. Trade continued unbroken, although some of the routes were now controlled by the Assyrian authorities. Ashurbanipal (668–626 B.C.) was to be the last Assyrian king who had to "pacify" the region, by further restricting the power of Baal I of Tyre and Jakinlu of Arvad.

An analysis of the Assyrian lists of booty and tithes is extremely informative as regards the variety of the articles imported from Phoenician cities or produced there. From the 9th century B.C. we find gold, silver, tin, copper, and bronze bars in the lists, as well as metal vessels. The quantities, like the 9,480 lb (4,300 kg) of gold delivered from Tyre to Tiglathpileser III, may perhaps be exaggerated, but they do reflect the prestige of the coastal towns. The elephant hides and tusks (presumably the tusks of the same animal) are a reminder of the high regard in which Levantine ivory work was held, while the colorful robes of linen and purple or red wool are evidence of another tradition that had lasted a thousand years. Finally the lists mention various types of wood and exotic animals among the commodities recorded by the Assyrian scribes as of particular interest.

This wealth of raw materials was also due to the efficient trade network in the Mediterranean. The Phoenicians, with a comprehensive policy of expansion, for the first time made this their own trading area. In addition to the bridgeheads already mentioned they set up numerous trading posts on Malta, Sicily, and Sardinia. The network of Phoenician trade had reached this impressive size even before the end of the 8th century B.C., after which Phoenician relations with the Etruscans were to reach their peak. And finally the foundation of the first Carthaginian colony on the Balearic islands towards the middle of the following century was evidence of the decline of the city of Tyre. Carthage was to replace Tyre as the most important center on the coast. It then assumed control of the western "Punic" Mediterranean, where it came increasingly into open conflict, with the Greeks from the late 6th century B.C., and later with the Romans.

Art in the Golden Age

Initially the trading posts in the north that set up the small sanctuaries in Simyra (Tell Kazel) and Irqata (Tell Arqa) experienced an upswing, but this was suppressed by the Assyrian annexation of the kingdom of Amurru in 738 B.C. and by the suppression following the uprising of 720 B.C. The

Pendant with carnelian scarab set in a gold ring (enlarged detail above), Bolsena, Etruria

Second half of 6th century B.C.
Carnelian; width 3.1 cm
Staatliches Museum Preussischer
Kulturbesitz, Berlin

There was an extremely lively and fruitful cultural interchange between the Phoenicians and the Etruscans which included art as well as trade. This Phoenician seal is evidence of that, as it is set in an Etruscan ring. The seal shows the young sun god Horus crouching on an altar shaped like a pylon (or a gateway) amid marshy land. Isis is said to have once hidden the young god Horus in a marsh.

Assyrian deportation policy and the severe regime imposed by the conquerors left little scope for the development of a regional style, and there is only sparse evidence of a Phoenician tradition. The monuments in Arvad, on the other hand, reflect this tradition in a spectacular way. Although they actually date from the time of the Assyrian threat, the reliefs demonstrate the independence the island city was able to preserve. In Byblos this period is only recorded in a few inscriptions and a handful of fragments from "necropolis K," but these are comparable formally with the ceramics from the necropoli around Sidon, Tyre and the Akko plain. Until the excavations in Beirut yield results one must go to the region south of Sidon to see widespread archaeological evidence of Phoenician settlements. These have a typical architecture which enabled Phoenician influence to spread far beyond the borders of the core region. In Sarepta a temple and craftsmen's quarter have been partly uncovered. However, high quality ashlar masonry appeared at the start of the first millennium B.C. in other areas of the Syria-Palestine coast as well. In the Phoenician temple of Kition (Cyprus) and the Phoenician fortress of Khirbet Ras el-Zeitun (Cabul) the stone blocks are laid in alternating rows of headers and stretchers or between groups of pillars – the latter producing a kind of stone half-timbered effect that was developed in north Syria in the Late Bronze Age. In Judah and Israel this masonry is often to be found with palmette capitals (proto-Aeolian capitals), a type frequently copied in Phoenician art. This also applies to the windows with triple stepped frames and balustrades with columns crowned with flowers, the shafts adorned with three flower cups.

Without sufficient finds from the Phoenician mother towns one must use the evidence that has been revealed in the settlements of their trading partners or found in the ruins of their Assyrian conquerors, after being paid as tithes or taken as booty in wars. In the first case attention focuses mainly on Cyprus and the Aegean. Salamis, Kition, Amathus, Kourion, Pahos, Tammassos, and Idalion are only some of the sites on Cyprus that have provided material evidence of Phoenician presence. The evidence is either in the form of sacral architecture (Kition) or tombs (Tamassos); there are also opulent collections of luxury goods such as furniture and accessories inlaid with ivory (Salamis) and beakers in precious metals (Kourion, Idalion), large numbers of which were also found in the Assyrian palaces. Sites in Crete have yielded objects imported from the east that were stored in the Idaic caves, the bethels uncovered in Kommos and bowls and jewelry from Knossos (Tekke) and Fortetsa. Often these objects are adorned with heraldic motifs, which were certainly used by several cities in Phoenicia, which was then a highly active colonial power.

Hence an increasing number of sites bearing traces of Phoenician trade are to be found in the west,

as on the Aegean islands of Rhodes and Samos, in Kilikia in southern Anatolia and the Nile delta in Egypt. Nevertheless, the true character of the trading communities active there (whether these were itinerant or settled has not yet been definitely established), and the artists and artisans is still a matter for imaginative interpretation.

Owing to the circumstances of its development the art of this period of expansion is on the whole cosmopolitan. The works show a combination of ideas that have been adopted with elements from a very independent tradition; they are made to suit the taste of the local market and some include elements of non-Phoenician craftsmanship. Hundreds of ivory tablets that once decorated magnificent furniture are

Opposite

Woman at a window, Arslan Tash
c. 900–800 B.C.
Ivory; height 5.9 cm, width 4.2 cm
National Museum, Aleppo

Hundreds of ivory carvings have been found which came from the Assyrian palaces in Nimrud, Chrosabad, Arslan Tash, and other sites in the kingdom where the tithes paid by the conquered cities were kept. Many of these carvings once decorated magnificent furniture. This one shows the head of a woman in a window with a balustrade on columns with flower capitals; she is probably a priestess and temple prostitute.

A relief from Arvad
c. 850–700 B.C.
Limestone; height 50 cm
Louvre, Paris

This decorated floor slab, like two others that are now in the Louvre and the Musée des Beaux-Arts in Geneva respectively, are from a public or sacral building. The griffins and winged sphinxes on the reliefs indicate the role played by the sacred tree of life in Phoenician culture. The seat of universal harmony is guarded by animals and mythological beings, who supported the kings of the Phoenician cities in maintaining their power.

Opposite

Bowl from Idalion, Cyprus
Early 7th century B.C.
Silver-gilt; diam 13.5 cm
Louvre, Paris

The narrative frieze and the medallion on this bowl contain various motifs enabling the owner of this very fine piece to identify with the Tyrian city god Milkart or Reshef of Sidon. In the central medallion the pharaoh is seen defeating fleeing foes. Behind him stands a follower. On the inner frieze sphinxes are trampling on fallen warriors. On the outer frieze, figures, alternately a man with an Egyptian shanti and the god Bes, are engaged in battle with lions and griffins.

Ivory throne, Salamis
End of 8th century B.C.
Ivory; height 90 cm
Nicosia Museum, Cyprus

A throne decorated with ivory and a bed were discovered in a royal tomb in Salamis on Cyprus. Probably they were given to the local prince as part of the dowry of a Phoenician princess. The ivory tablets between the seat and the armrests depict a sphinx and the tree of life; these are the typical elements of Phoenician stone cult thrones, like that on the next page.

impressive evidence of this. As well as several series from workshops that were probably south Phoenician, other groups have been identified as products of Aramaic and Palestinian regions which were strongly influenced by Phoenician culture. The workshops here had access to Phoenician models through the trade in goods or through contact with itinerant artists. They incorporated Phoenician elements into local sculpture, as the reliefs of Karatepe in Kilikia show, into metal working and carving. The artists of the Phoenicians' political and economic partners began to adopt one particular characteristic of Phoenician art, the decoration of utensils and jewelry with recurrent motifs underlining the privileged status of the owner. At times it has been thought that the choice of themes or the inscriptions indicated the secular or religious function of the client for whom these artifacts were made, but it is difficult to determine the exact origin and meaning of the motifs as long as there are no comparable examples from Phoenicia itself. We, therefore, have to be cautious in interpreting the regional movements in art in the "colonial world" until archaeological explorations in the city centers along the Phoenician coast are resumed.

The end of Phoenician power

The collapse of Assyria, which had been growing weaker and weaker, opened the door to the Medes and Babylonians. It also enabled Egyptian influence to grow again in the Levant. The spread of characteristic objects of the 26th Egyptian dynasty (664–525 B.C.) in the Orient and the Mediterranean fits the historical picture. According to the sources the pharaohs prepared the way for their return to their former northeast provinces by lending intensive

Cult throne on the Eshmun podium, Bostan el-Sheikh

The sacral site of Bostan el Sheikh, 1 mile (2 km) northeast of Sidon, probably dates from neo-Babylonian times (end of the 7th, early 6th century B.C.). The cult site near the source of the Nahr el-Awali (Ydal in Phoenician, then "the river of Asklepios") only acquired importance in later centuries. An important sanctuary was set up there dedicated to the cult of the god of healing and the protector of the Sidonian royal dynasty, Eshmun. The cult throne in the shrine dates from the 5th century B.C. It has two winged sphinxes on each side. It stands on a plinth that is an imitation of an Egyptian pylon and is placed in the "basin of Astarte." It lies beneath the monumental Eshmun podium. Bas-reliefs on the great blocks of the chapel above the back of the throne bear the motif of gods hunting. They date from the 4th century B.C.

Pages 72–73

Burial towers in Amrit

The most important monuments in Amrit (Greek: Marathos) were built shortly before the start of the 6th century B.C., if not indeed at the end of that century. The *meghazil* ("spindle" in Arabic), two burial towers about 33 ft (10 m) high, bear either a hemisphere or a pyramid at the top. They made a deep impact on travelers and scholars who rested here. Four erect lions line the base of the first tower, which like its neighbor stands over a subterranean rocky chamber which once contained several sarcophagi in stone or clay.

support to the revolts that broke out there in the 8th to 7th centuries B.C.

At the end of the following century Pharaoh Psammetich I intervened in military operations in the Levant (616 and 610 B.C.), and his son Necho II won several victories over the Babylonians before Nebuchadnezzar inflicted a heavy defeat on him at Carchemish in 605 B.C. The Phoenician cities do not appear to have played an active part in these campaigns. However, the good relations that existed between Phoenicia and Egypt are evident from the permission given to establish a Phoenician colony in Memphis (the "Tyrian quarter") and the establishment of a domain of the pharaohs in the Lebanon to harvest cedarwood. The rock steles left by Nebuchadnezzar in Wadir Brisa and Wadi el-Sabra, however, proclaim Babylonian hegemony over the petty princes of the coastal towns, like the stele at the mouth of the Nahr el-Kelb, which he ordered to be erected on one of his many campaigns.

Egypt pushes for greater control

Egypt continued its efforts to gain influence in the Levant. Necho II hired Phoenician sailors, and the Greek historian Herodotus ascribes the voyage around Africa to them. Necho's son Psammetich II

(595–589 B.C.) employed Phoenician mercenaries. Shortly after his reign his successor Apries (589–570 B.C.) is believed to have led an army against Sidon and defeated Tyre at sea; it was subsequently besieged by Nebuchadnezzar from 585 to 572 B.C. It is surmised that these actions were directed against the Babylonians, but the available sources are contradictory. And although Tyre did not capitulate to Nebuchadnezzar it was forced to acknowledge Babylonian dominance, which lasted until the Persians gained power during the conquest of Babylon by Kyros II.

The revision of the Tyrian constitution which was undertaken at this time may have been dictated by the Babylonian court. For seven years the traditional dynastic succession was replaced by the election of judges who ruled the island city.

The restoration of the monarchy in 556 B.C. did not mean a return to the glory of former days. Egypt had not only successfully broken the Phoenicians' monopoly of sea power, it had also given preference to trade with Greece. Greek trade was also growing steadily in the waters where the Carthaginian ships had replaced those of their Tyrian mother city.

Egypt's diplomatic and military interventions in Phoenicia are also evident in archaeological finds, objects of pharaonic art found in Arvad, Byblos, Sidon, Tyre, and Akko. How great Egypt's impact was on the indigenous folk art and religion is evident from hundreds of Egyptian amulets and seals and local imitations of them found on Phoenician soil or even exported to the west.

The presence of the Babylonians was more permanent and more important politically and historically, but it is only substantiated by the three steles already mentioned and a number of seals in the conical octagonal form characteristic of this period. Of the architectural finds the pyramidal core of the temple of Eshmun in Sidon (at Bostan el-Sheikh) which has a ramp to the entrance and a reservoir of water, is dated from this time, although some questions of interpretation are still open. In view of the sparse contemporary material the brief popularity of a particular motif in local stone carving is of particular importance. There are depictions of divinities standing on a bull or a lion. A stele from a Phoenician shrine at Tell Daphne in the eastern Nile delta repeats this motif, which in fact reflects the influence of neo-Babylonian art rather than archaic Phoenician work. Sparse as a report on the artistic activity of this period has to be, one must point out that the contribution from Mesopotamia was evidently great enough to influence so traditional a domain as religious iconography.

Monumental cippus of the Eshmun shrine, Bostan el-Sheikh

The monumental cippus, or small tomb, bears a capital that has been taken from another monument. The figures of bulls, the traditional symbol of masculinity and fertility, project from the front and sides. Similar capitals have also been found in Sidon and on the island of Arvad. They are evidence of the influence of decorative building at the court of the Achemenides.

Sacred spring, Amrit

The *maabed* ("altar" in Arabic) of Amrit is a sacred spring, whose central chapel is surrounded on three sides by galleries. It is entered through a columned hall at the front. The shrine was hewn out of the rock. The *naos* or "Egyptian niche" rises above the mass and was once decorated with a Syrian castellated frieze and an architrave in the tradition of Asia Minor. The architrave bore a winged sun disc. Judging from the dedicated sculptures found in votive trenches around the shrine, pilgrims gathered here in order to pray to the gods of healing such as Eshmun, the great god of Sidon, Asklepios, the Egyptian god of folk medicine and Heracles-Melkart, a syncretic form of the Tyrian god of protection and the Greek hero who was identified with Melkart. For lack of archaeological evidence the shrine is dated at the start of the Persian age.

The Persian age

The incorporation of the Levant in the 5th satrapy of the Persian kingdom opened the way to a new blossoming of artistic and cultural life. That this was possible despite the many international and regional political entanglements was due to the important strategic role that the Phoenicians played among the Persian colonies. As a base for operations against Egypt and Greece the Phoenician cities were treated relatively benignly, and their trading activities were encouraged. Locally they enjoyed a degree of political independence. The Phoenician fleet was a major part of the Persian army, and it was used against Egypt and the Greeks with the city kings commanding their own contingents. More Phoenician vessels again sailed the Mediterranean, and relations with the colonies were intensified. In particular, the presence on strategically important Cyprus was strengthened – evidently with the intention of countering the Greeks. In the north Arvad resumed the role of a leading center and it is

mentioned, with Tyre and Sidon, as the founder of Tripolis. Its fleet supported the Persian Achaemenid dynasty both in their war against the Medes (490–449/8 B.C.) and beyond. Under Xerxes I (486–464 B.C.) King Uzibaal is said to have personally commanded his own warships.

On the mainland almost opposite Arvad lay Amrit, with its important holy spring whose healing powers drew many pilgrims. The altar was a monolithic *naos* in the Egyptian style placed in the center of an artificial lake. The basin fed by the spring was surrounded with porticos that could be entered through a monumental gateway. The identity of the gods worshipped here has been deduced from finds in trenches that were depots for votive gifts, *favissae*.

The inscriptions on the statues found here, which are in the Cypriot and Egyptian style, mention Eshmun, the Sidonian god of healing, and Melkart, the god protecting Tyre. In the vicinity are numerous tombs which contained sarcophagi of basalt, Paros marble or fired clay. Memorials were erected over some of these tombs. As with the examples in the

Clay sarcophagi, Amrit

First half of 5th century B.C.
Clay; height 179 cm, width 47 cm (left),
height 187 cm, width 50.5 cm (right)
Tartus Museum

Thanks to the discovery of these clay
sarcophagi in 1996 in a tomb in the north of
Amrit, another group of sarcophagi, examples
of which in basalt and marble and a fragment
in clay had already been found, can now be
ascribed to the workshops in Arvad. Work
started on this new series towards the end of
the 5th century B.C. It shows the contribution
made by the native artisans, who may have
included Cypriots.

Podium from the Persian Age, Byblos

Byblos experienced a new golden age under the Achaemenids, of which the widely distributed artifacts, particularly the remains of a grandiose architecture, are impressive testimony. Although the columned hall built by Yehawmilk is known mainly for the inscription on the famous stele, one may well stand amazed before this foundation of a fortress that dates from the same time. Our picture shows one of the projecting corners of its facade. It is decorated with a lion's head, the traditional symbol of royal power that is omnipresent in the art of the Phoenician city of Byblos from the end of the 2nd millennium.

Below

Stele of Yehawmilk, Byblos

5th century B.C.
Limestone; height 114 cm
Louvre, Paris

Yehawmilk is shown presenting a bowl to his mistress, the goddess Astarte in the Geblitic pantheon, who was known as "the lady of Byblos" (Baalat Gebal). The inscription is one of the longest ever found in Phoenicia and it tells of the restoration of the portico in the temple dedicated to the goddess. This appears to be the temple that is illustrated on a votive tablet that is now in the Louvre. Not only did the king of Byblos wear Persian attire at this time, contemporary coins (5th century B.C.) also show the king of Sidon dressed in the Persian style.

Opposite

Drinking horn in the form of a wild boar's head, Sheikh

5th century B.C.
Attic ceramic with red figuration;
height 17.8 cm, diam. 12 cm
Department of Antiquities, Beirut

The ascendancy of the Persians brought a time of peace and prosperity to the Plain of Akkar in north Phoenicia, and urban centers like Simyra (Tell Kazel) and Irqata (Tell Arwa) recovered their former economic strength. Although Phoenician vessels joined the Persians in attacking the Greek coast the Phoenician cities opened their doors to the Greek world. This fine drinking horn in Attic ceramic with red figuration shows that cultural influence. It is from a tomb of the 5th century B.C. found in a village necropolis on the Nahr el-Kebir river (the Eleutheros of Antiquity).

various necropoli on the fringe of Tartus (Antarados) and its hinterland, the style of these works betrays the hand of Ionian sculptors whose work was also being copied in Sidon. The sarcophagi of clay in the Egyptian style, on the other hand, suggest the work of Cypriot master craftsmen.

If the political upswing of Arvad can be largely explained by the island city's thousand-year reputation as a sea power, it would have been less spectacular without the resurgence of agriculture in its mainland territories (*peraia*). The excavations at Tell Sukas in the north of Tartus, or at Tell Kazel in the south, afford an exemplary picture of these flourishing centers where the rich manufacturers were easily induced to buy (and sell on) the imported Attic luxury vessels. The same phenomenon is to be found in the Akkar plain in Lebanon, where the influence of Hellenism is evident in the material culture of sites such as Tell Arqa or Tripolis. However, the latter has so far only been accessible to archaeologists through underwater excavations of wrecks that sank in front of the two sea harbors.

Further south Byblos also finally experienced a renaissance, and this was expressed mainly in monumental architecture. It is evident in the restoration of the Baalat-Gebal temple by King Yehawmilk and the construction of an imposing fortress in the Achaemenid style. The king is depicted on a monumental stele dressed in Persian mode, but

The Throne of Astarte, Ain Baal

2nd century B.C.
Limestone; height 73 cm, length 39 cm,
depth 39 cm
Department of Antiquities, Beirut

The prototype of this throne from Ain Baal in the district around Tyre is shown on the sarcophagus of Ahirom (see p. 56). It is good evidence of the continuance of the traditional religious ideas in Hellenic times. The inscription on another example from the same region and depictions on seals suggest that cult furniture of this nature was also used in the Astarte cult.

Silver ring with amethyst scarab, Magharat Tablun

Towards 500 B.C.
Silver, amethyst, gold; diam. 7 cm
Department of Antiquities, Beirut

Despite the precious materials, the decoration on the underside of the scarab is a common motif in Phoenician carving at the end of the 6th and the early 5th century B.C. The divinity is shown on her throne, flanked by a sphinx. She is greeting a woman who is worshipping her (probably a priestess), and who is just approaching a vessel of incense. The winged sun disc and stars can be seen above.

for their heraldic depictions on coins and seals his successors preferred a style and iconography that are clearly indigenous in origin.

Thus art reflects the relative autonomy that the Persian rulers initially conceded to the city governments of Phoenicia in a wide variety of ways.

We owe it to the excavations that have been carried out in the center since 1994 that Byblos, too, is known to be among the settlements that experienced an upswing during Persian times. Lebanese archaeologists have uncovered the traces of a housing settlement around the southern harbor, which is mentioned in a report by a sailor, Scylax, around the turn of the 5th century B.C.

Sidon made use of the favorable times to resume its role as the most important metropolis. The city profited from the Babylonians' siege of its rival Tyre to strengthen its economy, in which glass production and purple dyeing are known to have played a major part. The support given to the Persians in their war against the Greeks by Eshmunazar I's fleet was rewarded with various gifts and privileges. Paradoxically, this open conflict with their Greek rivals in sea trade did not prevent Sidon from keeping its doors wide open to Greek influence, as the preferences of contemporary artists show. The phenomenon is evident in sacral architecture in the reliefs on the "podium of Eshmun" in the sanctuary of Bostan el-Sheikh, and it is also evident in the

decoration of sarcophagi, some of which are particularly unusual examples and may possibly date from the last dynasts of the city. Nevertheless the sculptors – like the potters and seal engravers – retained the style, iconography and typology of their forefathers. The indigenous stylistic features actually experienced a new upswing, of which the genres mentioned contain much evidence. The fact that Sidonian art maintained a tradition that had lasted a thousand years is all the more remarkable in view of the repeated devastation of the city. The destructive wars in Assyrian times were followed by those of the Persian age. In 346/345 B.C. Artaxerxes III Ochos put down a rebellion that had been started by King Tabnit II with the help of Pharaoh Nektonebos II.

Unlike Sidon, Tyre refused to open its gates to Alexander the Great when he reached the Phoenician coast in 331 B.C. The city first enters biblical history at the start of the Persian age, when in conjunction with Sidon it played a part in the renewed reconstruction of the temple at Jerusalem. The circulation of Tyrian coins in Palestine confirms the biblical story of the resumption of Phoenician business activities in Palestine. These appear to be related to the restoration of Tyrian authority in Galilee. Tyre's power extended to Sarepta in the north and Mount Carmel in the south. The city also played an important role as a component of Persian military might. Under the Persian King Kambyses (530–522 B.C.) it refused to use its ships against Carthage, but Tyrian kings are to be found commanding their fleet against Greece in the 5th century. The time up to the conquest by Alexander the Great is barely documented. However, Tyre hardly had the opportunity to derive benefit from the losses Sidon suffered after the revolt against Persia. The dam built by the Macedonian troops under Alexander to link the city with the mainland and which sealed its fate became a regular bridgehead to a new civilization that retained only isolated memories of its glorious past.

Opposite

Statue of a young prince, Eshmun temple, Sidon

5th century B.C.
Marble; height 48 cm, length 42 cm,
depth 58.5 cm
Department of Antiquities, Beirut

This marble statue was found in a *favissa* in the temple of Eshmun north of Sidon. According to the inscription it is Baalchillem, son of King Banaa of Sidon. The inscription asks for the blessing of the master, Eshmun of the Ydlal spring.

Jean-Baptiste Yon

The Greco-Roman Era
Cultural fusion in a Hellenistic setting

323 B.C.–337 A.D.

Rear of the Temple of Bel, Palmyra

Located in northern Syria on the caravan route between the Euphrates and Damascus, the ancient desert city of Palmyra became an important trading center. The Temple of Bel (32 A.D.) was surrounded by a colonnade, with capitals of gilded bronze which have not survived. The triangular merlons along the cornice are a Mesopotamian influence.

Detail from the "Sarcophagus of Alexander," Sidon

Last quarter of the 4th century B.C.
colored marble; total length 318 cm,
height of the sculpted section 58 cm
Istanbul Archeological Museum

This sarcophagus was found in Sidon and depicts the battle between Alexander and the Persian king, Darius. It demonstrates how popular the myth surrounding Alexander was in the years after his death, even in a city with strong Phoenician traditions.

The ancient world – A merging of cultures

Alexander the Great's conquest of the Levant (336–323 B.C.) was a crucial point of departure for the entire region. Although the Greeks of the classical period had indeed maintained many and close links with the Orient, it was the arrival of the Greco-Macedonian forces under Alexander's command that served as the decisive prelude to the region's integration into the Greco-Roman world. It was this world, dominated first by Hellenistic Greece and later by the expanding Roman Empire, to which the Levant belonged until the Arab conquest in the 7th century and in which it occupied an important place, both culturally and politically, for almost the entire period.

Perhaps the most fascinating theme which emerges is the way in which the local populations took up first the Greek, then the Greco-Roman civilization, and adapted, accepted, or rejected it. Depending on the prevailing conditions, these stages sometimes happened concurrently. After all, the conquerors were not entering a region without a past. Indeed, they were preceded by very rich civilizations which, in turn, had some influence on Hellenism. Evidence of the local cultures, some of which remain obscure due to a lack of historical source material, can be found in various aspects of Hellenistic life, such as religion, art, architecture, and politics. The monuments of this era, for example, blend native elements with those of Greek architecture. The interplay of all these factors eventually led to the development of new cultures, and so it was that the Christian faith – to give but one example – evolved in precisely this climate. Christianity found acceptance at the end of the period, and can be considered an original product of the meeting of civilizations in the Near East.

Any account of the region's history during this 600-year period must necessarily focus on the coexistence, consolidation, and fusion of different cultures. At the same time, however, new trends also resulted in the birth of independent cultures, and these, too, were able to adapt and thrive.

The Hellenistic era

The Levant, which was part of the Persian Achaemenid Empire, fell into the hands of the conquerors from Macedonia and the rest of Greece without appreciable resistance. When Alexander died in 323 B.C., however, his huge new empire, stretching from Greece to the Indus, disintegrated. His successors fought amongst themselves for around 30 years, until the situation was resolved at the beginning of the 3rd century B.C., when the Levant became a divided land: the Seleucids, whose territory stretched from Asia Minor to India, held the north, whilst the south fell to the Ptolemies, who primarily ruled over Egypt. This state of affairs lasted for almost the entire century, despite a number of conflicts as both kingdoms tried to unite the region under their own rule. The Seleucid king Antiochus III, known as Antiochus the Great (223–187 B.C.), eventualty gained control of southern Syria at the end of the Fifth Syrian War, and it was during his reign that the dynasty reached its zenith.

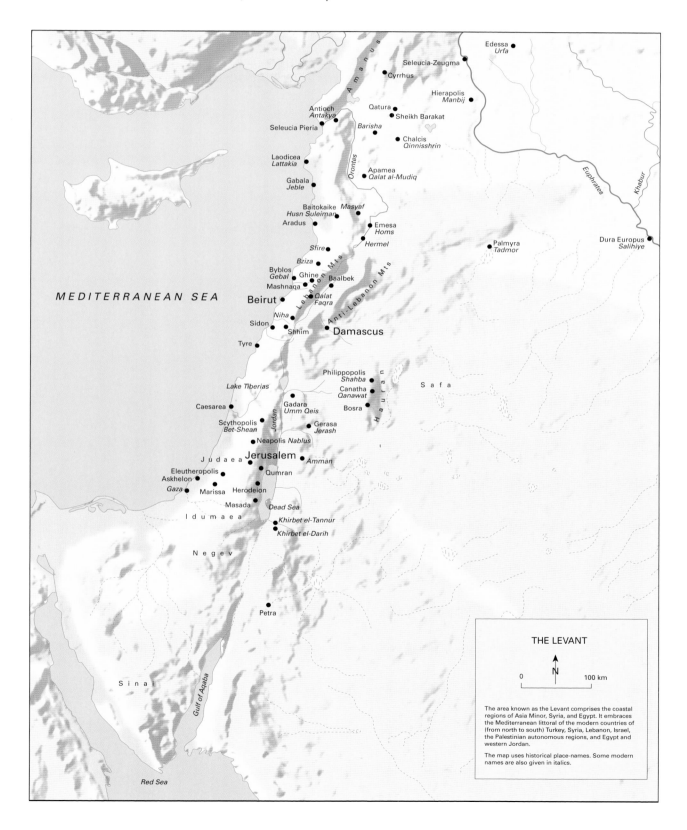

THE LEVANT

N

0   100 km

The area known as the Levant comprises the coastal regions of Asia Minor, Syria, and Egypt. It embraces the Mediterranean littoral of the modern countries of (from north to south) Turkey, Syria, Lebanon, Israel, the Palestinian autonomous regions, and Egypt and western Jordan.

The map uses historical place-names. Some modern names are also given in italics.

The capital of the Seleucid kingdom was originally SeHeucia, which lay on the Tigris near Babylon, but it soon changed to the northern Syrian city of Antioch on the river Orontes. The kingdom whose former heartland had comprised Mesopotamia and Babylon now looked primarily to the Mediterranean world, from where its rulers and their Greek subjects originated. With the loss of first the eastern (Bactria and later Iran) and then the western provinces (Asia Minor), however, its highly heterogeneous territory was gradually reduced in size and eventually confined to Syria. Seleucid power waned even further from the middle of the 3rd century B.C., when the Parthians of the Arsacid dynasty established themselves in Iran; attempts at re-conquest, such as the campaign which Antiochus III led as far as Bactria in central Asia (212–205 B.C.), were unsuccessful. Although the Parthians' conquest of Mesopotamia between 141 and 129 B.C. eventually brought them to the Euphrates, they never managed to make any long-term gains in Syria, where the Seleucid kingdom had been destabilized by dynastic rivalries and lay open to the rise of local powers. Cities, and above all other dynasties, continued to compete with the Seleucid rulers, until the kingdom finally disappeared from the map in 63 B.C., when the Roman general Pompey made Syria a Roman province – just one example of Rome's increasing intervention in oriental affairs from the end of the 3rd century B.C.

Urbanization and the influence of Hellenism following Alexander's conquest

The beginning of the Hellenistic period was characterized by the founding and "refounding" of *poleis*, particularly by the Seleucids in northern Syria. These new city-states were urban centers surrounded by a politically dependent rural area or *chora* which can still be identified today by mile- or boundary stones. In some cases these cities replaced or were built on top of existing native villages, and were given Greek names.

The economy of the ancient world was based mainly on agriculture, and so the land that ensured the *polis* its supply of provisions was of vital significance. Thus, the most important cities founded by the Seleucids in northern Syria (Antioch, Apamea, Laodicea and Seleucia Pieria) were each surrounded by an area of land for agricultural use, and this would probably have been divided up amongst the newly arrived settlers from the Greek world. It is estimated that a total of around 30 *poleis* had been founded by the middle of the 3rd century B.C., by which time the trend appears to have run its course. These cities were not established purely for military or economic reasons, but were also intended to act as kernels of Greek civilization. They provided settlers with the framework essential for life, and at the same time facilitated the integration of the indigenous population with the Greek settlers.

Bottom right

Frieze from Tomb I, Marissa

The presence of a three-headed Cerberus below a Greek inscription is typical of the Hellenized people who used this necropolis.

Bottom left

Front view, Iraq al-Emir

The lion frieze and the general shape of the building both establish a Hellenistic influence. The megalithic construction, however, is more reminiscent of Iranian models.

Detail from a lion frieze, Iraq al-Emir

A frieze decorated with lions ran right around the 430 sq ft (40 m square) "country residence," which was surrounded by an expanse of water.

Little is known about the beginning of this era other than the fact of the conquest itself, and the lack of source material has sometimes led historians to talk of the "problem of Hellenistic Syria." The local population evidently appeared to find the Greek model of civilization attractive, however, and this is nowhere better demonstrated than in the rapid transformation of the cities along the Phoenician coast into Greek *poleis*. Despite the swiftness of their Hellenization, which was aided by long-established contact, a consciousness of their own past remained alive and well in these cities. They retained their native names, and their inhabitants probably continued to speak the local language, Phoenician, into Roman times.

Old cities, new buildings

Despite Phoenician elements, Sidon, Byblos and Tyre very quickly became Greek, and subsequently Greco-Roman *poleis* in the classical mold. One piece of evidence for this was provided by the discovery of graves in Tell Maresha (the Hellenistic Marissa, around 21 miles (35 km) southwest of Jerusalem). Wall paintings at the site are strongly influenced by Ptolemaic Egypt, but the inscriptions show that a

settlement of Greek Sidonians were among those who made use of the necropolis. The names are both Greek and Phoenician, and were probably subject to a local Idumaean influence, although the language used is primarily Greek. In addition, the existence of a Sidonian colony such as Marissa in the interior of the country in the 2nd century B.C. must also indicate the vitality of the Phoenician city-states on the coast.

A further example of the phenomenon of Hellenization is the "country residence" of Iraq al-Emir some 20 km west of Amman, which has been studied in great detail since 1976, thanks to Franco-Jordanian excavations. This curious edifice, a blend of architectural traditions, was built by the Jewish Hyrcanus dynasty, a branch of the Tobiad family, shortly before the Seleucid conquest of southern Syria in the 2nd century B.C. Although abandoned even before it was completed, the building reflects the influence of Hellenism on the architecture of the region. However, some features, such as its megalithic construction, deviate from this style – evidence for the existence of a hybrid culture.

Few archeological traces of this period remain, often because later construction work has taken place on top of the Hellenistic structures, as still happens to this day. In the case of Dura Europus (Salihiye), a city founded on the Euphrates by the first Seleucids,

Frieze from Tomb I, Marissa

The frieze is particularly remarkable for its Greek inscriptions giving the names of the animals depicted. Here, a leopard is shown in a hunting scene. The decoration is influenced by contemporary Alexandrian painting.

View of Sidon

The ancient remains in the foreground testify to centuries of continuous settlement, a situation which does not always facilitate archaeological investigation.

Spindle-shaped vessel, Dura Europus

c. 140–125 B.C.
Glass; height 17.5 cm, max. diameter 2.7 cm
Yale University Art Gallery, New Haven

This perfume vase, which would have been used for cosmetic purposes, was found in the ruins of Dura Europus. It is one of a group of designs also known to have been in use in Cyprus and Egypt during the imperial era – evidence that goods were often exchanged.

the situation is scarcely more favorable. The city was abandoned after being captured by the Persians in 256 A.D., around 600 years after it was founded, and the fact that it was not resettled has enabled a certain number of discoveries to be made, particularly from the Parthian and Roman periods. The city walls and foundation outlines are of vital importance as regards Hellenistic Dura Europus, but otherwise there are very few traces of structures dating from that time. The checkerboard foundation pattern, also known as the Hippodamian system (after Hippodamus, an architect from Miletus), is typical of Hellenistic settlements, and had been used by the Greeks since at least the 5th century B.C. Around 60 identical *insulae*, or islands, were set around an *agora*, alongside which ran the main road; evidently the settlers (possibly veterans of Alexander's army) were originally allotted parcels of land of equal size. The surrounding city walls enclosed an area of around 100 acres (40 hectares).

It is clear that the city walls were not erected until 150 years after the city's foundation. At first, a citadel overlooking the Euphrates provided protection for the city and controlled traffic on the road running beside the river. Then, from the end of the 3rd century B.C., the threat from the Parthians led to the construction of a protecting wall. In the end, however, the Seleucids were unable to prevent the capture of the town in 135 B.C. – a consequence of the loss of the eastern part of their kingdom.

Dura Europus was relatively small in comparison to the cities founded in northern Syria (such as Apamea or Antioch), which usually covered larger areas of around 200 hectares. Nevertheless, it was important both in military terms and as a trading center. As in other cities, settlers were probably allocated plots of agricultural land in and around the surrounding area.

It is not until the middle of the Hellenistic period that relatively extensive archaeological remains are to be found, and these clearly demonstrate the influence of Hellenism in the cities and their immediate environs. In the rural areas, where the majority of the Syrian population lived, however, archaeological evidence is a great deal scarcer, with the result that only fragments of the real picture are available to us.

The end of the Seleucids

Neighboring lands and the lesser dynasties within their own kingdom both played a crucial role in the end of the Seleucids. Foremost among those who exploited the loss of power forced upon the Seleucids in the latter years of their rule were the most powerful Greek cities (Apamea, Seleucia, Sidon and Tyre), although in the less Hellenized areas and the border regions certain other kingdoms also made an appearance. Chronologically, the first major anti-Hellenistic crisis was the Hasmonean revolt. This culminated in 152 B.C. in an independent Judaea ruled by the Hasmonean dynasty, which proceeded to pursue an expansionist policy that frequently brought conflict with neighboring peoples. Their disputes with the Nabataen kingdom, which was also in the ascendant around this time and which will be discussed in detail in another chapter of this book, are just one example of this. Nevertheless, classical authors also mention other Arab or Aramaic dynasties throughout the Seleucid kingdom, such as the

Ituraeans in the Lebanon Mountains and the dynasties of Prince Sampsigeramus around Emesa (Homs), or those of King Abgar in Edessa. The rise of these small kingdoms is an indication of the way in which local forces profited from the decline of Greco-Macedonian power.

Sources from the Hellenistic period have very little to say about the indigenous culture, but this does not mean that it had disappeared. On the contrary, the rural population and a large proportion of the urban population spoke a Semitic language (Aramaic, in its various dialects), although an Arabic influence can also be detected, as in the Nabataean kingdom, for example. Indeed, onomastics and religion provide evidence that the Arabs played an increasingly important role as they continued their penetration of the region, despite the fact that they themselves were largely Aramaicized. More information becomes available at the end of the Hellenistic period, particularly concerning the existence of nomadic peoples of Semitic extraction on the edges of the urbanized and Hellenized zones.

Our own sources, themselves largely of Greco-Roman derivation, tend to overemphasize the Hellenization of the region. In reality, it was a peripheral phenomenon which mostly affected the cities – at least at the end of the Hellenistic era. There is no doubt that beyond the gates of even the largest Greek cities, such as Antioch, the population was predominantly Semitic and was influenced by Greek culture only on a very superficial level.

From the beginning of the 1st century B.C., the whole region was confronted with the rapid advance of Rome. Roman generals had defeated Mithridates, king of Pontus (southwest of the Black Sea), before becoming lords over the whole of Asia Minor following two wars between 88 and 63 B.C. At the same time, the inhabitants of Antioch, tired of the dynastic wars, turned to the king of Armenia, Tigranes, who proceeded to annex Syria in 83 B.C. However, his kingdom was unable to withstand the Romans for long (he was defeated by Lucullus in 69 B.C.), and after a few further incidents, including a final return of the Seleucids, Pompey made Syria a Roman province. Thus began a new era, lasting at least three centuries, which a large body of evidence shows to have been a prosperous time for the Levant. The eastern border was fixed along the upper reaches of the Euphrates, and remained unchanged until the end of the 2nd century A.D. Further to the south, where the river changed direction, the boundary ran through the middle of the desert to the Nabataean kingdom. Until the beginning of the 1st century A.D., Palmyra was a part of the Empire in name only; the status of the desert on the region's eastern boundary remains unclear. Generally speaking, very little is known about the exact course of the border through the desert, since these regions were in the hands of nomadic peoples whom the Romans found as difficult to control as the Parthians had.

Child's shoe, Dura Europus

c. 200–160 B.C.
Leather, iron studs in the sole; length 17 cm
Yale University Art Gallery, New Haven

The relatively dry climate aided the preservation of objects, such as this shoe, which sank into the glacis or slope constructed by the Romans. Documents on parchment and papyrus have also survived.

Hellenistic citadel, Dura Europus

The citadel controlled the Euphrates valley, seen here in the background. The first Greek garrison stood on this site, which had been settled since the time of the Assyrians.

View of Caesarea

The port of Caesarea owed its prosperity in part to King Herod. It was primarily a Greek city, and its inhabitants supplied the governor with troops.

Pax Romana

At first, the territory covered by the Roman province of Syria did not entirely correspond with that of the Seleucid realm. Pompey and his successors, and later on the first emperors, refrained from systematically eliminating the kingdoms and principalities which both dissected the province and at the same time formed its least Hellenized areas. Instead, the Romans preferred to make use of local rulers to carry out their policy of Romanization, which was de facto also a policy of Hellenization. This strategy, resulting in gradual integration into the Roman Empire, was also pursued by the Romans in Asia Minor.

The most important kingdoms in the Roman Empire's sphere of influence lay in the south, namely the Nabataean kingdom and the areas ruled by the heirs of Herod. The latter were finally annexed in 92/93 A.D. as a result of the policy of Hellenization, that is, pacification and urbanization using client kings. Herod the Great (41–4 B.C.) is the most famous of these rulers, and his founding of the port of Caesarea is a good example of the process: theoretically autonomous, the city was in reality a dependency of Rome, its loyalty displayed in its name. Herod resolved to redesign the city, which until then had been called Stratonus Purgus (Straton's Tower), and rebuilt it in monumental fashion. The harbor created at that time, by means of the construction of a dyke, became one of the most important in the region. It was from here that the Apostle Paul was transferred to Rome as a prisoner. In addition, a Latin inscription found in Caesarea mentions Pontius Pilate, the Roman procurator of Judaea (26–36 A.D.), with whose name everyone is familiar due to his part in the crucifixion of Jesus. In fact, the province of Judaea was amalgamated with the province of Syria in 6 A.D., and the ruling procurator resided in Caesarea with a significant garrison.

One aim of using client kings in the process of Hellenization was to pacify the less accessible regions (a task the Greek cities found very difficult to accomplish) and thus pave the way for their integration into the Roman Empire. To this end, Herod built a series of fortresses across his territory which enabled him to control the less secure areas of the kingdom. However, one such fortification was built in the immediate vicinity of Jerusalem, the center of his kingdom – an indication that the Jewish population was not entirely sympathetic to his pro-Hellenistic policies, and that he had to be prepared for resistance from within his own ranks.

The final stage in the integration of the client states west of the Euphrates took place in 106 A.D. with the annexation of the Nabataean kingdom, which had become the province of Arabia. By and large, the fortunes of the region during this period were dictated by the Roman policy of peace, which encouraged growth and prosperity. Relations with the Parthians continued to be problematic, but peace, albeit a peace under arms, had been reestablished after the Roman proconsul Crassus was defeated at Carrhae (in what is now southeast Turkey) in 53 B.C., and any acts of aggression tended to originate with the Romans rather than the Parthians. In the interior of the Empire, the annexations were largely

accomplished without great turmoil and uproar. Judaea, however, became a center of unrest, which culminated in a revolt between 66 and 70 A.D., which was finally brought to an end when the Romans captured Jerusalem and then Masada.

Fortress at Masada

Herod made use of this craggy peak to help him control the surrounding region, and it was exploited again during the first Jewish War. The precipitous location of the fortress enabled it to withstand the Roman army during a long and difficult siege which lasted until 74 A.D.

Complex with bath-house, Herodeion

This complex lies at the lower part of the site developed under Herod, and includes a bath-house. The fortress itself stood on the hill behind.

The uneven pace of Hellenization

At the start of the 2nd century A.D., a time often considered to be the golden age of Roman Syria, some areas of the region had been Hellenized to a greater degree than others. There were three main urbanized zones: first, the Phoenician coast, with extensions southwards as far as Gaza and Ashkelon; secondly, the *poleis* of northern Syria between the Euphrates and the coast; and lastly, in the south, the Decapolis, a group of (originally ten) cities mainly situated east of the Jordan, but also including Scythopolis in the west and Damascus in the north. However, both the Phoenician cities and those of the Decapolis (the latter being native settlements which had been converted into *poleis*) retained their Semitic names throughout – a sign of their true origins. In these cities, unlike those founded by the Seleucids, the native tradition generally remained strong. The social elite, however, were sufficiently Hellenized for Rome to entrust them with the administration of the *poleis*, because here, as everywhere in the eastern part of the Empire, Hellenization and Romanization were synonymous. The language used in this eastern region was Greek. Only the Roman army and a few colonies such as Beirut used Latin in official documents.

Outside the Hellenized areas, zones remained in which the degree of urbanization was small, and in which native cultures continued to be the dominant influence. These were primarily mountain and desert regions, or remote areas such as Palestine and the Syrian interior. Although a small number of cities were indeed located in these regions, they frequently had their own, independent cultures – one example being the isolated city of Palmyra, in the middle of the Syrian steppe.

The organization of the region

One feature which brought at least some unity to the region, and certainly facilitated Roman control, was the construction of roads. These were built first along the coast, then through the desert toward Palmyra (during the Flavian era, 69–96 A.D.), and later, after the annexation of Arabia (106 A.D.), south toward the Red Sea. Construction projects followed in quick succession under the emperors Trajan, Aurelius, Verus, Severus and their successors, particularly during times of heavy military activity. The campaigns they and their generals conducted were primarily directed against the Parthian kingdom, as was the case with Trajan (98–117 A.D.), who returned to an offensive policy which had been more or less abandoned since the 1st century B.C.

Trajan's Parthian campaign brought him as far as the Arabian-Persian Gulf, although his conquests beyond the Euphrates were subsequently relinquished by his successor, Hadrian (117–138 A.D.).

Above

Roman arch, Damascus

The Roman arch opposite the Temple of Jupiter (now the great Umayyad Mosque) is one of the last remaining relics of the Roman era in the city of Damascus.

Ruins, Scythopolis

Scythopolis was also known as Nysa, since it was here that Dionysus was said to have buried his wet nurse of that name. The city had a separate cult worshipping the god. These columns were probably destroyed in the earthquake of 749 A.D.

Arabia, on the other hand, was annexed without recourse to war. Peace was maintained until 162 A.D., when a Parthian campaign to Syria provoked a Roman counteroffensive, culminating in Mesopotamia being retaken by the Roman general Avidius Cassius in 165 A.D., albeit temporarily. This time, however, the Romans retained control of the banks of the Euphrates, largely due to the fact that they finally succeeded in occupying Dura Europus. Mesopotamia was annexed yet again during the time of Severus, who in 194 A.D. also reorganized Syria by establishing the province of Coele Syria (capital: Laodicea, later Antioch) in the north and separating it from the province of Phoenicia (capital: Tyre) in the south.

Although the Pax Romana was maintained within the region's borders more or less until the 3rd century A.D., a few events did disturb the peace. A second Jewish uprising (under Bar Kochba, 132–135 A.D.) led not only to heavy emigration, but also to a power struggle between Gaius Pescennius Niger and Severus, both of whom sought to succeed Commodus. In the end it was Severus who emerged as the victor and new emperor, in 193 A.D.

Bust of Isis with Horus, Ashkelon

This bust of Isis with Horus served as decoration for the city's forum, which dates from the 3rd century A.D. The cult of this Egyptian goddess is thought to have spread throughout the eastern part of the Greco-Roman world; Ashkelon, famous for its Greek culture, was no exception.

Archway on a colonnaded road, Tyre

The ancient Phoenician city of Tyre was also a provincial capital of the Roman Empire. These ruins are part of a monumental archway on the colonnaded road which ran past the necropolis at the entrance to the city.

Exedra of the Imperial Temple, Shahba

Dedicated to the father of Emperor Philip I "the Arab," this temple and the square in front of it dominated the town of Shahba, which became a *polis* following Philip's rise to power.

Coin bearing a portrait of Zenobia

c. 272 B.C.
Bronze
Bibliothèque Nationale, Paris

The fortunes of Zenobia, Queen of Palmyra, are the basis of legends recorded by Arab chroniclers in the Islamic era. They tell of the battles between nomadic tribes which form the background to the rise of Palmyra in the 3rd century.

The crisis

In contrast to the previous century, the 3rd century A.D. saw a Roman Empire characterized on the one hand by internal instability, and on the other by continued war with the Parthians and later the Sassanids on its eastern border. The new Sassanid dynasty in Persia, which came to power in 224 A.D., pursued a much more aggressive policy in this region of the Empire after 230 A.D., and saw its armies advance as far as Antioch. It was in this context that Dura Europus was captured after a siege (256 A.D.), leaving behind a great deal of archaeological evidence. In the end, several factors contributed to the destabilization of the Empire after 235 A.D. Not only was the eastern border under threat, the northern and western borders were also subject to attacks by Germanic peoples. These simultaneous offensives encountered a Roman army whose leaders were engaged in a power struggle; since the emperor was held responsible for military defeats, circumstances were very favorable for army leaders who sought to usurp power and restore order. For this reason, and also because of the threat from the Sassanids, emperors often went to the eastern provinces in person, in order to reassert their authority.

Attention was increasingly focused on the Orient during this period due to the fact that, for the first time, natives of Syria were becoming Roman emperors. Severus (emperor from 193–211 A.D.) had married into an important family from Emesa, and his successors, his son Caracalla and his great-nephews Heliogabalus and Alexander Severus, were descended from dignitaries and priests of the sun cult in Emesa. Similarly, the emperor Philip I (244–249 A.D.), to whom the revealing epithet "the Arab" was applied, came from the small town of Shahba in the Hauran. He made Shahba a *polis*, gave it his name (Philippopolis), and aided its enormous development.

The crisis in the Roman Empire during the 3rd century A.D. need not be dealt with in great detail here, although the tragic fate of the emperor Valerian (253–260 A.D.), who died in captivity after being defeated and taken prisoner by the Persians, should perhaps be mentioned. The inhabitants of the eastern provinces played an increasingly important role in the struggle against the Persians. This echoed the way in which control in Gaul was usurped by the Gallo-Roman Postumus, who, although not desiring a break with Rome, did wish to defeat single-handedly the invading Germanic "barbarians." In the Orient, the princes of Palmyra began their bid for power under Odenathus. His wife Zenobia took over in 267 A.D. as a highly educated regent for her son Wahballat (who was still a minor), and in 270 began a campaign of her own. As Mistress of Syria she undertook the conquest of Egypt, Arabia, and Asia Minor, and eventually broke away from Aurelian, who had been emperor since 270 A.D. Zenobia was unable to resolve the threat of conflict with Rome by diplomatic means, and Aurelian, having already conquered the kingdom of the Gauls in the west, now led a campaign to the east (272–273 A.D.), where he succeeded in defeating the Palmyran troops and putting an end to Zenobia's quest for power. To a certain extent, the reign of Aurelian heralded the end of the crisis in the Orient, even though the wars against the Persians still continued. The eastern border at that time lay along the Tigris, which meant that the battle zone was far away from Roman Syria.

The rise to power of a ruler of Illyrian descent, the emperor Diocletian (284–305 A.D.), marked the real turning point for the Roman Empire. During the time of the Tetrarchy (the joint rule, established by Diocletian, of two Augusti and two Caesars), the Empire's administrative and military set-ups were both completely reorganized. In this way the provinces were remodeled (see the chapter on the early Byzantine period) and work began on a series of fortifications along the borders, affecting even Palmyra. Particularly well-known is the Strata Diocletiana (Diocletian Road), which was lined with fortifications, and ran from the Euphrates via the Palmyran region to Damascus. Other branches ran south of Damascus toward Arabia, and as far as the Red Sea. Although these roads had existed before Diocletian, the construction project as a whole clearly

dates from the time of the Tetrarchy and points to heavy military activity in the region. The aim was evidently to monitor the nomads on the steppe, who had no doubt become much bolder following the end of the might of Palmyra, which had controlled the tribes until 272 A.D.

The period of the Tetrarchy also saw the last great persecution of the Christians, from 303 to 305 A.D. In fact, Christianity had very quickly separated itself from Judaism, and spread throughout the Mediterranean area in spite of the persecutions ordered by Decius and Diocletian. Constantine the Great (324–337 A.D.), on the other hand, who reunified power in the Empire in his own favor and continued with certain reforms initiated by his predecessors, pursued a very different religious policy: The Edict of Milan (313 A.D.) guaranteed Christians freedom of worship. This was a decisive break with the previous era, and, despite an evident degree of continuity, signaled a new phase in the history of the Levant.

Diocletian's Camp, Palmyra

Entrance to the *principia* (headquarters of the Roman garrison) at the top of a monumental flight of steps. The building dates from 301 A.D. Its importance is a reflection of Palmyra's new military role.

Theater, Gadara

Ancient records confirm the reputation of this *polis* as a "city of culture." The existence of a theater illustrates the Hellenization of Gadara during Roman times.

The blossoming of urban life

Urban development and the Hellenization of the region went hand in hand under the Romans, perhaps even more so than in the Hellenistic era. A brief survey of its cultural achievements reveals that Syria's culture was well integrated with the trends that were shaping the Greco-Roman world. In fact, this integration had been taking place across the entire Seleucid kingdom, from the beginning of the Hellenistic period onwards. As is also the case with literature, the few inscriptions which have been found east of the Euphrates use the same language and system of writing as those discovered in the Mediterranean.

Education and culture – Writers and philosophers

Cultural continuity across the various Hellenistic regions can be explained on the one hand by the common origins of the settlers, and on the other by continuing cultural exchange between the kingdoms. Although Oriental Hellenism lasted only a few years in the regions north of India (i.e., until the period when the Parthians broke off relations with the rest of the Greek world), the situation regarding Syria was, of course, very different, due to its constant contact with the Mediterranean region – contact which became even stronger after the Roman conquest. It is not surprising, therefore, that the Levant has produced so many scholars and writers since the Hellenistic era. Many of them are known to us only as names in the works of later authors, but their existence alone testifies to there being schools of philosophy in cities such as Apamea. In other words, there was a system of education that allowed intellectual endeavor to flourish. Particular emphasis should be given to education's role in the spread of Hellenism, accomplished through the schools that were to be found in many *poleis* in the Orient. In this way, cities contributed to the maintenance and dissemination of a culture which, although reserved for an elite, had a direct or indirect effect on a large proportion of the indigenous population. One may rightly wonder, therefore, whether the mother tongue of the most famous author of the Imperial age, Lucian of Samosata (119–c.180 A.D.), may, in fact, have been Aramaic. A native of Commagene, a province north of Syria, he left behind a series of works concerned with the Levant, and in particular with the cult of Dea Syria (the "Syrian Goddess") in Hierapolis, a city close to the Euphrates.

Numerous other writers and philosophers can be cited. Although fewer in number, perhaps, than their counterparts from Asia Minor or Greece, they always followed the intellectual currents which characterized the period in general. Antioch certainly did not have the status of Alexandria, and did not produce many names of note before the 4th century A.D. (among them the rhetor Libanius, who lived from 316 to 393 A.D.). The neighboring city of Apamea, by contrast, produced two philosophers worthy of mention, a few centuries apart: Poseidonius (135–51 B.C.), a historian and Stoic philosopher, and contemporary and friend of Cicero; and Numenius (second half of the 2nd century A.D.), who represented the beginnings of Neoplatonism. The cities of Phoenicia and the south, however, yielded numerous authors and men of letters. Not to be overlooked in this respect is Gadara (Umm Qeis), dubbed the "Attica of Syria" by the poet Meleager, who was born there. Part of the Decapolis, Gadara was the home of several great names of classical literature, including Philodemus, an Epicurean philosopher and another friend of Cicero; and Oinomaus, a Cynic philosopher of the 2nd century A.D. It is remarkable that the region was able to maintain its intellectual tradition at the end of the Hellenistic era, since the political situation at that time was anything but stable. Under such circumstances, it is perhaps less surprising that in 79 B.C., another philosopher from the Levant was to be found in Athens: Antiochus of Ashkelon, who taught Cicero there. His move to Greece was a sign of intellectual vitality – he became head of the Athenian Academy – but may also have been a judicious retreat from a region made dangerous by continued wars. Two historians are worthy of note from the following period: Nicolaus of Damascus (born c. 64 B.C.), who moved in the royal circles of Herod the Great; and more importantly, Flavius Josephus (37–100 A.D.), who was descended from a family of Jewish priests. Although at first he took part in the revolt against the Romans, Josephus later switched his affiliation. Part of his historical oeuvre was written in the capital of the Roman Empire (*History of the Jewish War* and *Antiquities of the Jews*), as well as his autobiography – one of the first examples of that genre.

The most famous writings originating from this region, however, are the various works, written in Greek in the course of the 1st and 2nd centuries A.D., which comprise the New Testament. Their status and literary merit are difficult to assess, but their influence was greater than that of other contemporary works. Essentially, they are the first writings of a tradition which developed further in the works of apologists such as Justin of Neapolis (Nablus) in Palestine, or Tatian, who probably came from Mesopotamia, and which heralded the prime of the early Byzantine period.

The wealth of literary creativity found in the last century of the Seleucid kingdom was not repeated until the end of the 2nd century, when the same cities were again represented: from Tyre came Maximus, an author with Platonic tendencies; one hundred years later, Neoplatonism finally gained acceptance

through another native of Tyre, Porphyry, who was born in 233 and whose real name was Malchus. Iamblichus of Chalcis was a further Syrian representative of this movement. Emesa produced Fronto, a rhetor who spent his career in Athens, and whose nephew, the philosopher Longinus, also spent a lengthy period in the Academy there. The aforementioned Porphyry was the most significant of his pupils. The novelist Heliodorus, author of the *Aethiopica* and likewise from Emesa, may also have lived at this time. Although the above-mentioned authors all wrote in Greek, there were some works produced in Latin, such as those of Ulpian, a jurist from Tyre who received his training at the famous School of Law in Beirut, a Latin-speaking colony. The School played an important role in this cultural context, and its pupils were to be found throughout the Roman Empire.

The fact that many of these philosophers, historians and rhetors were able to conduct the majority of their careers outside Syria, and indeed primarily in the intellectual capitals of Athens or Rome, is testament to the level of education to be had in Syrian cities. However, it may also be an indication that anyone wanting to progress in their career found

Main colonnade, Apamea

The northern section of the main colonnade, which was partially funded by the city's wealthy notables. Apamea was home to the Stoic philosopher Poseidonius.

Theater, Bosra

There has been a theater in the capital of the province of Arabia since the beginning of the 2nd century A.D. The structure was converted into a citadel during the Islamic period, and this helped preserve one of the best examples of classical theater architecture.

it necessary to leave Syria for centers with a better intellectual reputation.

Nevertheless, there was clearly a thriving Greek culture in the Levant, a movement which had begun just a few decades after the arrival of the Greco-Macedonian conquerors. Whether the previously-mentioned intellectuals were descendants of these immigrants or native Syrians was not important for the prevailing Hellenistic culture. As Plutarch remarked in his *Life of Alexander*, the king had an educative effect on Asia. It is certainly the case that only a thin layer of the population was truly affected, namely those who also possessed economic power.

Even so, the works of Greek culture had a considerable influence, which, thanks to Syrian and Arabic translations, continued even after the end of the Roman Empire.

The monumental nature of city design

The lack of theaters dating from the Hellenistic era in Syria is perhaps indicative that Hellenization was restricted to a relatively small elite. Other signs pointing to the same conclusion include the small number of Greek inscriptions from that period, and the fact that no Greek sporting contests took place before the advent of the Roman Empire, apart from in Sidon and Tyre. Then, however, venues sprang up all over the region. Of these, the most famous are the theaters in Bosra, including one of the most complete theaters of the Roman world, the theater in Palmyra, which was probably not completed, and the theater in Amman, with its impressive gradient. Literary sources and archaeological remains indicate the existence of at least 50 Roman arenas in the Levant. This includes those in the cities of Apamea, which had one of the largest theaters in the Roman Empire; Laodicea (Lattakia); Antioch, which had several theaters; Cyrrhus and Gabala (Jeble) in northern Syria; Beirut and the city-states on the coast; Philippopolis (Shahba); Canatha (Qanawat); and Gerasa (Jerash), which had three theaters. Another famous venue is the stadium in Tyre, one of the best-preserved and most-studied, although there is also a stadium in Antioch. In addition, hippodromes have been discovered in Antioch, Bosra and Gerasa.

Over the course of time, contests took place ever more frequently in the most urbanized zones, which made these buildings essential. In Arabia (except for Bosra) and in the desert (Palmyra), on the other hand, such contests were unknown. Nevertheless, certain events in Syrian cities attracted competitors from all over the Empire, and similarly, Syrians took part in contests throughout the Greco-Roman world – a further sign of Syria's integration during the Roman era.

These venues offer just one example of the monumental appearance which characterized the cities of the Roman Orient. Such buildings formed a

Theater, Amman

The theater in Amman lies at the foot of the citadel in the heart of the modern city, and is a fine example of the way in which Roman architecture made use of the surrounding terrain, in this case giving the *cavea* a dizzying gradient.

bridge between the culture of the intellectuals and the part of that culture which was accessible to the urban population as a whole. However, this is only one feature of the transformation which left its mark on the cities of the Levant. The extant remains provide ample evidence of the wealth and the rush to develop which can be traced back to the Roman conquest.

Theater, Philippopolis

The theater is located near the imperial temple and is very well preserved. Its small size and somewhat severe appearance are characteristic.

Southern theater, Gerasa

The skene or *frons scaenae* of the theater (end of the 1st century A.D.) is divided into three exedrae and was frequently altered. In both complexity and decoration it is comparable with those in other Syrian theaters, such as at Apamea or Palmyra.

Stadium, Tyre

The stadium is located near the monumental arch. Arcades link it to the colonnade and tie it into the urban landscape.

Theater, Byblos

The small theater in Byblos, following restoration work which shifted it right up to the shoreline. The facade with niches at intervals along the foot of the skene is typical of theaters in the Levant.

A good example of the monumental nature of city design following the Roman conquest is Apamea (Qalat al-Mudiq), whose main street is over a mile (2 km) long and 115 feet (35 m) wide. The road runs in a north-south direction, bounded by a Corinthian colonnade which was erected in stages during the period between the reigns of Trajan and Aurelius, as part of reconstruction work following an earthquake in 115 A.D. A census conducted by the Syrian governor Quirinius in 6/7 A.D. revealed the number of citizens to be 117,000, and put the total population of the city and its surrounding territory at the beginning of the Christian era at around 500,000 inhabitants. There are very few figures for the ancient world as precise as these. An understanding of the urban framework within which this population lived is readily gained from the large-scale structures (thermae – public baths – and nymphaea – pleasure houses with fountains and statues) and the residential buildings. They testify to the prosperity of the city, and the houses close to its monumental center clearly belonged to the wealthier citizens.

In both Apamea and Antioch, magnificent mosaics served as illustrations of wealth. Here again,

however, the Hellenistic age is not represented, and it is not until the early Byzantine period that there are a large number of examples. As for the Roman era, mosaics have been preserved in Apamea (dating from the 1st century A.D. onwards) and also in Palmyra, Philippopolis, and Eshmoun (near Sidon).

Gerasa is another example of a city with an astonishing monumental character; its colonnaded streets, modeled on those in Antioch built by Tiberius, are characteristic of Roman Syria, where such structures may have been developed. In any case, they are frequent here – found in Palmyra, Bosra, and Damascus, as well as Gerasa. Urban life was centered around these streets, which were lined with public buildings such as theaters (in Palmyra), temples (in Gerasa), and nymphaea. The colonnaded streets served to connect the most important buildings, giving a new shape to public spaces whilst at the same time parading the wealth of the city.

Arches, monumental gateways, and squares were often used to break up the monotony of extremely lengthy streets, and added to their decorative and aesthetic character. In addition, the fact that there were shops and also public buildings beneath the

Colonnaded road, Gerasa

The spectacle offered by colonnades such as these illustrates how Gerasa came to be known as the "city of 1,000 columns."

Main colonnade, Palmyra

The plinths halfway up the columns supported statues of patrons and benefactors. A small inscription beneath each one recorded their honorable deeds and gave general information about where they were from. A transverse colonnade leads to the tetrapylon, which divides the main street into sections.

Right

Mosaics, Eshmoun

Remnants of a mosaic which probably dates from the beginning of the 4th century A.D. and appears to depict the four seasons.

Main colonnade, Apamea

These columns (middle of the 2nd century A.D.) with spiral fluting can be found near the agora and the temple to the goddess Fortuna, and are one of the most outstanding sights of the city.

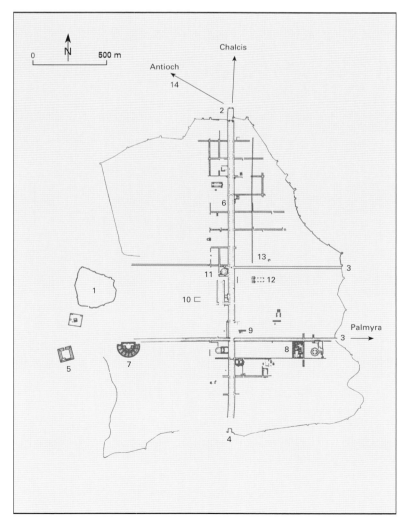

Plan of Apamea

Apamea's main road runs north-south for more than 2 km and is bordered by Corinthian colonnades along its length. Residential buildings, thermae and aqueducts are located nearby. The theater in the west of the city can be easily identified.

1 Acropolis, 2 North gate, 3 East gate,
4 South gate, 5 Caravanserai, 6 Main colonnade,
7 Theater, 8 Building with triclinium,
9 House with atrium, 10 Temple of Zeus-Belus,
11 Rotunda, 12 Baths, 13 Aqueduct, 14 Necropolis

Triple arch, Palmyra

This ingenious construction seamlessly joins two sections of the main colonnade where the road changes direction toward the Temple of Baal.

Right

Plan of Palmyra

1 Diocletian's wall, 2 Museum,
3 Peristyle houses, 4 Churches,
5 Basilica (new excavation),
6 Temple of Baal-Shamin, 7 Main colonnade,
8 Temple of Allat, 9 Transverse colonnade,
10 Temple of Arsu, 11 Tetrapylon,
12 "Caesareum," 13 Agora, 14 Annex to the agora,
15 Senate, 16 Theater, 17 Baths of Diocletian,
18 Temple of Nebo, 19 Temple of Bel,
20 Necropoli

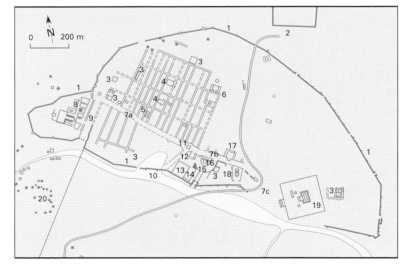

colonnades makes it likely that such streets functioned almost as a gathering place for the citizens. This new architectural framework for city life no doubt contributed to Hellenism taking root in the customs of the urban population, a process in which the thermae, as places to relax and socialize, were extremely important. Nevertheless, it may legitimately be suggested that in some cases the Roman influence prevailed over the truly Hellenistic elements of city design, namely in the organization of the city grid around two main axes, instead of the scalar Hellenistic checkerboard pattern around a central agora. However, oversimplifications should be avoided.

Other features which shaped the urban landscape were the aqueducts necessary for supplying the sometimes heavily populated cities with water, and the city walls, with gates opening onto the main road. During the Roman era of peace and into the 3rd century A.D., the condition of these ramparts was often neglected. Under the Seleucids, by contrast, they had been the cities' pride and joy, no doubt due to the fact that they were regularly called upon to help defend the population.

Opposite, top

Temple of Baal-Shamin, Palmyra

This small prostyle temple stands in the courtyard of a group of buildings and dates from the beginning of the 2nd century A.D. The god Baal-Shamin, whose name means "Master/Lord of the Heavens," was probably introduced to Palmyra by tribes from southern Syria.

Southern baths, Bosra

Like all Greco-Roman cities, the capital of the province of Arabia had bathing facilities – an essential element of classical civilization.

Mosaic of Gaia, Philippopolis

Second half of the 3rd century A.D.
272 x 332 cm
National Museum, Damascus

This very famous mosaic is from Shahba (Philippopolis) and depicts a range of allegorical figures: the woman and children in the center represent Earth and all its fruits, whilst time is personified by the figure on the left holding a wheel.

Nymphaeum, Gerasa

The nymphaeum lies at the midpoint of the
main road. The facade is a 72 feet (22 m) exedra
with statues in its niches, reminiscent of the
skene in a theater.

Oval forecourt and Temple of Zeus, Gerasa

This oval court borders the Temple of Zeus
(foreground) to the south, with a view along
the main road to the north. The Temple of
Artemis can be seen to the northwest.

Aqueduct, Caesarea

Caesarea was supplied with water via two aqueducts constructed during the reign of Herod. The more monumental of the two was renovated under Hadrian, and has now been partially freed from the sand which buried it for so long.

Factors underlying economic success

What were the reasons behind the prosperity of the cities? First and foremost, perhaps, the activities of Herod the Great – both within and beyond his kingdom – should be mentioned. His pro-Hellenistic stance, to which reference has already been made, led him to embark on a program of beautification in certain cities, among them Damascus, Antioch, Beirut, Tyre, Byblos and Ashkelon. Although there were some instances in which the influence of imperial authorities played a role (as seems to have been the case in Antioch, according to Flavius Josephus), it appears from surviving inscriptions that local benefactors often financed the construction of edifices which improved the appearance of their city.

After Herod, the cities began to fill up with monuments donated by the wealthy, particularly during the 2nd century A.D., which marked a high point in the prosperity of the region. These donations were just one feature of an active civic life modeled on that of contemporary Asia Minor. Syria's epigraphic record in this respect is not as extensive, but sufficient inscriptions survive honoring such patrons. They show that rivalries existed between the leading figures, who vied for supremacy in their city. On a broader level, the rush of construction can be understood only by taking into account the citizens' desire that their city should be the most magnificent – another respect in which the Hellenistic tradition was alive and well. This is also shown in the civic institutions known to have existed even in small city-states in the Hauran. Nevertheless, the fact that there were enormous differences in the degree of Hellenization, differences which become even more apparent with regard to the rural areas, is, of course, beyond doubt. The social elite in the less Hellenized

Latin inscription on aqueduct, Caesarea

This Latin inscription honors the work of a special detachment of the 2nd Trajanic Legion who repaired or rebuilt the aqueduct under the emperor Hadrian.

cities – the top officials and council members – may not have adopted Greco-Roman names, but they did participate in a civic life comparable at least in principle with that in Antioch or Apamea.

In the main, the *poleis* owed their material wealth to the surrounding rural areas, which provided them with products to consume, process and exchange. Syria's importance as a center of commerce is often emphasized, and we may rightly recall the activities of the Phoenicians in this respect. In Roman times, the prosperity of a city such as Palmyra was primarily rooted in its role as an intermediary in trade between the Orient (as far as the Indus) and Rome. However, this was just one of the pillars of Syrian wealth. The region's cities were important economic centers which benefited from the conditions created by the Roman Empire (new markets, the Pax Romana, and population growth) and the accessibility of numerous ports. These circumstances made possible the development which can still be seen today in the form of archaeological remains. Syrian traders, for their part, set out for the provinces of the Roman Empire; there is evidence of this in Italy, and also in Spain and Gaul (particularly around Lyon). At the same time, finds at sites outside Syria bear witness to the exportation of products from the Levant, although the majority of goods produced were probably intended for the local market. The Levant was famous for the quality of its luxury goods, principally glass (Sidon), metals (Antioch), and textiles (Damascus, Gerasa, Laodicea). The purple dye obtained from the murex mollusk long made Tyre wealthy and famous. Some ceramics were imported, although recent research has shown that a few workshops producing *terra sigillata* ware, which was common during the Roman period, must have been located in or around Syria.

Thaim's epitaph, Genay

c. 3rd century A.D.
Stone; height 112 cm, width 53 cm, depth 42 cm
Musée de la Civilisation Gallo-Romaine, Lyon

This inscription commemorates Thaim, son of Julianus. A Syrian from Canatha (Qanawat) in the Hauran, he worked as a trader in Gaul during the second half of the 3rd century A.D.

Hadrian's Arch, Gerasa

The monumental Hadrian's Arch stands 500 m from the south gate and marks the entrance to a zone set aside for further expansion of the city (which never occurred).

**Bust of a woman,
Hypogeum of Shalamallat, Palmyra**
*End of the 2nd century B.C.
National Museum, Damascus*

The jewelry and sumptuous fabrics worn by this woman show that she was wealthy. The bust is remarkable for its fine detail.

Hypogeum of Yarhai, Palmyra

This richly ornamented hypogeum has been reconstructed in the museum at Damascus, enabling the busts and sarcophagi to be viewed as a coherent whole rather than as separate pieces with no context.

Artistic diversity – Palmyran styles of dress

Works of sculpture from Palmyra vividly reflect the richness of Syrian and especially of Palmyran arts and crafts during the first three centuries A.D. Research into the necropoli of this oasis has revealed one of the most important bodies of art in Syria, and even in the entire Empire. Due to the popularity of Palmyran sculpture since it was rediscovered in the 17th century, busts and reliefs originating from Palmyra can be seen today in museums all over the world. These consist mainly of pieces used to seal tombs. We also find reliefs on sarcophagi, and a few statues in high relief, which were also frequently used as grave ornamentation. From the early 20th century onwards, it has been possible to undertake a classification of this body of art and to reconstruct its development, thanks to dates inscribed on some of the pieces uncovered. Particularly characteristic are the evident stylization and the front-view presentation, which probably has an oriental legacy.

This type of art also allows us greater insight into the civilization of Roman Syria. The busts depicting women, for example, illustrate the craft of the jeweler in a variety of ways; similarly, the decoration on the

Relief depicting a person at a banquet, Palmyra
Beginning of 3rd century A.D.
Limestone; height 55 cm
Palmyra Museum

This person, portrayed being served a drink at a banquet, is wearing the typical Iranian costume of the Palmyran nobility. Note the rich ornamentation of the clothing.

clothing, together with the rare finds of textile remains in tombs in Palmyra and Dura Europus, demonstrate the luxuriousness of some costumes.

External cultural influences

Palmyra is highly representative of a hybrid culture, incorporating Greek, Semitic, and also Iranian influences. Some members of the social elite, for example, were depicted in long-sleeved tunics and pants – a style of dress of Iranian origin – whilst others chose Greek clothing in the form of a short-sleeved, knee-length tunic, over which a *himation*, a coat covering the whole body, could be worn. A more local costume is frequently seen in sculptures of armed men found in and around Palmyra. In these, the long-sleeved tunic is worn over a large piece of cloth which was wound around the waist and covered the legs, but was open at the front to enable the wearer to ride a horse. The female costume of local origin was simpler; the most characteristic feature was a scarf used as a kind of veil to cover the hair, the latter often being held in place with a diadem. Presumably, it could also have been used to veil the face, but we do not know whether this was indeed the usual practice.

Palmyra represents only one slice of Levantine culture. Cities with a Hellenistic culture, such as Antioch or Gerasa, probably preferred the Greek style of dress. In some respects, however, Syrian culture was indeed a hybrid, if only because in places, it allowed diverse artistic traditions to coexist in the same city and produce their own, distinctive works. Like Palmyra, therefore, the sculpture of the Hauran could also be said to have its own particular stylistic characteristics. As the following pages show, temples and other sacred structures were the highest form of expression for this art, and borrowed elements from various traditions. Secular structures, on the other hand, were less of a mixture of styles, although certain features, such as the colonnaded street, may have been local inventions which subsequently spread to the rest of the Empire.

Fragment of woolen clothing, Dura Europus
Beginning of 3rd century A.D.
Wool; width 11.9 cm, length 24.6 cm
Yale University Art Gallery, New Haven

This woolen fabric comes from a piece of clothing worn in Dura Europus early in the 3rd century A.D. It is likely that the inhabitants of Dura Europus used less luxurious fabrics than the citizens of Palmyra.

Cornice depicting the Judgement of Paris, Suweida

2nd century A.D.
Basalt; length 1316 cm, height 52 cm,
depth 18.5 cm
Louvre, Paris

This scene, which takes a typical theme from Greco-Roman mythology, has been executed in a style characteristic of southern Syria.

Onomastics and the language of the Roman Levant

Onomastics (the study of names) provides a good indication as to the extent of Hellenization, even if Greek inscriptions are the only ones considered. It shows that Hellenism had taken root most firmly in the areas which had been first to feel the Greek influence, namely the cities of northern Syria, and above all, those of the Decapolis. In such places it is no longer possible to distinguish between the native population which adopted Greek culture and the descendants of settlers from Alexander's time. Elsewhere, the inhabitants retained their traditional names, even if they spoke Greek. In some instances, such as in Palmyra, they had dual names; the Greek

name Zenobia, for example, was Bat Zabbai in Aramaic, and people used either version, depending on which language they knew or happened to be using at the time. Inscriptions in stone were the privilege of the most wealthy, and it is therefore almost impossible to tell how many inhabitants of Syria actually spoke Greek. In any case, there was clearly a connection between use of the Greek language and membership of the upper stratum of society, even in Palmyra. It is possible that the gradual increase in the use of native names in inscriptions was due to a generally rising level of prosperity. In the early days of the Empire, only the tiniest proportion of the population was literate, namely the rich city dwellers who had economic power. Now, however, with increasing urbanization and the rise of the professions, less Hellenized people also had access to the written culture which was a feature of the ancient world.

Nevertheless, it appears from contemporary reports that the majority of the population – from the Jews to the Nabataean Arabs – spoke Aramaic. In the border regions the local languages and scripts were primarily used: Aramaic in the Nabataean kingdom and in Palmyra; and Safaitic, an old northern Arabian dialect, east of the Jordan. Syriac, an Aramaic dialect from Mesopotamia, was just as much the language of culture in one region of the Christian Near East as Greek. It experienced a degree of growth from the 2nd century onwards thanks to the theologian Bardesanes, a native of Edessa whose teachings lay somewhere between Christianity and heresy. In Palmyra, inscriptions were mainly written using the local Aramaic alphabet, and, if later sources are to be

Fragment of the Book of Enoch, Qumran, Cave 4

Copy, first half of 2nd century B.C.
parchment; width 17.7 cm, height 17.5 cm
Archaeological Museum of Palestine
(Rockefeller), Jerusalem

The Book of Enoch is one of the most important of the Apocrypha (those works not included in the accepted canon of the Old Testament). The Aramaic original was lost in antiquity, but sections of the Aramaic text were found for the first time at Qumran.

believed, the farmers immediately beyond the gates of Antioch, the capital of the province, knew no Greek and spoke only Aramaic.

In the zone between Hierapolis in the north and Qumran on the northwestern shore of the Dead Sea, there were areas in which native customs continued to prevail. These areas also produced important material demonstrating the coexistence of different cultures. The manuscript scrolls found in Qumran are among the most significant sources relating to the doctrinal shifts which were preoccupying the Jewish community at the time. Although they are primarily concerned with just one of a number of sects, they nevertheless provide history in general with important information about the languages used in the region. Other documents from the same zone, known as the "Babatha archives," show that the various dialects of Aramaic, including Nabataean, existed alongside Hebrew and Greek, and that in some cases, particularly in the field of law, a Greco-Roman influence can even be identified.

Rock massif, Qumran

The famous Dead Sea Scrolls were found in caves in this rock massif. A Jewish religious community (probably the Essenes) lived in the nearby settlement.

The strength of native traditions outside the cities

In the Roman era, records provide an increasingly clear picture of the native population. This is connected with a phenomenon whose origins go back at least as far as the 1st millennium B.C., namely the arrival in Syria of peoples from the Arabian peninsula. These "Arabs" (the term is used here in a linguistic sense) formed several groups, of which the Nabataeans are probably the best known. Mention should also be made of the Ituraeans, who settled near Damascus at the end of the Hellenistic era. Evidence provided by onomastics and the cults shows that a proportion of the population of Palmyra was also of Arab origin. Like the Nabataeans, they were exposed to a very strong Aramaic influence, and both peoples wrote inscriptions in Aramaic rather than Arabic. There are many indications that the language of everyday use was Aramaic, even in the Nabataean kingdom. There were other Arab peoples to be found in Mesopotamia, particularly in the steppe region of southern Syria and in northeast Arabia. These tribes are usually characterized as Safaitic, although they did not form a homogenous community. They are known primarily for leaving behind thousands of inscriptions, especially in the region of the southern Syrian steppe, and also in cities such as Bosra, and even as far as Palmyra. They were groups of nomads who occasionally cultivated the land, if climatic conditions were favorable, as traditional Bedouins still do to this day. Above all, however, their way of life was based on rearing dromedaries, horses, and sheep in migrant herds. This way of life was more or less the same for all the nomads, although not all were necessarily of Arab origin. The tribes often became at least partially settled. In the case of Palmyra, for example, this contributed indirectly to the city's prosperity. The nomads and the newly settled groups maintained their connections, and this explains how the Palmyran traders were able to control the routes which ran straight through the desert from Palmyra to the Euphrates, in order to conduct trade. Livestock production was extremely important for these tribes, as it was for the Safaites. A series of rural settlements has been discovered in the mountain region northeast of Palmyra, and these may perhaps have been the stud farms which supplied the pack animals for the caravans and the animals to be ridden by those who accompanied them.

The role of agriculture

Although very little is known about the rural world, its dominant role in this period cannot be questioned. The majority of the population lived on the land and made their living through agriculture – the nomads were simply an exception. A large proportion of these agricultural areas were under the control of the cities and their inhabitants. It is known that certain cities, such as Antioch, Apamea, and even Canatha in the Hauran, possessed a huge amount of surrounding territory, as was also the case with the Roman colony of Beirut.

A few plots of land, such as those occupied by temple complexes, did not belong to the cities. The most famous of these is the Temple of Zeus at Baitokaike (Husn Suleiman), in the mountains above Aradus. Its independence from the city had already been recognized during the time of the Seleucids, and continued in the Roman era. Some areas were imperial property, such as when a legacy of the Seleucid kings was involved. The best-known example of this is the Forest of Lebanon, control of which was partially entrusted to imperial procurators. A large number of boundary stones from this region have been preserved, which were put in place during the time of Hadrian (117–138 A.D.). Other lands belonged directly to autonomous villages, the existence and internal organization of which have been proven, primarily in southern Syria. Only later did the most important of these villages become *poleis*, a sign, perhaps, of the delayed Hellenization of their inhabitants.

The arrival of the Seleucids had already resulted in changes in land ownership around the larger new cities such as Apamea. However, Roman cadastral surveys exist for the limestone massif between Aleppo, Antioch, and Apamea, and also for the area around the city of Canatha in the Hauran. These surveys, which can be deciphered using boundary stones and from the shapes of the plots, were probably carried out in order to bring new regions under cultivation and increase production.

Stone with Safaitic inscription, Safa

1st century B.C.
Basalt; height 50 cm, width 40 cm
Louvre, Paris

Above the inscription giving the name of the engraver is a scene depicting a hunter and a lion.

Agricultural activities provided food for Roman Syria as well as a proportion of its exports (wine, fruit, and textiles from animal breeding). However, the various regions were not equally blessed as regards opportunities to exploit the land. Agriculture along the Mediterranean coast (cereals, olives, and wine) had little in common with agriculture on the steppe, which stretched to the Euphrates in the east and to the Arabian desert in the south. Dry farming (farming without artificial irrigation) was possible in many places here, hence the cereals crops in the Hauran and on the plains around Chalcis (Qinnisrin). Irrigation structures appear to have been rare (although a few examples do exist, such as in the oasis of Damascus and in the region around Palmyra), and the region's major river valleys, essentially those of the Orontes and the Euphrates, were certainly important for agriculture. Wine was produced in the areas around Laodicea and Damascus, and in the Hauran and Palestine. A proportion of this yield was exported. The north-Syrian limestone massif produced olive oil, an industry which first began to develop during the 2nd century, but only subsequently experienced real growth. Agricultural activity, of which the above are but a few examples, was clearly varied and extensive, and seems to have spared the region the crises of survival that affected other parts of the Empire. Nevertheless, bottlenecks in the supply of food did occur in some cities, although these were largely due to transportation problems rather than to crop failures.

Temple, Husn Suleiman

The ruins of this temple are the imposing remnants of a site of cult worship which goes back to pre-Hellenistic times. However, the wall in which this doorway is situated dates from the 3rd century A.D.

Several reliefs, including this one depicting a seated woman, can be seen along a path cut into the rock leading up to a monumental altar. As in Ghine, where the same stylistic features are found, this is a tomb relief.

Necropolis, Tyre

The necropolis dates from the imperial and Byzantine periods and runs beside a road. The site was made famous by the discovery of a number of decorated sarcophagi, some of which were imported, primarily from Greece (Attica).

Necropoli and temples

The manner in which the wealth of the social elite radiated beyond the *poleis* is demonstrated by the necropoli, which can be found throughout the region, and which often formed a link between the cities and the surrounding territory. It was precisely here that we see a blend of diverse influences, because far from being purely conservative, these burial areas were entirely susceptible to whatever was currently fashionable. Tombs served the local aristocracy as spaces for self-promotion and self-presentation, and as places where they could compete with one another using all the resources of art and architecture. Magnificent tombs were not an invention of this era, some earlier examples also exist. Nevertheless, burial monuments from this period can be found in increased numbers throughout the region, located more or less in the vicinity of the inhabited areas. In the case of the "Mausoleum" at Hermel in Lebanon, which dates from the last years before the rise of Rome (1st century B.C.), the monument marks the burial site of a local dynasty. Its relatively isolated location may indicate a desire that it should dominate the surrounding area. This type of structure was common in the region, both in northern Syria, east of Antioch, and in the south (the Hauran). There is even an example in Jerusalem, Absalom's Tomb, a monolithic cube, partly hewn into the rock. It dates from the same period as the Hermel Mausoleum, and serves as a memorial covering the entrance to the burial chamber.

On occasion, the function of these monuments as tomb sites has been brought into question. There can be good reasons for this, which have led to theories linking them with cults as well as with burials. Reliefs at Ghine (in the Lebanon Mountains) showing a man battling an animal were thought at first to depict the

"Absalom's Tomb," Jerusalem

Partly built (upper section), partly hewn into the rock, this structure is typical of the monuments known as *nefesh*, which were memorials to the dead rather than tombs in the literal sense.

Tomb relief, Ghine

Hunting is a theme frequently encountered in tomb decoration. Here, a man is fighting a lion or bear. The woman seated on the right is clearly unconnected with the scene.

mythological struggle of Adonis with a wild boar, thus favoring their interpretation as a site of cult worship. It is more likely, however, that they depict a hunting scene – the animal more closely resembles a bear – which was one event in the life of the person whose tomb lies a few meters away. Similarly, it has sometimes been suggested that the Altar of Mashnaqa, which dates from the beginning of the Christian era, was dedicated to the Cult of Adonis. There is no evidence to suggest this, however, and as at Ghine, the presence of reliefs at the site must be considered in relation to the tombs located nearby. On the other hand, it is highly likely that there were monuments to the Cult of Adonis in the Lebanon Mountains, for according to legend, that is where the god died.

"Mausoleum," Hermel

This structure, around 82 feet (25 m) in height, dates from the 2nd or 1st century B.C. It is decorated with hunting motifs, perhaps commemorating the activities of the deceased, who was probably a local prince.

Rock tomb, Qatura

Jebel Sheikh Barakat, above the village of Qatura, is well known as the site of an altar to Zeus, and contains a small number of Roman tombs with reliefs depicting the deceased and their families.

Sarcophagus, Bet Shearim

Jews from many communities in the Near East were buried in the necropolis at Bet Shearim. The discovery of this sarcophagus (4th century A.D.) showed that although Jewish custom strongly prohibited the depiction of living beings, the rules were occasionally breached.

Necropoli – Mirrors of society

In most cases, tombs of varying shapes and sizes were collected in rambling necropoli. As in the rest of the classical world, these were situated outside the cities in order to make a clear distinction between the world of the dead and the world of the living.

The most common form of tomb was an underground chamber known as a hypogeum, which often served as a communal burial site. These were generally built for a single family, but could also be used by several groups, sometimes for purely economic reasons. One type of hypogeum, hewn into the rock of a hillside, was extremely common, although it was not actually a Syrian pattern. Examples can be seen at Qatura, in the limestone massif of northern Syria, where burials have been dated to between 100 and 250 A.D. The reliefs depict figures, and are cut quite roughly into the rock. They have parallels throughout the region as far as the area around the River Tigris in Mesopotamia.

Other necropoli united people who were primarily linked by a shared religion. The best-known example of this is the necropolis at Bet Shearim, which expanded significantly during the 3rd century A.D. It was a burial site for Jews from numerous communities in the Near East and as far away as Mesene in Lower

Mesopotamia. Curiously, the majority of inscriptions are in Greek, although Aramaic and Hebrew texts can also be found at the site.

Palmyra provides the greatest wealth of evidence, both in the number of hypogea which have been discovered and in the frequency of the inscriptions. Among the information revealed by these inscriptions are details of various procedures involving burial sites, such as the sale of a portion of burial space by its owner. Whereas before we could only theorize, this knowledge allows us to reconstruct a more accurate picture of such practices.

Tombs were sometimes richly decorated, particularly with paintings. This trend is illustrated in Marissa, which has an example dating back to the Hellenistic era, and in Palmyra. It can also be seen in other areas, such as in Sidon on the Lebanese coast, in the mountain region around Masyaf in western Syria, and in Seleucia-Zeugma on the Euphrates.

Ceiling of the Elahbel Burial Tower, Valley of Tombs, Palmyra

Each of the stuccoed coffers is decorated with a rosette. In the center, four busts stand out in relief. Two of these are priests, as shown by their cylindrical headgear.

Tomb of the Three Brothers, Palmyra

Between the images of winged Victory carrying the busts of the deceased are the spaces intended for the corpses. The artwork as a whole imitates architectural decoration.

Valley of Tombs, Palmyra

The western approach to Palmyra ran through this valley. Inscriptions reveal that each tomb was reserved for the family and descendants of the person for whom it was built.

The Elahbel Burial Tower, Palmyra

Named after the person for whom it was built, this is one of the best-preserved burial towers in Palmyra. It dates from 103 A.D. and stands at the extreme western edge of the necropolis.

Opposite, below

Burial temple, Palmyra

Although it borrows features from religious architecture, this structure is very probably a tomb. It is located at the end of the main colonnade, just at the point where the town gives way to the necropolis.

Burial sites in Palmyra clearly display a Western influence, although the front-view presentation of the figures in their reliefs more closely reflects the local tradition. They are characteristic not only of hypogea, where they appear in large numbers, but are also seen in the other two main types of Palmyran burial monument, namely burial towers and, from the 2nd century onwards, burial temples. Such structures can be found in other locations as well, but Palmyra contains the greatest number of examples.

The most famous of the great Palmyran necropoli is the Valley of Tombs. It runs alongside the road to Emesa (Homs) and the Mediterranean, a route used not only by the caravans responsible for the city's prosperity, but also by Greek and Roman visitors.

Necropoli which developed alongside a road were a typical feature of the Roman Empire in its heyday. There are examples in Syria and Asia Minor, just as in Italy (beside the roads leading out of Rome or in Ostia). The phenomenon is believed to have been connected with the wealth of the *poleis*, in that

the members of the elite competed with one another by building imposing burial structures in the most visible locations. This was certainly the case in Palmyra, where the numerous inscriptions confirm the architectural facts. The location of certain monuments, such as the burial temple which completes the view along the main colonnade, demonstrates the prominent status of the traders who formed the local aristocracy and who tried to shape the urban landscape. Several memorials were built one after another on a hill at the entrance to the city, a location which not only dominates the road but can also be seen from the center of Palmyra, and this could be interpreted as an architectural expression of family rivalry among the social elite.

Valley of Tombs, Palmyra

A number of these tombs date from the ninth decade A.D.; as though the city's top families had been attempting to outdo one another.

Characteristic features of Levantine temple complexes

The relatively isolated location of burial monuments such as the one at Hermel can be compared with that of rural temple complexes, many of which lie far outside the urban zones. This phenomenon is not unique – the rural areas of Greece also contain isolated sites of cult worship – although certain elements appear to be typically Semitic. The largest coherent collection of such temple complexes is located in the Lebanon Mountains north of the Bekaa Valley. There are also examples in northern Syria in the zone around Jebel Barisha and Jebel Sheikh Barakat, which confirm the existence of cults relating to several deities, including the "Altar of Zeus" dedicated to the god Zeus Bomus. The present-day isolation of these sites can be misleading, as some were clearly surrounded by a small settlement in their heyday. The temple complex at Husn Suleiman is one such example, and it enjoyed a certain independence from the neighboring city of Aradus. In addition, the most important sites of cult worship produced settlements which sometimes developed into *poleis*. This was the case with the Dea Syria/Atargatis complex at Hierapolis in Syria, and the Jupiter Heliopolitanus complex at Baalbek in Lebanon. In some instances, however, isolation helped preserve the buildings, in contrast to

Temple, Shhim

This little temple in the mountains east of Sidon dates from the 2nd century A.D. It was converted into a winepress during the Christian era, when a small settlement developed at the site.

Temple decoration, Shhim

The decoration of the little temple at Shhim features reliefs around the doorway and a winged sun on the cornice.

Temple, Husn Suleiman

The temple stands in the middle of the complex and was built over the ruins of an older structure. In the podium is the window of a crypt which may have been part of that original edifice.

Inscription, Qalat Faqra

This inscription marks the construction of the building by one Tholom, son of Rabbomus. The necessary funds were provided by the Temple of the "most mighty" God (unnamed).

Hierapolis, where any remains have disappeared. Re-use of temples in the following era also aided their preservation: some were converted into churches, as at Bziza in the Lebanon.

As was usual throughout the region, the temple complexes of the Lebanon Mountains contained several structures within a surrounding wall: a temple, one or more monumental altars, banqueting halls for religious gatherings, rooms for various other purposes and pools for ritual washing. To these were sometimes added a columned aedicula (*naiskos*) and betyls (sacred stones, sometimes in the form of columns or pillars). At Qalat Faqra the different parts of the complex, including the altar and temple, are a considerable distance apart. Another building nearby (dated to 43–44 A.D.) carries a dedication to the emperor Claudius and is thought to be a treasury. Sometimes, as at Sfire, the surrounding wall encloses several temples; alternatively, different temples, each with their own peribolos (sacred precinct), can be found in close proximity to each other, as at Qasr Naous. Of course, all these features are also typical of the large temple complexes in city locations, such as at Gerasa, Baalbek or Palmyra; in the Hauran (at Sia/Si); or further south, in the Nabataean region (Khirbet el-Darih, Khirbet el-Tannur).

It has long been known that places of sacrifice were very important for the Semitic cults. This type of monument is described in the Old Testament, and can also be found in the Nabataean world. They are

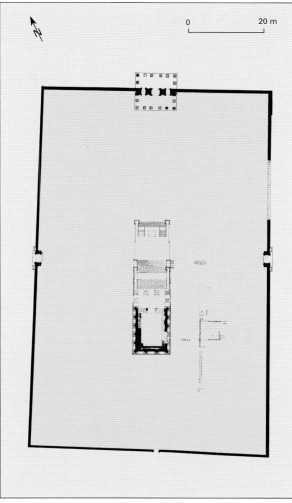

Plan of the temple complex, Husn Suleiman

The layout of the temple complex at Husn Suleiman is typical of the region. The temple itself stands in the center of a large courtyard which also contains various other buildings required for cult practices.

Niche aedicula, Qalat Faqra

Behind the little niche aedicula (foreground) are the monumental altar on the right and the "treasury" of the Temple of the "most mighty" God on the left.

Temple complex, Sfire

The line of the enclosing wall and the ruins of two Roman temples can readily be identified. The hilltop location, dominating the surrounding area, is characteristic of this type of complex.

attempts to get physically closer to a particular deity – hence the more or less systematic construction of monumental altars, which would be ascended in order for sacrificial rites to be performed on the roof terrace or in a corner turret. The same idea is sometimes expressed in the design of the temples themselves, in the form of stairways at their corners. Locations where such altars can be seen include Dmeir – near Damascus – and Palmyra.

A common arrangement, characteristic of the Roman influence, has the temple rising above a podium with steps in front. The decoration, too, often points to a Greco-Roman inspiration – with added local color, of course, resulting from adherence to certain decorative features (such as the door surrounds) rather than the introduction of local details from other artistic genres. In the interior of such temples, things were somewhat different. The cella was clearly divided into two parts, one of which formed the *adyton* or *thalamos*. Although there was no partition wall, a curtain must have hidden this "Holy of Holies" from prying eyes. In addition, the *thalamos* was often elevated, further emphasizing the separation of the two sections. This was the case in the temples of the Lebanon Mountains, and also in Palmyra, where the Temple of Bel, in particular, has a very peculiar arrangement.

The Temple of Nebo, Palmyra

This niche aedicula, probably used for storing cult images, stood between the monumental propylaea and the temple itself. In the background is the city's most important cult site, the Temple of Bel.

Opposite

Eastern Temple, Qasr Naous

The eastern temple, as it is known, was built on a podium and had a double row of columns in front of its facade.

Temple of Bacchus, Baalbek

This famous portal has survived the centuries, and is lavishly decorated with plant motifs which contrast with the classical appearance of the interior.

Below, right

Temple interior, Niha

A monumental flight of steps leads up to a kind of terrace, which forms the *adyton*.

Reconstruction of the temple interior, Niha

This reconstruction clearly shows the cella divided into two parts. A baldachin probably screened the *adyton* and its cult figure.

Religious diversity – The gods of the Levant

As in other parts of the Roman world, the inhabitants of the Levant showed great loyalty to their religious traditions and native deities. An important example is Hierapolis, in northern Syria. Although, like Palmyra, the city had a council and Greek institutions, it was closely linked with the cult of a local deity, Dea Syria (Atargatis), a goddess familiar to us through the writings of Lucian of Samosata. The Syrian character of this cult, which dates from before Alexander's conquest, is emphasized both in the name of the goddess (Dea Syria, the "Syrian Goddess") and in its ritual practices, which must have astonished the Greco-Roman population. Relics of this sort survived all over the region.

In the cities founded by the Macedonians, on the other hand, the situation was a little different, because there was less of a native tradition to uphold during this period. Even in these cities, however, some of the population were of local extraction, and their traditions and customs were either retained or adapted. The assimilation of Zeus and Bel (Baal) in Apamea, for example, demonstrates that even in such an apparently Greek city, religious influences were diverse.

Relief of Atargatis and Hadad, Dura Europus

2nd century A.D.
Limestone; height 40 cm, width 28 cm
Yale University Art Gallery, New Haven

One of the Greek names for Atargatis was Dea Syria ("Syrian Goddess"). She is usually identified by the lions around her throne.

Relief of a sun, Qasr Naous

This relief of a bust representing the sun lies near the ruins of the western temple. It probably had a decorative function and was not directly related to the cult. The sun sometimes forms a triad together with the moon and subordinate to the master of the heavens.

What is apparent, is that the Levant did not have a single religion, but rather a whole group of deities which varied from one place to another, in keeping with the cultural and geographical diversity of the region. Each locality retained its own particular pantheon, although various influences sometimes resulted in modifications. Leaving aside Judaism and Christianity, the cults in Phoenician cities had little in common with the cults which Arab nomads introduced to places such as Palmyra or the Hauran (or more generally, to the province of Arabia), although they certainly had a common foundation. Palmyra is a special case, however, in that it combined influences from Syria (the god Baal-Shamin), Mesopotamia (the god Bel, a local variant of Baal) and Arabia (the goddess Allat) with a significant local tradition. This led the city to be in the peculiar position of having at least two supreme deities, who were known as Zeus in the Greek language and Baal-Shamin and Bel in Aramaic, and who each had their own temple.

Certain temples (such as those in the Lebanon Mountains) were dedicated to specific local deities who were often associated with a particular location, such as a mountain peak. Often, however, the gods were given collective names taken from the Greco-Roman pantheon – Zeus, or Jupiter/Helios, for example. Some cult sites are known to us only through their archaeological remains, and in many of these cases it is no longer possible to identify the god to which the temple was dedicated. At Qasr Naous, for example, the discovery of a single relief depicting the sun has led to the assumption that the temple at the east of the site was dedicated to the sun god (Helios, in Greek), although there is no other evidence to confirm this.

The fact that native deities were often equated with Greek gods can be extremely confusing. The name Zeus, for example, can encompass a whole variety of different gods across the Levant, with only one thing in common: locally, each was considered

to be the leading deity. The situation in Palmyra has already been described; in Damascus and Baalbek, Zeus was probably Hadad, although it would be wrong to assume that this name signified the same deity in both cases, since their characteristic attributes were quite different. The number of supreme gods ruling the cities, such as Melkart in coastal Tyre, Heliogabalus in Emesa, Zeus Turmasgada in Caesarea, or Hadad and Atargatis in Hierapolis, is one more reflection of the diversity of the local pantheons.

Great Temple, Qalat Faqra

View of the great temple, which was surrounded by a wall. An inscription tells us that the complex was dedicated to a "most mighty God," whose name, in keeping with an ancient Semitic tradition, is not recorded.

Temple of Baal-Shamin, Palmyra

The exterior is classical in appearance, whilst the design of the interior is more in keeping with a Semitic cult, and includes an *adyton*.

The great temple complexes of Palmyra and Gerasa

All the supreme deities of the local pantheons had temples dedicated to them. Some of these sites are better known than others, but all have features characteristic of the diverse influences which affected the region. The temples of Bel in Palmyra, of Zeus and Artemis in Gerasa, and of Jupiter Heliopolitanus in Baalbek, are some of the most stunning monuments to have survived from this period. In addition, these complexes are both a demonstration

and a product of the various forms of hybrid culture which existed at the time. They were decorated using specific, classical models, whilst at the same time elements were retained which, in the local cultural context, were significant for the cult and its practices. Architecturally, therefore, these ambitious projects were not identical, and it is conceivable that the Roman influence may have had a hand at different stages in their design.

The Temple of Bel in Palmyra is the legacy of an old local cult (whose god retained his native name even in Greek inscriptions), and was plainly a focus for the city's civic life. The entire population would gather there during festivals, even though the religious life of the tribes was centered on other temples, such as the Temple of Baal-Shamin. Because the relevant records are lacking, the rituals associated with this cult remain largely obscure. Reliefs from the entablature of the temple, however, do provide a few clues as to the ceremonies performed here. Incense offerings and processions evidently played a part, as did mythology – a particularly good example of which is a scene depicting the gods fighting a giant who is part serpent. All the figures are presented facing outwards, a style which has become known as Parthian art.

The temple itself has some unusual features which make it unique in the classical world. The exterior plan is reminiscent of the Temple of Artemis

Plan of the Temple of Bel complex, Palmyra

The temple stands in the middle of a large, almost square courtyard measuring 210 x 205 m. This was surrounded by a high wall, joined on three sides to a colonnade with two rows of pillars. Inside the western wall containing the entrance to the courtyard was a row of taller columns.

Entablature from the Temple of Bel, Palmyra

The entablature supporting the roof of the temple included mythological scenes as part of its decoration. Here, a row of gods (depicted facing outwards) battles a giant.

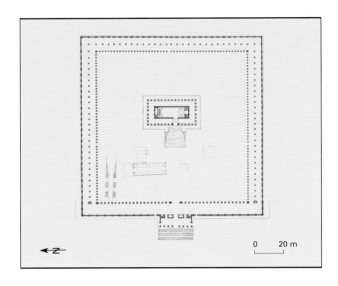

Entablature from the Temple of Bel, Palmyra

Relief showing a sacrificial scene. For a long time, the custom of portraying people facing outward was believed to have originated in the Parthian kingdom. Now, however, the term "Greco-Oriental" art is usually preferred.

at Magnesia (in Anatolia), albeit in a modified form to accommodate the particular requirements of the cult. Access to the temple was not from the shorter side, but through a portal on the longer western side set slightly south of the mid-point. This created space for two *thalamoi* at the narrow ends of the interior, which fulfilled the same function as in the Lebanese temples and were similarly elevated. An inclined surface in front of the southern *thalamos* no doubt allowed the objects kept inside (an image of Bel or a betyl, perhaps) to be retrieved during processions – one relief shows just such a scene. Surrounding the temple was a large peristyle with architectural features that were typical of the region, such as the propylaea at the entrance to the temple precinct. The temple was dedicated (unfinished) in 32 A.D., and the complex as a whole was probably completed during the 2nd century, more than 150 years after work began.

Temple of Bel, Palmyra

The gigantic portal in the western side of the temple is reached by a ramp and is strangely skewed. This arrangement is also found in the temples of Mesopotamia, but contrasts with the otherwise classical exterior of the monument.

Below

Temple of Bel, Palmyra

The peribolos wall surrounding the sacred precinct can be seen in the northwest corner. The complex (200 x 200 m) was bordered by four porticos, whose columns supported a roof covering the space between the portico and the wall.

Temple of Jupiter, Baalbek

In a direct line from the hexagonal forecourt are the large altar courtyard, its two altars and the steps leading up to the temple.

The temple complex at Baalbek

The great temple complex at Baalbek, like the Temple of Bel in Palmyra, was built on a site associated with a cult. This time the deity took on the name of a Roman god, Jupiter, no doubt because Baalbek-Heliopolis was a Roman colony.

As so often happened, however, the Latin name actually hid that of a local Hadad or Baal, a male diety who continued to be depicted in traditional fashion in a close-fitting sheath garment, carrying a whip, and accompanied by two bulls. The Temple of Jupiter Heliopolitanus was completed during Nero's reign (54–68 A.D.), although the final elements of the complex were not in place until the middle of the 3rd century. A flight of steps and a three-part gateway led first to a hexagonal courtyard. This in turn opened onto the main peristyle, which displayed some of the key architectural features characteristic of the region: a pool for ritual washing, and two altars, the older of which was discovered to have been a relic from the Hellenistic period.

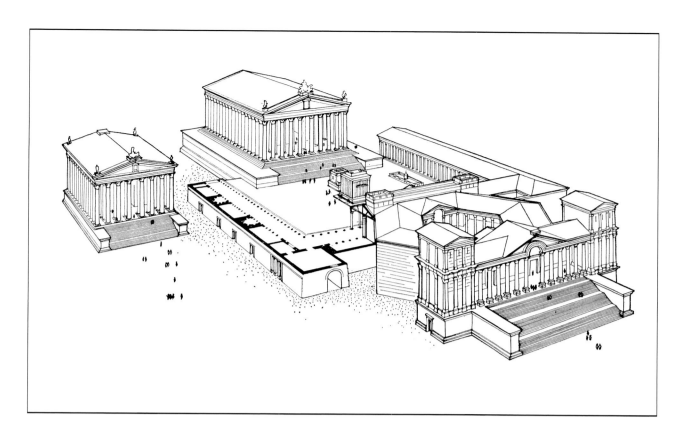

Reconstruction of the Temple of Jupiter complex, Baalbek

Access to the complex was via a perron leading up to the propylaea, a colonnaded entrance hall. This adjoined a hexagonal forecourt, unique in the ancient world, which had three portals opening on to the large altar courtyard. Corinthian arcades enclosed this second courtyard on three sides, with the Temple of Jupiter bordering it on the fourth.

Temple of Jupiter, Baalbek

One of the two pools used for ritual washing can be seen in front of the exedrae adorning the courtyard.

Temple of Jupiter, Baalbek

The large courtyard contained two altars. The smaller and older one had been restored and stood at the foot of the temple steps; it had been in the exact center of the site's original courtyard.

Below, right

Monumental stone block, Baalbek

This block is an exact match for some of those used in the pediment of the Temple of Jupiter (a *trilithon*, from the Greek "with three stones"). This one, which never left the quarry, weighs around 985 tons.

Jupiter Heliopolitanus, Baalbek

2nd-3rd century B.C.
Bronze; height 38.5 cm, base 14.7 x 12.7 cm
Louvre, Paris

This bronze statue was found in the environs of Baalbek. It is a very vivid depiction of the form taken by the deity who was worshipped at Heliopolis/Baalbek. The traditional appearance of Jupiter Heliopolitanus – dressed in a sheath garment and accompanied by two bulls – was retained.

The other, larger altar took the form of a tower with an internal staircase up to the altar terrace – a further example of Semitic cult practices being performed in temple complexes. The temple itself was also raised, standing on a podium around 65 feet (20 m) high. Some of the blocks in its substructure weigh 985 tons (1,000 tonnes). The colonnade running around the temple further emphasized its elevated situation, although only six of these 65 feet (20 m) columns are still standing.

As at other sites, more temples are located nearby. It is possible that Jupiter Heliopolitanus was the chief deity in a triad, and if so, he would have been accompanied by Atargatis and a third, Semitic god, whose name is unknown, but who could be equated with several deities, such as Hermes/Mercury or Dionysus/Bacchus. It was to the latter that the peripteros at the foot of the Temple of Jupiter was probably dedicated. Like its neighbor, the Temple of Bacchus also stood on a podium, but is not as old (dating from around 150 A.D.), and is better preserved. It is mainly remarkable for the rich decoration of the surrounding peristyle (particularly its cornice) and the interior. Inside the temple is a platform for an aedicula which would have contained an image of the deity – another example of an *adyton*, or Holy of Holies.

Temple of Bacchus, Baalbek

The elaborate ornamentation of this colonnade using plant motifs is very similar to the decoration in the Temple of Jupiter, although of a later date (around 150 A.D.).

Temple of Jupiter, Baalbek

At the far end of the great courtyard and at the top of this monumental flight of steps was the Temple of Jupiter itself. The internal structures have been largely destroyed, but there must have been an *adyton* here.

Temple of Bacchus, Baalbek

Compared with the Temple of Jupiter, from which it is separated by an enclosing wall, the Temple of Bacchus is much less imposing in scale. The exterior has a peristyle of narrowly spaced columns and is clearly oriented toward classical models.

Opposite

Temple of Bacchus, Baalbek

Probably the most striking feature of the temple's interior decoration are the Corinthian half-columns, which create niches in the walls.

A little further away are two more temples. One is round, of unique design, and probably dates from the 3rd century. Although known as the Temple of Venus, its true dedication is not known. The neighboring rectangular temple is older and similarly anonymous.

The rich decoration of these temples, which is particularly evident on the doorways and ceilings, is highly typical of Roman Syria and combines classical and oriental decorative elements. Traditions from a variety of regions can be identified, ranging from Rome and Anatolia (which maintained its influence) to Mesopotamia and Iran. From the middle of the 1st century A.D., however, they outgrew their cultural confines and formed a separate, Syrian tradition. The predilection for using plants as a decorative motif is particularly evident in Baalbek, although there are also numerous examples in Palmyra. This opulent style, sometimes characterized as "baroque," spread throughout the region from the 2nd century and was used for all sorts of buildings, although the temples are the most characteristic. There was no uniformity of decoration, however, and contrasting regional variations can be readily identified: along the Phoenician coast, for example, designs were closer to classical models, whilst in the south the Nabataean and Arabian influence was apparent. Nevertheless, even the southern zone followed Greco-Syrian models – at least in the cities, as the great temple complexes in Gerasa and other cities of the Decapolis demonstrate. The Temple of Artemis in Gerasa is one of the largest. It dates from the middle of the 2nd century A.D. and dominates the main road and its porticos, to which it is linked via a monumental propylon (entrance gateway).

Round temple, Baalbek

This monument has been attributed to the goddess Venus and is unique in the ancient world. The combination of a round structure with a portal interrupting the circle in front produced one of the most original creations of the "Roman baroque."

Temple of Artemis, Gerasa

These propylaea, the monumental entrance to the Temple of Artemis, linked the city's most significant temple complex to the main road and its porticos. The decoration and complexity of the architecture proclaim to passers-by the site's importance.

Above, left

Temple of Bacchus, Baalbek

The temple's *adyton*, raised on a platform as in the Temple of Jupiter, is well preserved. The structures which must have screened the cult objects no longer survive, however.

Left

Temple of Bel, Palmyra

Unlike the ceiling of the northern *adyton*, which depicts the zodiac, there are no figures on the ceiling of the southern one. Instead, the decoration consists of a central, stylized flower surrounded by hexagonal coffers and a pattern of squares and triangles.

Tradition and progress

Relics of the culture which existed in the Levant before Alexander's conquest can be found in the fields of religion, language and onomastics, albeit dressed in Greek clothing. At first, Greek influence was indeed superficial, even in religious matters: what lay underneath remained unchanged. In time, however, it became more pervasive, and a whole section of society was transformed. The legitimization of Greek values in the region's civic and political life is proof of this. Histories of classical antiquity tend to focus on the superficiality of Hellenization in the Near East, emphasizing what made the region different from the western parts of the Empire. Hellenization continued throughout the Roman era, although the rate of change varied. It is difficult to believe that the social elite did not genuinely accept the values which allowed their integration into the Empire. At the same time, however, it was quite possible for them to retain attitudes and beliefs from their native backgrounds.

The fundamental changes which occurred in the Near East after the Macedonian conquest are not hard to detect, and are confirmed by numerous sources. It is likely that the most Hellenized members of the elite preserved selected traditional practices only, whilst at the other end of the spectrum, farmers in the more remote areas would have been familiar with and able to assimilate at least some aspects of Hellenism (as translated into statues, images on coins, or buildings, for example). The picture we have today is distorted, because the only sections of society accessible to researchers are usually those with sufficient resources to have commissioned inscriptions or even donated temples for the use of their fellow citizens. The region was certainly affected by Hellenism, but at the same time retained its native characteristics, and this resulted in the evolution of a separate and to some extent original, vital culture, in which existing traditions were modified in order to create new ones.

Opposite

Temple of Bacchus, Baalbek

Access to this Corinthian peripteros was through a tall portal. The cella inside the temple is richly decorated with reliefs and includes an *adyton*.

Ceiling of the Temple of Bacchus, Baalbek

The hexagonal coffers on the ceiling of the peristyle contain busts representing Syrian cities. Their floral borders add to the overall impression of "baroque" decor.

Laïla Nehmé

The World of the Nabataeans

A kingdom between Syria and Arabia

312 B.C.–106 A.D.

Khaznet Firaun from the mouth of the Siq, Petra

The right side of the Khaznet Firaun ("Treasury of the Pharaoh") as seen from the Siq. In the lower section of the façade is an equestrian figure representing one of the two dioscuri, either Castor or Pollux. In the upper section two figures can be seen: on the left is a Winged Victory and on the right is an Amazon, who swings an axe above her head.

The age of the Nabataean kings

The Nabataeans were a people of Arab origin who first appeared on the historical stage in 312 B.C. They disappeared from the political map four centuries later when their kingdom was annexed by the Romans in 106 A.D. Originally nomadic shepherds, they soon came to play an important role in the region's trade in luxury goods. The considerable wealth they accrued from this commerce led to the Nabataeans adopting a different way of life; they gradually became settled and built cities which bore comparison with Palmyra and Gerasa (Jerash). They also developed an individual culture which combined local traditions with foreign influences. Nabataean rock architecture, ceramics and writing –

to name but three aspects of their culture – have an original and easily recognizable "signature." At the height of its territorial expansion their kingdom covered virtually the entire Levant south of Damascus; this presence naturally meant that the Nabataeans made a significant contribution to the region during classical antiquity.

The first recorded mention of the Nabataeans can be found in the work of the Greek historian Diodorus Siculus of Sicily: in volume XIX of his "Historical Library," he wrote of a conflict between the Nabataeans and the Greeks in 312 B.C. The entire political history of the Nabataeans is marked by their foreign relations – be they friendly, hostile, or belligerent – with the powers who struggled for supremacy in the region: these were the Hellenistic kingdoms (the Ptolemies in Egypt and the Seleucids in Syria), the Roman Empire and the Jewish–Hasmonean dynasty whose independence was recognized by the Seleucid king, Demetrius Nicator, in 141 B.C.

The cities and territories of the region were constantly changing hands as a result of both intensive diplomatic activity and the fluctuating fortunes of war, but the Nabataean kingdom can roughly be said to have covered the area between central Arabia in the south and Damascus in the north; the western border approximated to today's Negev Desert and in the east to the Wadi Sirhan, which today forms part of the boundary between Jordan and Saudi Arabia. This territory includes relatively fertile areas (the Hauran plain in Syria and the Transjordanian high plateau) as well as deserts (Negev, Arabian). Agriculture was not always possible due to the aridity of the region, and so, at the beginning of their history at least, the Nabataeans' considerable wealth was earned from their role as

Nabataean inscription, Umm el-Jimal

Nabataean inscription which reads: "This is the *nefesh* of Fahru, son of Sullai, praeceptor [tutor] of Gadimat, King of Tanuk." The inscription was written in two languages, Greek and Nabataean; the Greek version was found in the eastern part of the city. Both texts name Gadimat, who ruled in el-Hira c. 270 B.C. The bilingual text is associated with the more recent Nabataean inscriptions.

Map: THE LEVANT

MEDITERRANEAN SEA

Beirut
Lebanon Mts
Ituraea
Anti-Lebanon Mts
Dmeir
Damascus
Palmyra
Eufraat
Khabur

Galilee
Lake Tiberias
Hippos
Qalat el-Hosn
Yarmuk
Haoeran
Gadara
Umm Qeis
Adraa
Deraa
Bosra
Zerqa
Umm el-Djimal
Gerasa
Djerash
Amman
Jordan
Perea
Judea
Jerusalem
Hisban
Ammon
Gaza
Dead Sea
Madaba
Dibon
Arnon Wadi Mugib
Rhinocolura
el-Arish
Elusa
Khalutza
Beer Sheva
Mampsis
Rabba
Karak
Moab
Hasa
Qasr Gheit
Nessana Nizzana
Sobata
Shivta
Oboda
Advat
Edom
Khirbet el-Tannur
Khirbet el-Darih
Negev
Buseira
Shobak
Wadi Araba
Petra
Humeima
Hisma
Wadi Rum
Aila
Elat
Akaba
Sinai
Gulf of Aqaba
Myos Hormos
Ouseir
Red Sea
Leuke Kome, Hegra *Medein Salih*, Dedan, El-Ula
Wadi Sirhan

0   N   100 km

The area known as the Levant comprises the costal regions of Asia Minor, Syria, and Egypt. It embraces the Mediterranean littoral of the modern countries of (from north to south) Turkey, Syria, Lebanon, Israel, the Palestinian autonomous region, and Egypt, and also western Jordan.
The maps use historical place-names. Some modern names are also given in italics.

middlemen in the trade of frankincense, spices, and other valuable commodities rather than as tillers of the soil.

Their caravans made their way up from southern Arabia – known by the writers of antiquity as "happy, or flourishing, Arabia", *Arabia Felix* – to harbors on the Mediterranean, whence their goods were transported by ship to Alexandria and European ports. The lands ruled by the Nabataeans were criss-crossed by desert tracks whose main routes can today be reconstructed by plotting and linking the more important of the region's caravan stations. Foremost amongst these was, of course, Petra. The capital of Nabataea in antiquity, the city is today an internationally important archaeological site and tourist destination.

Uncertain origins

In spite of the efforts made by historians to discover the original homelands of the Nabataeans and find traces of their existence from before the end of the 4th century B.C., none of the theories proposed in the last 20 years has been confirmed unequivocally. A possible clue as to the origins of the Nabataeans is provided by the Semitic word *nbt*, "appear, bring forth." Used exclusively in names from southern Arabia it may be the root from which the word *nbtw*, or "Nabataean," is derived. Their mastery of water storage and irrigation techniques can also be cited as

an explanation of their origins; the peoples of southern Arabia were also extremely adept at applying such technology. Others have proposed northeastern Arabia – present-day Kuwait – as the ancestral homeland of the Nabataeans. This idea is either based on the dubious correspondence of a place-name mentioned in ancient texts with a location bearing the same name today, or by referring to the equally questionable relationship between the language of Nabataean inscriptions and the language of the Arabian peoples of Mesopotamia in the neo-Assyrian era (10th to 7th centuries B.C.). The area between Mecca and the central Arabian oasis of Dedan (el-Ula) has been suggested as the original country of the Nabataeans, but investigations in this region are still in their infancy. Yet another theory maintains that the Nabataeans are a confederation of tribes known as the Qedar, who lived in Syria and northern Arabia from the 9th to the 4th centuries B.C.

The only assumption of which we can be relatively certain is that the *nbtw* named in Nabataean inscriptions had nothing in common with either the Nabayati of the Assyrian chronicles of Assurbanipal (669–627 B.C.) or the Nebajot of the Old Testament (Isaiah 60:7). It is difficult to determine precisely when they migrated to Edom (in the south of Jordan). By 312 B.C., however, they had settled in the region around Petra because it was in that year that Greek troops besieged their fortress; and it is with this episode that the Nabataeans enter the works of the Classical Greek and Latin authors of history.

Wadi Rum

The valley of the Wadi Rum – "Iram" in Nabataean and medieval Arabic texts – lies around 60 miles (100 km) south of Petra. The broad dry valley is lined by steep cliffs and became widely known as one of the locations for the film *Lawrence of Arabia*. The Nabataeans founded a settlement here with a temple in honor of the goddess Allat; this shrine was discovered in 1931.

Wars with the Diadochi – The account of Diodorus Siculus

The details of the Nabataeans' battles with the Diadochi can be found in the comprehensive description by Diodorus Siculus (vol. XIX, 94–100). One of Alexander the Great's successors, Antigonus I Monophthalmos ("the one-eyed"), ordered an offensive under the command of his general Athenaios, probably with the intention of seizing the Nabataeans' valuables. Athenaios knew that the Nabataean men of combat age would gather every year at a type of market, leaving behind all their goods – as well as women and children and the elderly – at a certain "rock" (Greek *petra*). Athenaios therefore waited until this meeting was taking place and then with 4,000 foot soldiers and 600 cavalrymen attacked the hideout. The Nabataeans were surprised in the middle of the night; several were either killed or captured and Athenaios made off before sunrise with booty worth 500 silver talents as well as great quantities of myrrh and frankincense. It was only after marching for 25 miles (40 kilometers) that he gave the orders for his troops to set up camp. In the meantime, the Nabataean warriors had learned of the attack; they immediately set off in pursuit of the Greeks, surprising them in their sleep and killing almost all the infantry and a large part of the cavalry.

Returning to their rocky fortress the Nabataeans composed a letter in Syrian – that is, in Aramaic – to Antigonus condemning his actions. In order to placate them, Antigonus claimed that his general had acted on his own orders. However, Antigonus was in fact already preparing for a second attack – this time with 4,000 foot soldiers – plus a 4,000-strong cavalry under the command of his son, Demetrius. The Nabataeans had remained on their guard even after receiving Antigonus' assurances and they positioned sentinels in the hills who, by lighting beacons, would warn their own people of a Greek advance. They also stationed a garrison in Petra, and hid their herds of livestock in the desert and other places accessible only to themselves.

The Hills of Edom, south of Wadi el-Hasa

Edom means "red" in Hebrew, and was the name given to Esau because of the color of his hair. The Edomites lived here during the Iron Age; they refused to allow Moses to cross their land, and were constantly feuding with Israel. The Nabataeans settled in this region at the beginning of the Hellenistic epoch.

View from the High Place of Sacrifice, Petra

View into the valley basin to the west from the peak of Jebel el-Madbah. To the left is the Umm el-Biyara massif where the Nabataeans sought refuge during an attack by the Greeks in 312 B.C. To the right is the Deir massif. The Wadi Musa runs through the basin from east to west.

Demetrius' siege was unsuccessful. The Nabataeans sent him a message declaring that it was unreasonable to fight against people who had no desire to be slaves, and who possessed neither water, grain, nor wine, because their customs were different from those of the Greeks. Demetrius eventually gave in and withdrew, taking with him gifts and several hostages.

Diodorus Siculus' description is a treasure trove of information about the Nabataeans of the Hellenistic era. According to him they had appeared in the region around Petra at the end of the 4th century as a tribe of nomadic shepherds, and met as a community only once a year. Their campsite on these occasions was the valley of Petra – a natural fortress which required no protective walls. Today it is believed that their real refuge was the Umm-el-Biyara massif, which was as inaccessible in Nabataean times as it is today. Diodorus Siculus described the land of the Nabataeans as an inhospitable region with poor soil and little water. The Nabataeans, however, were experts at building underground cisterns for rainwater and then concealing them from the eyes of strangers. Endowed with a fierce sense of liberty they lived, according to Diodorus Siculus, in the open air and did not build houses – a rule which was followed by the entire tribe, since houses were deemed too vulnerable to enemy attack. Some Nabataeans were camel breeders, while others concentrated on rearing sheep. Many of them, however, were already involved in trading perfumes and spices on the Mediterranean, an occupation which earned them enormous wealth.

Area near the acropolis, Avdat

At around the beginning of the 1st century A.D., Avdat in the Negev desert was an important stopping place for caravans on their way from Petra to Gaza. It was also an important religious center dedicated to the cult of the divine Nabataean king Obodas I (96–85 B.C.), who gave his name to the city. According to A. Negev, who discovered the city, agriculture replaced trade as the chief economic activity after the town was destroyed by a fire in the second half of the 1st century. For several hundred years Avdat flourished as a center for sheep, goat, and camel breeding.

The first kings of Nabataea

For the next 50 years after the events of 312 B.C. nothing more is heard of the Nabataeans – and even in the years after that their presence in Transjordan is merely intimated. In 259 B.C. we learn of a shipment of grain to the "people of Rabel" – probably one of the first Nabataean kings. These words were written on a papyrus belonging to the Egyptian merchant Zenon, who was acting on behalf of the minister of Ptolemy II Philadelphos (ruler of Egypt from 282–246 B.C.). Another papyrus relates that Nabataeans had settled in the Hauran region and it is from this period that the oldest Nabataean inscription dates. It was found in Elusa in the Negev and tells of a certain "Haretat, King of Nabataea" who was the first to bear the royal name of Aretas.

Syria was constantly fought over by the Ptolemies and the Seleucids, before finally falling into the hands of the latter in 198 B.C. The rivalry between these two powers lasted until the reign of the Seleucid king Antiochus IV. Epiphanes, who sought to establish the Greek cult of Zeus Olympios in all the cities of his kingdom – including the temple of Jerusalem. With this draconian measure, however, he attracted the hostility of most of the Jewish nation. As a consequence of the rebellion which broke out in 167 B.C., Jason, the official high priest of Jerusalem and a supporter of Antiochus' policies of Hellenization, was forced to flee the city. At first he sought refuge with the Ammonites before moving on to Petra, to "Aretas, *tyrannos* of the Arabs" (2. Maccabees 5:8) who may be the same king mentioned in the inscription from Elusa.

Several years later, in 163 B.C., there was a friendly meeting in Hauran between the Nabataeans and the leaders of the Jewish uprising, Judas and Jonathan Maccabeus (1. Maccabees 5, 24–26). Finally, in 160 B.C., Jonathan requested that "the Nabataeans as his friends ... look after their many arms." (1. Maccabees 9:35). Descriptions such as these testify to the good relations which Hasmoneans and Nabataeans continued to maintain with each other.

The Nabataeans and Hasmoneans

These friendly contacts came to an end during the reign of the Nabataean king Aretas II (120/110–96 B.C.), due to the aggressive policies pursued by the Jewish–Hasmonean king Alexander Janneus, who occupied Gaza, the Nabataeans' most important port, in 97 B.C.

Aretas I's successor, Obodas I, (c. 96–85 B.C.) defeated the Hasmoneans in about 93 B.C. in a battle in the Golan Heights. Three years later Alexander Janneus returned the regions of Moab and Gilead, which he had conquered, to the "king of the Arabs"; both territories lie east of the Jordan between Lake Tiberias and the Dead Sea. The Jewish king was at that time involved in a conflict with the Seleucids and had no wish to fight on two fronts at once.

Enlarged by the addition of this land, the Nabataean kingdom grew significantly and would almost certainly have begun to cause the Seleucids – whose own power was on the wane – increasing concern. This is perhaps the reason why Antiochus XII led two campaigns against the Nabataeans in 88 and again in 87 B.C. The second of these wars ended in total defeat for Antiochus when the Nabataean king managed to lure the Seleucid troops into the Negev desert. Antiochus himself was killed in this battle and the majority of his troops starved to death in the desert.

Obodas I died two years later and it is probably he – and not another Seleucid king of the same name – who was buried in the Nabataean city of Oboda (Avdat) in the Negev, and was worshipped as a god after his death. This information is provided by the "Ethnika" of Stephen of Byzantium – a 6th century B.C. lexicographer – who described Oboda as "a place of the Nabataeans ... where the divine king is buried." The tomb has never been found. In Petra, on the other hand, there are holy sites dedicated to Obodas I; he was the only Nabataean king to be worshipped as a god.

He was succeeded by his son Aretas, the third king of this name (84–63 B.C.). His epithet – Philhellenos, or "he who loves the Greeks" – appears on bronze coins which he had minted in

Damascus. He ruled the Syrian capital, whose inhabitants had called on him to be their patron, for 12 years from 84–72 B.C.

In 82 B.C. conflict with Alexander Janneus erupted again and ended with the defeat of Aretas III, who lost 12 cities in Moab and Edom as well as several Mediterranean ports. After both Alexander Janneus and his wife both died in 67 B.C. their sons, Hyrkanos II and Aristobulus, quarreled over the succession, the latter forcing his brother from both the throne and the office of high-priest. Hyrkanos, however, had an Idumean adviser named Antipater who was married to a Nabataean noblewoman. At the suggestion of Antipater Hyrkanos sought refuge with Aretas, promising the king the return of his 12 lost cities if he would support his cause. Marching at the head of an army allegedly 50,000 strong, Aretas defeated the troops of Aristobulus, who withdrew behind the walls of Jerusalem. The Nabataean king then began to lay siege to the city.

At this time the Romans were moving relentlessly forwards into the Near East. M. Aemilius Scaurus, envoy of Pompey, the then consul, was called on by representatives of both parties to mediate in the dispute. Scaurus sided with Aristobulus and forced Aretas to break off his siege on pain of being declared an enemy of the Roman people. Aristobulus pursued the retreating Nabataeans, defeating them in a battle in the Jordan valley in 64 B.C.

A settled existence?

Apart from the Jewish historian Flavius Josephus, the most important source of information on the final years of the 1st century B.C. is the Greek geographer and historian Strabo. His work contains details of the lifestyle of the Nabataeans, and he describes them as living in established settlements (Geographia XVI 4:21–24 and 26). Why these former nomads should decided to become settled is not known; according to Strabo they had allegedly become so eager for property that anyone who reduced it was publicly fined, while those who increased their wealth were honored (Geographia XVI 4:26).

In marked contrast to previous ages the Nabataeans now owned luxuriously furnished houses of stone. Strabo was also full of praise for their system of government. At this time large numbers of Romans and other foreigners were also to be found in their capital, Petra: they were said to be the only ones to provide the courts with work, since the Nabataeans studiously avoided conflicts with one another.

Architectural relief, Petra

This relief shows an Eros flanked by two lions. It belongs to a series of sculptures influenced by Alexandrine and Hellenistic art.

Lion Gryphon Temple, Petra

The Lion Gryphon Temple is one of the most important in Petra; this view shows the middle section seen from the south, with the colonnaded street in the background. A podium or *motab* was located in the cella, which was flanked by ten columns. The temple owes its name to the motifs on several of the capitals. It is known to have been built by 27 A.D. at the latest and was probably dedicated to a goddess, perhaps al-Uzza or Isis.

Commemorative coin of Marcus Aemilius Scaurus

58 B.C.
Silver drachma
Bibliothèque Nationale, Paris

This coin shows the subjection of Aretas III after the Roman victory of 64 B.C. The Nabataean king is shown kneeling and holding the reins of a dromedary.

Coin of Aretas IV

9 B.C. – 40 A.D.
Silver drachma
Bibliothèque Nationale, Paris

This coin shows the Nabataean king Aretas IV crowned with a laurel wreath.

Roman hegemony and the Battle of Actium

The Roman province of Syria, established by Pompey in 64 B.C., filled the vacuum left by the collapse of the Seleucid royal house. Pompey was also forced, however, to secure the Roman Empire's southeastern border, which adjoined the Judaean and Nabataean monarchies. In yet another complication surrounding the Hasmonean succession – Aristobulus had become impatient and did not wish to wait for the Roman verdict in his dispute with his brother – the Romans changed sides to support Hyrkanos. In so doing they allied themselves with the Nabataeans, who had always favored the older of the two brothers; a common front was therefore created on both sides of the Jordan.

In 62 B.C. this did not prevent the Romans from marching against Petra; the real motives for the campaign are obscure, but once again they may have had to do with ambitions to seize the wealth stored in the city. The two sides did not clash because the Nabataean king was prepared to pay a tribute of 300 silver talents. In memory of this supposed victory the Roman legate Scaurus had commemorative coins minted in Rome on which Aretas III (84–62 B.C.) is depicted kneeling on the ground in front of his dromedary.

It is assumed that in the period between 62 and 60 B.C. the Nabataeans were ruled by a king named Obodas II. The only proof of his existence is provided by several coins stamped with the numbers 1, 2 and 3 – the years that a king of this name reigned.

The temptations posed by the conquest of Arabia with its riches was almost certainly the main motive for the Syrian proconsul, Gabinius, to renew operations against the Nabataeans in 55 B.C., and this campaign ended with their defeat in war.

Malichus, the first king of this name, succeeded Obodas II to the throne in 58 B.C. During his 30-year reign he faced the difficult task of having to take sides in the internal struggles of imperial Rome – first between Caesar and Pompey, later between Mark Antony and Caesar's murderers Cassius and Brutus, and finally between Mark Antony and Octavian. In 47 B.C. Malichus provided Caesar with support, sending him mounted troops when the Roman leader was in difficulties in Alexandria. A few years later, however, he took the side of the Parthians, who were making incursions over the Romans' eastern border; after the Parthians were beaten back by the Romans in 39 B.C. Malichus was rebuked by the imposition of a punitive war tax.

In the famous battle of Actium on 2 September 31 B.C., Octavian – later to be known as Augustus – won control over the Roman Empire with his victory over Mark Antony and Cleopatra. On the eve of the battle Malichus I had sent troops to Actium in support of Mark Antony, and in order to encourage the victorious Augustus to forgive him, he had Cleopatra's ships, which were anchored off the Gulf of Suez, set alight. The queen, who now recognized the inevitability of Roman rule in Egypt, committed suicide by exposing herself to the bite of a poisonous snake. After Cleopatra's death the Ptolemaic kingdom became a province of the Roman Empire. The kingdoms of Judaea and Nabataea, which lay on both sides of the Jordan valley, were now hemmed in to the north by the province of Syria and to the south by Roman possessions in Egypt.

In Judaea, Herod the Great, appointed king by the Romans, had attempted with their approval to liquidate the Hasmonean dynasty. He now enlarged his kingdom by adding to it the cities of Gadara (Umm Qeis) and Hippos (Qalat el-Hosn), as well as several Mediterranean ports including Gaza – towns confiscated from the Nabataeans. A new king – Obodas III – succeeded Malichus I to the Nabataean throne and pursued a less ambitious foreign policy.

From the campaign of Aelius Gallus to the reign of Aretas IV

In order to control the trade in luxuries, Augustus sent 10,000 soldiers under the leadership of the prefect of Egypt, Aelius Gallus, into Arabia Felix in 25 B.C. Included in this army were 1,000 Nabataeans commanded by Syllaios, the *epitropos* of Oboda III. This unscrupulous and power-hungry individual was to lead the army on its march through the desert. Their destination was the kingdom of Saba on the southwestern tip of the Arabian peninsula. For reasons which can generally be attributed to Syllaios' treachery, but which were also due to unfavorable conditions – especially a scarcity of water – this campaign was a complete failure.

Strabo describes how, at the time of Gallus, goods unloaded at Leuke Kome (Wejh) on the east coast of the Red Sea were transported via Petra to the Mediterranean port of Rhinocolura (el-Arish) south of Gaza. However, in the early 1st century A.D., when Strabo wrote of the so-called Arabian campaign, the transport route led directly by ship to Myos Hormos (Quseir) on the west coast of the Red Sea. From there goods were taken by a caravan route up to Koptos, situated on the Nile, which was easily accessible by boat from Alexandria. Because the Nabataeans only controlled the overland passage, this displacement of trade routes by the Romans meant that they suffered heavy losses.

In 9 B.C. Aretas IV (9 B.C.– 40 A.D.) ascended the Nabataean throne. He was almost certainly not a son of Obodas III, since his real name, Aeneas, was not a dynastic title. Augustus, enraged that Aretas IV had appointed himself king without first asking his permission, at first refused to recognize him and even rejected the gifts Aretas sent him.

In Judaea, King Herod the Great died in 4 B.C., and ten years later the kingdom became a procuratorial province of the Romans. His son, Herod Antipas, Tetrarch of Peraea and Galilee, had married

a daughter of Aretas IV, whom he divorced in 27 B.C. She returned to her father, who, in revenge, attacked the territory of the faithless husband.

The flight of the Apostle Paul from Damascus, described in the second letter to the Corinthians (11:32–33), occurred in 37 A.D., between the end of the reign of the Roman Emperor Tiberius and the death of Aretas IV. The gates of the city were being guarded day and night by the garrison of the "ethnarch of King Aretas," the individual in question being the head of the Nabataean community in Damascus, who wanted to arrest Paul. The apostle was let down in a basket from a window in the city walls and so made his escape. The presence of an ethnarch with responsibility for guarding the city gates leads one to believe that Damascus was temporarily occupied by the Nabataeans – although there is no other evidence to substantiate this.

Aretas IV probably died in 40 A.D., since there are no coins or inscriptions which can be dated beyond the 48th year of his reign. Several large buildings in Hegra and Petra were erected during his reign and point to the Nabataean kingdom having reached a cultural zenith. Nabataean inscriptions also reached their greatest extent under Aretas IV.

Theater, Petra

The openings in the wall above the terraced seating are Nabataean tombs which were destroyed during the construction of the theater.

The "Nabataean" arch, Bosra

This arch once stood in the center of the city and marked the transition from the old to the newer parts of the city which were built at the end of the Nabataean era, probably under Rabel II. He chose Bosra, which lay in the middle of fertile plains, to be the second capital of his empire.

Malichus II and Rabel II

Malichus II (40–70 A.D.), the son of Aretas IV, succeeded to the throne without any apparent problems. During his reign the decapolis remained outside the kingdom, but Nabataeans in Hisban and Madaba gradually began to acquire the fertile lands of the Transjordan. Madaba was the seat of a Nabataean governor. The southern coastal strip of the Dead Sea from the mouth of the Arnon – today the Wadi el-Mudjib – was also part of the Nabataean kingdom. The northern boundary of the Nabataean Negev, however, is not as easy to define; similarly, it is not known which of the Mediterranean ports were used by the Nabataeans, because caravans coming from Oboda were able to reach Rhinocolura as easily as they could Gaza. Nabataea also bordered on northern Arabia as far as Hegra and perhaps even the Sinai as well. In the east, in the oasis of Dumat el-Djandal, the reconstruction of a Dushara shrine is recorded in a dedicatory inscription from the fifth year of Malichus II's reign, and this fact allows us to assume that Nabataeans were also resident here.

The son of Malichus, Rabel II (70–106 A.D.) ascended the throne at a very young age. Coins featuring the portrait of the king as well as that of his mother, Shaqilat, testify to a regency during the first five years of his reign. On later coins, Shaqilat's place is taken by the two successive wives of the king. It was during this period that Bosra, in the Hauran region, rose to become one of the powerful cities in the kingdom, and Nabataean agriculture developed in the Negev and southern Syria. In the valleys around Oboda, dam complexes have been found in connection with rectangular stone tubs engraved with inscriptions from the reign of Rabel II.

Petra and the Nabataeans after their incorporation into the Roman Empire

In 106 A.D. the Nabataean kingdom finally lost its political independence: Trajan incorporated the annexed territory into the Roman Empire as the Provincia Arabia. Bosra became the capital, probably because of its location in a densely populated and agriculturally productive region. It appears that the annexation proceeded quickly and without any great conflict. Already in the year 107 A.D. a Roman soldier wrote to his parents in Egypt that he was dazzled by the magnificence of the goods brought to Petra by caravan. Although Petra had lost its position as capital, Roman governors continued to hold their court sessions there and one of them, Sextius Florentinus, even built a tomb in the city. In the wake of Nabataean annexation the city was given the status of a *metropolis*. Between 111 and 114 A.D. a great Roman road, the Via Nova Traiana, was built to connect Syria with the Red Sea. Since it ran through Petra, that city continued to play its part in the trade between Arabia, Syria, and the ports of the Mediterranean.

There are virtually no written references to the city from the second half of the 2nd century A.D. Under the Roman Emperor Heliogobalus, c. 221/222 A.D., Petra became a *colonia*. When Diocletian redistributed the imperial provinces in 295 A.D. the Provincia Arabia lost the Negev as well as the cities of Aila (Aqaba) and Petra, which were allocated to the province of Palestine. In 358 B.C. this area was renamed Palestina Salutaris, with its own capital city – Petra – and independent of Palestine proper. An earthquake in 363 destroyed parts of the city, which went into decline and began to show signs of decay. It was not until the middle of the 5th century that the city experienced a certain turnabout in its fortunes.

The first Christians appeared in Petra at the beginning of the 4th century, but pagans remained both numerous and active as a report by Barsauma, the founder of the east Syrian church, showed. During a journey to the region between 420 and 423 he arrived, according to his account, at a large city by the name of Reqem-at-Gaia, which closed its gates to him. He threatened to declare war against the town and then to burn it if he and his 40 companions were not admitted. For 40 years there had been no rain in the region but when he finally entered the city so much water fell from the skies that the city walls collapsed in the deluge. The heathen priests were immediately converted.

The urn tomb, one of the largest burial structures in Petra, was transformed into a cathedral in 446 A.D.

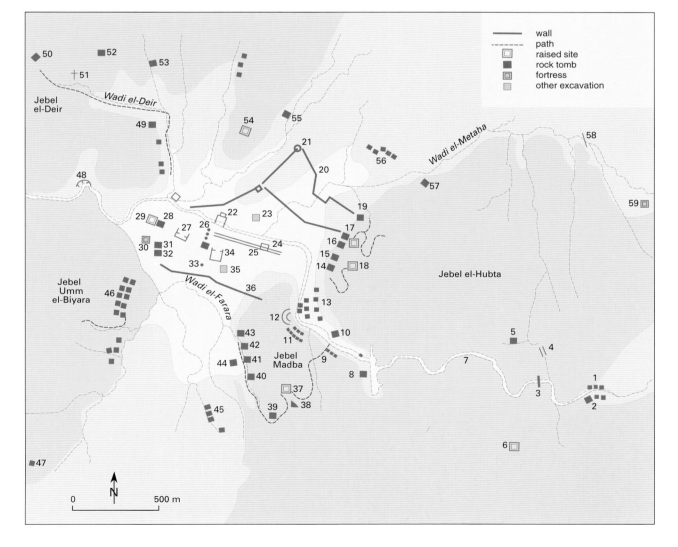

Ground plan, Petra

1 Block tombs, 2 Obelisk tomb, 3 Dam, 4 Tunnel, 5 Eagle niche, 6 el-Medras, 7 Siq, 8 Khaznat al-Faroun, 9 Tomb no 67, 10 Uneshu tomb, 11 theater necropolis, 12 theater, 13 necropolis of el-Hubta, 14 Urn tomb, 15 Silk tomb, 16 Corinthian tomb, 17 Palace tomb, 18 cult platform on el-Hubta, 19 tomb of Sextius Florentinus, 20 northern city walls, 21 Conway tower, 22 Lion Griffin Temple, 23 Byzantine church, 24 nymphaeum, 25 colonnaded street, 26 Temenos Gate, 27 Qasr el-Bint Firaun, 28 museum, 29 cult site of el-Habis, 30 Crusader fortress of el-Habis, 31 Incomplete Tomb, 32 columbarium, 33 Zibb Firaun, 34 Great Temple, 35 excavations of el-Katute, 36 southern city wall, 37 High Place of Sacrifice, 38 obelisks, 39 Lion Fountain, 40 Garden Temple, 41 triclinium near the Tomb of Statues, 42 Renaissance Tomb, 43 Tomb with Broken Pediment, 44 Tomb of Statues, 45 tombs at the Wadi el-Nmer, 46 necropolis at Umm el-Biyara, 47 Serpent Tomb, 48 stone bridge in the Wadi Siyagh, 49 Lion triclinium, 50 el-Deir, 51 hermit's cave, 52 Qattar el-Deir, 53 Urn Biclinium, 54 cult platform of el-Meesera, 55 Turkmaniye Tomb, 56 necropolis of Moghar el-Nasara, 57 Dorotheos House, 58 aqueduct, 59 Crusader fortress of Wueira (Li Vaux Moyse)

Johann Ludwig Burckhardt, known as Sheik Ibrahim

Sebastian Gutzwiller
c. 1830
Oil on canvas; height 105.5 cm, width 69 cm
Historical Museum, Basel

The Swiss explorer Johann Burckhardt (1784–1817) was commissioned by the London African Society and traveled throughout Syria, Egypt, and Nubia under the name of Sheik Ibrahim. It was he who discovered the Jordanian city of Petra. His travel writings on the Near East were published in 1819. Burckhardt died from food poisoning at the age of 33 in Cairo

Opposite

El-Hubta necropolis, Petra

View of the Urn Tomb as well as the two levels of the Byzantine arcade from the 5th century A.D., when the tomb was converted into a church. The arcades supported a terrace in front of the tomb.

and consecrated by Bishop Jason. Two other churches on the right bank of the Wadi Musa were examined in the 1990s by teams of US scholars; this period can also therefore be illuminated by archaeological evidence. In one of the churches – of the so-called *basilica* type – the floors of the aisles are covered with polychrome mosaics featuring medallions with objects (amphorae, candelabra, baskets, and so on), as well as animals (birds, peacocks, fish) and people. In the south aisle is a mosaic with a central row of rectangular pictures showing the four seasons, the ocean, the earth, and wisdom; all of these are accompanied by Greek inscriptions. In a small room adjoining the northeast of the church a considerable collection of charred papyri has been found, the remains of which are under examination. These documents date from the 6th century and are mainly bills of sale, but there are also wills, various business contracts, inventories, and so on.

In 636 Christian–Byzantine domination of the region came to an end with the battle of Yarmuk. During the Umayyad Caliphate, which was based in Damascus, the area around the Jordan enjoyed the favor of the new rulers because it was situated on the route to Mecca. When the Abbasids came to power, however, the Islamic capital was moved to Baghdad, and Petra, now far from the pilgrims' trail, was left to its fate.

Baldwin I breathed life back into southern Jordan in 1116 at the time of the Crusades when he built the castles of Shobak as well as of el-Habis and Wueira (Li Vaux Moyse) near Petra; these events will be related in a later chapter. In 1276 the Mameluke

sultan Baybars stopped in Petra on his way from Cairo to Kerak. The city then slid into obscurity until it was rediscovered by the Swiss traveler Johann Ludwig Burckhardt in 1812, who unveiled its splendors to a European audience.

Religion and the shrines of the Nabataeans

The Nabataean religion was polytheistic and belongs to the pre-Islamic religions; gods were depicted as idols in the form of betyls. Characteristics of the cult were blood sacrifice, the existence of sacred precincts – the *haram* – and, finally, the importance of processions and sacred communities.

In the numerous archaeological sites of Nabataea, especially those at Petra, shrines play almost as prominent a role as tombs. In contrast to the latter they were often built in remote or inaccessible locations, and it often happens that they are overlooked by visitors. For a long period it was the sheer omnipresence of the sacred that led people to believe that Petra was nothing more than a single, gigantic shrine where the Nabataeans worshipped their gods and buried their dead. Though this is certainly a tempting idea, there is little evidence to support it. Nevertheless, the city's shrines – from the simplest to the most magnificent – are an expression of a strong sense of religion which permeated the everyday and formed the very basis of life itself.

High Place of Sacrifice, Petra

At the left of the two trees is a betyl niche framed by standards with crescent moons. In the lower background to the left can be seen the Urn Tomb with its terrace and portico.

The betyls

Most Nabataean gods were depicted in the form of betyls, stones carved in the shape of columns. The term has its origins in the Semitic root *beth-el*, which can be translated as "the House of God." The betyl is therefore a divine dwelling place, and through it the Nabataeans were able to worship their gods.

Although they tended to worship cult images as gods, this practice cannot be referred to as litholatry, because it was not the stone itself that was venerated. Valuable information is provided by the Suda, a Byzantine lexicon. Though this dates from the 10th century, its authors drew on much older sources, and it contains a description of the betyl of the Dusare – the Greek expression for Dushara – the main god in the Nabataean pantheon: this was a black, rectangular stone four feet high and two feet wide which was devoid of facial features. It rested on a gold-covered pedestal. The Nabataeans made sacrifices to the betyl, pouring over it the sacrificial blood which was said to be their libation. The entire temple shone with gold, according to the Suda, and there were a great many offerings.

With the exception of the gold and the specified height and width, this description applies to the hundreds of betyls carved into the rocks of Petra and Wadi Rum in Jordan as well as Hegra (Medain Salih) in Arabia. They almost always stand in a niche – ornamented or unornamented – whose size, form, and décor were generally decided by the donor himself. Various elements – pilasters, pediments, friezes, acroteria, crescent moons and other types of decoration – could be combined according to the wishes of the patron. This freedom of expression provided for a great diversity of forms – to the joy of both archaeologists and travelers.

As described in the Suda, betyls were mostly rectangular. Apart from several examples with a slightly curved top edge – which merely represents a modification of the rectangular type – there is only one well-known exception to this rule. This is the Dushara betyl which can be seen on coins from the Syrian–Jordanian border town of Adre (Daraa) and which is located in a niche in the Siq, the long ravine through which Petra is approached. A Greek inscription relates that it was donated by a *panegyriarches*, a festival director from Adraha, who was probably a member of a delegation which had traveled to Petra. As the Adraha betyl is egg-shaped, some scholars believe that it represents a mountain, in particular the Shara massif which itself towers over Petra.

The Suda goes on to state that the betyls were bereft of images – that is, that they did not feature any figurative forms. This is true for 99 percent of those betyls whose worked surfaces had neither reliefs nor ornamental designs. A small number of betyls which are generally described as anthropomorphic or "eye idols," however, show stylized facial features in

which the eyes or the nose – less frequently the mouth – are depicted generally as geometric shapes and forms.

The last piece of information in the Suda concerned the pedestal which formed the base for the betyl. In Nabataean inscriptions it is known as a *motab*. The root of this word is *ytb* and its approximate meaning is "to sit down." The betyl therefore "sits" on a *motab* which can take a variety of forms: a simple trapezoid base under the idol; a podium such as can be seen on the coins of Bosra or Kerak; or a genuine, stepped podium fitted with a tenon joint to allow a portable betyl to be inserted into it.

Betyl niches can be found everywhere: along the processional routes to the cult sites where they served as places of prayer; in the middle of the remains of houses where they were used as family shrines; and close to funerary monuments and chambers, where the god was able to watch over the tomb and surrounding area.

High Place of Sacrifice el-Madhaba, Petra

The steps lead up to a *motab* on which betyls were placed during cult ceremonies.

Coin of Trajanus Decius and Herennius Etruscus, Bosra

251 A.D.
Bronze
Bibliothèque Nationale, Paris

On the reverse of the coin is a *motab* depicted as a low, stepped podium which supports a betyl in the form of a column. This main betyl is flanked by two other smaller betyls or vases.

Sanctuary, Umm el-Biyara

Pictured here is a low rock shelter from the northwestern edge of the Umm el-Biyara plateau. A Greek inscription indicates that the shrine was dedicated to "Zeus the Redeemer." In one of the well-preserved niches is a betyl on a stepped pedestal. On the altar of another niche another tiny betyl can still be seen. Sacrificial offerings were secured to the loops hewn into the rock.

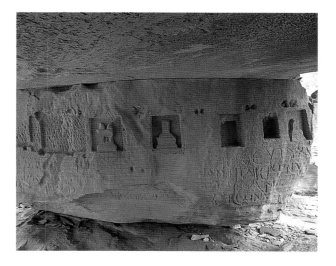

El-Dair, Petra

This structure has a two-story rock façade
ordered by eight columns and pilasters. The
upper floor has a tholos in the center of a
broken pediment. The monumental building
may have served members of a *thiasos* as a
banqueting hall in honor of their god Obodas,
who is named in a nearby inscription.

The triclinia

Often the shrines are attached to enclosed or
hypaethral "banqueting halls." These are so-called bi-
or triclinia – feasting halls with benches (Gr.: *kline*)
running around two or three sides of the room. They
were also sometimes arranged in the shape of a
horseshoe, in which case they were called *stibadium*.
They served as meeting places for religious
communities, so-called *thiasoi*, who gathered there to
venerate a god, a king or a deceased person. In some
instances inscriptions in the rooms provide
information on the names of members and enable the
god or king being worshipped to be identified. Other
inscriptions refer to a *rab marzeah* or "head of the
thiasos." These gatherings were described by Strabo
as sacred feasts celebrated by groups of 12 or 13
persons and attended by two female musicians. Each
guest was allowed to consume no more than 11 cups
of wine and the king himself served his guests. This
last detail mentioned by Strabo was interpreted as a
democratic gesture, but should in fact be seen in the
context of the king's relationships to his subjects
within the tribe: the king's behavior was more that of
a tribal sheik than a Western monarch. Excavations in
the interior of the el-Dair, one of the most magnificent
monuments in Petra, uncovered a triclinium (if only
in the form of low terraces) which may have been
used by members of a *thiasos* which met to honor
the divine king Obodas I. An inscription found
nearby mentions "Ubaidu, Son of Waqih'el and
his companions of the *thiasos* of the God,
Ubdat [Obodas]."

Sacrificial sites

The sacrificial sites were generally laid out as unroofed shrines cut into the rock. They are characterized by their dominant position in the local topography and the easy access provided by one or two processional roads. In Petra there are several such sites on the summits of the hills overlooking the lower town.

The most famous sacrificial site in Petra is the High Place of Sacrifice whose Arabic name, el-Madbah, means "place of sacrifice/slaughter." Two processional streets lead up to the site by means of several hundred steps. It comprises a courtyard lined with benches for the participants, in the middle of which the priest probably stood on a slightly elevated platform. Opposite were two podia, the first of which had several steps leading up to the *motab* where the betyls were placed during the ceremony; the second was the sacrificial altar and had a basin carved into it with a channel used for collecting the blood of the sacrificial animal.

In Petra each of these cultic sites had its own cistern carved into the living rock into which rainwater was directed down special channels. This water was then transferred into smaller basins and used for ritual purification or for cleaning the trappings of the cult after each use. It is not known how often these ceremonies took place, but they were probably observed according to a precisely determined calendar in which the seasons may well have played a role.

High Place of Sacrifice, Petra

The *motab* and basin for ritual purification to the left of the High Place of Sacrifice can still be clearly seen. The steps lead up to a basin set into the rock which may have been intended to collect the blood of sacrificial animals. It is not known for certain whether the stone slab in the foreground was used as an altar.

Below

Obelisks at the High Place of Sacrifice, Petra

The obelisks, which were created by the site being quarried around them, are generally considered to be monumental betyls. They perhaps once marked the entrance to the *haram*, or sacred precinct, of the most important sacrificial site in Petra.

Groups of niches

These sacred sites, which can accommodate anything from two to more than one hundred niches, are always located in protected spots far from the hustle and bustle of the city. As a rule one niche in each group has a particularly prominent status expressed either in its size, decorative scheme, its position or theme.

Such is the case, for example, at the Qattar el-Dair – the so-called dripping shrine in the northwest of Petra. It is located beneath a rocky outcrop on the way to el-Dair and is named for the water which seeps out between two layers of rock, filling a series of interconnected basins "drop by drop" (Arab.: *qattar*). A triclinium as well as numerous inscriptions testify to its use by *thiasoi*. A betyl in the form of a so-called cross of Lorraine is dedicated to the "God in Bosra" meaning one of the Nabataean gods – probably Dushara.

Sid el-Madjin lies in a natural rock rotunda at the mouth of a narrow wadi in the extreme northeast of the el-Hubta massif. In winter the surging rainwaters here wash away everything that stands in their path. Dozens of different idol niches are carved into the rock of the rotunda and the walls of its access route. Close by there are several "banqueting halls," and one can well imagine that Nabataeans came to this special place to erect or dedicate a betyl to a favorite god. An inscription in the rock wall identifies one of the donors as a "servant of the goddess al-Uzza," while another expresses the hope of appearing "healthy and well before Dushara and all the gods."

Another example of such groups of niches is provided by the shrine dedicated to Zeus Soter in the west of the Umm-el-Biyara plateau, which rises to the west of Petra. In the walls of a natural rock bay are several niches with altars or betyls on pedestals. The carefully worked niches and the paleographic sketch formed by Greek inscriptions lead one to assume that this monument was built at a later date.

The "chapels"

The so-called "chapels" form the last category of rock shrine. They are caves with at least one of the cult object types – betyl or altar – hewn into the rear wall of the cave. The best-known of these shrines, the "Obodas chapel" in the el-Nmer massif to the south of Petra, was dedicated to the divine king of the same name. This is indicated by a dedication in the chapel's interior which refers to a "statue of the God Ubdat [Obodas]." A niche in which this statue may have been placed takes up the rear wall of the chamber.

On the el-Dair plateau a peristyle is positioned in front of one of these rock chapels, whose rear wall displays a great Hellenistic niche with gables and pilasters. No definitive statement can be made about the precise function of these chapels – of which there are more than 30 in Petra – as additional information on them is lacking.

Sid el-Madjin, Petra

Large, double-framed niches and betyl in the northern side of the shrine.

Northwest wall of the Djebel el-Hubta, Petra

Alcoves and a small niche with three hollows on the right inner wall of a cult chamber. Traces of the system used for sealing off the chamber can still be distinguished.

Opposite

Sid el-Madjin, Petra

Niches in the southern side of the rotunda of the shrine of Sid el-Madjin. This sacred site has more than 100 niches and is located in a wadi which is regularly flooded by winter rains. The shrine was probably not dedicated to any single deity; many Nabataeans carved niches here in honor of their favorite god.

Centre right

Qasr el-Bint Faroun, Petra

View of the front and side of the temple. The 75
ft (23 m) high Qasr el-Bint – the best preserved
temple in Petra – has even retained part of its
cornice. It was built at the end of the 1st
century B.C. in the middle of a broad temenos.
The façades were decorated with painted
stucco. The temple served as a place of worship
for either a single god – such as Dushara – or,
as the tripartite *adyton* seems to indicate, a
trio of gods.

Reconstruction of the façade of Qasr el-Bint Faroun, Petra

This reconstruction shows that the external
walls of the temple were ornamented with
stucco in the antique era.

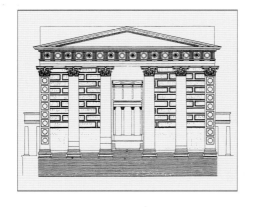

Ground plan of Qasr el-Bint Faroun, Petra

The cella is divided into three rooms, the
central one being the inner sanctum.

Right

Qasr el-Bint Faroun, Petra

Interior of the first long cella in Qasr el-Bint
Faroun. Towards the front of the building it
developed into a pronaos or vestibule. The cella
was reached from the pronaos through the
door in the wall to the left.

The temples

Temples belong to a more precise and predetermined
plan for the architecture and layout of a city; they are
more difficult to build because their construction
requires the commitment of considerable resources.
Fawzi Zayadine, a contemporary expert on the
culture of the Nabataeans, has divided Nabataean
temples into two principal groups: the first has a
central podium in the cella while the other possesses
a tripartite cella. In the first group the podium was
often a simple cube surrounded by an ambulatory.

Steps led up to the podium, on which the idols were
erected – as in the temple of Khirbet el-Darih, where
three depressions are set into the flagstones of the
platform in a diagonal line. Around these recesses are
small holes through which the sacrificial blood was
able to run off into bowls positioned below.

In the second group the cella is divided into
three rooms, of which the central one was the inner
sanctum. Its rear wall could be fitted with a podium
to serve as a pedestal for the betyl. The Qasr el-Bint
Faroun is probably the most famous and best
preserved temple in Petra and it, too, was built

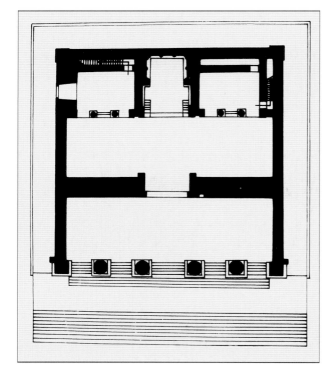

according to this scheme. This massive building towered over the neighboring sacred precinct of the temenos 218 x 66 yds (200 x 60 m), which was laid out at the end of the main street. The tripartite cella was situated at the rear of the temple, its central room being occupied by a podium 1.40 m high which had two small staircases, each of seven steps. The two rooms to the sides were probably also used for cult purposes as well as providing access to the roof of the temple. This recalls once again Strabo's description of the function and use of the temples: he wrote that the Nabataeans would erect an altar on the roof and worship the sun by daily offerings of libations and incense (Geographia XVI 4:26).

The temples complete the list of shrines used for the veneration of the Nabataeans' gods. Who were these gods and how many were there? What were their characteristics? In what form were they worshipped? How can we prove the existence of their cults? Although these are questions which we can only answer by resorting to information which is often incomplete and ambiguous, the following section will endeavor to present a picture of the Nabataean religion and its practices.

Qasr el-Bint Faroun, Petra

The Temenos Gate. This gate stood at the end of the colonnaded street and in front of the temenos for the Qasr el-Bint Faroun (seen in the background).

The gods of the Nabataeans

The Nabataean religion was polytheistic to the core, and its pantheon numbered no fewer than 20 gods. Knowledge of these divinities is derived from coins and inscriptions which explicitly mention them, as well as from betyls and figurative depictions such as sculptures and statuettes. Perhaps to an even greater extent than their art, the Nabataean pantheon was the result of a syncretic approach which fused various systems of belief. It developed from the Edomite gods, as well as those from central Arabia, Syria–Palestine and the Greco-Roman world with which the Nabataeans came into contact at an early stage. Not all of these gods can be found at every Nabataean site, and some gods were clearly favored in certain parts of the kingdom. There is no evidence that the goddess Allat, for example, was present in the pantheon at Petra – though she was worshipped in the south, in Wadi Rum, and in the north, in the Syrian region of Hauran. In contrast, the Egyptian goddess Isis was venerated exclusively in Petra. The differing emphasis placed on these gods can be explained by the fact that the Nabataean pantheon reflected the ethnic diversity of the various regions of their kingdom. Laws relating to the appropriation of gods from neighboring cultures, for example, seem not to have existed. This variety is evidence, above all, of the lack of a national god: the phenomenon of a people identifying with their god – as was the case with Israel and Yahweh – was alien to the Nabataeans.

The Goddesses

Al-Uzza, "the Strong," was without doubt the most popular of the Nabataean gods. A bilingual Greek–Nabataean inscription found on the Aegaean island of Kos indicates that she was the equivalent of Aphrodite, the Greek goddess of love. In the Greek version of the text, in fact, "Aphrodite" appears in the same place as does "al-Uzza" in the Nabataean. She was also worshipped in connection with other gods in Wadi Rum. There, she appears twice in the shape of an anthropomorphic betyl – once beside a plain betyl whose inscription names the "Lord of the Temple" (perhaps Dushara), and again beside another anthropomorphic betyl identified from an inscription as being that of al-Kutba, goddesses of writing and trade. In Petra at least two inscriptions describe their authors as "servants of the goddess al-Uzza." This goddess is also named in two dedications belonging to the niches which line the access routes to the cult sites. In one of them al-Uzza appears again beside the "Lord of the Temple." And it is she again who is venerated at the side of Dushara in Qasr el-Bint Faroun. In Petra the Aphrodite cult is documented by a fragment of an inscription in Greek which came to light during excavations at Qasr el-

Bint al-Faroun; it names the goddess of love together with Zeus Hypsistos, "the most high." One of the best-preserved papyri to survive to the present day, known as the "archive of Babata," points to the existence of an aphrodision, a shrine to Aphrodite in Petra which in Roman times was used by the city council as a documents archive. Finally, several sculptures found in Petra have been interpreted as depictions of the Greek goddess.

Al-Uzza is not the only goddess to be represented in the form of an anthropomorphic betyl. The Syrian fertility goddess Atargatis was also so depicted; her betyl stands in the Wadi Siyag, which had one of the most plentiful supplies of water in Petra.

Papyri found in Upper Egypt describe Petra as one of the centers of the cult of Isis. As the sister and wife of the god of death, Osiris, Isis was also considered a guardian of the dead. Her worship by the Nabataeans was the result of the commercial and political ties which existed between the Nabataean nation and Egypt. In Petra there are at least two shrines dedicated to her: both are rock niches with statues of the goddess. In the first, situated on the edge of the city, the figure of the goddess – later decapitated by iconoclasts – sits on a throne with a podium depicted in profile; the folds of her cloak and tunic are finely worked, and the knot of Isis can be seen on her breast. Near the niche, carved Nabataean graffiti indicate that pilgrims visited this shrine, which lay close to the caravan route from Petra to Egypt. The second Isis shrine consists of several niches, some of whose reliefs are badly eroded. One shows the enthroned goddess seated on a stool whose sides are carved into the rock. An inscription on both sides of the niche dates the shrine to the year 25 B.C.

Opposite

Section of the façade from the Khaznet al-Faroun, Petra

The upper right half of the facade of the Khaznet al-Faroun ("Treasury of the Pharaoh"). In the tholos (upper left) there is a sculpture of an Isis-Fortune figure with cornucopia in her left hand. To the right of the tholos in a recess (here in shadow) is a winged goddess of Victory. Still farther to the right is an Amazon wielding an axe.

Place of Isis worship, Petra

This shrine is in a gorge which reaches up to the right bank of the Wadi Siyagh and it is difficult to gain access to it. Four niches are particularly interesting: from left to right can be seen a figure of Isis; a badly eroded figure; a betyl set into the rock; and a niche with basin for ritual purifications. At both sides of the left-hand niche is an inscription from 25 B.C. in which the name of Isis can clearly be made out.

Anthropomorphic betyl, Petra

1st century B.C.–1st century A.D.
Yellowish sandstone; height 32 cm, width 20 cm,
circ. 14 cm
Archeological Museum, Amman

On the base of the stele is a Nabataean inscription; it does not name the goddess but describes her as "the goddess of Hayyan, son of Nibat." The Egyptian goddess Isis may have been meant; she corresponded to the Nabataean goddess al-Uzza. The hollow in the middle of the laurel frieze at the top of the stele originally contained the basileum, the attribute of the Egyptian goddess. The stele is framed with pilasters with a raised diamond frieze and rests on a molded pediment. The eyes, into which precious stones were once set, almost disappear under the eyebrows. In contrast to most anthropomorphic stelae this example has a full-lipped mouth. It was found in the Lion Gryphon Temple.

Isis was also depicted in the form of an anthropomorphic betyl. One of them is crowned by a headband in the center of which can be seen the fertility emblem of Isis – a sun disc surrounded by horns and ears of wheat. In another example the Isis emblem was made of precious materials and set into a recess in the middle of the headband. Clay statuettes from another temple in Petra, known as the Lion Griffin Temple, show Isis in an attitude of mourning – an allusion to her grief for the murdered figure of Osiris. This posture was borrowed from depictions of the Greek goddess Demeter lamenting the abduction of her daughter Persephone by Hades, the god of the underworld. Finally, Isis also had a central place at the Khaznet al-Faroun. Her symbol decorates the central acroterion of this monument, which is more a mausoleum or tomb than a temple. The various depictions of Isis quite clearly show several of the goddess's many aspects: she appears as a grieving widow and a guardian of the dead, as well as a goddess who grants fertility and life.

We have already mentioned al-Kutba, who appeared in Wadi Rum in connection with al-Uzza. She was probably venerated by the Nabataeans as a female divinity; as goddess of writing she can be related to the Babylonian god of the planets, Nabu, who represented the planet Mercury and was considered the scribe of the gods in Babylonian and Aramaic mythology. His cult was probably introduced during the ten years King Nabonid of Babylon (556–539 B.C.) spent in northern Arabia. As a scribe Nabu was also the guardian of the tablets of fate and, more importantly, he was the god of prophecy.

Allat and Manat (Manawat) are the last of the goddesses in the Nabataean pantheon to be discussed here. The former is the equivalent of Athena and was the most important Arabian goddess in Roman times. She is not named in any of the inscriptions in Petra, and was depicted there only once with the attributes of Athena in a relief found near the tenemos gate of Qasr el-Bint Faroun. An inscription in Wadi Rum describes her specifically as she "who is in Bosra."

Manat is the goddess of destiny, particularly that which is the lot of mankind. In the grave texts of Hegra she is referred to eight times. Occasionally her name is mentioned in conjunction with what seems to be her attribute, the *qaishah*, a modification of the Arabic *qais* or "measure." The *qaishah* of the goddess might therefore have been the cubit, the symbol of the correct measure.

The male divinities

After they settled in Edom, the Nabataeans adopted the Edomite god Qaus, the god of storms and life-giving rain. He is attested to in theophoric names such as *zydqws*, "Qaus has increased," or *qwsntn*, "Qaus has given." He is also named in a Nabataean inscription from Bosra in which a certain Muaynu dedicates a basalt eagle to him. The shrine of Khirbet el-Tannur was also consecrated to Qaus, and it is here that we find a depiction of the god with the features of the Syrian divinity Hadad, god of storms and rain; flanked by two bulls he is seated on a throne casting a thunderbolt. His name is mentioned in two other inscriptions found in the same place.

Dushara was the main god in the Nabataean pantheon. His name is more a description of place; its approximate meaning is "he who is from the Shara [mountains]" – the range of mountains to the east overlooking Petra. His is the name which appears most frequently in inscriptions. He is alternately called the "God of Gaia" (the antique name of a village close to Petra), "God of Medrasa" (a still current term for a part of Petra), or "God of our Lord"

(meaning the reigning Nabataean king). An impression of his importance can be gained from the place he occupies in the list of divinities: texts refer to "Dushara and all gods" or "Dushara and the other gods." An inscription which Syllaios had carved in 9 B.C. during a stay in Milet in Asia Minor indicates that Dushara was considered the equivalent of Zeus – yet another indication of the importance of this central god.

The linking of Dushara and Dionysos, the Greek god of wine, is indicated in a relief in Wadi el-Farasa in Petra: a portrait medallion which was perhaps once surrounded by vine-leaves is situated directly above a typically oblong Dushara betyl. A coin from Bosra shows on its reverse side the image of a youthful, robed God with luxuriant hair who can be identified as Dionysos; the inscription reads "Bostrenon Dusares." Finally, a relief fragment from a pilaster was found in Petra on which the god was depicted with vine-leaves in his hair and his attribute, the thyrsus, in his right hand. The pictorial record is confirmed by Hesychios, a Byzantine lexicographer of the 5th century, who wrote that for the Nabataeans Dionysos was Dusares.

In the 4th century Dushara was described by Bishop Epiphanios of Salamis in his essay against heresy ("Panarion") as the son of a virgin. In order to show that pagans had taken up the idea of the virgin birth of a god by themselves, he quoted – amongst others – the example of Petra where, according to Epiphanios, songs were sung in the temples of the idols in honor of the virgin, who was called Chaamu in Arabic, and of her son, Dusares.

Most tombs in Hegra, as well as the Turkmaniye tomb in Petra – the only one to have a long inscription on its facade – were under the protection of this god. The owners attempted to protect their tombs from potential grave-robbers by employing the threat of a curse from Dushara.

Still other male divinities are known from the Nabataean capital – for example the main god of the Syrians, Baal-Shamin, who was named in Wadi Rum along with Dushara and who possessed his own temple in Wadi Musa. His symbol was the eagle, for which reason it can be assumed that the monument generally known as the "eagle niche" in Petra was consecrated to him. His name also appears in several dedications in the region around Bosra.

Shai el-Qaum, "the companion of the tribe" was the patron god of caravans. A Nabataean soldier donated an altar to him in Palmyra in which he is described as the "god who drinks no wine." He was obviously worshipped in Hegra too, since he is mentioned in an inscription near an Adihula niche. Finally, his name is found in a dedication from 96 A.D. found in Ghariye, in the Nabataean region of Hauran.

Cultic rites

One of the few things that can be assumed about Nabataean cultic rites was that these ceremonies involved processions. In Petra numerous processional routes leading to the shrines were used, and one can imagine the priest or his assistants carrying the betyl to the High Place of Sacrifice along these paths before finally setting it up on a *motab*. The same ritual was probably followed in Khirbet el-Tannur and Khirbet al-Darih. The arrangement of

Sid el-Madjin, Petra

In this picture can be seen two niches from the entrance to the rotunda of the shrine of Sidd el-Madjin; under the right niche is the engraved inscription "before Dushara and all the gods."

Relief of Dushara, Petra

Dushara, the main god in the Nabataean pantheon, corresponded to the Greek god of wine, Dionysos. His portrait medallion pictured here is located in the Wadi el-Farasa and was situated above a typically rectangular Dushara betyl.

Processional route, el-Hubta

This processional route carved into the rock leads to the peak of el-Hubta; it was completely restored by the Department of Antiquities in Petra and opened to the public in 1996.

Temple, Khirbet el-Darih

Adyton of the temple with an in-built *motab*. Steps at the side (added later) lead up to the podium, where holes for erecting betyls are still visible. A narrow passageway led around the *motab*, which was surrounded by columns and richly ornamented corner pilasters. Under the podium there are two crypts.

several courtyards in front of the temple, as was the case in Khirbet el-Darih, was obviously connected with the way in which the sacred area was gradually approached and perhaps also with a division of the believers into various categories such as women, men, novitiates, priests, and so on. The benches at the sides of these courtyards, such as those found at Qasr el-Bint Faroun or Khirbet el-Darih, were probably intended for the participants who took a greater or lesser role in proceedings. Offerings in the form of aediculae – niche-like shrines, such as those attested to in the Hauran area on the basis of basalt fragments – may also have been placed there.

Ancient sources – the Suda and the descriptions of Strabo – talk of libations being offered to the gods. The devices on the podium at Khirbet el-Darih as well as the bowl-like depressions in front of several betyls confirm the historical record. Because blood was offered in some of these libations, the question is raised as to the nature of the sacrifice. The climax of the ceremonies was probably the sacrifice of an animal on an altar such as is known to have taken place at the High Place of Sacrifice. The monumental altar in front of Qasr el-Bint Firaun also served this purpose. This was not so, however, with the dozens of other altars hewn directly into the rock. Like other rock monuments – such as the *motab* laid out in the form of a seat – they testify to a some uncertainty amongst believers as to the precise meaning of the various cult objects.

The very high number of small places of prayer – in Petra there are several hundred – together with the vast numbers of names of the faithful scored into the rock near these shrines, underlines the importance of religion in everyday life. Similarly, the large numbers of cultic drawings on rock surfaces in the quarries of the Nabataeans are an expression of the all-pervasive presence of the divine at every moment of existence. It was not merely a matter of chance, therefore, that temples were always built in prominent locations such as at Khirbet el-Tannur, Khirbet el-Darih or Petra, where the Qasr el-Bint Faroun with its tenemos was laid out at the end of the city's main street.

The Nabataean shrines in Petra, in Wadi Rum and in Hegra illustrate, in a manner of speaking, the words of the Arab historian Hisham Ibn al-Kalbi from the 8th century, who reported that those Arabs unable to erect a temple or a statue simply set up a stone in front of a temple or other location and then held their ritual processions as if they were dealing with an authentic temple.

Block tomb, Bab el-Siq

One of the three free-standing block tombs, the "Dijn Tombs," on the right bank of the wadi at the entrance to Petra. This tomb rises up from a stepped pedestal and is crowned by a smaller ashlar block. On the eastern side is the entrance to a burial chamber with two shaft tombs.

The world of the dead

A short tour of the ruins of Petra quickly demonstrates the importance accorded to the dead in Nabataean society. The facades of over 600 tombs are lined up on the terraces and rock walls of the mountains which surround the center of the city. For a long time the sheer omnipresence of these tombs fueled the belief that Petra was never a proper city. Although research carried out in the last 20 years has meant that speculation of this kind has had to be abandoned – it is now known that Petra was a wealthy and lively commercial center which was home to numerous foreigners – the tombs still remain the most prominent element of the city's visible remains.

The fact that in Hegra there are different types of tombs from the same era (in contrast to Petra, the grave monuments there are often dated by inscriptions on the facades) has rendered redundant the theory proposed at the beginning of the 19th century, which held that there was a connection between the typology of the tomb and the date of its construction. In the 1970s these ideas were replaced by the more convincing notion of a relationship between the type of tomb and the social status of its owner. The tombs, in their combination of "oriental" and classical stylistic facades, did not develop over time, therefore, but were always a matter of choice for the individual owner. Since the beginning of the 1990s it is the development of architectural ornamentation within each tomb type which has been the main focus of interest. A precise examination of several key elements – for example the profile of the moldings, the capitals, and the frieze – at selected tombs in Petra has allowed them to be divided into six (temporal) groups within which the architectural ornaments are homogenous. Each of these groups is classified under one particular monument which could be dated with absolute certainty, either from archaeological finds or from inscriptions. To describe these architectural ornaments here in detail would go beyond our scope; the typology of the tombs on the other hand, though no longer having anything to say about their chronological order, still continues to be valid.

El-Hubta necropolis, Petra

This necropolis does not contain any so-called "royal tombs"; instead there are dozens of modest tombs of various sizes which belong to the category of classical tombs featuring either crowsteps or facing steps. Seen from the High Place of Sacrifice, they represent the southern part of the necropolis.

Obelisk Tomb, Petra

The tomb owes its name to four obelisks (or *nefesh*) which crown the upper part of the facade. The monument consists of two levels: a triclinium at the bottom and a burial chamber in the upper section. In the niche between the two central obelisks stands a robed figure, which today is missing its head.

Opposite

Mouth of the Siq, Petra

The only access route to Petra was the Siq, the gorge formed by the dry bed of the Wadi Musa, just over 1 mile (2 km) long. At the extreme right of the picture can be seen one of the few funerary monuments in Petra – in this case a Hegra tomb – to have a chamber located between two rows of crowsteps.

Typology of tombs in Petra

With the aid of the typology of Petra's funerary monuments, these memorials can be read according to a simple and easily remembered code.

The *nefesh*, consecrated to the memory of a particular individual, was separate from the actual grave. The word is derived from the Semitic and means "breath, soul, person." A *nefesh* takes the form of a pyramid or an obelisk – sometimes on a cube with a stepped base – and may be surmounted by a pyramidal point or a type of finial.

Generally *nefesh* were situated along connecting roads, so that they were visible to passers-by. They are less frequently found in the interior of tombs, of which the most impressive example is a large funerary monument opposite the theater, whose burial chamber has a *nefesh* carved out of the rock of one of its walls. Two of them have been more closely

identified from two Nabataean and one Greek inscription. The four obelisks of the facade of the "obelisk tomb" over the Bab el-Siq, as well as the statue in the central niche, can be interpreted as symbols of the dead who are buried inside.

Pit tombs, of which there are several hundred in Petra and elsewhere, are the most spartan of burials. They are simple, oblong depressions hewn into the rock with an inset edge to allow a lid to be fitted. Some of these tombs have two or three circular depressions at the sides to receive libations. The deceased were interred either without a shroud or cloaked in leather burial garments, the remains of which have been found in the necropolis of Khirbet el-Darih.

Shaft tombs, on the other hand, were more complex communal graves, and they can sometimes only be differentiated from the previous tomb type with difficulty. They were often filled in at a later date and therefore appear to the observer to be pit tombs. The entrance to these tombs leads into a shaft in whose walls footholds were carved to allow a descent into the burial chamber. The chamber itself was placed 2–3 m underground and furnished with either pit tombs or *loculi* – wall niches, in which the dead were interred.

All tombs with ornamented facades – with the exception of those which remained unfinished – possess a burial chamber in the middle of the rock which is distinguished by a varying number of *loculi* and/or pit tombs. Not all burial chambers, however, necessarily have a decorated facade: in Petra there are almost 200 such examples, which form a link between tombs excavated from the ground and tombs with facades. For lack of any particularly distinguishing features, however, we shall not pursue this group further.

The so-called crowstep tombs display one or two rows of crowsteps in relief in the upper third of the facade. Originally Persian or Assyrian, this motif may have found its way to Nabataea via Phoenicia, where it occurs in the shrine of Amrit. Below each row of crenellations, as well as above the lowest, were carved moldings, and there was usually a flat band beneath the lowest of these. Above the otherwise simple doors of these tombs there may be a ledge or groove carved into the rock into which was placed a stucco cornice (and not a board with the name of the owner, as had previously been suggested). Pilasters sometimes also support an architrave and a triangular pediment.

The upper third of the facade of the so-called "double crowstep tombs" has two rows of crowsteps only, which are supported by a cornice composed, from bottom to top, of fillet, astragal and cyma reversa. In two meticulously worked groups – the "proto-Hegra" and the "Hegra" tombs – these basic forms were joined by other ornamental elements. The first of these types is characterized by corner pilasters which frame the facade. Instead of an architrave their capitals support a fillet. The second type has, in addition, an Ionic entablature over corner pilasters which is separated from the cornice with its cyma reversa by an attic. Occasionally the corner pilasters are complemented by engaged quarter columns; two demi-columns between the door of the tomb and pilasters further articulate the facade. In some of the tombs dwarf pilasters can be found in the otherwise unadorned attic zone, where they serve as a continuation of the corner pilasters and demi-columns of the facade. One of the tombs in the necropolis of Moghar el-Nasara has a frieze with shields and mythological figures in relief.

Arch tombs form their own category, but are relatively rare. Their facades are framed by pilasters which support a single or double round arch in whose center there may sometimes be a circular carved ornament reminiscent of a phial.

Finally there is the hellenized type of tomb such as the so-called statue tomb or the broken pediment tombs of Wadi el-Farasa. Instead of crenellations these single-story monuments have triangular pediments over the entablature which recall the structure of a Greek temple facade.

Due to the complexity of their facades, which can be up to five stories high, the large funerary monuments cannot be reduced to any of the types described above.

With the exception of the Khaznet al-Faroun all the so-called royal tombs are located in the necropolis at the foot of the el-Hubta massif. These tombs were so named for their monumental character and in particular because they contained inscriptions which mentioned the names of a Nabataean queen and her *epitropos*, her plenipotentiary for western affairs of state. Nonetheless, there is no overwhelming evidence that the Nabataean kings were in fact buried there; the tombs may equally have been the last resting place of high-ranking individuals.

Entry to a shaft tomb, Petra

View of the rectangular entrance to a shaft tomb. The entrance to these complex communal graves led into a shaft which finally ended in a burial chamber 6–10 ft (2–3 m) below the ground.

El-Hubta necropolis, Petra

Tomb in the southern part of the necropolis at the foot of el-Hubta. The height of the facade was determined by the height of the cliff into which the tombs were carved; the size of the chambers probably also determined their cost.

Theater necropolis, Petra

This necropolis is among the oldest in Petra and is situated at the entrance to the city. The various tomb types are worth noting: they include those with steps, arches, or crowsteps. Above some of the doors are horizontal slots which supported ornaments.

Burial chamber, Petra

This burial chamber is provided with three *loculi* in the rear wall. In both right-hand loculi burial recesses have been hewn from the rock.

Opposite

The "Corinthian Tomb," Petra

The facade of the tomb consists of three horizontal orders: semi-circular pediments at the bottom, a broken pediment in the middle, and a *tholos* framed by the two halves of a broken pediment at the top.

Elevation of Nabataean tomb facades, Petra

Tomb facades with (from left to right) a frieze with a double row of crowsteps, an attic with two sets of facing steps, a frieze with a single row of crowsteps, and a crown of crowsteps.

Two proto-Hegra tombs, Petra

Proto-Hegra tombs are half-crenellated tombs whose facades were framed by pilasters with Nabataean capitals. They have only a single element in the entablature – an Egyptian cavetto cornice. Hegra tombs, on the other hand, display two more finely worked constructions in the entablature.

Tomb of Statues, Petra

A view of the Tomb of Statues in the Wadi el-Farasa from the interior of the triclinium opposite. The tomb's facade features a design of demi-columns and corner pilasters and is surmounted by a flat pediment and blind attic. Between the columns there are three tall, framed niches with statues (each composed of six stacked limestone blocks), of which only the central figure in armor has been well preserved. The tomb is, somewhat misleadingly, known as the "Tomb of the Roman Soldier" after this armored figure.

Opposite

Khaznet al-Faroun, Petra

The Khaznet al-Faroun ("Treasury of the Pharaoh") in all its magnificence. This tomb is considered an example of the Hellenized type, since its facade recalls those of Greek temples.

Tomb with broken pediment, Petra

This tomb in the Wadi el-Farasa has also been described as "Hellenized" because, like the Khaznet al-Faroun, it adopts elements from Greek temple facades.

"Columbarium," Petra

The purpose of this peculiar monument at el-Habis has still not been fully explained: was it a tomb (the small niches serving as shelves for receiving cinerary urns) or was it functional (possibly a dovecote)?

Necropolis of Umm el-Biyara, Petra

The necropolis of Umm el-Biyara lies at the foot of a massif of the same name. Petra's highest mountain served the Nabataeans as a refuge during an attack by the Greeks in 312 B.C.; only a single track led up to the summit. The tombs occupy only the lower accessible slopes of the mountain.

Burial rites

One of Strabo's informants, the Greek philosopher Athenodorus, claimed that the Nabataeans regarded their corpses as dung; Heraclitus had written that the dead had to be deposited outside because they were considered more repugnant than dung. Even the kings were buried beside piles of manure according

to Strabo (Geographia XVI 4:26). Some scholars are of the opinion that this description has resulted from writers mistaking the Aramaic word *kpr*, "tomb, gravestone" for the Greek *kopros*, "dung." According to this theory Athenodorus probably heard the Nabataeans say they laid the bodies of the deceased in *koprin*, and concluded that they had little respect for their dead. Still others have been reminded of the custom of exposing the corpse to the elements as it was practiced in Iran. The remark can be explained perhaps still more simply: some of Petra's cemeteries are situated on the outskirts of the city close to areas which have been identified as ancient trash heaps.

Apart from Strabo, literary sources provide no accounts of Nabataean burial practices; we are forced to rely instead on archaeological evidence and approximately 50 surviving Nabataean burial texts, of which some 38 are from Hegra.

Nabataean burials do not appear to have followed any prescribed formula. Jordanian burials as well as those of the Negev show different methods for dealing with the corpse: they may have been

simply wrapped in textile or leather shrouds, buried in lime, or wholly or partly cremated. Some of the dead were laid in sarcophagi of wood or stone; in addition, traces of the sort of resins used in Egyptian mummies have been found on the shrouds. There were even cases of second burials, when the remains were removed from one site and reburied at another. The majority of tombs contained burial offerings: clay vases, oil lamps, terracotta statues, jewelry, coins and small bronze bells. Thanks to excavations which began in 1997 in the necropolis of Khirbet Qazone on the Jordanian side of the Dead Sea, we will soon know more about burial customs. The 22 tombs excavated so far prove that only one corpse was buried in each pit grave; their heads were facing south and they were wrapped in shrouds made from old pieces of clothing.

The tombs were seen as the inviolable property of a particular group of people who, where inscriptions have recorded the names of their members, are often recognizable as families. According to these texts they were "subject and consecrated to" a god – generally Dushara – and placed under his protection. Grave robbers, who were obviously feared by the owners of the tombs, were placed under a curse and could rely on being visited by divine wrath. The inscriptions of the Hegra tombs can be described as a type of legal document, since they listed all those persons who were allowed to be buried there. In some of these inscriptions there is even a reference to a copy of the burial text being stored in the temple which contained the municipal archive.

Tombs were not infrequently connected to a triclinium, and it can be assumed that feasts in honor of the dead were held. The obelisk grave in Petra is the most telling example of this, since tomb and triclinium occupy two floors in the same monument. Family members would gather on the occasion of such a feast; in the case of a dead king the assembly was composed of participants in the *thiasos* who gathered in his honor.

In conclusion it can be asserted that the dead, contrary to the claims of Athenodorus, were treated with particular respect by the Nabataeans. The measures taken to protect the tombs; the burial offerings given to ease the transition into the next life; and the libations and celebrations of feasts for the dead are all evidence of a desire to cherish the memory of the deceased.

Triclinium at the Tomb of Statues, Petra

The most conspicuous elements of the "Bright Hall," a triclinium in the Wadi el-Farasa, are the pilasters with intervening niches and the stone bench which runs parallel to three of the walls.

Rock-cut house, Wadi Siyagh

The terraces above the Wadi Siyagh are riddled
with rock-cut chambers which could be
reached from the wadi by means of stairs. This
area was one of the largest residential quarters
in Petra.

Rock chamber in a dwelling, Petra

To the right of the opening of this rock-cut
chamber on the eastern slope of el-Habis are
the remains of stucco decoration.

Dwellings

Following an examination of the gods and the necropoli of the Nabataeans, it could now seem inappropriate to discuss the living. Their world has been the poor relation of archaeological research into this era; the rather unprepossessing domestic architecture of these regions of the Near East, whose temples and tombs offer much "better" objects for research, has few friends. Fortunately, this situation has improved in the last few years, and much more light has been shed on the domestic life of the Nabataeans.

Reports by Diodorus Siculus and Strabo have provided us with two very different accounts of Nabataean domestic architecture. The first concerns the period at the end of the 4th century B.C. and describes the Nabataeans as follows (Historical Library XIX 94): "They live in the open air and call the desert their homeland which has neither rivers nor such springs as could provide a foreign host with water. It is a law amongst them to cultivate neither grain nor any such plant as might provide them with nourishment, nor to consume wine or build houses."

At this time therefore it seems that the nomadic or semi-nomadic Nabataeans lived in tents which they could erect or dismantle as they pleased, and this assumption has been reinforced by excavations carried out by the University of Basel on a hill south of Petra's city center. Archaeological strata were found here which bore traces of a settlement, and they have been interpreted by scholars as the remains of a tent settlement from the period between the end of the 2nd and 1st centuries B.C.

Towards the end of the 1st century B.C. the situation was completely different. Strabo, upon whose account we are dependent for knowledge of the period, mentions that the Nabataeans' houses were expensive because they were constructed of stone. A Nabataean house was discovered on the same hill as the tent settlement mentioned above, and it revealed two phases of construction in the period between the end of the 1st century B.C. and the beginning of the 2nd century A.D. This house had a number of rooms, two of them being laid out in the shape of an atrium. One of the rooms opened out on to a large, irregular courtyard; the dwelling was of a single story only and was covered by a flat roof. After its violent destruction at the beginning of the 2nd century, the building stood empty for around 200 years before the site was used once again: Roman finds can be dated back to 419, at which time an earthquake destroyed the complex completely.

In 1996 the same Swiss archaeological team began excavating to the south of the house and discovered a second residence from the 1st century A.D. Its walls of up to 10 feet (3 m) in height had survived, and showed unusually well-preserved polychrome paintings in the first and second Pompeian style.

Lion Fountain, Petra

The "Lion Fountain" is situated in the Wadi el-Farasa at the ascent to the High Place of Sacrifice. Water fed through a canal flowed over the head of a lion carved into the rock.

In spite of such discoveries we should not ignore the fact that most dwellings in Petra were either partly or wholly hewn out of the rock. They were single or multi-roomed dwellings, sometimes with windows, and opened on to natural terraces which may have had small structures such as animal pens or simple sheds. Niches were used as built-in cupboards, and so-called "hour glasses" were set into the walls: these were two large holes bored next to each other and separated by a stirrup to which various objects could be attached. Furniture was extremely meager and probably consisted of little more than a few ceramic items for everyday use, sacks of straw as mattresses and several implements. Light was provided either by "windows" carved high into the wall or oil lamps which were placed in special recesses in the walls. The inhabitants of Petra obtained their water either from the springs of the Wadi Musa, which flowed into the city along a channel hewn into the rock, or from rainwater cisterns. In Petra there were over 200 cisterns of various sizes which provided water in even the driest periods.

Little is known about the Nabataeans' diet. An examination of bones found during the excavation of a dwelling at the foot of the Djebel el-Hubta showed that the occupants consumed only poor-quality sheep meat. The small number of bones at this site might indicate that there was little meat in the local diet, but this conclusion is based on too small a sample to generalize about the whole population.

Stele with a human head in relief, Khirbet Rizqe

1st century B.C.–1st century A.D.
Brownish sandstone; height 26.5 cm,
width 24 cm
Archaeological Museum, Amman

The eyes of this strongly stylized face – or *nefesh* – are almond-shaped while the nose is in the form of an elongated pyramid.

Victory goddess with the Zodiac, Khirbet el-Tannur

End of the 1st century B.C./beginning of the 1st century A.D.
Limestone; height 73 cm, width 33 cm, circ. 36 cm
Archaeological Museum, Amman

Originally the Victory figure held aloft a bust relief of the patron goddess Tyche which was surrounded by the 12 signs of the Zodiac; today this is housed in the Museum of Arts in Cincinnati. To the right of the head of Victory can be seen the star sign for Pisces.

Arts and crafts

Nabataean burial sites have been the subject of investigation since the beginning of the century and have yielded a variety of art objects as evidence both of the vitality of Nabataean craftsmen and the development of an artistic style which testified to local as well as external influences. The statues, statuettes, jewelry and ceramic items today housed in museums in Jordan, Europe, and the United States provide an insight into the wealth of some Nabataeans, and are material evidence of their love of well-crafted objects. The majority of these items, however, are religious or funerary in nature rather than being drawn from everyday life. Several were probably imported from Alexandria or other places, though the numbers of such objects are insignificant. The many workshops of Petra and the cities of the Negev were active and supplied a flourishing and growing market.

Sculptures

Sculpture as such was not practiced widely by Nabataean artists, who showed a certain fondness for the relief. The various materials used – sandstone and limestone in Petra, limestone in Khirbet el-Tannur and Khirbet el-Darih, basalt in the Hauran region – led to the use of different techniques and favored the development of distinct styles.

The large numbers of betyls proves that the Nabataeans clearly preferred not to depict their divinities in figurative form. The first departure from this custom can be seen in the "eye idols." The stelae of Khirbet Rizqe, a pre-Islamic shrine in the south of Wadi Rum, belong in this category. These are memorial stelae which were meant to represent the deceased or pilgrims. One of them depicts a roughly stylized human face; its almond-shaped eyes have deep slits and the long, slightly projecting nose becomes broader towards the bottom. It has not been possible to date these stelae precisely.

Hellenized sculptures which appear from around the end of the 1st century B.C. take their forms from the art of Alexandria and Pergamon. This group is represented by the reliefs of the Khaznet al-Faroun and Qasr el-Bint Faroun as well as a series of relief fragments found in the 1950s near the temenos gate of Qasr el-Bint. They belonged to a lost building which was perhaps located on the site of the gate. One of the most noteworthy is a head of Dionysos with full cheeks and slightly parted lips, his hair bound by a band around the forehead and his head crowned by vine leaves and grapes.

In the same series is a frieze from which several fragments showing weapons and trophies have been found. One of these perhaps served as the central ornamental device on a shield, and shows a head framed by long curly locks of hair reminiscent of a Medusa. The figure's solid necklace of overlapping scales is closed by a knot. The expressive character of the face, reinforced by the knitted brow and the roughly worked stone, shows the influence of the art of Pergamon. On the left of the fragment can be seen the lower part of a cuirass.

The Hellenistic–Syrian style (generally dating from the 1st century A.D.) can be seen in several reliefs in Khirbet el-Tannur as well as a sculptural group found in 1954 in the rubble of the temenos gate at Qasr el-Bint. The latter includes the bust of a

Architectural relief of Dushara-Dionysos, Petra

1st century A.D.
Yellowish sandstone; height 36 cm, width 55 cm
Archaeological Museum, Petra

This depiction of Dionysos was found at the Temenos Gate beside a bust relief of the Greco-Roman gods of Athena, Hermes, and Melpomene.

Frieze, Petra

End of 1st century B.C.–*1st century* A.D.
Limestone; height 34 cm, width 40 cm, circ. 39 cm
Archaeological Museum, Amman

This fragment of a relief featuring the head of Medusa belonged to a frieze which probably decorated the Temenos Gate or the altar of Qasr el-Bint Faroun.

goddess (possibly Serapis), a bust of Hermes, a winged head with sideburns and a winged Fortune holding a palm branch in one hand and a cornucopia in the other. The most remarkable of the finds amongst the reliefs of el-Tannur is a winged goddess of victory who carries in her upraised arms a medallion with a tyche bust surrounded by the 12 signs of the Zodiac. In contrast to the usual sequence these are divided into two groups of six which correspond to a spring and an autumn calendar. The Nabataeans employed this sequence because their year was defined by the agricultural festivals of spring and autumn. The goddess wears a long robe tied with a ribbon under the bodice and held at the shoulders by two clasps in the form of rosettes. The triangular face has simplified features and eyes with outsized pupils, its hair parted down the center, and the figure wears a jeweled band on its upper left arm composed of individual rings.

Two reliefs from Khirbet el-Tannur seem to show evidence of Parthian influences. The stylization of the face is more extreme here than in the relief just described. The first shows an alto-rilievo bust of the goddess Atargatis or Derketo. The rosette surrounding her is enclosed in a frame whose four corners there are acanthus leaves. The face of the goddess is oval and displays angular features. Her superb head of hair, which falls in spiral plaits to her

Atagartis, Khirbet el-Tannur

*End of the 1st century B.C.–beginning of the
1st century A.D.
Limestone; traces of red paint; height 27cm,
width 36 cm, circ. 47 cm
Archaeological Museum, Amman*

Parthian influences have been detected in the
strongly stylized facial features of this bust of
the goddess Atagartis.

Statue of Artemis, Petra

*2nd century B.C.
Bronze; height 120 cm
Archaeological Museum, Amman*

This bronze of Artemis is slightly smaller than
life-size. Although it was discovered in Petra, its
origins have yet to be explained. The goddess is
shown running, with her left foot still on the
ground, and she wears a fastened tunic. The
statue was apparently discovered around 20
years ago, but details of the work have yet to be
published. It is presently undergoing
restoration, and experts have estimated that it
dates from the Hellenistic era, more precisely
from the 2nd century B.C.

shoulders, is covered by a veil with a motif of two fish
facing each other. The goddess also wears a tunic
with a zigzag collar – though a necklace may in fact
be depicted – the folds of which are very imprecisely
worked. The second relief shows the head of the god
Hadad whose visage is also represented in simplified
form. He has a full head of hair as well as a strong
beard twisted into a spiral; the face is dominated by
large eyes which lend the figure an imposing gaze.

According to Fawzi Zayadine the sculptures of
the Hauran region, whose rough finish is at least
partly attributable to the hard basalt of the area,
overlap with the Hellenistic–Syrian style. These
works are local products whose indeterminate
chronology is based solely on stylistic criteria. The
first of these recognized styles, which cover the two
centuries before and after Christ, merits a short
explanation at this point. The works of this group
show geometric forms in their bodies, while
symmetry and frontality characterize representations
of both animals and people. The treatment of
schematic details in relief could be described as
graphic. A further characteristic is the frequent habit
of attaching extra material to the relief to form
protruding elements.

Finally it should be mentioned that a bronze
statue of Artemis was found by Bedouins in one of
Petra's wadis in the 1970s, although details of the
pieces were not published until 1996. Belonging to
its own stylistic category it is thought to date from the
2nd century A.D. and depicts a goddess running; the
left leg is the standing leg while the right has been
reconstructed. The figure wears a short tunic fixed at
the shoulder with two clasps.

Pottery

The most famous items of Nabataean pottery are
known as "eggshell ware" due to their extremely
delicate construction. They were made from a type
of red clay found near Petra. These ceramics were
either unfinished, given a covering of engobe,
painted or provided with a relief decoration.
Nabataean pottery – which was apparently not
exported – has been found in large quantities in all
the culture's burial sites. The most important ceramics
workshop, that of Zurrabe near Petra, was excavated
in 1980; this dig uncovered a number of kilns, all of
which had been in operation until a relatively late
date. The Nabataeans adapted techniques and forms
from the potters of the Hellenistic era, but showed
great originality. The spectrum of ceramic forms
covers hemispherical bowls, bowls with ring bases,
and vessels for ointments and perfumes
(unguentaria), as well as oil lamps made by using
negative casts.

The unpainted pottery intended for everyday use is obviously more widespread than painted ceramic items. In some parts of Petra the visitor can only walk to the accompaniment of the crunching of broken pottery underfoot, and one only need bend down to pick up a handful of shards. Unpainted pottery is divided into three chronologically successive groups, which are dominated by open forms. The first of these (first half of the 1st century B.C.) includes the types derived from Hellenistic forms: large diameter steep-walled dishes with slightly in-turned rims, plates and bowls with slightly in-turned rims, as well as those with convex rims. These red or orange ceramics are often covered with a red-brown engobe. At 0.3 to 0.6 cm thick these pieces are, however, far removed from the delicacy of "eggshell ware."

The forms of the second group (second half of the 1st century B.C. until around 20 A.D.) are more elegant and their thickness has been reduced by around half to 0.2 to 0.3 cm. The most representative finds include bowls with in-turned rims or vessels with protruding rims. The surface is no longer covered with engobe and their appearance is dominated by the bright orange color of the clay. Several of the pieces had white engobe applied to the outside below the rims.

The third group (around 20 to 100 A.D.) encompasses still more elegant forms: shallow bowls with steep or ridged walls as well as small, deep bowls. At the same time the hemispherical bowls with in-turned rims from the second group can be found, though those with protruding rims are absent. The walls of the items are very thin and the clay was fired until it was "hard as metal."

Less common – and the object of illegal excavations – are the painted shards which are often removed from tombs and sold to tourists. These were exceptionally costly items which owe their reputation to the care lavished on their execution. Painted ceramics were also chronologically divided into three groups according to the form and typology of the decoration. The three phases form a single stylistic development which is not actually marked by any abrupt transitions.

The first group (second half of the 2nd century until the first half of the 1st century B.C.) largely consists of relatively deep bowls with a thin, pale red layer of engobe and hastily executed decoration. The decoration consisted of straight or wavy bands which intersected at the base of the vessel. The interior of the rims were sometimes decorated with pearl motifs and their lines replaced with dots. The second group (second half of the 1st century B.C.) is characterized by thin-walled bowls with palmette motifs which radiate out from the base or which are distributed concentrically over the surface of the vessel. The rims of these vessels are slightly curved, and the painted patterns of rays show a slight bulge halfway up the surface. The third group (1st century A.D.) consists of very fine, small-rimmed vessels decorated generally

with stylized palmettes as well as various geometric motifs and cross-hatching on the base.

Figurative paintings of people or animals occurs less frequently than the depiction of vegetable motifs. There are, however, rather clumsily painted pieces on which birds and donkeys can be seen. Both animals and people were represented naively and non-naturalistically.

For pottery featuring a relief decoration small circular molds with the desired motif in the "negative" were used, and were applied to the still fresh clay prior to firing. The motifs were generally formed from a combination of lines, dots, ovals and lozenges. In another technique, stamps were employed to create the relief decoration found on bowls, perfume vessels, and jugs.

Bowl, beaker and cup, Petra

1st century A.D.
Red clay; pink engobe
Bowl: height 6 cm, diam. 15 cm, painted brown (interior) and black (exterior)
Beaker with horizontal rim: height 7.6 cm, diam. 9 cm
Cup: height 7.4 cm, max. diam. 7 cm, base diam. 4.5 cm
Archeological Museum, Amman

Painted Nabataean ceramics such as these were probably considered luxury goods, although they have been found in great quantities in Petra. The distribution of this extremely common type of pottery is generally taken as proof of an autonomous Nabataean culture.

Terracotta statuettes

When the kilns of Zurrabe were excavated, numerous terracotta statuettes were found depicting gods, animals, and people. The Egyptian goddess Isis was a popular motif in this folk art. One of these statuettes shows her seated and clutching the corner of her robe with her left hand; her head, crowned with stylized lotus blossoms and a crescent moon, is slightly inclined in an attitude of grief and is supported by her right hand. Also well-preserved is a piece showing a group of musicians as they probably appeared during a *thiasoi*. Two women sit on either side of a man on a bench, and all three have their feet on a sort of cushion. The woman at the right plays a lyre, her counterpart an unknown stringed instrument, while the man plays a double flute. Both women are clothed in veils and tunics with a V-neck and piping. The man's hair is held in a band, and his robe features twisted braid trimming at the hem. Also among the statuettes is one of a clean-shaven, naked young man; several examples of this type, with its raised right hand, feature a crescent moon in the form of a pendant. The figures have been interpreted as either a god or a votive statuette. There are also pieces which show a bearded figure with a pointed cap representing a priest. Of the animal statuettes the most common are those of dromedaries and horses in full harness; occasionally they are mounted.

Nabataean culture – A tribute

In spite of several attempts by the Greeks and, later, the Romans to seize the wealth of this nomadic, trading people the Nabataeans were able to maintain their independence for over 400 years. They achieved this through diplomacy and the creation of client structures as well as the exercise of military strength. On today's map their territory would stretch from Arabia through the Negev to Jordan and Syria. They established numerous cities, employed hydrological techniques, and succeeded in creating agriculturally productive land in a hostile environment. Their most impressive monuments were their cities whose most famous works – the rock tombs of Petra – have survived in an excellent state.

The material culture of the Nabataeans (several examples of which – such as architectural decoration, jewelry or coins – have not been discussed here) testifies to the high degree of perfection achieved by this civilization. The development of their own alphabet to record their language – a dialect of Aramaic – is further proof of this. The magnificent tomb inscriptions at Hegra and a text at the Turkmaniye Tomb in Petra are of the greatest elegance. Arabic script was developed from Nabataean, and some of the first inscriptions in the Arabic language were written with the aid of the Nabataean alphabet: this is evidence of the great respect still accorded this script two to three hundred years after the disappearance of the independent Nabataean kingdom.

Petra, the former capital of Nabataea, is on UNESCO's World Cultural Heritage list and attracts tens of thousands of visitors every year; this means that monuments threatened by natural erosion are being subjected to even further stress. French and German research programs are endeavoring to find solutions which will enable the rock of this ancient city to be safeguarded for future generations.

Group of musicians, Petra

1st century A.D.
Orange terracotta; height 8.7 cm, width 9.2 cm, circ. 2.5 cm
Archaeological Museum, Amman

Groups of musicians such as these with double flutes and lyres probably played during the ceremonies of the *thiasoi*.

Opposite

Tomb entrance, Petra

Conspicuous features in this detailed view are the magnificent colors on both sides of the door as well as the marked erosion of the lower half of the doorframe. The upper section consists of a stepped entablature supporting a triangular pediment.

Damaged facade of a tomb, Petra

Groups of researchers are carrying out intensive work to find solutions to the problem of wind and sand erosion, as well as ways of preventing the damage caused by rising damp.

Pierre-Louis Gatier

The Levant during the early Byzantine era

The Golden Age of eastern Christianity

4th–7th century A.D.

The Great Shrine, Qalat Seman

The Great Shrine at Qalat Seman dates from
the 5th century A.D. and is dedicated to St.
Simeon Stylites. Simeon had a column built in
the vicinity of the village so that he could live
his life of asceticism halfway between heaven
and earth. This is a view of the central octagon
and the east wing of the cruciform shrine.

Christianity asserts itself in the eastern empire

In the early 4th century A.D., the Roman Empire was shaped by two developments in which Constantine the Great (324–337) played a decisive role. First of all, with the Edict of Milan of 313, he ushered in a positive policy towards Christianity. The persecution of the Christians stopped and Christian religious services were first tolerated and then encouraged, until in 337, on the day before his death, Constantine himself was baptized.

This enabled Christianity to establish itself firmly in society, and the only one of Constantine's successors to attempt to return to paganism, Julian (361–363), who was dubbed Apostata, or "the renegade," was unable to achieve this goal. On the other hand, in 324 Constantine founded a second imperial capital, Byzantium, situated at the point where the Black Sea met the Aegean Sea, between the Balkans and Asia Minor, which became Constantinople, and in 330 it was dubbed the "New Rome."

The founding of Constantinople was a watershed in the division of the Roman Empire. Although during

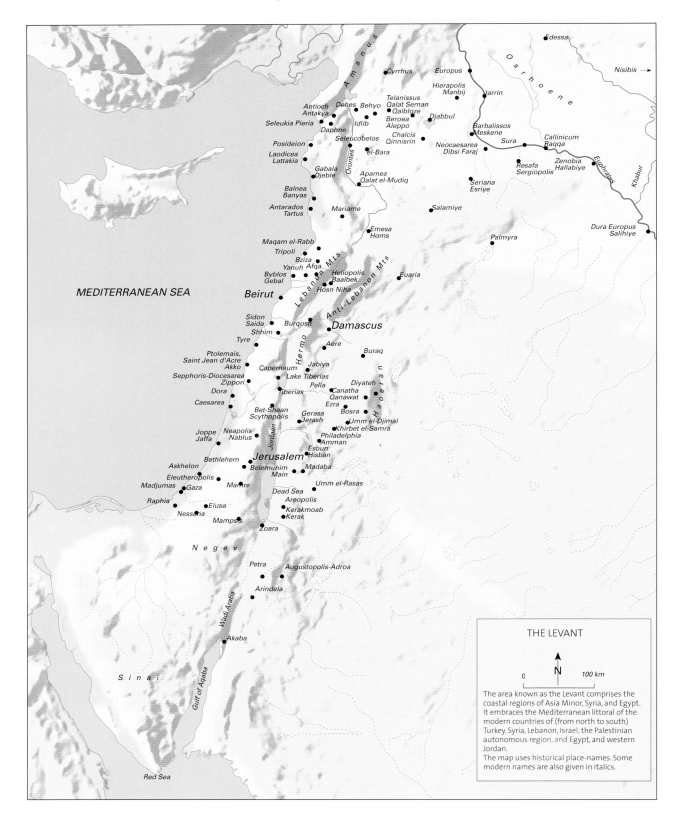

THE LEVANT

0   100 km

The area known as the Levant comprises the coastal regions of Asia Minor, Syria, and Egypt. It embraces the Mediterranean littoral of the modern countries of (from north to south) Turkey, Syria, Lebanon, Israel, the Palestinian autonomous region, and Egypt, and western Jordan.
The map uses historical place-names. Some modern names are also given in italics.

the 4th century the two halves of the Roman Empire – the western half, administered from Rome, and the eastern half, administered from Constantinople – were ruled by a single emperor, ultimately it split into two halves. The last emperor to rule both halves of the Empire simultaneously was Theodosius I, who died in 395.

Historians usually refer to the eastern empire, ruled from Constantinople, where Christianity gradually asserted itself, as the Byzantine Empire. It should not, however, be forgotten that its inhabitants regarded themselves as Romans, whether they lived in the Crimea, in southern Egypt, on the Tigris, or by the Danube. Western historians tend to regard the end of classical antiquity and the beginning of the Middle Ages as being marked, among others, by the events of the 5th century, marking the end of the history of Rome as the imperial capital, be they the sacking and conquests of Rome (in 410, 455 and 472) or the overthrow of the last western Roman emperor Romulus Augustus in 476. However, for the eastern Mediterranean this demarcation of events is irrelevant. Here it was the Muslim campaigns which began in the 630s which marked the end of the period of classical antiquity. Nevertheless, since early Islamic civilization can also be regarded as the heritage of Byzantium, it can be regarded as a historical transition rather than a break. The three centuries from the beginning of Constantine's reign until the Islamic campaigns by the Muslims are defined as the early Byzantine period. Sometimes parts of this period, or all of it, are described as early Christianity or late antiquity.

The territory of the Levant does not quite coincide with the Byzantine diocese described as "Oriens." This diocese embraced a group of provinces that covered areas from the south of Asia Minor all the way to the Red Sea, including the Sinai desert. It included Cyprus and extensive areas east of the Euphrates. However, the heart of this diocese, stretching from Gaza in the south to Cyrrhus in the North – or from the Negev to the Amanus, the mountains between Cilicia and Syria – can be defined as the early Byzantine Levant. The area's present division into different countries of course no longer reflects what it was in antiquity, and one should take care to distinguish the Byzantine provinces of Phoenicia, Syria, Palaestina, and Arabia from their present-day successors.

Today the term "Byzantine" is rarely used with positive connotations. The taint of decadence attached to these times is, however, the result of historical prejudice and is in no way a true reflection of reality. The early Byzantine era was substantially a time of economic development and population growth in the Levant. Archaeologists have established that population density, comparable only to that of the end of the Bronze Age, was not repeated during the subsequent Islamic era until this century. Because of the increasing number of villages, the growth of

cities, the construction of fine buildings, the development of crafts and the abundance of artistic creativity, the early Byzantine era can be regarded as a golden age.

Even though the period can certainly be described as a period of flowering, it should not be forgotten that it was shattered by a deep crisis during the mid 6th century. The end of Byzantine (or Roman) rule in the Levant was marked by a disastrous political decline and a long-term economic downturn. Despite the difficulties of these final decades, however, archaeological finds and the remains of buildings, as well as the works of literature and art that were created here, are evidence of the vitality of Byzantine civilization. There is no region where the culture of these three centuries is so abundantly evident as that between the Amanus Mountains and the Sinai desert.

Basilica, Qalbloze

The basilica at Qalbloze, in the northern Syrian limestone massif, is one of the most outstanding examples of early Christian architecture.

Excavations, Bet She'an

The tell of Bet She'an, overlooking from the northeast the city of Scythopolis, formerly the capital of the province of Palaestina Secunda, where remains from many periods, including the early Byzantine period, have been revealed.

Large urban residence, Bosra

Bosra is the ancient city of Bostra, capital of the Byzantine province of Arabia. This large residence is also known as "Trajan's Palace."

The geography of power

The whole Byzantine Empire was divided into extensive administrative districts known as dioceses, established by the reforms of the Roman emperor Diocletian (284–305). The diocese of "Oriens" was ruled by a civil administrator known as the *comes Orientis*, and a military commander known as the *magister militum per Orientum*. Both of them lived in Antioch, the capital of the diocese. This principle of separating civilian and military authority was reflected further down the administrative hierarchy: the provinces which came under the diocese were administered by governors posted to the individual provincial capitals, for example Antioch, which was the capital of the small province of Syria Prima. Military commanders, or *duces*, were only found in the frontier provinces. Thus for the region of the Levant, from north to south, we know of a *dux* for Osrhoene, one for Syria and Euphratensis, one for Phoenicia, one for Arabia and finally one for Palestine.

From the reign of Constantine to that of Heraclius (610–641), the last Emperor, who ruled the Levant before the Muslim conquest, the provinces were repeatedly reorganized to make them smaller and more numerous. This trend had already begun in the previous era; it was continued and implemented with increasing frequency up until the reign of Justinian

(527–565). At that time the provincial administration in the region west of the Euphrates was made up of the following provinces: Syria Prima with its capital Antioch (Antakya); Syria Salutaris with its capital Apamea (Qalat el-Mudiq); Theodorias with its capital Laodicea (Latakia); Euphratensis with its capital Hierapolis (Membij); Phoenice Prima with its capital Tyre; Phoenice Libanensis with its capital Emesa (Homs); Arabia with its capital Bostra (later Bosra);

Centrally planned church, Bosra

View of the chancel apse of the church (6th century), dedicated to SS. Leontius, Sergius and Bacchus.

Palaestina Prima with its capital Caesarea; Palaestina Secunda with its capital Scythopolis (Bet She'an); and Palaestina Tertia (or Salutaris) with its capital Petra.

The general trend of reducing the size of the provinces can be put down partly to administrative problems and partly to the wish to prevent too much power from falling into the hands of the governors. Another reason was to enable taxes to be collected and justice to be administered effectively. During the early Byzantine period control over the provinces from Constantinople was heightened. Again, it was for the purposes of curbing power that the *duces* only commanded frontier troops stationed in camps and forts, known as *limitanei*; in case of war, the nucleus of the troops deployed was the central army.

Inside the provinces, the polis made up the most important framework for exercising power in the Greco-Roman tradition. The Roman Empire could be described as a federation of cities, and this is what the early Byzantine empire to some extent remained. A polis consisted of a capital, and the surrounding area from which the city drew its resources, known as the chora. The leading citizens belonged to the curia, which was responsible for governing them and for bringing in taxes; the status of the curia member was hereditary and obligatory. Public peace and the smooth running of the system depended on good relations between the curias and the provincial governors. The "Letters" and "Speeches" of the orator Libanius, a late 4th-century curia member from Antioch, illustrate the complexity of the system of authority in the cities. Relations were strained at the time between the ordinary curia members and the *honorati*, a group of persons higher up in the hierarchy, made up of the former high officials and military officers. The curia members, on whose behalf Libanius spoke, valued their privileges and the traditional ideology of the polis, which in their view should be self-governing, so it was difficult for them to quietly accept the inconsiderate interference of the central authorities. Due to the heavy burdens of office they carried, some of them did however avoid the office of curia member. This was made possible through a variety of functions and offices, for instance joining the priesthood. In this way the number of curia members gradually declined, despite all the emperor's efforts to increase them.

Excavations, Bet She'an

The city's nymphaeum was destroyed during the earthquake of 749.

Remains of a settlement at Mampsis

This major settlement in the province of Palaestina Tertia, with its city walls and garrison, probably became a polis in the 6th century.

The growing number of poleis during the Byzantine era illustrates how this structure functioned. Settlements that grew around military camps, such as Sura on the Euphrates, were given the title and status of a polis, as were villages such as Euaria in Phoenice Libanensis, Gabala in Syria Prima or Mampsis in Palaestina Tertia. In addition to these there were settlements founded in Hellenic times that for centuries had had a nominal presence, and which were promoted to the status of polis in the early Byzantine period. Examples are Seleucobelos at Apamea and Europus in Euphratensis. This phenomenon, common throughout the Levant, particularly applied to the areas which had been least urbanized during the early Roman period.

The province of Palaestina Tertia provides a good example of the development of the poleis. It developed in stages, spreading from areas south of Gaza or south and east of the Dead Sea, which had previously been part of the provinces of Palaestina and Arabia. The poleis founded during the early Roman period were very few in number. They were the capital Petra, Kerakmoab (Kerak), and Areopolis (Rabba) east of the Dead Sea. Of the military bases that were named as poleis, Ayla (Aqaba) on the Red Sea was the most important. Numerous new poleis also emerged: these were Augustopolis-Adroa, east of Petra, Arindela, Zoora, Mampsis, Bitarus, Elusa, and Saltus Hieraticus, a former imperial estate. In the late 6th century, to these were added Mamspara as well as the two districts Pentakomia and Metrokomia. The element *kome* (Greek: "village") indicates that they were former villages or groups of villages (*pente* being the Greek for "five") which had grown in status.

Numerous cities throughout the Levant were given names reflecting their devotion to the emperor, or in some cases the privileges they had acquired. Under the Constantinian dynasty the name Constantia was frequently used: both for Antarados and Madjumas at Gaza, two ports that were promoted to the status of cities, as well as a city in the province of Arabia which is present-day Buraq. Other examples from Syria include Leontopolis, which replaced the old name of Callinicum (Raqqa), and Burqush, which was named Iustinianupolis. Other changes of name reflected the religious traditions of a city, or a wish to underline its sanctity. For example, Antioch was renamed Theupolis, the "City of God," Jerusalem was simply called "Holy City," and Resafa was named Sergiopolis or "St. Sergius' City." These names, which were tantamount to titles, were part of the competitive strategy that existed among the cities. The poleis of a single province, and also the capitals of neighboring provinces, were in constant competition. The creation of the province of Theodoria, whose capital was Laodicea, was the result of an old hatred between this city and Antioch, the capital of Syria Prima, at whose cost the new province was created. In Euphratensis the capital Hierapolis was in competition with Cyrrhus (which became Hagiopolis) and with Sergiopolis (Resafa) in its function as provincial capital, as well as with Antioch, the capital of the diocese of Oriens. Not only did local pride, privilege, and titles play a role in this competition, but also tax concessions and rivalry for the emperor's favor.

From the 4th century onwards the Church tended to reflect the Empire's structure in its administrative division. The provincial capitals, or metropoles, were under the authority of the metropolitan bishops, who were ranked above the bishops of the other cities. Above these were four patriarchs, whose seats were in the diocese capitals of Rome, Constantinople, Alexandria, and Antioch. The Patriarch of Antioch enjoyed only limited authority and was only provisionally established, having to resist threats to his authority twice in the course of the 5th century. The first was in 431, when the Bishop of Cyprus was given the privilege of autocephaly, which in effect released him from his subordination to Antioch, and the second was in 451, when Juvenal, Bishop of Jerusalem, succeeded in elevating his bishopric to the status of patriarchate. He was even given the opportunity to control Palaestina Prima, whose capital was the city of Caesarea, in order ultimately to prevail over the three provinces of Palestine. After freeing himself from subordination to Antioch, Juvenal tried in vain to annex the province of Arabia and its Bosra-based metropolitan bishop to Jerusalem; however, Arabia remained under the authority of Antioch.

Internal view of city walls, Resafa

These 6th century city walls served to protect the pilgrims' shrine of St. Sergius.

Each polis was ruled by a bishop and was, within the ecclesiastical province which coincided administratively with a province proper, subject to a hierarchical order, although this did not prevent internal conflicts from arising. The cities and their bishops competed strongly for the title of Metropolitan Bishop, and bitter struggles were fought within the hierarchy below. The sense of competition between individuals or poleis (known in ancient Greece as *agones*), was reflected in various ways in the early Byzantine period.

Monumental northern gate, Resafa

The gleaming gypsum rock of which the buildings of Sergiopolis (Resafa) were built resembles marble.

The hierarchy of power

The villages were the smallest administrative unit, and these were situated in the territory of poleis and subordinate to them. The curia members there had the task of collecting taxes for the central authorities in the villages. They were also responsible for raising taxes, and their estates acted as security. It is not currently known wheater village officials existed, and, if so, what status they had, or the degree to which villages could manage their own affairs. What has come down to us, such as the title of *pistikos* coined for the Province of Arabia, at least shows that the upper stratum of village – society did exercise some form of power. Some villages managed to upgrade their status to that of a polis, where a town wall, a port, a market, or public baths gave them a civic appearance. In the ecclesiastical sphere, some villages were the seats of chora or rural bishops, who were subordinate to the polis bishops. Later on, the *periodeutus* replaced the chora bishop, and under the leadership of the bishop exercised local authority at a lower level. Here again there was fierce competition, in which the strongest emerged with the

status of a see and the title of polis. An example is Belemunim (Main), which in the 6th century achieved promotion, thus attaining independence from the territory of Madabas in Arabia.

Unlike the settled inhabitants, very little is known about the nomads inhabiting the region. The emperors had an interest in winning tribes over to them in order to make use of their military capabilities. Their method was to recognize the authority of the most influential tribal chieftains by bestowing on them official titles, such as that of the phylarch, having them baptized and paying them for their loyalty and participation in military operations. The use of so-called Saracen or "camp bishops" made it possible both to guarantee a certain degree of religious independence for the phylarchs, and to guarantee the nomads' involvement on the side of the Christian emperor. The Ghassanid phylarchs profited most from this policy, which proved very costly for the empire and never worked smoothly, since there was too much mistrust on both sides. The Byzantines never seemed able fully to control the complex distribution of power in the world of the Arab tribes; revolts, acts of treachery, and raids were part and

View of Hallabiye

The northern wall, the "law courts," and the citadel rising above the Euphrates.

parcel of relations between the Empire and the tribal chieftains.

The head of the state apparatus was the emperor, whose power had grown significantly compared with that of the Roman emperor. This was further reinforced by the religious aspect of his office. The emperor's seat was Constantinople, which made him even more unreachable, although emperors during the 4th century are reported to have spent long periods in Antioch – in particular Constantius II, who stayed there from 337 to 350, and Valens, who stayed there from 371 to 378. Their stays were not connected with military operations on the eastern front. Others spent less time there, such as Julian the Apostate (361–363) who was passing through on his way to the east in 362 and wrote his "Misopogon," a satire against the inhabitants of Antioch who mocked him for his philosopher's beard.

Some two or three centuries later, in the year 630, Heraclius moved into Jerusalem to return the True Cross, which he had reclaimed from the Sassanids. Otherwise, the Holy City played host mainly to women of the imperial family. In 326 St. Helena, Constantine the Great's mother, joined a pilgrimage to Jerusalem, where she was said to have discovered the True Cross; the empress Eudocia, Theodosius II's wife, visited the holy shrines from 438 to 439, and settled in Palestine in 442, dying there in 460. Her granddaughter followed her example in 471.

Civil engineering works carried out under Constantine during the 4th century and under Justinian in the 6th century offer examples of the emperor's decisive role in building. Constantine set in motion a program for religious buildings at holy shrines: the Church of the Holy Sepulchre in Jerusalem, the Church of Eleona on the Mount of Olives, the Church of the Nativity in Bethlehem and the Terebinthian shrine at Mamre near Hebron. This policy also embraced Tyre and Antioch, where he funded magnificent cathedrals. Justinian's buildings in the Levant are innumerable, starting from the city walls of Zenobia (Hallabiye), Cyrrhus or Chalcis, to more modest structures, such as a large cistern in Madaba and the hospice of Bosra, and magnificent churches such as the Nea, the "New Church" in Jerusalem. Justinian had Antioch rebuilt after its destruction by an earthquake in 526. The Levant was particularly favored by the emperor's generosity, both in the fortification of cities threatened by the Persians and in the decoration of existing holy shrines. Thus the empress Eudocia, according to a contemporary author, had so many churches, monasteries, and hospices built for the poor and the elderly that it was impossible to count them.

Mosaic, Madaba

Each building on this mosaic is a church symbolizing a city-state. The mosaic is from Main, the Byzantine Belemunim.

Byzantine coins

4th–6th century
Bronze/gold; diam. approx. 20 mm
Museo Nazionale Romano, Rome
Musée d'Art et d'Histoire, Geneva
private collection, Munich

The four gold coins depict the great rulers of Constantinople who reigned from the 4th to the 6th century (left to right): Constantine the Great (324–337), profile with a diadem, Valens (364–378), "resitutor republicae," in profile, Theodosius I (379–395), profile, and Justinian (527–565), full portrait, wearing a crown and carrying an imperial orb.

Kharab Shams

Located on the North-Syrian limestone massif, the village has two churches based on basilica ground plans: the old church in the foreground and the church from the 6th century in the background, seen from the south.

War and peace

The most important threat to the Byzantine Empire was from the east. Rivalry between the Mediterranean world and an empire that was centered in Lower Mesopotamia and in the highlands of today's Iran had existed for a long time. This situation, which had been replayed frequently in antiquity, characterized international relations as a whole between the 4th and 7th centuries. Byzantium's military problems with the empire of the Persian Sassanids weakened both sides and ultimately led to the disappearance of the Sassanid Empire and the collapse of the Byzantine Levant during the 7th century.

The Sassanid dynasty had in the 3rd century taken over from the Arsacid dynasty, which stood at the head of an enormous empire stretching from today's Central Asian republics in the east to Afghanistan and Pakistan. The place where the Byzantines and the Sassanid empires met was the valley of the Euphrates and in southern Khabur, where Circensium, a fortified Byzantine city, had long served as an outpost. The Khabur valley itself was in Byzantine hands, but to the north the Taurus valley, with the massif of Tur Abdin and the cities of Amida, Dara, and Nisibis, as well as the entire region between the Khabur and the Tigris, was an extensive

region in which the rivals frequently clashed in border disputes. The Byzantine provinces of Osrhoene and Mesopotamia, east of the Euphrates, largely acted as a buffer for the northern regions of Syria up to a line joining Palmyra, Emesa, and Tripolis. Further to the north Armenia felt the pressure of the two powerful rivals.

The conflict between the Sassanids and the Byzantines was primarily that of two empires that regarded themselves as having sole entitlement to supremacy, and whose official ideologies appeared to deny the other's right to existence.

Religion was a primary factor in the conflict. In the Persian empire, the caste of the wise men, the high priests of the Mazdaist religion, played an important role in several waves of persecution against the Christians. The Christians were regarded as internal enemies, or a "fifth column" working for Byzantium. The teachings of Nestorius, which had previously been tolerated in the Byzantine Empire, were proscribed by the Council of Ephesus in 431, after which its followers had emigrated to the neighboring Sassanid Empire. The Sassanid kings realized that it was in their own interests to tolerate and use this group of Christians, who no longer aroused suspicion of treachery. Nestorianism was therefore able to develop considerably in Lower

Mesopotamia, and many Nestorian missionaries set out to convert the distant lands of Central Asia, the Persian Gulf and southern India. The Sassanid rulers themselves remained faithful to the religion of their forefathers, although they would not hesitate to marry Christian women.

Commercial interests can also be seen as playing a part in the conflicts, although they can also be regarded as simple levers used to exert pressure. The best-known episode of this kind is the adventure of the oriental monk who, under orders from the Emperor Justinian, had used a hollow staff to smuggle silkworms into the Roman Empire. The Persians had tried to prevent the spread of silkworms in order to protect their role as intermediaries in the silk trade. Although this story may to some extent be apocryphal, it does illustrate the importance of luxury goods in international trade, and the Sassanid empire's advantageous position. The Byzantines for their part regulated the sale of metals which were used to produce weapons.

The conflict between these two large empires also led to pacts with the Arab tribes of the vast steppe lands that bordered the Fertile Crescent. Thus two rival groups emerged: in Lower Mesopotamia, the city of el-Hira had since the 3rd century been the residence of the Lachmid dynasty which for its part exercised influence over the tribes allied with the Persians; a similar role on the other side was from the 5th century onwards played by the Ghassanid tribe, whose allegiance to Byzantium was obtained by the bestowing of official titles in the manner described above. Of these titles, the most frequent one was that of phylarch, which originated as a general term to describe an Arab tribal chieftain, but then became the official rank of the captain of auxiliary troops fighting for the empire. The highest-ranking title was that of king, which was given to the Ghassanid ruler al-Mundhir in 580.

Djabiya in the Golan Heights, one day's travel south of Damascus, where the Ghassanids often resided, cannot be described as their capital, as they had various strongholds distributed over several provinces. It can therefore be assumed that a building outside the city walls and to the north of Resafa served as al-Mundhir's audience chamber. As we have seen, Resafa was named Sergiopolis in honor of the Christian martyr St. Sergius. Historians regard it as possible that the Ghassanids used the gatherings of the Arab tribes making the pilgrimage to Sergiopolis as an opportunity to display their power and to gather the Arab chieftains. In each war between Persians and Byzantines, troops of their Arab allies accompanied the armies in their campaigns, or carried out independent operations.

Nonetheless, relations between the Byzantines and their allies were strained and distrustful. There were three main reasons for this. One of these was the Byzantine emperor's wish to concede as little independence as possible to the phylarchs, whom he tried to treat as appointees rather than allies. Secondly, the Ghassanids professed Monophysitism, a Christian doctrine that was suppressed under Justinus I (518–257) and his nephew Justinian (527–565) and most of their successors. Finally the allies expected substantial payments to guarantee their allegiance, payments which the Byzantine treasury frequently failed to pay, which in turn led to dissatisfaction and revolts.

Triumphant ruler's medallion, Qalat el-Marqab

6th–7th century
Chased gold
Medallion: length 6 cm, diam. 5.4 cm; pendant: length 9.3/9.5 cm
Louvre, Paris

Picture of a triumphant ruler on a chariot, flanked by the winged goddess of victory.

From Justinian to the Persian conquests

The early 6th century marked a turning point in the military history of the Levantine provinces. Until Justinian's reign they, unlike the regions bordering with Persia, had not suffered war on their territory. At the end of the 3rd century the Roman Empire had achieved its greatest expansion eastwards in the campaigns of Galerius (296–297). This gave the Romans territories beyond the Tigris. Throughout the 4th century the clash of weapons resounded all along the eastern front. From 337 to 350 Constantius II fought the Sassanids – a period when he also stayed in Antioch. The war was resumed in 359. The new emperor, Julian the Apostate, arrived in Antioch in 362 in order to prepare for a campaign aimed at Lower Mesopotamia and Ctesiphon, the capital of the Sassanid empire.

Thanks to the soldier Ammianus Marcellinus (who, although from Antioch, wrote in Latin), we have a report of this campaign and its failure. Ammianus sympathized greatly with Julian, although he did not hesitate to expose his mistakes in his reports. In July of the next year, the emperor was killed in battle. His insignificant successor Jovian (363–364) negotiated peace in the empire and secured the retreat of the army in return for important regions, including the city of Nisibis east of the Euphrates, which was regarded as the shield of the Orient.

Although it had ended in disaster, Julian's campaign did not have any major implications for the Levant, or at least no more than did Valens' later wars from 370 to 378 and Anastasius I's wars from 502 to 505. The operations concentrated on the regions east of the Euphrates, and in particular on the regions between the major cities of Amida (Diyarbakir), Nisibis and Edessa. Syria, which was the Byzantine army's main support in the rear, probably had more problems than just the passage of the army. Generally, however, the 5th century was a long period of peace for the Levant.

After Justinian's reign, however, things changed. The focus of the 527–531 war was a major operation by the Persians' allies, the Lachmidiae. In 529 northern Syria was subjected to Persian raids which reached as far as the chora of Antioch. After four years of war with Khosrow I of Persia, Justinian made a peace treaty in which he made many concessions. However, in 540 the war was resumed by the Persians, and continued – a number of cease-fires aside – until 562. Many cities were occupied and sacked, including Sura, Beroea (Aleppo), and in particular Antioch in the year 540. The Persians did not try to occupy the territory, but to weaken it by looting, destroying cities and mass deportations of the population. The rural population, although contemporary authors scarcely mention it, suffered more from this than the urban population.

Church and city walls, Hallabiye

The church, viewed from the citadel, with the south and east city walls, overlooking the Euphrates.

In 572, Justinian II (565–578) resumed the war, which lasted for a total of 20 years, and was continued by Tiberius II (578–582) and by Maurice (582–602). This long period was marked by the capture of Apamea in 573, in which 292,000 people were said to have been deported. The environs of Antioch were again laid waste. This phase of the war affected only northern Syria.

One disadvantage for Byzantium was that in 590 and 591 Maurice had helped Khosrow II of Persia to regain the Sassanid throne from his rival, Bahram, a Persian general. In 591 the emperor finally managed to impose peace on the Persians, but when Phocas the usurper had him assassinated in 602, Khosrow II invaded Syria and Asia Minor. The Persians soon captured and pillaged all of the cities up to Jerusalem, which fell in 614. The invaders removed the True Cross from the holy city, which became deserted as a result of massacres and deportations. Thus Syria and Palestine were under Persian rule from 611 to 629. The Emperor Heraclius (610–614), who in 610 overthrew Phocas, started a reconquest of Asia Minor in 622, after which he invaded Mesopotamia. His counter-offensive ousted the Persians from Palestine and Syria, and in 630 he was able to take the True Cross back to Jerusalem.

However, the scale of the destruction caused by the Persian occupation of the Levant should not be overestimated, even if Jerusalem was badly affected. Internal tensions between Jews and Christians, Monophysites and Chalcedonites, between desert nomads and settled people, were revived and re-kindled. The Persians, however, allowed the Christians to repair buildings that they had destroyed in Jerusalem, and they tried, having supported the local religious minorities – the Jews in Palestine, the Nestorians or Monophysites in Northern Syria and along the Euphrates – to reinstate the local balance of power. The Persian conquest was something of a dress rehearsal for the events that were to be played out during the later Islamic conquest. Cities, led by their bishops, negotiated the reopening of their gates. However, any resistance was violently suppressed, and the conquerors skillfully employed religious differences to help achieve this.

Given this chaotic history of war, the long peaceful interval which lasted until 529 A.D. is remarkable, as it spared the Levant the consequent devastation. However, the disputes between the regions put great strains on it. Between 529 and 613 only Syria was sacked, after which war broke out in southern Syria and Palestine. Aside from this, internal conflicts, tribal rebellions, or Jewish and Samaritan uprisings broke the apparent peace of the Byzantine Levant.

The most manifest effects of the period of numerous battles can be seen in the remnants of fortifications of cities in the Levant, of which the best preserved are those in the valley of the Euphrates, in Zenobia (Hallabiye), Barbalissus (Meskene),

Neocesarea (Dibsi Faraj), and in Resafa in the Syrian plains. The majority of cities strengthened or rebuilt their fortifications, as can be seen in Palmyra or Cyrrhus. The city of Chalcis (Qinnisrin) was fortified by the engineer Isidorus of Miletus, who is famous for his major role in the construction of Hagia Sophia in Constantinople.

Tower, Umm el-Rasas

The fort of former Mefaa was built for protection against the nomads of the Jordanian desert (Provincia Arabia). Later the fort grew into a large settlement with a watchtower in its center.

Population and settlements

The Levant was inhabited by groups which, although distinguishable according to various criteria such as language, religion, origin, and lifestyle, cannot be divided into neat categories. In addition, the terms used by ancient writers are not very accurate, which means that administrative districts and populations were often confused. For example, the word "Phoenician" at that time was used to describe all the inhabitants of both the provinces of Phoenice Libanensis and Phoenice Prima. A citizen of Palmyra, Damascus or Emesa would thus be described as a Phoenician, as would somebody from Tyre, Berytos (Beirut) or Ptolemais (Akko or Acre).

Modern historians uses the term "Arab" to describe peoples whose mother tongue was Arabic or which belonged to the Arabic language group. In the old days, "Arab" meant any inhabitant of the Arabian peninsula. However, it was also used to describe people who lived in certain steppe or desert zones on the fringes of settled populations, as well as the populations of cities and regions temporarily ruled by dynasties stemming from nomadic peoples. In this way Emesa or Edessa were sometimes described as "Arab." Everyone from the province of Arabia was called an Arab, such as the Roman Emperor Philippus Arabs (244–249), who was born in the Hauran region. The original nomads, some of whom were settled to a greater or lesser extent, were sometimes designated as "Saracens" (a term of unknown origin), "Scenites" (tent-dwellers), or with the biblical terms of "country-dwellers" or "Ishmaelites." There are also references to Scenite Arabs. It was only after the Muslim conquest that the Byzantines described their conquerors as Arabs. Although there is no doubt that the Byzantine Ghassanid auxiliaries were Arabs in the linguistic sense of the word, it is hard to ascertain to what degree the Levant was Arabic before the conquest. We should bear in mind that Greek papyrus scrolls of the 6th century, which were found in Petra in 1992, actually use Arabic forms in their toponyms and vocabulary, indicating that they were in use in this particular area of Palaestina.

The Levant was largely bilingual: some people spoke Aramaic, while others spoke Greek. Part of the population probably spoke only Greek, although most of them were probably not actually descended from Greeks who had settled in the Orient. Then there was a wide range of people who spoke and used both languages to varying degrees.

Recent excavations, Sepphoris-Diocesarea, Zippori

Buildings of varying sizes and differing functions have been uncovered in the residential districts.

Opposite, above

Mosaic with animal designs, Bet She'an

Some floors of houses and public buildings were covered with mosaics depicting mythological scenes, animals, plants or just geometric patterns.

Opposite, below

Excavations, Bet She'an

Scythopolis was the capital of the province of Palaestina Secunda. These columns were toppled by the earthquake of 749.

The Jews can be clearly distinguished, since their religion prescribed endogamy, which meant that they could only marry other Jews. After the revolts against the Roman emperor Hadrian and their subjugation during the 2nd century, they seemed to disappear completely from Jerusalem and its environs. Even if they were occasionally mentioned in relation to the city, particularly with reference to the remains of the Temple of Herod (which remains today, in the form of the Wailing Wall), they did not actually live in the city but had been banished from it. Nevertheless, at the end of the 6th century they seem to have resettled there. Jews were frequently found in Palaestina Secunda, both in the country, around Lake Tiberias, in the Golan heights, or the plain of Djesreel, as well as in the cities of Tiberias, Sepphoris-Diocesarea (Zippori) and Scythopolis (Bet She'an). Most of the ports along the Levant coast had Jewish communities, from Posideion in the north to Madjumas near Gaza in the south. Caesarea, Ptolemais, Tyre, and Berytos also seem to have had their own Jewish quarters. The Jewish Diaspora around the Mediterranean, in the Sassanid empire and on the Arabian peninsula was quite large, although there was also a "local Diaspora" concentrated in the inland cities of the Orient, and, occasionally, in the country. The Samaritans were comparable with the Jews. A religious community of Jewish origin, they also settled in Palestine, particularly around Neapolis (Nablus) and near the shrine of Mount Garizim in Palaestina Prima, as well as in the cities of Caesarea and Scythopolis.

Population structure and numbers

Historians know almost nothing about the birthrates, mortality and life expectancy, or family composition in the Levant during the early Byzantine period. Their assumptions are based on the structure of many pre-industrial communities, which would make the population of the early Byzantine Levant largely resemble that of medieval Europe, with a high birthrate, a high mortality rate, particularly among children, and a short average life expectancy.

However, it is not easy to estimate the total population, or the urban population. Ancient authors have left us some statistics. At the end of the 4th century, Antioch, the most populous city of the Levant, was according to the Greek Church Father John Chrysostom the home of 100,000 Christians. However, figures like these have to be treated with care, as in those times accurate population counts were impossible.

Old Church, Kharab Shams

The Old Church of Kharab Shams, seen from the south side. The other 6th century church was built on the hill in the background (not visible in photograph). Kharab Shams is one of the many villages on the northern Syrian limestone massif whose ruins bear witness to the region's flowering from the 4th to 6th centuries.

A period of growth

Numerous archaeological excavations carried out in the Levant, as well as the study of abandoned villages in the limestone hills of northern Syria, in the Hauran, the Golan or the Negev, make it possible to establish that this region was most densely populated in the early Byzantine era. There is hardly a locality which does not contain structures from late antiquity. A tell – an artificial mound – could come into being by different populations settling at the same place through the centuries, as for example Deinit tell near Idlib, which was abandoned in the Roman period. However, in the early Byzantine period houses and a church were built at the foot of the artificial mound and on its incline. Using the flat peripheries of the tells also would appear to have been common at that time.

Two examples illustrate the density of human population: a study of 120 archaeological sites along the two roads leading from Jerusalem to Joppe (Jaffa) on the coast shows that 90 of them were mainly Byzantine and at 70 of these there were no earlier remains. Studies of the Syrian plain between Salamaniye and Aleppo in the west and the Euphrates in the east yielded similar results. Two major periods of settlement increased in importance: the Middle Bronze Age and the Byzantine era, the latter being far more significant in terms of the number of archaeological sites.

Villages were built everywhere, some of them, such as Khirbet el-Samra in Jordan, around a fort along a main road, and others, such as Seriana (Esriye) in the Syrian plain, around a disused pagan temple. Deep into the Negev, or in arid zones far eastwards, new settlements arose around staging posts, military buildings, springs, and wells. Diyate, on the edge of the Safa, is an example of how these peripheral zones were colonized. Umm el-Jimal developed around a Roman fort, using building materials from a Nabataean village which had been abandoned during the 3rd century. A wall was built around the settlement, extending about 870 yards (800 m) from north to south and about 650 yards (600 m) from east to west, thus making it the size of a small city. In addition to settlements such as these, there are also isolated farms from that time. They were often built in arid zones where the opportunities for farming were limited.

The development of villages

The number of villages and their size increased. In the limestone massif of northern Syria between the ancient cities of Antioch, Apamea, Beroea (Aleppo), and Chalcis, more than 100 villages were built on the hills of Jebel Seman, Jebel Halaqa, Jebel Barisha, Jebel Ala, Jebel Dueili, Jebel Wastani, and Jebel Zawiye – the largest and southernmost range. The entire area stretches about 60 miles (100 km) from north to south, and stretches a maximum 30 miles (50 km) from east to west, and is inaccurately known as the "dead cities" of northern Syria. They were not in fact cities which in any way – administrative status, appearance, or function – differed from villages. These abandoned villages, as they should properly be called, remain as substantial archaeological sites, which are being examined building by building and

room by room, revealing both the various construction phases of the houses, and the expansion of the settlements. The studies indicate that the period from 350 to 550 A.D. was one of continuous and sustained growth.

With no exact figures for the cities, the number of inhabitants has to be deduced from the studies of the buildings, although this is a contentious method. In Gerasa in Jordan, numerous churches in and around the center of the city as well as outside the city wall suggest a growth in population. The promotion of villages to the status of polis is a further indication of continued population growth.

View of the village of Bamuqqa

This village in the northern Syrian limestone massifs had two churches. The northern hills belonged to the Syrian capital of Antioch. Its growth depended on the prosperity and markets of the city.

Houses, Umm el-Jimal

This village was among the largest settlements of the province of Arabia, and due to its location on the edge of the plain even had a surrounding wall. The Byzantine village developed around a small Roman fort, and has an unusual internal layout, since inside the city walls there are isolated groups of houses, which have been interpreted as being the quarters of various Arab tribal groups.

Travelers and pilgrims

The Levant had a fairly regular influx of travelers visiting the holy shrines of Christendom, but the majority of pilgrims remained in Palestine for only a few weeks. In Syria in particular, the call of a monastery or a holy man was enough for disciples from all around to be attracted and to settle.

Alexander Akoimetos, who was born in the Greek islands and then lived in Constantinople, left there to settle in a monastery in northern Syria. Women from Roman high society, such as Paula and her daughter Eustochium, who are known from a cemetery in Bethlehem, moved to Palestine in 385 and lived the rest of their lives there in piety. They used their wealth to fund the construction of hospices and monasteries. St. Hieronymus lived in one such monastery from 389 to his death in 420. Another pious aristocratic woman, Paula's cousin Melania the Younger, spent the last years of her life in the nunneries of Palestine which she had founded. In addition to these famous personalities there were many monks from other parts of the empire, such as Chariton from Iconium in Asia Minor, who was one of the founders of monasticism in Palestine. Euthymius and Sabas, who founded monasteries in the Judaean desert, also originated in Asia Minor.

The foreign monks in Palestine occasionally organized separate communities within the same monasteries to enable them to speak their native language, or they set up separate monasteries. These communities included Latins, Thracians, Georgians (Caucasian Iberians), Copts, Armenians and Syrians. Texts and inscriptions reveal that large numbers of monks came from all corners of the Empire, from as far afield as Spain and Gaul or the Caucasus and the Sassanid empire.

Apart from monastic circles, there does not seem to have been much eastward migration from the western parts of the Empire. On the other hand, migration from Syria towards the west was fairly commonplace. Evidence of the emigration of Syrians are tomb inscriptions in Rome, Ravenna or Salona. Emigration from the chora of Apamea, the Anti-Lebanon Mountains or the province of Arabia seems been more widespread than from the more heavily populated inland regions, and concerned people of more modest status than Georgius the silk merchant from Antioch, who in 552 donated an estate to the church in Ravenna. As we have seen, in the 200 years from 350 to 550 A.D., the Levant enjoyed a population boom. An abundance of labor played an important role in economic development, although one

Baptistry, Bamuqqa

The numerous baptistries in northern Syria show that the baptism of children gradually became common practice in the villages. Adults were baptized in the city cathedral.

Cornice, Beshindlaya

Cornice with decorations characteristic of Syria in the Christian age: a medallion with a cross and floral motifs. The motif here is the spiny-leafed acanthus, which is typical of Christian art in the region during the 6th century.

Pyramid tomb, el-Bara

This Christian-era tomb is situated in one of the largest villages in northern Syria.

consequence of it was the overloading of rural areas and probably also overpopulation. However, in the middle of the 6th century a variety of factors brought about the end of this phase of growth. The wars that led to catastrophic devastation in northern Syria from 529 onwards were accompanied by epidemics. Starting in Egypt in 541, the bubonic plague was probably carried by ships across the Red Sea, and it raged throughout the empire. For over a century it flared up repeatedly, and its effects in the Orient have often been compared with those of the Black Death that engulfed Europe in 1348. The church historian Euagrius, who survived the plague, had first caught it in his childhood, and according to his report it returned on four occasions, including in 560/561. Among the reasons for the disastrous effects of the plague and for its spread were the highly concentrated urban and rural population, as well as their contact with travelers and soldiers.

The coincidence of crisis factors – a much larger population, in tandem with limited farming resources, as well as military conflicts and epidemics – allows us to assume that the decline of the population in the Levant, accompanied by an economic downturn, began in the mid 6th century.

and overland transport was slow. Throughout the Levant, pulses such as peas and lentils complemented the staple diet.

Animals were indispensable for plowing and tilling, and for transportation. The numerous Byzantine houses that have been preserved in the Hauran all have their own animal stalls, which can be recognized by rows of feeding troughs on the ground floor.

Agricultural methods seem hardly to have developed. In northern Syria, olives were mainly crushed by means of stone rollers; these were rolled back and forth in basins filled with olives by means of handles. This simple process made it possible, in a region where wood was scarce, to use only stone parts, but as a fairly laborious method it was only viable in comparison to the use of highly perfected presses thanks to the wide availability of labor.

A great distinction was made between crops requiring irrigation and those that did not. Irrigation systems were at the height of their development in the Byzantine years, and catered for far more than the requirements of individual gardens. Irrigation makes it possible to obtain higher yields from traditional crops, while many other crops cannot be grown at all without it. In Diyate, in a much drier zone east of the Hauran, farming was only possible with irrigation. The village was only able to exist thanks to its systems of levees, dams and channels that allowed the little water from the hillsides to be channeled to the terraces, and to direct the water from a seasonal river into the fields in the valley.

The Negev, where the average annual rainfall can vary from 90 mm at Nessana to 200 mm in Beersheba, is the region with the most highly perfected irrigation system. The principle is to capture trickles of water over a wide area and to collect them with a minimum of loss.

In the Syrian plain remains of large barrages have been found, but above all huge structures of foggaras (or qanats) – underground conduits designed to catch water and to channel it from star-shaped networks to a lower-lying central collector.

Building and maintaining these water systems must have been a large part of the work of the Byzantine farmers. Without the necessary skills in hydraulic engineering it would hardly have been possible to open up new areas in mountainous regions, and especially in the plains. Only the northern Syrian limestone hills seem to be almost completely lacking in water systems, because the very friable and absorbent soils here immediately soak up the rainwater. The few cisterns set up around the fields completed the system of waterworks.

Ampulla with cross, Beirut

5th/6th century
Clay; height 7 cm, length 5 cm
Department of Antiquities, Beirut

This phial was used by pilgrims to store sacred oil.

The economy – The importance of agriculture

Agriculture played a dominant role in economic output, and the majority of the population was engaged in it. In the ancient Mediterranean farming system, the most important crops were cereals, wine, and olives. Some areas specialized in growing a single crop. The limestone massif of northern Syria, where the arable land was littered with rocks and the soil was relatively poor, was used mainly for planting olive trees. Many regions were famed for their wines, in particular the areas around the coastal cities of Gaza and Askalon. Vineyards covered part of the Hauran and the region of Capitolias further south. Large wine-presses have been found in northern Jordan and in the Hauran. In many Lebanese coastal settlements, and in the foothills of the Lebanon Mountains, numerous olive presses have been found. Cereals were cultivated mainly in the plains, such as the region around Bosra, which was Syria's granary. According to records, there were also areas of specialized cultivation – of figs near Bosra, plums near Damascus, walnuts in Lebanon, and dates around the Dead Sea. In the main, however, mixed crops predominated, even in the specialized regions. Concentrating on one particular crop was simply not viable, as there was a large rural population to be fed,

Craftsmen and merchants

There seem to have been very few craftsmen and no merchants in the villages. Even pottery workshops seem to have been confined to the cities, and none at all are known to have existed in the chalk hills. Apart from agriculture, building was the only other major village activity. Surviving inscriptions therefore frequently mention bricklayers, stonemasons and carpenters. These seem to have served a number of villages, and tended to live in settlements whose size was halfway between that of a city and a village.

When they visited the cities, which they did for big religious festivals, the villagers survived on basic necessities, according to the writings of John Chrysostom. Itinerant traders also crossed the land, some traveling in groups, as we learn from the papyrus scrolls of Nessana. In addition, the country markets, which were often held on public holidays, allowed people to obtain goods and also acted as places of contact.

In Telanissus in northern Syria, a market used to be held at the foot of the monastery of St. Simeon Stylites, which St. Simeon was supposed to have been able to watch from his column.

The cities were of course preferred venues for manufacturing and trade. Inscriptions from Gerasa mention potters, smiths (or coppersmiths), traders, money-changers and goldsmiths. The fine ceramics that were produced during the 6th century in Gerasa, decorated with animals, plants, and themes from pagan mythology, as well as with crosses and saints, have been discovered in tombs throughout the northern half of Transjordan all the way to Capernaum and Scythopolis. In Bosra, which was renowned for the manufacture of weapons and of bells, there were guilds of goldsmiths, ironsmiths and wineskin makers, which made the city a center of the caravan trade. In the Life of Simeon Salos (the "fool"), there is a description of the ordinary people in the agora and the streets of Emesa. There were innkeepers and sellers of *posca* (a drink made of water, vinegar, and eggs), confectioners, a Jewish glazier and a wine merchant leading his mule.

The ports of the Levantine coast were particularly well known for their produce. In Tyre there were imperial workshops for the production of textiles, wool and silk, as well as purpling-houses – which also existed in Berytos. The list of trades which is to be found in the Tyre necropolis illustrates the importance of craftsmen who worked with purple dye, cloth and – as in Berytos – with glass. In addition there were also grain dealers, bakers, a fishmonger, a confectioner, a wine wholesaler, an olive oil supplier, vegetable gardeners, a coal-merchant, a sausage-maker, a *garum* (fish soup) seller, a second-hand dealer, a frankincense seller, a money-changer, carpenters, plasterers, a marble-carver, a smith, a locksmith, and a goldsmith. A part of the population in all major cities also consisted of ship owners and sailors. Many inland cities possessed workshops for imperial armaments or for cloth needed by the army or by government officials: Damascus and Antioch produced weapons, while Scythopolis produced linen clothing. Mattresses and blankets were made in Damascus, cheap clothing in Antioch. In wine producing regions such as Berytos, Gaza, and Ascalon, amphoras were manufactured .

With their craftsmen and merchants, who belonged to guilds and had to pay taxes and duties, the trades of the Byzantine Levant, often highly specialized, were almost of medieval standards. Small stalls that were set up in the streets or the colonnades – which were part of the majority of big cities – complete the picture. As the cities were places where consumers predominated, and where wealthy people lived, manufacturers of luxury goods must have also played an important role.

Opposite, above

Bangles, Beirut

Late 5th/early 6th century
Gold and semi-precious stones; diameter 10.2 cm
Louvre, Paris

The jewelers frequently mentioned in texts were also money-lenders. These bangles are finished with the heads of rams.

Flask, Syria

500–600 A.D.
Molded glass;
Height 15 dm, width 4.9 cm
Louvre, Paris

The Levant was famed for its glass. This flask has a cross on one side and a stylite saint at the back .

Cruciform pendant and earring, Tyre

6th century
Gold: height 2.5 cm/4.5 cm
Department of Antiquities, Beirut

Jewelry was used as decoration by families, but also added to its wealth. These ornaments were found in the necropolis of Tyre.

Domestic and foreign trade

The high cost of land transport made trade within the empire difficult. The main roads, or *viae publicae*, which were the successors to the Roman road system, were lined with milestones; the last of these contain inscriptions in praise of the emperor Julian the Apostate, although this does not mean that the roads were not subsequently maintained. Some stretches can be dated to Justinian's reign. Inns and roadhouses built at regular intervals were used by the public post services. The main roads ran from north to south: from Antioch to Apamea, Emesa, Damascus, Bosra, Philadelphia (Amman) and thence to Ayla (Aqaba) on the Red Sea.

For a long time it was believed that late antiquity was the period when the old road system was abandoned. However, all that can be established with certainty was that at this time no new major public roads were built. In addition to the main roads there was an intricate network of minor tracks and paths which were less convenient to use. They were almost impassable for wagons, so that here goods were usually carried on animals or by people, rather than driven in carts. There are few navigable rivers in the Levant. From Darkush onwards it was possible to sail down the Orontes. The Euphrates was navigable downstream, but was impossible to travel back up, and while the Dead Sea and Lake Tiberias could be crossed in small boats, the river Jordan was unnavigable. Transport therefore relied on the roads, and rivers were crossed by means of pontoon bridges (such as the Euphrates), stone bridges (like that at Cyrrhus) or by ferry (such as those that crossed the Jordan).

The best way of moving goods around was by sea. The ports, even less significant ones such as Madjumas near Gaza or Askalon, used their favorable situation for trade. A crossing from Palestine to Salonica or Constantinople could take from 13 to 20 days, while the return journey was quicker, and could be done in 10 to 12 days. The post system which used the overland routes, and which functioned very well, took six to seven times longer.

Seleucia Pieria, the harbor of Antioch at the mouth of the Orontes, was an important city which had a military role. Laodicea, Antarados (Tartus), which outshone the island of Arados opposite, Tripolis, which was famous for St. Leontios, Byblos, Berytos (Beirut), Sidon, Tyre, Ptolemais (Akko), Caesarea, Ascalon and finally Madjumas, by Gaza, bordered the Levant coastline from north to south. Good natural harbors, of which Tyre and Sidon were most important, were rare, but in many places additional harbor construction works were carried out. In Seleucia Pieria a new harbor was completed in 346. Often the "ports" were no more than fairly shallow, protected bays where the ships were pulled up onto the beach. What goods were traded through these ports is little known. In Posideion there are large quantities of *terra sigillata*, which was imported from Cyprus and north Africa. Excavations in Beirut have also brought such material to light, and it has been found in the majority of big excavations, together with what is termed phocaic pottery from Asia Minor.

Unfortunately we have no precise details about trade with the Far East and through the Red Sea. Palmyra remained a key city, whose fortifications were redesigned by Diocletian and then strengthened by Justinian. However, the city had to give up its role as a trading city, although since the defeat of Zenobia in the 3rd century it maintained its significance as a military post. Foreign trade was strictly controlled by the imperial authorities – both the Mediterranean and the Red Sea ports, all of which seem to have had customs posts, such as Ayla and the island of Jotabe (Tiran). The number of authorized trading points with the Persians was limited. For example, under Justinian only Callinicum on the Roman side and Nisibis and Artaxa further to the north on the Persian side were open for trade.

The scale of the caravan trade between the Arabian peninsula on the one hand and on the other the Province of Arabia, as well as the Palestinian and Syrian provinces, is still not known.

The economic crisis

We have already seen the importance of agriculture for feeding the rural population. The cities were big consumers of cereals and of oil, wine, wood for heating bath houses, wool, and linen. Monetary exchange was the normal form of trade in northern Syria, as the excavations at Dehes show. However, the economy proved to be unstable. The *Lives of the Saints* shows that spring rains which spoiled the first cereal crops, plagues of locusts, vineyard pests, and later on frost or, more frequently, long periods of drought, could spell disaster for the harvest. Due to the lack of flexibility of the markets and transport constraints, it was impossible to avoid starvation and the effects of epidemics.

Earthquakes and wars seem to have affected the cities of the Levant particularly severely during the 6th century. Antioch was shaken by numerous earthquakes, and in addition to this damage was that caused by the fires they started off. The two earthquakes of 526 and 528 were the worst of their kind and ultimately prompted the renaming of the Syrian capital as Theoplis ("city of god") in order to obtain divine protection. Phoenicia, too was subjected to this phenomenon. The famous earthquake of 503 devastated Ptolemais (Akko), Carmel and Tyre; the 551 earthquake, which was followed by flooding, destroyed Berytos (Beirut). If we add to this the aftermath of Persian military operations, we can date the decline or indeed the collapse of the urban markets to the 6th century.

Byzantine seal, Tyre

c. 570 A.D.
Seal: diameter 2.9–3.7 cm
Bibliothèque Nationale, Paris

Seal of two *kommerkiarioi* from Tyre. They depict the Byzantine emperor Justin II (565–578), his wife Sophia and his son, later the emperor Tiberius (578–582). The inscription gives the names of both merchants, Diogenes and Diomedes of Tyre, who were probably commissioned to supervise the production of silk.

Oil scales, Chime

5th–7th century
Bronze; length 39 cm
Department of Antiquities, Beirut

These scales were discovered beside an oil press, and are assumed to have been used for weighing olives.

At first, from 350 to 550, the economy of the Levant grew on the back of ongoing expansion. The increase of arable land in the mountainous and arid regions, and the constant establishing of new villages and the growth of existing ones played an important role here. The state of newly acquired arable land was fragile and needed intensive farming to produce only modest yields. It is possible that favorable climatic conditions contributed to this development, particularly in regions where a slight increase in rainfall could result in significant crop improvements. This phase was interrupted only by brief crises that resulted from bad harvests in one or two successive years.

In around 480 the extensive expansion into the limestone massif of northern Syria intensified due to the introduction of new technical developments. A growing number of large houses were built using new techniques. However, in around 550 it was no longer possible to stem the growing crisis. On the economic level, intensive over-use of the land by a much larger population played a role. In the plains and mountain regions the shallow topsoils became exhausted by excessive farming or grazing. Although entire regions were not abandoned en masse, a period of slow decline set in. The bustling villages lost their population and fell in size, the peripheral zones became deserted, while the cities acquired rural characteristics.

It is not certain whether this decline affected the entire region. It seems that the crisis spread only gradually from the north to the south. One of the explanations is military: the regions south of Emesa did not fall victim to the ravaging forays of the Persians, and the pressure from nomadic tribes to which the south was exposed was not really comparable. In addition, there were financial and commercial reasons: the influx of pilgrims and the trade they brought with them to Palestine, trade on the Red Sea, wine exports from Gaza, and also trade in farm products with the *Hijaz* were continued. The downward trend thus did not seem to emerge before the turn of the century. The lengthy Persian occupation of the south from 613 A.D. then contributed to a further decline by cutting Palestine off from the western regions.

Christianity – Conquest and division

Our aim here is not to trace the long journey of Christianity from its origins in Palestine to the Edict of Milan of 313, which marked the end of the persecution of Christians. Instead, we will turn our attention to the main features of its organization in the Levant in the early 4th century when Constantine, whose aim was more than just to tolerate Christianity, introduced a policy of state support for the church. The two centers of emerging Christianity in the Levant were Palestine and Antioch. The Christian communities in Palestine seemed to be quite numerous in the late 3rd century, although they were rarer in Syria. In Phoenicia Christianity was spreading; it even found supporters in the province of Arabia and was known in Edessa in the province of Osrhoene.

An unusual archaeological find gives us a rare insight into the life of a small community during the 3rd century: in Dura Europus (Salihiye) on the Euphrates, an embankment was constructed along the substantial city wall in 256 to provide protection against the Sassanids; despite it, the city was overrun and sacked in the same year. The remnants of the settlement lying beneath the embankment have been well preserved, and include a vast synagogue, a mithraeum (meeting hall for followers of the Cult of Mithras), and a private house that in around 230 had

been converted into a *domus ecclesiae*, or a house that was also a church. The building retained its old floor plan and has a courtyard surrounded by rooms and a portico. The largest ground-floor room, which consists of two former living rooms, and which could accommodate 70 people, measures 41 x 17 ft (12.65 x 5.15 m). It seems to have been an assembly room, since its eastern end has a small dais designed for orators or preachers. The other main room is 25 x 14 ft (7.60 x 4.22 m). This is a baptistry, as a square font indicates. The walls were decorated with mural paintings. Over the font is the Good Shepherd, and directly below him are Adam and Eve plucking the forbidden fruit. The long northern wall shows the curing of the lame and Christ walking on the water, while the southern wall depicts a garden scene, presumably the Garden of Eden, a woman carrying water, who may be Rebecca, as well as David and Goliath and the women at the tomb. This Christian iconography emphasizes the salvation that believers expected to achieve by baptism. The general appointment of the *domus ecclesiae* gives an idea of the scale of Christian gatherings even in the first half of the 3rd century.

Some way away from this Christian building, a fragment of parchment was found. This originates from the "Diatessaron" of Tatian, a Syrian Apologist of the 2nd century. This work, which is the earliest known collection of gospels, was later condemned by the church together with Tatian's doctrines. The

Murals, Dura Europus synagogue

The biblical scenes depicted in these frescoes on the walls of the synagogue in Dura Europus (c. 245 A.D.) are a blend of pagan elements with Persian and Greek influences. This fresco, from a section on the west wall, includes a panel with the Ark of the Covenant in the land of the Philistines. The panel above it depicts the pharaoh, and beside it is Moses as an infant.

Mithra killing the bull, Sidon

Late 4th century A.D.
Marble; height 74.5 cm, length 88.5 cm
Louvre, Paris

Mithra is an ancient Indo-Iranian deity. The cult of Mithra originated in Iran, as the god's Iranian vestments show. It was widespread in the Roman empire, particularly among soldiers, and for a long time was a serious threat to Christianity. The sculptures in the shrine of Mithra in Sidon illustrate how popular the cult was in the Roman empire, and also how widespread paganism was in the 4th century.

manuscript is, like the few inscriptions in the baptistry, in Greek, and may have been translated from Syrian. The Christian community of Dura Europus would have consisted primarily of the Christian men of the garrison stationed there.

Bishops came from all over the empire for the ecumenical Council of Nicaea in 325. Their numbers included many Syrians, Phoenicians and bishops from Arabia. The list shows how widespread Christianity was in the Levant. Modest cities such as Aere in Arabia and Gabala (Djebele) or Balnea (Banyas) in Syria were represented at the council by their bishops. It is remarkable that there were no representatives of cities south of a line between Esbun, Jerusalem, Eleutheropolis, and Gaza, a very lightly urbanized part of Palestine and Arabia. This has given rise to a dependence on the density of the network of cities to indicate the degree of Christianization. Evidently, there were fewer people who professed Christianity in the country than in the cities, where craftsmen, merchants, and even the ruling classes and the curia members accounted for the majority of Christians, although the upper ranks of the nobility and members of the intelligentsia, who felt more closely bound to the traditional Greek culture, were likely to have been more hesitant in accepting Christianity. During the 4th century the renewed struggle between paganism and Christianity, although not always violent, was waged under biased conditions. The emperors who succeeded Constantine, with the exception of Julian the Apostate, favored the Christian faith. A number of decrees of this time ruled against ties between civic life and traditional religions. A law of 356 banned sacrifices and ordered that temples be closed down. In 381, 385 and 391 Theodosius I gradually outlawed pagan religious services. As a result of these proscriptions it became practically impossible to observe public sacrifices and civic religious festivals, that is those aspects of tradition that had become most strongly institutionalized. It was the closure of the temples that finally disheartened the pagans.

Remains of a church, Ghine

When a village was built within the walls of the pagan shrine of Ghine in the Lebanon Mountains, the temple was converted into a Byzantine church.

The struggle against Paganism

The years from 380 to 390 were marked by the destruction of the temples. For example, the *praefectus praetorio* of Oriens, Cynetios, carried out a campaign in the region; groups of radical monks raged through the country. Markellos, the bishop of Apamea, organized the destruction of the Great Temple of the Oracle of Baal in the center of that city. However, when he attempted to attack the temple of Aulon, Markellos was killed by enraged farmers. Other major attacks were carried out in Heliopolis (Baalbek) in Lebanon, in the Palestinian town of Raphia, in Petra, and in Aeropolis, which lay east of the Dead Sea. Finally, in Gaza Bishop Porphyrios (396–420) was given the support of the empress Eudoxia in the form of auxiliary troops. Seven of the temples in the city were looted and destroyed. The most famous one, the temple of Marna, the main deity of Gaza, resisted initially, but finally soldiers set fire to the cella of the building. On the site of the ruins a church was built, echoing the circular floor plan of its predecessor.

Some temples were converted into churches. In Damascus, the city's most important religious building, the temple of Jupiter Damascenus, became the church of St. John the Baptist. Important shrines in the countryside were also Christianized, such as the shrine of Afqa in Lebanon. In Heliopolis a church was put up in the courtyard of the great temple of Zeus. Other temples, such as those of Qalat Faqra, Hosn Niha, and Qasr el-Banat ad Shhim were situated next door to basilicas, while the temples in Ghine, Maqam el-Rabb, Yanuh and in Burqush on the Syrian side of Mount Hermon were converted into churches. Many rural temples in Lebanon seem simply to have been abandoned. In the cities many temples were retained, as the buildings were considered part of the monumental architecture of the cities.

The fight against paganism during the 4th century was not restricted to the public aspects of religion. Theodosius also banned worship in the home. During the 5th century, pagans were forbidden to take up certain occupations. Justinian even forbade pagans to make wills, receive inheritances, or to testify in court. Finally, in 529 A.D., he ordered that all pagans be baptized.

Traditional pagan religions were concentrated in two main areas. One of these, which had originated in neo-Platonism, was that of philosophy and mysticism, while the other, which was closer to folk traditions, included soothsaying and astrology, which kept the two currents in close association. In late antiquity, people of all religions and philosophies shared a desire to foresee the future, to be able to influence fate and to protect themselves against disease and misfortune. The dying paganism sought refuge in the ways of sorcery and magic, which sometimes verged on occultism. Those in power were particularly mistrustful of sorcery, as such secret consultations often related to the fate of the emperor himself. Major trials, such as the trial of Scythopolis in 359 A.D., were particularly targeted against its practitioners, but it was also used as an opportunity to get rid of political opponents, practicing pagans and anyone else who happened to be in the way. It would therefore be inaccurate to ascribe religious fanaticism solely to rampaging monks or Christian emperors, and to regard it as a one-way process. The brief period in which Julian the Apostate was in power was characterized by anti-Christian riots and the destruction of holy sites, relics, and churches.

It would be equally one-sided to assume that compulsion alone had brought about conversion. Christianity's focus on the individual conscience, morality, and salvation played an important role in its growing popularity. The religion, which was spread by people of exceptional character, was less of a doctrine than an effective aid to people, and the worship of saints and prayer offered succor in the case of disease, mourning, the vicissitudes of life, natural disasters and problems in public life. Shrines such as those of Simeon Stylites the Younger, a Syrian ascetic of the 6th century, as well as relics and religious paintings, had their influence on everyday life. A large number of mass conversions were the result of remarkable events, such as the case of Alexander Akoimetos, who during his travels stopped to rest overnight at an abandoned temple at Chalcis (Quinnisrin). When challenged by an upper-class pagan citizen, he reputedly was given a sign in the form of a bolt of lightning, which set the building ablaze. After this the city's inhabitants joined him.

In the country religious unity seemed to prevail, an impression confirmed by hagiographers in their descriptions of the lives of the saints. Theodoretus, a church historian and bishop of Cyrrhus, succeeded in converting 200 villagers in the city's environs in his campaign against the Marcionite Doctrine. One of the monks whose life Theodoretus describes in his writings converted an entire pagan village in Lebanon in one session.

In the cities, by contrast, different religious groups lived side by side; for a long time groups of dissidents sought refuge there, and it is not surprising that more Jews lived in the cities than in the countryside. Neighboring rival cities often held opposing religious views, at least as far as the majority of their populations were concerned. Antioch, for example, was primarily Christian during the 4th century, while its neighboring rivals remained pagan. These neighbors were Beroea (Aleppo), Laodicea, and Apamea, which housed the neo-Platonic school and was held as a bastion of intellectual paganism.

Two of the main factors that determined the influence of Christianity related to its specific morality. Even heathens like Julian the Apostate were impressed by the effectiveness of neighborly love effected under the church's organization. Institutions to help the poor, the sick, travelers, widows, old people, and orphans came into being with early Christianity, and from the 4th century onwards enjoyed a marked upswing. In Jerusalem, the construction of monasteries and churches was accompanied by the building of hospices from the time of Melania the Elder until the reconstruction of Justinian's Nea, or "new church," to which were attached two hospices with 200 beds.

These welfare institutions consolidated Christian communities around their bishop, ensuring him an important role in the city. Christian sexual morals were from the pagan point of view a further decisive trait of the Christian religion. Groups of virgins, and widows who renounced remarriage, aroused awe and wonder.

Mosaic, church choir, Ghine

A characteristic feature of 6th and 7th century churches is the decline of figurative decorations, which were partially or wholly replaced by geometric patterns, indicating iconoclastic tendencies. The center of this mosaic still features an eagle.

Below right, opposite below

Mosaics, Zippori

These mosaics are from the early Byzantine period. Their content, still pagan, show Amazons, the tribe of women warriors, who under their queen Penthesilea assisted the Trojans during the Trojan War.

The status of Jews and Samaritans

We have already seen the geographical distribution of the Jewish population of the Levant, with communities that were widely distributed through cities, had a special presence in the ports, and had a strong urban and rural concentration in Palaestina secunda. The Jewish patriarch lived in Tiberias. He was recognized by the Christian emperors as he had been by their predecessors, and often held an important position in the administration. The patriarch's position was hereditary, but with the death of its last male representative, Gamaliel VI, the institution died out in 429 A.D. Until then, the patriarch appointed the head of the Sanhedrin, responsible for the synagogues, established the calendar for rituals and was the supreme judge of his fellow believers. The empire's Jewish communities paid him a tax, the *aurum coronarium*, with the full cooperation of the state.

Numerous laws gradually diminished the rights of Jews; they were forbidden to marry gentiles, to own non-Jewish slaves and to practice law or take up most public posts. Attacks on synagogues were only nominally punished, despite their frequent proscription through legislation. The burning of the synagogue of Callinicum (Raqqa) caused a deep controversy between Bishop Ambrosius of Milan and Emperor Theodosius. The emperor wanted the synagogue to be rebuilt by the bishop of Callinicum, who had been considered responsible for it, but he had to give way. Julian the Apostate was the only one of the emperors who with his anti-Christian policy was in favor of the Jews. The most difficult time for the Jews seems to have been the beginning of the 7th century, when the emperor Heraclius forced them to be baptized, which resulted in making the Jews enemies of the Byzantine Empire just before the Islamic conquest.

In 352 there was a Jewish revolt against Gallus (351–354) who was appointed as emperor of the east. Sepphoris-Diocesarea (Zippori), near Nazareth, was occupied by rebels after they massacred the local garrison. Christians and Samaritans were the victims of the rebels, who appointed Patricius as their king. Gallus' troops, however, recaptured the town and wrought havoc against the rebels.

The Samaritans, who were not on good terms with the Jews, were treated by the authorities in much the same way as the Jews were. During the 5th and 6th centuries they were subjected to the same persecution and restrictions. Two revolts flared up as a result of attacks against their shrines. The Christians' attempts to remove the mortal remains of Eleasar, Ithamar, and Phineus from a Samaritan temple caused the first series of revolts. After the destruction of a Samaritan temple on Mount Garizim, where the church of St. Mary was subsequently built, the revolt continued. In 529/30, another uprising occurred under Justinian, which was much more long-lived and serious, and was accompanied by greater massacres and persecution than the first one. In both of these cases, the Samaritans, who refused to recognize the legitimacy of the empire, had appointed their own king.

Remains of settlement, Zippori

Sepphoris-Dioceserea (Zippori) had a large Jewish community. These are excavations carried out in the 1990s.

"Syrian Bible in Paris"

6th century A.D.
Height 33 cm, width 25 cm
Bibliothèque Nationale, Paris

This Bible in the Syrian language illustrates how widespread the use of the Syrian language and culture was in northern and eastern Syria. Most of the texts from Syrian literature deal with theological subjects, and express above all the beliefs of the Nestorians and Monophysites. The painting has obvious stylistic parallels with contemporary Byzantine illuminations, and depicts Maximinus Daia as pharaoh, with Moses.

Divisions among Christians

Almost from its inception, Christianity was divided by opposing doctrines. The intervention of the emperor in church life altered the controversies from the 4th century onwards. For example, the Council of Nicaea was instituted by Constantine himself in order to deal with the threat of disunity through the Arian controversy which concerned the nature of Christ. In doctrinal schisms the problem of the authority of the church often arose, and the question of an individual's personal belief often hinged on which bishop he believed. Believers and the clergy made their choice, and the authorities made theirs, and attempted to impose it, either by force, by persecuting heretics and banishing or imprisoning bishops and monks, or by persuasion and attempting to mediate between the quarreling factions.

The main controversy at this time related to the divine nature of Christ. For the Egyptian priest Arius, a disciple of Lucian of Antioch, Christ himself was not divine, but should be regarded as God's creation. The Council of Nicaea of 325 condemned Arianism and formulated the first official recognition that Christ was equal (Gr: *homousios*) with God the Father. The Arians opposed the Nicaeans (or Catholics), but after many regional councils themselves split into numerous factions which either drew finer distinctions or amplified the difference between the Father and the son. The see of Antioch underwent a deep crisis between 330 and 418 because of differences between members of the various Nicaean and Arian factions and divisions. In 374 A.D. there were four rivals quarreling over the title of bishop, and it was not until 418 that the Nicaean Alexander succeeded in imposing himself as the sole bishop of Antioch.

The so-called school of Antioch can be ascribed to three theologians who came from Antioch: Diodorus, bishop of Tarsus, Theodore, bishop of Mopsuestia, and Theodoret, bishop of Cyrrhus. Nestorius, a Syrian monk who studied under the first two, became patriarch of Constantinople in 428. Together with the Antiochene theologians, he supported the doctrine of the dual nature of Christ (Dyophysitism). This related not to the relationship between father and son, but to the relationship between the divine and the human within the person of Christ himself. In reaction to Arianism, the school of Antioch propounded a theology that the human element in Christ was separate from his divine nature. Nestorius was then opposed by Cyril, the patriarch of Alexandria.

In his view, Christ's reincarnation as man gave him a single nature, where the divine and the human merged, this being the doctrine of Monophysitism. Soon afterwards, during the middle of the 5th century, Pope Leo the Great conceded that Christ was a single divine entity, but with a dual nature, one human, one divine. This compromise soon became known as the Chalcedonian creed, after the council which conceded it. The issue of the humanity of Christ, which was practically denied by the Monophysites and greatly emphasized by the Nestorians, led to two different concepts of the Virgin Mary. The Monophysites and Pope Leo regarded her as the "Mother of God," while the Nestorians by contrast regarded her as the "Mother of Christ," who had borne the human nature of Christ. A variety of beliefs were concealed behind these opposing views. The Nestorians' Christ was in his suffering humanity close to the believer. For the Monophysites, however, his divine might stood to the fore.

These differences in opinion also reflected issues of regional and cultural identity and the rivalry that this engendered. The Arian crisis developed against the background of competition, at first between Alexandria, Constantinople, and Antioch, with numerous Arians among the bishops of Syria and Palestine, such as the famous Eusebius of Caesarea (260/65–339). The crisis of Nestorianism pitched the theological doctrine of the school of Antioch against that of the Alexandrine creed in Egypt and the church of Edessa in Osrhoene. There were many Monophysites in northern Syria in the 6th century, although Palestine as a whole tended to reject them. It is certain that it was above all on the Syrian mainland and along the Euphrates that Monophysitism succeeded in finding support in regional cultural identity, and was expressed in a literature in the Syrian language, and whose center was Edessa. Even if it was an expression of nationalism, it was expressed there more diffusely and less strongly than in Egypt, which was largely Monophysite, and people fully supported the church of Alexandria.

The most outstanding personality of the age was Severus, the Monophysite bishop of Antioch. In 488 he was baptized at the temple of St. Leontius in Madjumas and took up a monastic life. Severus was ordained as a priest by an exiled bishop, and in 512 becoming bishop of Antioch. But when he was banished in 518 by Justin I, he went into exile, finally dying in Egypt. Severus was one of the great Monophysite theologians as well as an outstanding organizer, whom the Monophysites could thank for the expansion of their influence in Syria.

There were many turns in this religious controversy. In 431, Nestorius was dismissed by the Council of Ephesus. This condemnation sealed the fate of the Nestorians, who became increasingly marginalized in the 5th century. The closure of the school of Edessa by the emperor Zenon in 489 A.D. marks the end of the Nestorian influence in Syria. In the Sassanid empire the largest Nestorian communities appeared. During the following era, their missionaries spread their faith in Central Asia, China and the Arabian Peninsula, where it survives to this day.

The Council of Chalcedon in 451 sealed the success of the propositions of Pope Leo that Christ was a single divine entity, but with a dual nature, one human, one divine. The supporters of the Council, who were subsequently called Chalcedonians, opposed both the Nestorians and the Monophysites. Juvenal, bishop of Jerusalem, profited from the council, because by belonging to it he was able to enhance the status of his seat, and was made patriarch with power over the three Palestinian provinces. The revolts led by Monophysite monks, however, which accompanied Juvenal's return to Jerusalem, brought much burning and bloodshed, and the army had to intervene to ensure his safe arrival. The role of monks (and of believers) in these religious schisms, which had until then been limited to imperial and clerical circles, changed. The monks

were a link between these ruling groups and the people at large.

After Chalcedon the crisis intensified, particularly as two emperors, Zenon (476–491) and Anastasius I (491–518), tended to favor Monophysitism, while their successors, and in particular Justinian, returned to supporting the Chalcedonian view. Various attempts were made in vain to find a compromise.

Fragment of the emperor Anastasius' constitution, Umm-el-Jimal

The constitution of the emperor Anastasius regulated the administrative organization of the Orient.

Holy Cross basilica, Resafa

The main basilica, which is known today as the "Holy Cross" basilica, was reinforced in the Middle Ages with substantial flying buttresses.

In the 6th century not only the emperor, but also the patriarchs of Constantinople and the bishop of Rome were positively inclined towards the Council of Chalcedon. On the other hand, entire regions, such as Armenia and Egypt, were largely Monophysite. At that time opponents to the Edict of Chalcedon were only favored by the empress Theodora (527–548), Justinian's wife. After being forced into exile, it was she who supported the reestablishment of a Monophysite Syrian episcopate, which was led by a wandering bishop, Jacob Baradaeus. A parallel hierarchy ensued, with many cities having two bishops, one in the city supported by imperial power, and another in one of the many Monophysite monasteries of the Levant. This development started on the one hand in Bosra and on the other in Edessa, where Jacob Baradaeus successfully developed Monophysitism into his own teaching, whose supporters were called Jacobites. They for their part again split into two rival factions who quarreled a great deal, although their church retained its power until the coming of Islam. In Palestine their numbers appear to have reduced greatly around Gaza, a former center of the church, while in other areas there were none at all; in Arabia they were

represented primarily in the north of the province. In Phoenicia and in some of the chora of Apamea, they were scarcely encountered but they were widespread in the northern Syrian limestone massif and in Euphratensis, and they dominated the regions east of the Euphrates. For this reason in this area they preferred to use the Syrian written language. However, it should not be forgotten that many Monophysites in the Levant spoke Greek, and in particular Severus of Antioch.

The religious disputes were highly charged and tumultuous, although the actual violence committed was never high, even during the great persecution of the Monophysites during the 6th century. Violent death was rare, and a comparison with other ages shows that the later repression of heretics often resulted in much greater bloodshed. The result of this hatred and schism weakened the empire, and even more so Christianity just before the confrontation with Islam.

Joshua the Stylite, a Monophysite monk from Edessa, left a detailed chronicle of the disasters that befell the Byzantine east under Anastasius I in the form of starvation, earthquakes, and invasions during the early 5th century. However, he did attempt to protect the Monophysite emperor: he believed that it was not the emperor himself whom God wished to punish, but the Christians of Edessa, who celebrated a carnival inherited from paganism.

The increasingly broad participation of people in religious schisms during late antiquity was by no means purely academic. What was important for them – their salvation – depended on it; however, rather than eternal salvation in the next life, they were concerned with survival in this life, in the here and now. Traditional pagan religion and a good part of the Old Testament regarded events, regardless of whether they affected the individual, a group, or the state, as signs from God sent as warnings, punishments or rewards. Disease, infertility, military defeat, earthquakes, drought and bad harvest, or by contrast health, fertility, victory, and well-being, were all seen as part of God's designs and as expressions of his wrath or satisfaction. For this reason heresy was regarded as something that upset the divine order, and this was something of which everyone was especially fearful.

The power of the bishops

The bishops were the protagonists of religious schisms within Christianity. Their duty was to lead the Christian population of a city and to head the large numbers of clergy in the polis and the chora, to teach them and to baptize them. They controlled the administration of church property and increasingly assumed the role of the city's representatives before the authorities, which makes it understandable why there continued to be such fierce struggles for the bishop's throne.

At the time of their appointment bishops did not have to be priests, nor did they have to come from the city which they were to lead. For example, St. John Chrysostom, the great preacher from Antioch, was appointed patriarch of Constantinople (398–404). Bishops were not allowed to marry, although, like priests and deacons, they were allowed to be married at the time of their ordination. Bishops' children are frequently mentioned. Occasionally a clandestine system of nepotism emerges, with several bishops coming from the same family. Most of them were curia members and belonged to educated circles. They had often studied rhetoric, and sometimes law. A typical representative of these educated circles is Theodoret, bishop of Cyrrhus, whose letters, church history, and many works on exegesis have survived. They took their roles as preachers and educators very seriously. Severus of Antioch compiled large numbers of letters, sermons, and hymns. The Latin church father Hieronymus described Titus of Bosra as belonging to those who embellished their works so generously with the views and doctrines of the philosophers that it was impossible for the reader to tell whether he was supposed to admire the worldly knowledge in them or the religious scriptures.

The number of clergy was large. A spectacular example of this is the impressive list of clergymen found in the mosaics of the church at Evron, in the chora of Ptolemais. However, those in power strove to limit the number of clergy, who enjoyed certain tax exemptions, and to prevent the church from appointing curia members, whose appointments freed them from taxation, although they were able to find proxies. Deacons who also practiced another profession were quite common. The assets which the bishop had under his control included state donations which were frequently made, usually for a specific purpose such as the construction of a church, or for extraordinary assistance to be distributed to the poor, in particular charitable donations and some of the proceeds of the chora parishes, and finally the total income from church property, which was partially tax exempt. The bishops' salaries in all cities were on a par with those of the provincial governors, and ordinary clergymen were also salaried. The bishops therefore managed considerable sums of money, and were thus heads of something resembling other administrative departments. This meant that a bishopric, particularly in the metropolises, had its own extensive bureaucracy. In Resafa the bishop's palace has been discovered by the apse of the Basilica of the Holy Cross ("Basilica A"). This building, in addition to a chapel, had a room for the archive and for the bishop's secretaries, which was known as a scriptorium.

An episcopal court heard trials affecting both the clergy and the laity. The expansion of the power of the bishops turned them into representatives of their cities; at a time when the stratum of curia members was beginning lose authority, their role in municipal politics grew. Theodoret wrote to the authorities to plead for tax reductions for his city. With the funds of his church he financed the construction of colonnades, two bridges, and an aqueduct, as well as the upkeep of the public baths. It seems that in Justinian's reign the bishops constituted an integral part of the administration, replacing the now redundant curia members, controlling the imperial civil servants and being responsible for providing for the population and for the construction of secular buildings. For example, John, the metropolitan bishop of Bosra, was given financial aid by Justinian for renovating the aqueduct and building a city wall, without involving the Arabian provincial governor at all.

Lamp, northern Syria

2nd half of the 6th century A.D.
Silver, partly gilded; height 14.5 cm
Abegg Trust, Riggisberg

This lamp, with its gold-leaf reliefs, was manufactured in the reign of Tiberius II Constantinus (578–582) in Syria, and was probably part of a larger church treasure. The inscription along the edge is addressed to a certain "Megalos, former consul and patrician of our very pious ruler." The bosses at the base and the alternating vines and palm leaves are reminiscent of ancient decorations.

Monks and ascetics, or the integration of a subculture

Monasticism emerged in Egypt at the end of the 3rd century A.D. It was originated by people who looked up to the example set by the martyrs of the Christian persecutions, who sought sanctity, and thus decided to cut themselves off from society. Initially they settled on the peripheries of villages, where they lived a strictly ascetic life of fasting, prayer, abstinence, and deprivation. Then, like St. Anthony (c. 251–356), they left the regions of the civilized world and sought refuge in the rocky wilderness surrounding the Nile. They were described as anchorites (people who had left the chora of the villages), or "monks" (from the Greek "monos," meaning "single" or "unified"). They tended to rally around one master, and soon groups of eremites (from the Greek "eremos," "wilderness") who lived in scattered units, or monks living in monasteries, known as cenobites (from the late Latin "coenobium," "monastery"), took shape. The "superior" or "hegemenos" headed the monastery. The term "abba," or abbot, was used to describe a respected senior monk, or "father," who was not necessarily a "superior." In Egypt, Pachomius was the first organizer of monastic life inspired by St. Anthony's anchorite community.

In about 330 A.D. the monasticists reached Palestine, thanks to Hilarion from the region of Gaza, a disciple of Anthony of Egypt, who set up his first hermitage at Madjumas. From there, his influence spread throughout the region. This first "Egyptian wave" was followed by a second movement over the 4th century around the holy cities of Jerusalem and Bethlehem. It was mainly westerners, including Roman aristocratic women such as Paula the elder and Melania the Younger, who founded convents in the cities; these were also related to pilgrimages. The third wave during the 5th century crossed the Judaean desert southeast of Jerusalem and surrounded the Dead Sea with a dense network of monasteries. The most prominent of these were the lauras and the hermitages of St. Euthymius, St. Sabas, and their disciples.

In northern Syria the monastic movement seems to have had its own origins. It gradually emerged out of an old form of asceticism practiced in the city and especially east of the Euphrates from sectarian movements. One of the founders of Syrian monasticism was Julian Sabas, a monk from Osrhoene, who lived a wandering life of constant prayer. From the 4th century onwards, the hermitages in the region of Chalcis were sufficiently renowned to attract the later church father Hieronymus, who had come from the west, and Alexander Akoimetos. The latter, who was the founder and abbot of a group of monks known as the akoimetes, left his post as an official in Constantinople for the purpose. The Syrian monks were distinguished by the extremity of their ascetic practices. Monks living in complete isolation would have themselves immured in small houses and communicated with the outside world only through a small opening. Some achieved records for fasting or for not sleeping, while others had themselves chained up. Alexander settled himself at the bottom of a large jar near the Euphrates, while Simeon Stylites lived at the bottom of a cistern.

Simeon Stylites, known as the Elder, was born in 390 into a farming family in Cilicia. After living with the ascetics for two year, he joined the Teleda Monastery near Antioch at a very young age. His very severe form of asceticism aroused envy among the other monks, as he lived for two years buried up to his chest in the garden, after which he wore a neckiron, stood on a wooden block without sleeping or tied a rope very tightly around his waist. Finally he was banished from the monastery and traveled to Telanissus (Qalat Seman). He lived for ten years outside the village chained by one leg and in seclusion on a rock in the mountains. He then had a column six ells (22 feet and 6 inches) in height built,

Gilded silver plaque from liturgical furniture with Greek inscription, Ma'arret en-Noman treasure

5th–6th century
Silver with gold leaf; height 29.6 cm,
width 25.5 cm.
Louvre, Paris

This illustration shows Simeon Stylites the Elder being visited by a male serpent asking him to cure its mate. The famous anecdote symbolizes the saint's refusal to cast his eyes upon women.

so that he could live on it between heaven and earth, exposed to the heat and the weather, on a platform that was too small for him to stretch out. From 422 to 459 Simeon lived on three or four columns, each one higher than the previous one, the last one being about 50–60 ft (18–20 m) high. Simeon is the best example of what the historian Peter Brown describes as a "holy man" of late antiquity, a man who demonstrated his God-given strength by deprivation and prayer which resulted in his great authority as protector of the villages. He also assumed roles in other aspects of life, as a preacher, lawyer, and healer, roles which encroached on the life of the church, where according to records, he soon played another role. He fought against the godlessness of the pagans, against the presumptuousness of the Jews, and at other times, by "recommendations" to bishops and officials, and by means of letters to the emperor, he broke up groups of heretics. When Simeon died, people flocked to his see his pillar. People gathered around his mortal remains, ascribing miraculous powers to them. His death caused disputes among the monks of his monastery in Telanissus, the surrounding villages, and right up to the highest authorities in Antioch, the patriarch and the commander of the militia. His remains were finally

taken under armed escort to Antioch. However, his other relic, the pillar in Telanissus (Qalat Seman) remained a focal point for pilgrimages. Thus Simeon Stylites founded "Stylitism" – living atop a pillar. This form of asceticism was imitated by many followers after his death, and spread both towards Constantinople and towards the Euphrates, although this individualistic, demonstrative and extremist form of monasticism flourished most in northern Syria. Numerous pillars have been found there, which had consisted of three sections, reflecting the Holy Trinity, in memory of Simeon. Simeon's last column became the focal point of a huge monastery and place of pilgrimage (St. Simeon's Monastery). His most renowned follower was Simeon Stylites the Younger, whose pillar stood on Mount Admirable near Antioch.

Shrine of Simeon Stylites, Qalat Seman

The largest shrine to Simeon Stylites was built in the 5th century. This is a northern view of the central octagon, with the remains of Simeon's column and the south entrance.

Main facade of the shrine of Simeon Stylites

The shrine stands on a terrace measuring 110 yards (100m) east–west and 430 yards (400 m) north–south, and is approached by the pilgrim's way from the southwest. In the southeastern corner of the terrace is the baptistry, which gives a view of the facade of the shrine in the south of the terrace.

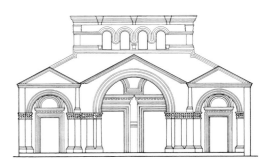

The Levant during the early Byzantine era **221**

Southwest monastery, Qalat Seman

One of the three monasteries, located in the southwest of the ancient village of Telanissus.

Animal mosaic in the old baptistry, Mount Nabo

The animal mosaic of this 6th century pilgrims' shrine shows Moses in the Cenotaph. The exotic human figures are leading an ostrich, a zebra and a giraffe (cameleopard). A monastery was built around the cenotaph to receive pilgrims. As at other places of pilgrimage, baptisms were carried out here.

Christian saints

The Palestinian holy man of late antiquity appeared more reserved, more tied to a monastic community and less cut off from the monks surrounding them, whose activities were directed more towards the development of monastic institutions. Nevertheless, the similarities between Euthymius and Sabas on the one hand and the holy men of Syria on the other outweighed their differences. Two holy monks, Barsanuphius and his disciple John, lived locked in their cells in the monastery of Seridus near Gaza during the 6th century. They communicated with each other and the outside world only via a messenger and via letters. The Levant is littered with

the remnants of monasteries in the countryside. Deir Dehes in the chora of Antioch is a typical rural monastery, situated near a village, and similarly supporting itself by farming. It consisted of a church measuring about 70 x 25 ft (20 x 7 m) with a basilica-type ground plan and two courtyards. Around these are buildings that were used for accommodation or agricultural purposes, including a tower and an oil press, so that churches, gardens, and other buildings constitute a self-contained unit. The monks' graves were beneath the church. Monasteries of this kind were most widespread during the 6th century.

The Martyrios monastery, named after its founder who was one of Euthymus' followers, has been discovered east of Jerusalem. It is of a kind different from that of Deir Dehes, distinct in its more close-knit population of monks, and by the fact that it took in pilgrims. The complex, which was almost square in shape, each side measuring about 200 ft (60 m), was surrounded by a high wall. The hospice for pilgrims was outside this wall, and the monastery seems to have been divided into two parts. The northern part, for the pilgrims, had a bath and a large refectory decorated with mosaics, while the southern part, reserved for the monks, is particularly remarkable for its communal burial chamber.

Written records and excavations also indicate the presence of monasteries in cities, for example those in Scythopolis (Bet She'an), Pella and Gerasa. However, monks tended not to live in cities.

The eremites of Antioch of the 4th century inhabited caves and hovels on the slopes of Mount Silpius outside the city walls. Jerusalem attracted monks and nuns more quickly than other places, this was due in the main to its holy shrines. Nunneries are to be found exclusively in the cities, as it was evidently inconceivable that they should be founded away from male supervision.

The appearance of monks in the towns testify to their gradual integration into society. The monasteries were under the control of the bishops, and from the late 4th century onwards, many bishops themselves were former monks. The agricultural life that was led in the majority of rural monasteries, the composition of parishes whose priests were monks, and the large-scale conversions which monks carried out made them the rural backbone of the church. On the other hand they were also able to provide a voice for popular Christianity.

During the religious schisms which have been described here, monks often became spokesmen for the people living in their area, as for example the Chalcedonians in Palestine and the Jacobites in eastern Syria.

Monastery, Mar Saba

The monastery founded by St. Sabas in the 5th century in the Judaean desert is in a protected valley between Jerusalem and the Dead Sea. It was the place where the great theologian John of Damascus (680–750) was active. Only ten monks live here today.

Pilgrim's ampulla, Jerusalem

6th–7th century A.D.
Tin/lead
Dumbarton Oaks, Washington DC

This ampulla depicts the veneration of the cross and the women by the tomb.

Above

Church of the Nativity, Bethlehem

The Church of the Nativity, built by Constantine, was renovated by Justinian.

Pilgrimages and relics

From the reign of Constantine the Great onward a new form of religious observance developed, which was closely bound to the substance of belief. Christ's human form and his life in Palestine, which was a historical fact, manifested itself in various physical forms that believers could see in person. The Holy Sepulchre, Bethlehem and the place where Christ was baptized by John gave pilgrims a venue for commemorating the events that happened there as well as for prayer. This applied both to the shrines of the Old Testament, the graves of the martyrs, and later also the monasteries, as the monks were successors to the martyrs.

The "Onomastikon," a list of Biblical sites, gives their exact location. The "Onomastikon" was compiled in the early 4th century by Eusebius, Bishop of Caesarea, and then translated from Greek into Latin by the Church Father Hieronymus.

These shrines, along with sacred objects, started to multiply rapidly during the 4th century. Constan-

tine, the church of Jerusalem and the church of the Levant in general dedicated themselves to building up a "holy geography" to suit their own purposes. Some more entertaining aspects of this were the stone where Christ was said to have fed the multitude with five loaves and fishes, the "fig tree of Zachaeus," and the "dung-heap of Chiobs" in Arabia. However, even believers were critical of such veneration of objects, regarding it as something far removed from the prayer "in spirit and in truth" of St. John's gospel.

The veneration of relics assumed an increasing importance; a typical example of this is the discovery of the True Cross by St. Helen, Constantine's mother. In the course of time the Cross was divided up and relics of it blessed other shrines, such as the Great Basilica of Resafa or the cathedral of Apamea. The "discovery" of a relic was regarded as the result of divine intervention, and was used as evidence of the truth of a cause. For example, the discovery of the head of St. John the Baptist in Emesa also served the city's ambitions, enabling it to rank alongside Damascus, as the second metropolis in the province of Phoenice Libanensis. In Sergiopolis (Resafa), the cult of St. Sergius played a similar role, while the cult of the True Cross helped Herapolis, the capital of Euphratensis, to gain in status. Here the inclination of ancient cities for *agones*, or competition, again expressed itself. To the importance of holy shrines and the status of the miracles that had occurred there were added older arguments: a city's age, its Greek cultural heritage, its myths, and the renown of its games and of its temples. These were complemented by the city's biblical traditions, its martyrs, the benefits of pilgrimages, and the beauty of its many religious buildings.

Relics could be multiplied by dividing them up. Fragments of relics were laid beneath altars. For example, a church in Esbun (today Hisban) in northern Syria had a bowl containing tiny splinters of bone which in turn was placed in a stone box. In Northern Syria, large sarcophagi were built as shrines for relics. These contained a hole in the top, so that oil could be poured in over the relics before it drained off into flasks through a hole in the bottom. In this way secondary relics were made for the use of pilgrims, which included the eulogios (small clay medallions) of St. Simeon and cloth that had been touched by relics, as well as soil from Palestine, water from the river Jordan, or oil that was burned in the lamps at shrines. Despite criticism, this passionate hunt for relics thrived, and went as far as the theft of the body of Jacob Baradaeus from the Casion monastery in Palestine by emissaries of the bishop of Tella. Relics were distributed mainly from one central holy shrine to subordinate ones, and they usually traveled from the east to the west. Conversely, at the end of the 6th century, an emissary of the bishop of Gerasa to Rome was given relics of Saints Peter and Paul by Pope Gregory I.

Pilgrimages, the cult of relics, and the beginning of icon worship were the expression of a religious system in which saints or holy men were intermediaries between God and man, "passing on" prayers from believers. The believers hoped that this would help them in their daily life, and expressed their gratitude in donations which were used to decorate churches and ensure the donor's welfare. In this way an economy of donations evolved, which is illustrated by the donation of valuable gifts as well as of the more modest votive tablets.

Stone relief of Simeon Stylites, Hama region

5th–6th century.
Dark basalt; height 78 cm, width 66 cm
National Museum, Damascus

This is one of many reliefs depicting St. Simeon Stylites (c.390–460), standing on his column.

Devotional objects, Qalat Seman

5th–6th century.
Clay; diameter 3/2.9 cm, depth 1 cm
National Museum, Damascus

These small medallions were used to ward off evil. They depict Simeon Stylites on his column. Pilgrims would take these devotional objects home from their pilgrimage.

Below

Reliquary, origin unknown

5th–6th century.
Stone; container: height 33 cm, length 52 cm, depth 26 cm; lid: height 16 cm, length 49 cm, depth 26 cm
Aleppo Museum

The hold in the lid was used to pour oil over the relics of the saint. The oil came out through a hole in the bottom of the reliquary, and was kept by the pilgrims in a container (flask or phial). This oil was believed to have the miraculous power of the original relic.

The continued survival of urban life

The cities of the Levant were not abandoned in the 4th and 5th centuries, as was the case in the west. Wealthy people tended to remain in their urban residences rather than retreat to the villas on their rural estates.

The early Byzantine cities largely retained the Roman characteristics they had inherited. Most of the changes were insignificant. Whereas the Hellenistic and Greek cities located their cemeteries outside the city walls for reasons of hygiene, the Christians saw nothing wrong with keeping the remains of martyrs in buildings in the middle of residential areas, because this meant that they were protected. Privileged cemeteries would then grow around a martyr's tomb, or around various holy shrines, such as in Jerusalem. The tombs of bishops, as in Resafa, benefited from having such important neighbors, and people who made large donations were also buried at holy shrines. However, due to limited space, the necropoli outside city walls continued to be used, as was the case in Tyre. The most renowned of Antioch's cemeteries is outside the gate of Daphne.

The most outstanding buildings of representing classical civilization were those used for public performances of various kinds – theaters, amphitheaters and hippodromes. These underwent some major changes in late antiquity. Theaters fell victim to the general condemnation of actors, as one-act plays tended more towards variety shows than classical drama. Mimes and pantomimists were associated with debauchees and prostitutes. The conversion of actors by saints is a recurrent theme in hagiographies. For example, Simeon Salos ("the Fool") is said to have crippled the right hand of a bawdy juggler at the theater of Emesa. It was then healed during a dream, after the juggler had sworn that he would never engage in such play again. These buildings were no longer maintained adequately by the curias or rich donors, because the attitude to donations had altered; previously the custom had been that by contributing to public buildings, putting on performances, providing food or holding banquets for their fellow citizens, the rich gained fame and public recognition. However, over time donations went increasingly to the poor and for Christian buildings. The theaters in Gerasa (Jerash) were given up in the 5th and 6th centuries, and at some point the hippodrome was converted into a kind of amphitheater, although this was only short-lived. Some of these public buildings became church offices, while others were converted into workshops and one was even used as an ossuary. Although bloodthirsty combat sports had been forbidden by Constantine, hunting games which succeeded gladiatorial combats were still popular in some arenas, and it cost the church considerable effort to

Bath-house and building with portico known as the "café" (andron), Serjilla

The village baths raised the status of Serjilla in comparison with the neighboring villages, and gave the settlement almost urban status. The bath-house and andron of this village community were situated in the market place. They were funded in 473 by a rich landowner called Julianus. Between the buildings is a cistern measuring about 12 x 40 yards (10 x 30 m).

Roman theater, Jerash

The Roman theaters in Gerasa fell into disuse in the Byzantine era. One of them was converted into a pottery workshop.

suppress them. In the cities, the supporters of the teams in games took part in riots, such as those of 507 in Antioch. As a result of numerous clashes between the "blues" and the "greens," the 520 Olympic Games to be held there were cancelled. Groups of supporters like this existed in the 6th and early 7th centuries in Antioch and Tyre, and they were also known in smaller poleis such as Gerasa. They were involved in numerous incidents of civil disorder and anti-Jewish pogroms.

The public baths or thermae were one of the adornments of the city, and were extremely popular. The construction of public baths allowed a smaller polis to join the ranks of the larger ones. Benefactors such as Thomas of Androna would donate baths to their fellow citizens. Thomas' view was that when he entered the doors of the bath, Christ had opened the doors to true salvation. Although many monks refrained from washing, the majority of saints were not averse to the use of baths. Barsanuphius of Gaza took an intermediate view. In his opinion bathing was not forbidden to people if necessity forced them there. Therefore, if they were sick and needed to use a bath, it would not be wrong. But for healthy people taking a bath meant that they were pampering their bodies, which led to relaxation, which led to weakness. However, bath-houses were often built by bishops such as Theodoret of Cyrrhus, who also paid for them to be maintained.

Opposite page

View of the village, Serjilla

Serjilla was between the 4th and 6th centuries one of the larger villages of northern Syria, boasting a bath house, large farmsteads, and a church.

Religious and secular buildings

One complex of churches in Gerasa consists of a three-nave basilica, the church of St. Theodore, a baptistry, and numerous annexes, as well as a bath-house. Situated in the center of the city, it was built on the site of a demolished pagan temple. Throughout the city, Christian buildings now took pride of place and were built in significant locations. In Gerasa, a city of medium size, archaeological excavations have brought to light at least 17 churches, most of these having remains of chapels and office accommodation attached to them. They include one diaconicon, and also a prison that was erected by bishop Paul in the 6th century for inmates who had yet to be convicted. It was therefore a building that symbolized a new approach to civic magnanimity and Christian love.

The early Byzantine city was defined above all by its fortifications. For example, in Euaria fortifications marked the village's promotion to a polis. Other distinctive features of a polis were Christian buildings, and a grid-plan street layout. Cities also maintained their main thoroughfares, such as that of Antioch, which was rebuilt by Justinian; it was 2 miles (3 km) long and, with its colonnades and adjoining shops, nearly 40 yards (35 m) wide. In Apamea, where some porticos were decorated with mosaics, the main north–south thoroughfare was half a mile (1 km) in length and without shops was almost 41 yards (37.5 m) wide. It seems to have had a network of streets laid out in a grid pattern, with a main street going from east to west in the southern part of the city. Mampsis in the Negev, which only became a polis at a later stage, made do with a relatively straight main street. Resafa had no colonnaded street, and there only seems to be one section of a street, extending about 160 yards (150 m), that runs in an approximately straight line.

The large squares which in Roman times had served as agoras for trade disappeared. In his "Description of Antioch," Libanius says that trade was conducted throughout the city. The old public spaces became more and more confined. In Gerasa a destroyed or an unfinished bridge was made inaccessible by the construction of a church, and the *macellum*, or Roman food market, was used to house a dyer's workshop, among others. At the same time in the 6th century the colonnaded entrances to buildings were increasingly occupied by traders. This was the start of a process which ultimately led to the broad streets being built over, leading to the emergence of the narrow souks and bazaars of the Islamic era.

The expansion of the church's sphere of influence and the contraction of public city spaces do not mean that the ancient city had completely vanished. For example, there is evidence of the survival of Roman civil institutions, such as a *quaestor*, or finance officer, mentioned in Bosra in the 5th or 6th century, or two ephors (supervisors) in Tyre in 597/598, who acted as market inspectors. Furthermore, private donors continued to have public buildings, particularly baths, constructed for their fellow citizens. These donors seem to have been primarily the senior state officials.

The main cities had administrative or semi-administrative buildings, such as the "Triclinos Building" in Apamea, which was the residence of the governor of Syria Salutaris. The residences of the wealthy were as opulent as the public buildings. In Apamea there were buildings with a floor space of 1,750–5,000 square yards (1,500–4,500 sq m) with monumental facades, giving them the appearance of palaces. They were built around large peristyle courtyards and had reception and dining halls. The upper stories probably contained the bedrooms. An important detail emerges in the 6th century, indicating a change in popular custom. The homes of the wealthy were now fitted with private bathrooms and lavatories, used in place of the public amenities that were gradually disappearing at this time. At the same time the peristyle courtyards of the houses in Apamea had wells and water basins, thus enabling the use of their own water supply. A building complex in Palmyra, which seems to be a house of citizens of

Street, Zippori

The main streets of the big cities were all flanked by arcades, and often paved with mosaics. Under the arcades were the shops.

medium standing, built over an area of 1,000 square yards (900 sq m) gives us an insight into its development from the 2nd to the end of the 8th centuries. An upper story was situated over part of the ground floor, while the rest was covered with a roof terrace. The house was probably divided into a visitor's wing around the northern courtyard and an area reserved for family life around the southern courtyard. In Jerusalem small three-room houses measuring 95–120 square yards (80–100 sq m) have been discovered, some with courtyards, but there are also houses with 350–450 square yards (300–400 sq m) of floor space, which have an inner courtyard and the remains of workshops. Apamea's biggest houses were sumptuously decorated, with marble plaques in the reception rooms, and tapestries suspended between the peristyle columns. Above all, however, they featured mosaics which depicted themes from Greek culture or indicating agricultural wealth, such as personifications of the earth surrounded by the seasons of the year, the seven sages, or mythological scenes. In Mariame (Mariamin) an exceptional mosaic from the late 4th century depicting a group of female musicians decorated the triclinium, or banqueting hall, of a magnificent house; of these, an organ and a zither player are particularly noteworthy. The mosaics are frequently the only insights we have into urban life in late antiquity.

What was the importance of mythological themes in the eyes of the upper stratum of early Byzantine society? Although the depiction in Apamea of Socrates surrounded by six wise men is undoubtedly from the era of Julian the Apostate and can be associated with the neo-Platonic philosophical school of the city, which was a passionate stronghold of paganism, it is probable that in many decorations the use of mythology served only to show the owner's education, or *paideia*. The mosaics of Antioch frequently display mythological themes, dating mainly to the 4th century; however, a set of ancient sculptures, including a crouching Aphrodite and Dionysius, seem to have been destroyed and buried only in the 6th or 7th century. It is not certain whether the owner of these figures was simply a nostalgic supporter of paganism, or simply a collector.

In the Levant, as elsewhere, classical culture was integrated with Christian culture. The continued existence of a system of an elite class explains this continuity from the classical world to late antiquity. All, or almost all, the higher officers, from bishops to the highest-ranking curia members and senior officials, studied rhetoric. Libanius, a teacher of paganism in Antioch in the 4th century, criticized the rivalry between the study of law, which was conducted in Latin, and the teaching of rhetoric in Greek at the school of Berytos. In reality, however, many of Libanius' students, who studied law, opened the way to high government positions after studying rhetoric, which taught them the techniques of oratory, from pleading to homilies.

"The Phoenix", mosaic (detail), Daphne

5th century A.D.
Size: width 600 cm, length 425 cm
Louvre, Paris

Daphne, situated above Antioch, was a suburb favored by the rich citizens of the town. It has numerous villas with mosaic floors.

In the country

It would be incorrect to depict the *paideia* of Hellenized cities as contrasting with the simplicity of Aramaic-speaking rural areas. In some regions, such as the coastal zones, Greek was the preferred language. For both Gaza and Antioch, on the other hand, we have definite evidence that the citizens, and not just farmers passing through, used Aramaic. Some rural areas, on the other hand, have large numbers of Greek inscriptions, such as Moab in Palestina Tertia, indicating that these areas were probably largely Hellenized. However, the focus tends to be more on the written rather than the spoken language. Greek reading and writing was taught almost universally, whereas the written Aramaic was rare outside Syria, as we have seen above. In the 5th and 6th centuries, villages determined the lifestyle of the majority of the population. The settlements consisted of houses that were erected without any specific building plan. The spaces between the houses were not paved as streets or squares, but simply remained as passages or unbuilt areas. Groups of houses were connected by means of winding alleys. The plans and arrangement of the houses were built to take into account the local topography and climate, and were usually huddled together and presented a closed external aspect.

They were also subject to various social conventions, such as not overlooking, or being overlooked by, neighboring houses.

The houses were designed primarily for agricultural life. One type of house which is prevalent in the northern Syrian limestone massif is a house fronted by a yard enclosed by a wall and bounded by various farm buildings. The ground floor was used to keep supplies and for animal stalls. A portico over the facade provided protection against the weather, and a stairway beneath it gave access to the living accommodation above, which usually consisted of two rooms, four at most. It can be assumed that these were bedrooms. Meals were probably prepared in the yard or under the portico.

This type of building can be found in areas where rural houses have survived, although there are numerous variations. Some houses were grouped together like small islands around closed, partitioned yards, as in some villages in northern Syria and the Negev. The use in Hauran of basalt, which could be hewn into long slabs and used for roofs, differs from the roof tiles which were laid on timber frames in the limestone hills. The impression from the Negev is of terraces of unbaked bricks that supported a traditional and serviceable system of branches and woven mats. The houses of Hauran comprise a

Large dwelling, Deir Seman

This three-story house, known as "house I," is substantially more opulent than the average house.

Opposite

External staircase, Umm-el-Jimal

Umm-el Jimal was an important village in the province of Arabia. This external staircase is built in a style typical of the region.

ground floor consisting of a row of identical rooms with outhouses at two different levels. The upper story, if there was one at all, was reached by a simple outside stairway on the front of the building.

Notable buildings

Buildings other than farmhouses are very rare, although some areas stand out from the average village by virtue of their large size and some prominent buildings. Umm el-Jimal, some 750 yards (700 m) from north to south and 550 yards (500 m) from east to west, is large, but particularly remarkable are its city walls and its 14 churches, making it one of the largest polis-type settlements. However, it has neither government offices nor a barracks, although for a long time it was assumed that such buildings had stood here. The arrangement of the buildings shows that there was no overall town plan. The only structures which can be regarded as public buildings are the large reservoirs, but being purely utilitarian they are not monumental in character. Throughout the limestone massif, where water is scarce, only seven particularly large villages had bath-houses. What were formerly regarded as "inns" because of the number of animal stalls they contained, are today thought just to be farmhouses. Hostels situated near shrines were maintained by monasteries, as were a number of hospices for pilgrims, travelers and the poor. It is unlikely that isolated villages far from major roads had hostels. The villages were thus shaped only by the agricultural pursuits of their residents.

Churches existed in almost all villages of the northern Syrian limestone massif. Villages in the province of Arabia have an impressive number: Rihab had nine or ten, Umm el-Jimal had 14, and Umm el-Rasas had almost the same amount. In the Syrian plains or the limestone hills, by contrast, the largest villages had no more than six or seven churches, as exemplified by Burdj Heidar east of Qalat Seman or by el-Barah. In addition to the monasteries, which were built far away from or on the periphery of villages, the other type of Christian building to be found is the baptistry. These occur above all in the chora of Antioch, where from the 5th century onwards they were constructed as self-contained buildings with a square floor plan.

Floor mosaic, Qabr Hiram

6th century A.D.
Marble/limestone
Louvre, Paris

Mosaic from the village church of St. Christopher, in Qabr Hiram in the province of Phoenecia Maritima.

Buildings, Umm el-Jimal

South view of a group of buildings consisting of a large building with a tower and a church, which is (incorrectly) known as a "barracks."

Basilica, Mushabbak

This basilica (view of the apse) stands outside a small village in northern Syria, and with its triple nave and columns is typical of the region.

These baptistries have small fonts for baptizing children, suggesting the strong Christian influence in rural areas. The baptistries at shrines such as Qalat Seman, where Simeon's monastery stood, were, like their urban counterparts, designed for the baptism of adults.

A study of the settlements shows that a social hierarchy existed in village communities. In the limestone massif the houses differ in size and ornamentation, as they do in Hauran, where a few opulent houses stand apart from the others, in particular some that include reception rooms with alcoves.

It is difficult to establish the nature of land ownership – whether the villages in the limestone massif were in the hands of estate owners who ran the estates themselves, or whether the wealth of large residences such as those in Apamea was based on the land rent received by their owners and thus on the work of the farmers in the chora. There is no record of any estate ownership, although written sources make frequent mention of villages belonging entirely to one owner. The available evidence should be interpreted with care, but it seems that the regions in the plains were more frequently in the hands of urban landowners who did not live there, while the mountain villages belonged to their inhabitants. Moreover, it is apparent that the estates of urban landowners and villagers were not always connected.

Basilica, Kharab Shams

The west front of a typical northern Syrian three-nave basilica.

Urban and rural churches

The churches of the Levant in the early Byzantine period occur in two variants which are found throughout the Mediterranean region: the basilica-type church and the centrally planned church. The basilicas are usually rectangular buildings divided into three naves by colonnades, although more modest single-nave buildings also fall into this group. Some exceptional basilicas even have five naves, such as the church of the Holy Sepulchre which

Constantine built in Jerusalem. The floor plan of the basilica is marked by its design, featuring a raised platform at the east end of the main aisle, surrounded by a low barrier, and the choir screen, adjoining the apse. This area, known as the presbyteries, was reserved for the clergy, which would celebrate the Eucharist here. Basilicas had various other features: a raised platform, known as the ameba and reached by a stairway, was designed for sermons. Examples have been found in the late 6th century churches in Gerasa and Arabia. In northern Syria, and in particular in the chora around Antioch, the center of the main nave features an elevated area, the bema. On the axis of the apse that faces the west and the congregation, a lectern was situated to replace the ambo. In the churches of Arabia tables stood by the pulpit, which were probably used for readings. The synthronon at the rear of the apse had a stone bench for priests and a raised plinth in the middle for the bishop. This arrangement has been found in the basilica of the Holy Cross (Basilica A), which additionally had a Syrian bema.

The plan of the basilica has a number of variants according to local customs. In the choras of Antioch and Apamea the apses are often flanked by two side-rooms, thus closing it towards the east. One of them, the diaconicon, served for the storage of valuable objects; it had built-in cupboards and a small door. It was almost never accessible from the side aisle, but opened towards the presbyterium. The other room, the martyrium, contained relics. It was easily accessible via a wide entrance, to enable the congregation to worship the relics. In the chora of Antioch, the churches were generally entered from the long south side, and the congregation would be split into two, with the men going to the front near the presbyterium, while the women went to the back. Otherwise, churches were usually entered from the west, and the congregation was divided along the length of the church, with the men on one side and

Basilica, Bosra

This basilica (viewed from the north) is associated with the tradition of Bahira the Monk and his meeting with Mohammed. In this celebrated encounter, Bahira recognized Muhammad as the Prophet.

Interior of the basilica of the Holy Cross, Resafa

The arches of the naves, supported by buttresses, are divided by arched columns. In the middle are the remains of a Syrian bema, the raised area reserved for the clergy.

the women on the other. If there were galleries, they were reserved for the women. Northern Syria is the only region where martyriums occur. Elsewhere in the Levant, relics were kept either under the altar or in the side chapels.

In the Negev, in Palaestina Tertia, many basilicas have a semicircular apse, and this in turn is flanked symmetrically by two more small semicircular apses. Northern Syria has a number of unusual buildings, such as the basilica of Qalboze, where the prominent apse is decorated on the outside by columns built directly against the outside wall. The design was

actually based on the church of St. Simeon Stylites in Qalat Seman.

The floor plan of the second type of Byzantine church, the centrally planned church, differs from the basilica in that the congregation's view is directed not towards the eastern end of the church, but to its center. The building can be cross-shaped, such as the church of St. Babylas in a suburb of Antioch, circular like the rotunda of the church of the Holy Sepulchre in Jerusalem, or a tetrakonchos (four conches) shaped building such as the centrally planned church of Resafa. However, more complex buildings can

also be found: an octagon set into a square, as George of Ezra's church in Arabia (now southern Syria), or a circle set into a square, as the church of St. John in Gerasa. Domes were often used to distinguish the central part of these remarkable buildings. The nature of the structure meant that relics were positioned in the center of the building, with more room for the ceremonies which the martyr's cult might involve. However, in most cases the centrally planned churches have retained the same layout as the basilicas, which are characterized by an apse. In addition, the centrally planned church was occasionally selected for large buildings where the cult of relics was less important than the wish to express the significance and sanctity of the place through its architecture. The cathedral of Apamea, like one of the largest churches of Seleucia Pieria, was built according to this design. Two centrally planned churches whose floor plan consists of a circle within a square have been discovered in Bosra. The smaller is the dedicated to Sergius, Bacchus, and Leontius. The scale of the other is enormous. It is not known which of the two was the cathedral.

Octagonal church, Gadara

This centrally planned octagonal church with a portico is unusual for a city. Urban churches were usually designed as triple-nave basilicas.

Opposite, below

Baptismal font, Submit

This cruciform baptismal font is in one of the apses of the basilica. Those being baptized descend the steps into the font, and then are submerged completely.

Basilica, Qalbloze

The Qalbloze church is one of the most remarkable example of buildings in northern Syria and of early Christian architecture. The apse embellished with closely standing columns imitates that of the shrine in Qalat Seman.

Decoration

These churches were embellished with lavish decoration. The walls often contained frescoes and marble plaques, or mosaics that unfortunately have not been well preserved. The flooring was sometimes marble, in the form of the very costly *opus sectile*, but more frequently was mosaic. These mosaics did not usually depict religious subjects, in order that the congregation would not step on them. In Huarte, in the chora of Apamea, however, an exception was made, and Adam was depicted in the Garden of Eden among the animals. There are countless mosaics with animal and floral motifs, geometrical patterns, or idealized scenes of rural life – and even, as is the case in Arabia and southern Palestine, portraits of the donors. In addition, the churches in Syria and Arabia contain pictures of buildings, churches, or cities. These decorations can be interpreted symbolically, with wild beasts symbolizing unrestrained passions, and peaceful landscapes symbolizing paradise. However, we should also bear in mind their purely decorative purposes and more obvious meanings. The donors liked to demonstrate the lavishness with which they dispensed their wealth, thanks to which they were able to make these offerings. An unusual mosaic has been discovered in Madaba, which consists of a map of the holy shrines of Palestine and Egypt, inspired by Esebius of Caesarea's "Onomastikon." It also served to underline Madabas' situation in the midst of many cities, and to emphasize its holiness.

All churches in the Levant had liturgical objects of bronze or precious metals, from lamps suspended from the ceilings or liturgical vessels to processional crosses. Large numbers of these have been found in the region of el-Riha in northern Syria, apparently buried in the early 7th century. These treasures, which have the names of donors inscribed on them, illustrate the importance of highly placed persons whose offerings had enriched the village church.

The end of the early Byzantine period

The Persian conquest, which was followed by a long period of occupation, marked the end of political stability in the Levant. The short intervening period of reoccupation by the Byzantines did nothing to improve stability, and the arrival of the Islamic conquerors in the 530s led to the disappearance of a simultaneously Roman and Christian civilization in regions where it had been particularly magnificent. Modern historians tend to underline three events that are related to the 6th- and 7th century Levant. First of all, partly because of the economic crisis, the Levant changed a great deal during the 6th century, entirely rejecting the Greco-Roman civic model that had been so prominent in the previous centuries. Secondly, what had remained, from the practice of Greek government to the models of monarchy from ancient civilization, only gradually disappeared in the Islamic period. Finally, Byzantium's downfall was the result of military defeats, and the relative passivity of the population of the Levant in response to the Persian and later to the Muslim invasions should not necessarily be regarded as the "natives" rejecting the "Byzantines." It was a precautionary measure in the face of a conquest which the Levantines regarded as transitory – an assumption in which they were mistaken – and which no one today regards as a disaster.

Basilica mosaic, Petra

This detail is part of the floor mosaic in one of the aisles of the large Byzantine basilica in Petra. In an addition to the building, 6th century papyruses were found. Petra was a major city in the Levant at least until the early 7th century.

Left and opposite

Mosaics, Madaba

In the 6th century and in the early Islamic period Madaba was a center of mosaic art. The floors made here often depicted animal motifs, and were even laid in churches.

Marie-Odile Rousset

Islam and the Crusades
Conflict of cultures

621–1291 A.D.

Umayyad mosque, Aleppo

This mosque was completely rebuilt by the Emir of
Aleppo, Nur al-Din, after being destroyed in a fire in
1169. The minaret was erected towards the end of the
11th century and is therefore the oldest Seljuk
structure in Syria.

The state of research

The study of medieval art and architecture in the Middle East is known as Islamic archaeology and art history, though this term tends to mask the complex reality of the material. This branch of scholarship has to concentrate on more than just the material traces left in the various lands under Islamic rule; like other areas of cultural studies it must also take into account the findings of a broad spectrum of disciplines. An extraordinary wealth of texts have survived from the Islamic era, for example, and these have contributed greatly to the focus and self-image of the field of archaeology and art history. The most famous texts in Orientalism have generally been those that are most accessible, while the results of field archaeology have unjustifiably received too little attention.

Objective knowledge of archaeological material, however, is constantly on the increase.

Europe first became aware of artifacts from the Islamic Orient in the 19th century, when the first collectors' items – which were by and large rare pieces of pottery – appeared on the antiques market. It is therefore not surprising that the first scholarly investigations from the end of the 19th century were directed towards these objects.

The reports of European travelers as well as the details provided by Islamic geographers led to the development of a historical geography at the turn of the 20th century. The study of urban geography was born in the 1920s, during which time noteworthy contributions were made by the work of Karl Wulzinger and Carl Watzinger on antique Damascus. The foundations for an architectural history of the region were created by the work of Keppel Archibald Cameron Creswell, James Allan, and, most recently, Michael Meinicke.

At the beginning of the 20th century, research was still mostly funded either by individuals or museums. Archaeological activity increased with the establishment of European institutes in the Middle East. Between 1910 and 1930 the first real excavations were carried out in al-Fustat (Old Cairo) and Samarra on the Tigris. By the time World War II broke out numerous important sites in Islamic archaeology had been examined and their details published in academic journals.

The history of the Crusades was the subject of independent investigations; the first work on the architecture of this period had appeared in 1871. At the end of the 1920s the first structures had been uncovered and Camille Enlart and Paul Deschamps began to publish their work on Crusader architecture. For many years theirs was the only work to deal with this topic. It was not until the start of the 1980s that Denys Pringle and Robin Brown again began to look closely at the fortifications, and to organize digs in Israel and Jordan. Systematic surveys of medieval settlements involving the participation of geographers have been conducted since the 1960s, although it is only since the 1980s that they have gained any momentum.

A glance at the publications produced during the 20th century shows that – along with so many other fields of research – the fate of archaeology of the Islamic period has been closely linked to the changing political climate in the region. The intense activity of the 1920s and 1930s was due to the English and French presence there. World War II, however, dealt a severe blow to the study of the humanities in general, while the regional conflicts during the 1970s prevented the continuation of research projects in the Levant. The 1980s may now be seen as the "heyday" of medieval archaeology. Since then, the Gulf War and the increased desire of the countries concerned to administer their cultural legacies themselves – as well as more limited financial support from European institutions – have led to a decline in research activity.

THE LEVANT

N

0   100 km

The area known as the Levant comprises the costal regions of Asia Minor, Syria, and Egypt. It embraces the Mediterranen littoral of the modern countries of (from north to south) Turkey, Syria, Lebanon, Israel, the Palestinian autonomous regions, and Egypt and western Jordan.
The map uses historical place-names. Some modern names are also given in italics.

The Islamic conquest of the Levant

The Arab–Islamic culture of the Levant grew out of the encounter between the new, rapidly expanding religion of Islam and the culture of the local population with its Arab, Byzantine, and Persian traditions. The monotheistic religion proclaimed by the Prophet Muhammad both provided the motive force for the unprecedented conquests of the new Islamic empire and laid the foundations for its intellectual traditions.

The Arab wars of conquest were surprising both for the speed of their success and the longevity of the movement itself. In barely a century this once nomadic people conquered the lands of the Mediterranean, from the Persian Empire to the borders of France. A string of military victories were won through a combination of the abilities of Arab generals such as Khalid ibn al-Walid – the conqueror of Syria – religious fervor, and the promise of booty.

The long-term success of these campaigns – which allowed the creation of a stable empire – can partly be explained by the Muslims' intelligent political strategy of tolerating the "people of the book" (believers in the book-based religions). This included Jews and Christians, and later covered Zoroastrians, Buddhists, and Hindus. The wars of conquest may have been religiously motivated but in general they did not lead to forced conversions. The "unbelieving" population in the conquered territories were given the opportunity to pay a poll tax in order to receive the status of "protected" citizens; they were then able to continue to practice their beliefs.

The Bedouin tribes, who had warred with each other during the Prophet's conflict with his home town of Mecca, clashed once again after his death in 632 A.D. This was the year 10 according to the hegira, the Muslim calendar which reckons the years using Muhammad's flight from Mecca to Medina in 622 A.D. as a base date. Muhammad's father-in-law, Abu Bakr, who was elected the first caliph (Arab.: "representative," "successor") knew how to exploit this energy, and he began the first campaigns to conquer new territory. The first attack in 633 was aimed at the Persian Empire, and Arab victory in the Battle of Qadisya in 636 brought them possession of the city of Ctesiphon on the banks of the Tigris. In the same year they founded the city of Basra at the mouth of the Euphrates, and a year later that of Kufa on the Euphrates.

In 634 the campaigns shifted in the direction of Syria and Palestine. Along the way the Arabs entered into an alliance with the Hassanids, one of the peoples nominally under Byzantine rule, but whose depredations on the territories of the eastern Roman Empire were staved off only by the more or less regular payment of Byzantine bribes. The Arabs

View of Jerusalem

The city and Haram al-Sharif (Temple Square) seen from the east. The Dome of the Rock with its golden cupola is one of the earliest and most important religious buildings in Islam.

achieved their first victory at Adjnadein in February 635 and by September Damascus had surrendered without a fight. Initially the Byzantine Empire, weakened by political instability and religious conflict, put only small contingents of troops into the field. The army they finally dispatched in 636 was crushed utterly at the battle of the Yarmuk river. At this point Byzantium abandoned Syria, and Damascus, the Byzantine provincial capital, was finally occupied by the Arabs. In the following year Arab troops took the cities of Baalbek, Homs, and Hama, and in 638 conquered Jerusalem – which also belonged to the Byzantine Empire – expelling the Jews but not the Christians. In 639 Muawiya I ibn Abi Sufyan, who later founded the Umayyad Dynasty, was appointed governor of Syria. In 641 Caesarea fell. This meant that the whole of Syria – which was known as Bilad el-Sham by the Arabs and encompassed all the territories of the Levant – was finally in Muslim hands.

The inhabitants of the occupied territories, once they had paid their poll tax, were now considered the subjects of a new ruler. He proceeded to bring to an end the war between Byzantium and the Persian Empire which had raged for 40 years to the great suffering of the local people. At first, few changes were instituted which affected the broader populace. Local rulers were able to retain their positions while the faction-ridden Arab army formed a military aristocracy which was essentially concerned with tax collection. For the most part, landowners were allowed to keep their holdings. State property, as well as the possessions of those who had fled or died, were allocated to Arab families who were then able to build up large estates. The Arab occupiers imposed a property tax, *kharadj*, on those landowners who did not convert to Islam, while Muslims were required only to pay a general tax on profits or to donate alms – a levy known as *zakat*.

As a consequence of their campaigns the Arabs now dominated the land and sea routes linking trade between the Mediterranean and the Far East. Islam gradually came to be accepted by the conquered peoples – either out of conviction or because it was to their advantage. Though the Muslim empire was fully formed at this point, it is still too early to speak of an Islamic culture as such; this was not to develop until the Umayyad era through the modification of Byzantine and Persian traditions. The Arab language – along with religion the most important element in founding a culture – also slowly gained acceptance.

The acquisition of the pre-Islamic legacy by the Umayyad caliphate in Syria

An important event which occurred at the beginning of the Islamic era was to dominate their entire history: while the Prophet was alive he had not made arrangements for a successor, and his community of believers split into groups led by different caliphs. The third caliph, Uthman, was murdered, and his elected successor Ali – son-in-law of the Prophet and father of the only male heirs, Hasan and Husein – was opposed by the governor of Syria, Muawiya I ibn Abi Sufyan, who assumed the role of Uthman's avenger. An arbitral decision called for by Muawiya's followers after the battle of Siffin on the Euphrates in 657 went against Ali, and Muawiya was declared caliph by his troops. Ali also fought against his previous supporters – the Kharijites – who had not supported him during the arbitration process, and it was a member of this group who finally murdered him in Kufa in January 661 – a date which marks the beginning of the Umayyad dynasty.

This conflict sealed the divisions in Islam: while the Sunnis recognize the first four caliphs as "righteous," the Shiites consider only the fourth caliph, Ali, to be the legal successor to Muhammad and their first *imam*, or spiritual leader. The Shiites, who split into still more groups in the course of time, were to remain a minority, but their concept of an *imam* directly inspired by God has profoundly influenced Islamic spirituality.

The century of Umayyad rule was marked by efforts at structuring and organizing the newly founded empire. Muawiya transferred the capital to the more central location of Damascus, meaning that Mecca and Medina were returned to their original functions as places of pilgrimage. There was unrest when Yazid I came to power (681–683) after the death of his father Muawiya. The Shiites declared Ali's second son, Husain, caliph; he was not able to overcome the military superiority of Yazid, however, and was killed, along with his entire clan, in Kerbala on the Euphrates in 680. At the same time, devout circles in Mecca supported Abdallah ibn

Al-Omari mosque, Bosra

The al-Omari mosque was probably built in 720 by Caliph Yazid II. The staircase on the façade may be an early form of minaret, with the muezzin calling worshippers to prayer from the roof of the building.

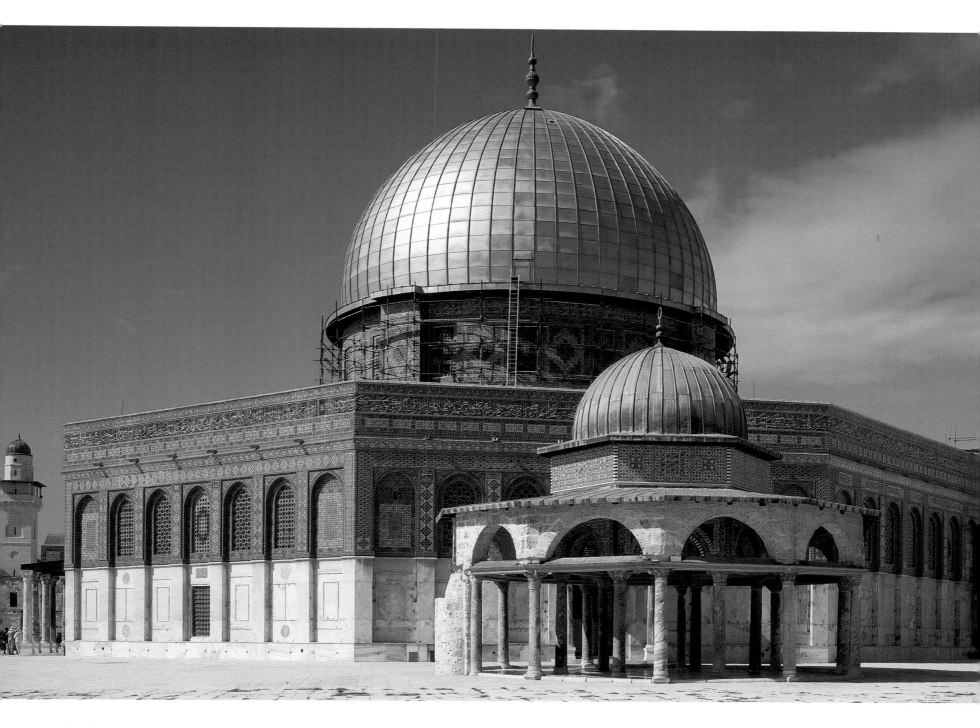

al-Zubair, who was son of a former companion of Muhammad.

The caliphate, however, survived all this upheaval and retained its base in Damascus. The reigns of Abd al-Malik (685–705) and al-Walid I (705–715) can be regarded as the pinnacle of the Umayyad dynasty. During this period an armistice was agreed with the Byzantine Empire, the Arabization of the administrative apparatus began, and the first Arab coins were minted. Syria was divided into districts corresponding to those of the former Byzantine administration: Qinnisrin, Homs, Damascus, Jordan, and Palestine.

The accumulated wealth of this new empire expressed itself in a burst of unprecedented creative activity – this was the birth of Islamic art proper. As religion was deeply intertwined with daily life, an architectural and decorative style sprang up which

was closely related to religious requirements. The caliphs were builders in the grand manner, and they employed Syrian and Coptic artists and craftsmen who provided the most important Byzantine contribution to the art of early Islam.

The Dome of the Rock, Jerusalem

The Dome was built at the time Islam was being introduced to the region, and its precise symbolism is still a matter for debate. Today however most historians agree that the Dome of the Rock was deliberately built in the historical heart of the Jewish and Christian worlds in order to underscore Islam's membership of the monotheistic tradition. The Dome of Chains in the foreground is said to have served Abd al-Malik (685–705) as a treasury.

Drum of the Dome of the Rock, Jerusalem

The magnificent colors in the interior of the Dome of the Rock are given added radiance by the light which enters through the drum's 16 windows.

Ambulatory of the Dome of the Rock, Jerusalem

The arcades in the ambulatory of the Dome of the Rock are still decorated with their original mosaics. The mosaics of the drum, on the other hand, were renewed in 1028. Located in the center of the building is the stone from which the Prophet is said to have ascended to heaven.

The Dome of the Rock

The oldest Muslim building to have survived the centuries more or less intact is the Dome of the Rock in Jerusalem. It was built between 688 and 691 during the caliphate of Abd al-Malik. Towering over the city, it belongs to a group of structures from the Umayyad period which were built on the site of the Solomonic Temple destroyed during the Roman occupation. At the center of the Dome of the Rock is the Al-Aqsa Mosque, while south of the platform the remains of substantial buildings, which probably served as palaces or for administrative purposes, have been unearthed.

The Jewish temple had been built on the spot where – according to the Old Testament – the angel of the Lord had stayed the hand of Abraham as he was about to sacrifice his son Isaac. It was on this site that the dome was erected. While Abraham – along with Moses and Jesus – is considered to be one of the most important pre-Muhammadan prophets. The site is also significant for being the place where, according to Arab sources, the Prophet journeyed at night to heaven.

The Dome is patterned after the centrally planned buildings of Byzantium, such as the church of the Holy Sepulchre.

The dome rests on a drum made entirely of wood; since 1994 it has once again been covered in plates of gilded copper and nickel as it was in Umayyad times. The central space of the building can be entered from all four points of the compass and is surrounded by two ambulatories separated from each other by an octagonal arrangement of columns. The dome and drum rest on another circular set of columns, so providing a vault for the rock. Underneath the rock is a cave known to Muslims as the "Fountain of Souls"; according to tradition the souls of the dead gather here to await the Day of Judgment. According to another tradition the rock tried to follow the Prophet on his ascent to heaven, and when the archangel Gabriel held it back he left behind imprints of his hands and feet.

The interior of the two-story drum is decorated with mosaics from 1082 while those of the lower section are the originals from 692. Above the arcades a Kufic inscription can be seen. The name of the builder, Abd al-Malik, was removed in 831 by the Abbasid caliph al-Mamun who replaced it with his own in an attempt to claim construction of the building for himself. The Dome has a powerful architectural significance in that it represents the beginning of a series of developments which would lead to Islamic religious architecture discovering its own unique forms and vocabulary.

The mosque

The typical ground plan of a mosque was developed from that of an Arab courtyard house, and was modeled on Muhammad's house. In contrast to churches, the exterior is a smooth wall rather than a structured facade. Access to the interior is gained through a courtyard surrounded by porticos which provide shade. In the center is a well or fountain at which the faithful can undertake the prescribed ritual purification before prayer. The hall of worship itself is divided by sets of columns into aisles, so that the congregation can form into rows behind the *imam*. The *mihrab*, a niche in the middle of the wall facing Mecca, indicates the direction of prayer, or *qibla*. This *qibla* wall stands at right angles to a line drawn towards Mecca. The *mihrab* is the most richly decorated area of the mosque, and the bay opposite it is sometimes elevated and roofed over with a dome. To the right of the *mihrab* is the stepped pulpit, the *minbar* of wood or stone which is built parallel to the *qibla* wall and richly decorated. The minaret, from which the faithful are called to prayer, is a tower with an internal staircase and is normally located on the side of the mosque opposite the prayer-hall.

Interior of the al-Omari mosque, Bosra

The al-Omari mosque in Bosra also features an inner courtyard with shaded arcades and a central basin for ritual purification. The mosque was restored at the end of the 1930s, and it is not known for certain whether the courtyard originally had a roof.

Umayyad mosque, Damascus

The Umayyad mosque, along with the Dome of the Rock in Jerusalem, is one of the finest buildings of the early Islamic period. The arcade, pediment and mosaics of the façade of the prayer-hall were clearly inspired by the Byzantines. In the background the westernmost of the three minarets can be seen.

The Umayyad mosque in Damascus

Along with the Dome of the Rock, the Great Mosque of Damascus is one of the most important early Islamic buildings. It was built by al-Walid between 706 and 715 on the site of the cathedral of St. John. The external walls of the mosque are the courtyard walls of a former temple to Jupiter. Its ground plan served as a model for a great number of Near Eastern mosques. Enclosed by a high wall, the complex is divided into a courtyard and the hall of worship to the rear, whose three equal long aisles parallel to the *qibla* wall are cut in the middle by a wider, perpendicular transept. The external appearance is dominated by the central dome of the transept as well as three minarets which were all built in separate styles and redesigned after the Umayyad period. Located in the middle of the suk in the old town, the mosque is a place of peace and meditation; the massive courtyard (133 x 60 yards – 122 x 55 m) with its shaded porticos is a popular place to take a walk.

To the west is a small, octagonal domed building whose side-walls, resting on eight massive columns with Corinthian capitals, are decorated with mosaics. It was here that the Umayyad state treasure was stored; a similar building can be found in Jerusalem near the Dome of the Rock. The facade of the prayer-hall is dominated by the axial nave; its Byzantine pediment is ornamented with a magnificent mosaic on a gold ground. Although closely related to Byzantine art, the motifs do not feature any depictions of people, in accordance with the commandments of Islam. The pediment is decorated with arboreal motifs, and the mosaics on the walls of the treasury display luxuriant vegetation, or scenes of rivers, cities, or palaces. The other walls were decorated with marble. According to the Arab geographer al-Muqqadasi, this magnificent decorative scheme enabled the attention of Muslims to be diverted away from the imposing structures of Christian religious architecture.

Opposite, below left

Mosaics, Umayyad mosque, Damascus

The best-preserved of the mosaics, which were restored in the 1960s, are beneath the western portico. They were probably made by Byzantine craftsmen and may well depict a panorama on the Barada river.

Mosaics, Umayyad mosque, Damascus

These mosaics on a gold ground are in the vestibule beneath the western portico, and they depict architectural and vegetable motifs. In accordance with the strictures of Islam, however, there are no representations of people.

Mosaic, Treasury of the Umayyad mosque, Damascus

The treasury (Bait al-Mal) in the courtyard of the Umayyad mosque in Damascus is also covered with mosaics on a gold ground.

Al-Aqsa mosque, Jerusalem

This stone mosque was built in the 8th century and has since been altered a number of times. Its present form is derived from the period of its restoration between 1924 and 1943.

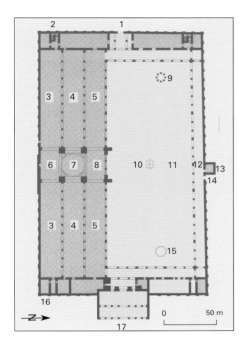

Ground plan of the present Umayyad mosque, Damascus

1 Western entrance, 2 Western minaret, 3 Southern bay on the *qibla* wall, 4 Central bay of the prayer-hall, 5 Courtyard bay of the prayer-hall, 6 Central bay in front of the *mihrab*, 7 "Eagle dome," 8 Northern bay of the central aisle, 9 "Treasury dome," 10 Purification fountain, 11 Courtyard over the antique *tenemos*, 12 Courtyard arcade, 13 Northern minaret, 14 "Gate of Paradise," 15 "Hour dome," 16 Eastern minaret, 17 Original main entrance

Opposite

Prayer-hall of the Umayyad mosque, Damascus

The original ground plan of the Umayyad mosque in Damascus has been completely preserved. To the left in the picture is the tomb of John the Baptist, which is an object of veneration.

The three aisles of the prayer-hall of the Umayyad mosque are supported by arcades with antique capitals and horseshoe arches. The dome of the transept, also known as the Dome of the Eagle, is situated opposite the *mihrab*. After being altered several times over the centuries it today has a Turkish appearance. Outside the hours of prayer there is a relaxed atmosphere in the prayer-hall; the believer comes here to pray, to relax, to study or to ask advice from one of the community's respected sheiks, who are usually seated beside the tomb of John the Baptist. According to Islamic legend, this marble monument contains the head of the saint, venerated as the herald of the prophet Jesus.

Of the Umayyad mosques in the region, the Al-Aqsa Mosque south of the Dome of the Rock in Jerusalem is also worthy of some discussion.

An examination of its architectural history has led to the conclusion that there were three phases of construction prior to the Crusades. The first building, 60 yards (50m) long, was built by Abd al-Malik. This structure proved inadequate, however, and al-Walid had the mosque extended northwards by around 22 yards (20 m), to where the wall of the façade stands today.

Al-Walid was also responsible for introducing the central aisle crowned by a dome. The prayer-hall was divided into 16 bays and opened out on to the square in front of the mosque through three monumental doorways. The ceiling was supported by cypress beams with a 14-yard (13-m) span and engraved coffering; it was reconstructed in 780 after being destroyed in an earthquake in 747.

Secular architecture

Secular buildings from the Umayyad era are generally known only from texts. An example is the so-called "Green Palace" of Muawiya, his "House of Government" (Dar al-Imara) which was situated to the south of the Umayyad mosque in Damascus. The most recent excavations in this area have shown that it was probably demolished when the quarter was redesigned during the Ayyubid or Mameluke periods. During this period another palace complex was built in Jerusalem below the temple mount and southwest of the Al-Aqsa mosque. Six great buildings have been discovered since the late 1960s, of which one is probably a mosque. The largest of them (91 x 104 yards/84 x 96 m) is thought to be a palace. The complex was connected to the Al-Aqsa mosque on the temple mount by means of a bridge.

The Umayyad palace was built at the far northern end of the fortress within circular walls from Roman times. It consisted of two sections arranged around courtyards, a connection being provided by a

Street of colonnades, Amman

This street of colonnades once connected the reception hall and chambers of the Umayyad Palace.

Reception hall of the Umayyad palace, Amman

The reception hall of the Umayyad palace in the citadel of Amman is decorated with a splendid series of niches, and was designed to leave the visitor awestruck. The ground plan with its four *iwans* is, like the decoration, borrowed from Persian architecture.

Hunting lodge, Qasr el-Kharane

Qasr el-Kharane has the character of a caravansarai in more than just its ground plan; it is also located at the intersection of two important roads in the Jordanian desert. Scholars were long unable to agree on the date of its construction by the Umayyads because of the marked Sassanid influences in its architecture and decoration.

Left

Interior, Qasr el-Kharane

Some rooms have direct access to the central courtyard, which was once surrounded by arcades.

colonnaded street. In the east are three apartments whose rooms were arranged around three sides of a courtyard. Two other dwellings bordered on the northern part of the complex. The palace was entered through a great gate known as a "Qasr" which was richly decorated with vegetal and geometric motifs.

The "desert palaces" were a different affair; these royal residences built by caliphs or emirs on the Syrian–Jordanian steppe provided a retreat from city life. These buildings range from small hunting lodges such as the Qasr el-Kharane to larger and more complex structures. They were situated near the routes used by wandering Bedouin tribes, whose support was vital to the lords of these palaces. They were also far enough away from the puritanical cities of Mecca and Medina for the pleasures of life to be enjoyed undisturbed.

Stables, Qasr el-Kharane

In the western wing of the ground floor are a vestibule and two large rooms with pilasters: the stables. The door frames are high, and halfway up the walls is a typically Sassanid decorative device of stucco moldings.

Fortress, Qasr el-Her el-Sharqi

The exact function of this small fort, built during the Umayyad era by Caliph Hisham (728–729), has yet to be determined. It has been claimed that it was a residential complex in the center of a large estate. At the left in the picture can be seen the minaret of a mosque from Ayyubid times.

Entry to the fortress walls, Qasr el-Her el-Sharqi

An arch in the interior of the entrance to the fortress walls of Qasr el-Her el-Sharqi. The paintings probably date from the Ayyubid or Mameluke periods.

Hunting, feasting, and poetry competitions enjoyed great popularity. Poetry, the preferred way of expressing emotions in Arab culture, achieved enormous importance in the Umayyad period. Along with the traditional themes of love, or the praise of Bedouin life, a kind of state-sponsored poetry developed at court, whose task it was to publish abroad the fame of the caliph.

To the east and west of the oasis town of Palmyra are two "desert palaces," Qasr el-Her el-Sharqi and Qasr el-Her el-Gharbi. They were probably founded on great estates from the Byzantine era, of which several still existed in Umayyad times. Several sections of wall enclosed vast precincts, in the case of el-Her el-Sharqi an area which measured some 2 x 4 miles (3 km x 6 km). Due to their location in the desert the irrigation systems of these complexes were of critical importance.

The water supply for el-Her el-Sharqi was provided by a system of pipes from el-Qawm, some 20 miles (30 km) to the northwest. A network of subterranean sewers, reservoirs and cisterns serviced the palace, and even enabled luxuriant gardens to be cultivated. Built on a square ground plan, the palace facade was dominated by corner and semicircular towers positioned at regular intervals. The decorative features of the facade have led scholars to doubt that the building would ever have been intended for defensive purposes.

The facade of Qasr el-Her el-Gharbi, which has been completely rebuilt in the Museum of Damascus, is decorated from the ground to the embrasures with stuccowork. The palace had also been furnished with sculptures depicting people, in the style of Palmyrian reliefs.

Another spectacular example of the facades of these "desert palaces" is the base of the gate facade from Qasr el-Mshatta, which was taken to the Museum of Islamic Art in Berlin in 1903/04. It is ornamented with vines, amongst which can be detected a great variety of birds, fruit and flowers.

The apartments of the "desert palaces" were generally accessible from a central inner courtyard partly framed by two-story porticos. An opulently furnished bath-house, the *hammam*, was naturally an indispensable part of these buildings, although it was often separate from the palace itself. More than just places for relaxation, these baths also had an audience chamber where the lord of the palace could receive his guests and listen to their concerns.

Plaster statue, palace of Khirbet el-Mafdjar

2nd quarter, 8th century
Plaster; height 195 cm (including base)
Archaeological Museum of Palestine
(Rockefeller), Jerusalem

This plaster statue allegedly represents the caliph Hashim. It once stood in a facade niche in the palace reception hall of Khirbet el-Mafdjar.

Rear of the palace, Qasr el-Mshatta

This building was probably begun around 744 by Caliph al-Walid II, and was not completed until after his death. The facade of the rear wall of the palace seen here was articulated by semi-circular buttresses.

Decoration at the entrance to the palace of Qasr el-Mshatta

743/744
Carved stone; length c. 460 cm, height c. 550 cm
Staatliche Museen Berlin, Preußischer
Kulturbesitz, Museum for Islamic Art

Decoration carved in stone at the entrance to the palace of Qasr el-Mshatta. The rosettes are decorated with acanthus leaves, with the vines in the background twisting their way to the top of the ornamentation. The two sides of the portal differ greatly in style and were probably completed by two different workshops.

Palace entry vestibule, Khirbet el-Mafdjar

There are benches on both sides of this vestibule as at Qasr el-Her el-Sharqi; the walls above them were entirely decorated in stucco.

Entry to the palace, Qasr el-Mshatta

The entry to the palace in Qasr el-Mshatta (in the foreground) was decorated with extraordinarily delicate stonework. A large section of the facade can be found in the Pergamon Museum in Berlin.

The frescos of the Quseir Amra (built 712–715) are extraordinarily diverse, and show scenes from the life of a prince. The pictures include hunts for onager (wild donkeys), female dancers, bath-house scenes, workers constructing the palace, and depictions of great deeds and legends, as well as a fascinating composition in which six kings from around the world seem to be paying homage to a Muslim prince. Amongst these decorative images are those of naked people. Such depictions disappear completely, however, at the end of the 8th century, after the rise of the Abbasids, who for religious reasons disapproved of such art.

As a rule these complexes were completed by the addition of a small mosque, houses of various sizes and store rooms. A good example of a total arrangement of this sort is provided by the complex at Djebel Seis, built by al-Walid I. Alongside the palace of Qasr el-Her el-Sharqi were found the remains of a settlement whose square ground plan (180 yards – 166 m – along each side) with four centrally positioned gateways is reminiscent of a Roman encampment. The mosque was located in the southeastern corner.

Above

Audience chamber and baths, Quseir Amra

In Quseir Amra only the audience chamber, baths (seen here from the south), and a building related to the water supply have survived.

Frescoes, Quseir Amra

The frescoes of the palace show scenes from the life of a prince. Depicted here is an onager (wild donkey) hunt from the ceiling of the frigidarium.

Frescoes in the vestibule of Quseir Amra

The paintings on the west wall of the vestibule (left) show scenes in a *hammam*, while above them there are depictions of an onager hunt. The depictions in the eastern aisle show various tradesmen at work building the fortress (right).

Left

Balustrade of the Great Fountain, Khirbet el-Mafdjar

This fountain, decorated with a balustrade, was located in the "courtyard of honor" at the palace of Walid ibn Yazid (724–743).

Opposite

Palace gate, Qasr el-Her el-Gharbi

The gate of the Umayyad palace was reconstructed by Nassib Saliby on the façade of the National Museum in Damascus. The stucco decoration shows the Umayyads' assimilation of Byzantine, Sassanid, and local ornamental styles.

Arches of the mosque at Qasr el-Her el-Sharqi

These arches were part of the mosque and can be found in the southeastern part of Qasr el-Her el-Sharqi.

Palace of al-Walid I, Andjar

The gracious arches of the façade for the great audience chamber were restored in the 1950s after being excavated by Emir Maurice Chéhab.

There are also other examples of this new type of settlement: al-Walid I, for example, built the Umayyad city of Andjar between Beirut and Damascus, in what is present-day Lebanon. This also had a square layout, with two main thoroughfares intersecting in the center, this junction being accentuated by a tetrapylon. Small shops were located to the rear of the arcades along the street. A palace stood in the southeastern corner of the complex, its facades built of alternating layers of ashlar and brick. To the north a *hammam* has been excavated, while the southwestern quarter was probably reserved for houses.

Other cities of this type are known, such as those found in Medinet el-Far on the banks of the Balikh in Syria and in Amman and Aqaba in Jordan. The largest of these, Ramla, was built by the caliph Sulayman (715–717); this, and not Jerusalem, was the capital of Palestine at the time.

In archaeological terms the abrupt transition from the Umayyad to the Abbasid period can be seen in the catastrophic destruction wrought by an earthquake in 747, which affected numerous sites throughout Jordan and Palestine–Israel; this natural disaster is often mentioned in medieval chronicles.

The glory of the Abbasids

The reign of the Umayyads represents a brilliant period in Levantine history. The power of the dynasty, however, was anything but undisputed. The religious divisions within Islam were still potent; the great clans in Mecca and Medina felt themselves disadvantaged by the rulers in Damascus and the great mass of converts from different ethnic groups rejected Arab domination. Syria was unable to counter these all-pervasive problems, and the Umayyad dynasty was finally toppled in an Abbasid revolt in the year 750. The Abbasids traced their ancestry to an uncle of the Prophet, al-Abbas. They organized an underground movement in Persia, where it proved easy to unite the discontented behind a common cause. In 747 the Abbasids took Merw, and in 749 in the great mosque at Kufa they appointed as caliph Abul Abbas el-Saffah, "the bloodthirsty." The army of the Umayyads was defeated in a battle at the Great Zab, a tributary of the Tigris, in 750. In order to prevent future uprisings from the defeated dynasty, Abul Abbas al-Saffah invited members of the Umayyad clan to a banquet on the pretext of seeking a reconciliation, only to have them massacred. Only one member of the clan escaped: Abd al-Rahman managed to flee to Spain where he later founded a new Umayyad dynasty.

The first century of Abbasid rule was marked by great political achievements. With the help of their viziers and a strongly centralized administration, the caliphs succeeded in maintaining order almost throughout the entire Muslim empire. After the short reign of al-Saffah, his brother al-Mansur (754–775) came to power. He reorganized the caliphate and founded a great intellectual and scientific movement. The heterogeneous Sunni ideology gradually came to predominate, and was the source of a new political base in the empire.

One of the Abbasids' first steps was to turn away from Syria, an Umayyad stronghold. The Abbasids looked to the east, to Persia. In 762 they founded a new city on the banks of the Tigris, the site of the later city of Baghdad. Madinat al-Salam, the round city, had a diameter of 2.5 miles (4 km) and was protected by a double ring-wall with moats 22 yards (20 m) wide. The palace and the mosque were located in the center of the city. Nothing has survived of the first town since its destruction in 813.

The caliph Harun al-Rashid, the "righteous" (786–809), is the best known of the Abbasids because of the stories from "A Thousand and One Nights" and the contacts he is said to have maintained with Charlemagne (he allegedly allowed the Frankish emperor to provide Christian pilgrims on their way to Jerusalem with an armed escort).

Abbasid mosque, Raqqa

This Abbasid mosque was built by Caliph al-Mansur in 772, and later remodeled by Nur al-Din, who also built the minaret in 1165.

Palace grounds, Raqqa

A series of palace buildings were unearthed during excavations at the Abbasid site of Raqqa. This picture shows excavations of the western palace.

The luxury of Harun al-Rashid's court is immortalized in legend, as are his piety and his triumphs over the Byzantines. However it was under his rule that the governors of Ifriqiya (north Africa) created autonomous empires which laid the foundations of the eventual breakup of the Muslim empire. In the dispute over his succession, al-Rashid's two sons, al-Amin – who was born to an Arab mother – and al-Mamun – who was born to a Persian mother – plunged the empire into a civil war from which al-Mamun (713–833) emerged the victor. This prudent politician was also a patron of philosophy and science and founded the "House of Wisdom" in Baghdad, which housed a great library and an astronomical observatory.

His brother, al-Mutasim (833–842), built the new capital, Samarra, 75 miles (120 km) upriver from Baghdad, in order to escape the religious tensions in the city. The new town also served as headquarters for his Turkish guard, who were distrusted by the inhabitants of Baghdad. By 892 eight caliphs had ascended to the throne in Samarra. Most of the city has survived; it extends over a distance of 25 miles (40 km), incorporating at least 13 palaces with enormous gardens. A complete plan of the city will soon be published, and the examination of pottery collected in the course of digging and surveying is

almost complete. This work has shown that Samarra flourished for a longer period than had previously been thought.

The main cities of the caliphate traded as far away as India and China. These ties encouraged the consumption of luxury goods and led to the development of a sophisticated culture which gradually spread throughout the Abbasid territories from Persia to Egypt, with the result that provincial cities tended to follow developments in Baghdad. One of the best known of these cities is Raqqa, at the confluence of the Euphrates and the Balikh. It was founded in 772 by the caliph al-Mansur on the Byzantine–Umayyad city of Callinicum, which had existed since the Hellenistic period. It was regarded as a second capital, whose task it was to secure control over the wealthy province of Djesire and to serve as an outpost against the Byzantines.

The city's horseshoe-shaped layout was to have been a more sophisticated version of the circular city of Baghdad. Two thirds of the city walls, built from unfired brick, have been preserved; round towers reinforce the wall approximately every 60 yards (53 m). Inside the walls the Great Mosque, restored under Nur al-Din in 1165/66, retained its original square layout: the strengthening of its outside walls with semicircular towers recalls the great

Mesopotamian mosques of Samarra. The three aisles of the hall of worship and the porticoes around the central courtyard were inspired by the Umayyad mosque in Damascus.

In the north of the city was a residential district in which several palaces were built. A series of these palaces was examined in the 1950s and 1980s. The rectangular complexes were of a considerable size (10,000 square yards/8,500 sq m /for Palace B; 22,000 square yards/18,700 sq m/for Palace C) and were divided into various areas: enormous gardens, private chambers for the prince's harem, a princely residence with a reception hall, guest apartments, baths, and mosques. The external walls were provided with semicircular towers. In Palace B the floor and parts of the walls of the audience chamber were laid out with sheets of glass which reflected the multicolored light entering the room through perforated slabs of stone and stucco. The wooden ceiling was painted and the stuccoed doorways displayed vegetal motifs – usually of grapes entwined in vines. In addition, there were frescoes and Kufic inscriptions in which the name of the caliph al-Mutasim was mentioned.

The water supply for this complex was provided by an older canal from the Balikh river and another laid out in Abbasid times from the Euphrates. The most recent research on the canals in the valley of the Euphrates has demonstrated the enormous economic importance of this system of supply: they enabled agricultural production to be increased throughout the entire region.

Excavations in Heraqla, 5 miles (8 km) to the west of Raqqa, unearthed a strange building which has no parallels in the Islamic world. A circular wall with four gates made entirely of stone enclosed a square structure whose sides were approximately 110 yards (100 m) long. Built on a large terrace, the building was reinforced with corner towers and had a series of inaccessible interior rooms whose walls were purely structural. The only functional elements are the *iwane* in the center of each side wall. These rooms, which were open on one side, generally adjoined a courtyard and have also been found in Abbasid architecture from the east of the empire. The building was probably never finished and it is difficult to attribute a particular function to it. According to written sources it was supposed to be a fortress built in honor of a beautiful Byzantine woman captured by Harun al-Rashid after his victory in Herakleia in Taurus. Today, however, it is thought that the building commemorates his defeat of the Byzantines. It remains the only example of platform architecture from the early Islamic era.

In most Levantine cities life took its age-old course during Abbasid times. Political neglect of the region by the Abbasid rulers is most probably why there are no large Abbasid structures in Syria. It cannot be concluded, however, that the Levant under the Abbasids was nothing more than a deserted stretch of land. Such notions have been steadily undermined by excavations in Jordan and Israel which have indicated Abbasid settlement at several sites.

The capital city of Ramla, founded by the Umayyad caliph Sulayman, was flourishing at this time. Inscriptions date the "Pool of Helena," a massive subterranean cistern, to the year 789, that is, the reign of Harun al-Rashid. The ground plan of six aisles is further divided into four bays by powerful arcades supported by cross-shaped columns. The entire structure is of carefully hewn stone and the slightly angular arches are one of the first examples of pointed arches in the Levant. The weight of the wall above the arcade is reduced by openings which serve to form a double arcade. A stairway on the northern side gave access to cisterns covered with stone slabs. A rectangular opening at the top of each vault made it possible for 24 people to draw water at the same time.

The third building phase of the Al-Aqsa mosque can also be dated to the epoch of the Abbasids, after the central aisle and two bays to the north of the dome had been destroyed in the earthquake of 747. The freshly plastered columns were painted to resemble marble. The building was described by al-Muqqaddasi, who wrote that the shrine had 26 entrances: seven in the north, on both sides of the main entry gate, and eleven in the east. The central part of the building was covered by a saddleback roof crowned by a splendid dome.

Stucco frieze in the western palace, Raqqa

The decorative style of this frieze is characteristic of the early Abbasid era.

Inscription on a cistern, Ramla

End of 8th century
Paper; length 140 cm; width 110 cm
Max van Berchem Archive, Geneva

This inscription on a cistern from Ramla dates from the reign of the caliph Harun al-Rashid (786–809) and was transferred to paper by Max van Berchem. The Arabic script used here is known as "Kufi."

Umayyad mosque, Aleppo

The mosque was completely rebuilt by Nur al-Din in 1169 after being destroyed in a fire. The minaret is the oldest Seljuk structure in Syria, and dates from the end of the 11th century

The decline of Abbasid power

After a century of brilliant achievements, the power of the Abbasids began quickly to fade. Their empires disintegrated and provincial governors founded local dynasties.

Until the destruction of Baghdad by the Mongols in 1258, the caliphs continued to be drawn from the same family. In reality, however, they had long since lost grip on power; they lived in increasing isolation from the people and gradually fell under the influence of Iranian and Turkish emirs. The caliph retained only a representative function on the basis of his religious position, while the emirs controlled the business of government and the army.

At the beginning of the 10th century the Hamdanid dynasty from Mossul (in present-day Iraq) extended their sway over Djesire as far as Aleppo. Sayf al-Dawlah (944–967) was able to build up a brilliant and stable principate which lasted until 1002. He devoted himself to waging war against the Byzantines and even plundered the St. Simeon monastery (Qelat Seman) in northern Syria. This incident brought him a reputation as a great warrior, but led to a revenge attack by the Byzantine emperor Nicephoros II Phocas, who plundered his city in 962. It was in the course of this conquest that the Byzantines wrested back control of Antioch, which was to remain part of their territories until 1085.

During this time Sayf al-Dawlah surrounded himself with artists at his court in Aleppo, and the splendor of his city far outshone that of Damascus. From documentary sources we know that several fortresses in the west of Syria belonged to the Hamdanid dynasty, including Qalat Burzei and the Château de Saône (Qalat Saladin). No buildings from this era have survived in their original state, however.

At the end of the 9th century the esoteric Shiite sect of the Karmates plagued the Syrian steppe as far as Jerusalem, with devastating raids launched from their oasis of el-Hasa on the shores of the Persian Gulf. The rise of rival caliphates can also be dated to the beginning of the 10th century; the Umayyads established their dynasty in Cordoba in 929, and the Fatimids had already founded their caliphate in 909 in Kairouan in present-day Tunisia.

The latter considered themselves direct descendants of Husain, son of Ali and Muhammad's daughter Fatima. Driven by the goal of uniting all the Muslim lands under their rule they attempted several times to capture the city of al-Fustat (Cairo) on the Nile. When, in 969, they finally succeeded, al-Fustat became their new capital. In the following year they asserted their control over the holy cities and continued with the conquest of Syria. This proved a difficult undertaking, however, as they encountered the opposition of the Karmates, who had their roots in the same Ismaili movement as the Fatimids. Around 980 their territories reached as far as Tripolis.

Fatimid power was based on the legitimacy of their caliph as the descendant of Ali, and was supported by a strong army and an excellent propaganda machine. Under their rule Egypt again experienced an upturn in its fortunes, and the court in Cairo became an important patron of the arts and crafts. During the reign of al-Hakim (966–1021) a number Christian churches were destroyed, including the Holy Sepulchre in 1003 – an event that deeply shook the Christian world.

In Jerusalem the Fatimids attempted to strengthen the sacral character of Islamic shrines. The al-Aqsa mosque was rebuilt, this time on a smaller plot, and was provided with mosaics inspired by Umayyad art. The caliph al-Zahir rebuilt the walls of the city in 1033 as well as the western gate, which was covered in mosaics. At this point Jerusalem began to take over the role of provincial capital from Ramla, which had been seriously affected by earthquakes in 1033 and again in 1068.

During this period of political and religious uncertainty the Seljuks were laying siege to the empire. Due to Mongol pressure – a people who themselves were under threat from the Song dynasty in China – whole tribes had begun to migrate to the west. From their homelands to the east the Seljuks conquered the territory of what is today Iran and concluded an agreement with al-Qa'im, then caliph in Baghdad. The caliph was anxious to rid himself of the supremacy of the Iranian Buyid dynasty (945–1055), since they were no longer capable of maintaining order in the empire. In 1055 the Seljuks marched on Baghdad and seized control of Mesopotamia. From now on they held the real reigns of power, while the Persian Grand Vizier Nisam al-Mulk was responsible for administering the empire. The caliph was left with only his spiritual office.

Fatimids and Seljuks

The Seljuk sultans attempted to crush the Fatimid caliphate in Cairo, which at this time controlled the south of Bilad el-Sham, but they found a determined opponent in the person of Badr al-Djamali, the prefect of Damascus. As a result they turned against the Byzantine Empire, and in 1071 under Alp-Arslan they destroyed the Byzantine army at Mantzikert, taking the *basileus*, Romanus IV, captive. This victory marked the end of Byzantine hegemony in Asia Minor and the beginning of the settlement of Cappadoccia and Armenia by the Turkmen.

At the same time Alp-Arslan's son Malikshah (sultan from 1072–1092) conquered first Mossul and Aleppo (1070) and finally all of Syria, including Damascus (1075). His brother Tutush, appointed governor of Syria, fought against the Fatimids; Jerusalem was first captured by the Seljuks in 1078, but changed hands several times in the years leading up to the First Crusade in 1099. Damascus too saw various Fatimid and Seljuk rulers come and go. The presence of the Seljuks and their wars with the Fatimids over ownership of southern Syria, as well as the weakness of the Byzantine Empire, began to unsettle Europe and gave rise to the idea of the Crusades.

The death of Malikshah in 1092 was the beginning of the end for the Seljuk empire. His children were still too young to succeed to the throne, and real power was exercised by their tutors, the *atabeg*, who divided up the various regions between themselves. After Tutush died (1095), Syria passed to his two sons – Ridwan in Aleppo and Duqaq in Damascus, who died in 1104. The real power behind his throne, however, was his *atabeg*, Tugtakin, who declared himself independent and founded his own dynasty: the Burids.

Around this time religious terrorism began to make an appearance in Bilad el-Sham. At the end of the 10th century a new Ismaili sect sprang up from a schism within the Fatimid movement. Its teachings were spread by Hasa al-Sabbah from Egypt to Syria and Mesopotamia, and finally to Persia. In 1090 he conquered the fortress of Alamut in the north of present-day Iran and used it as a base for his Assassins (Arab.: *hashashin*, "users or smokers of hashish"). The Assassins publicly murdered political personalities in order to strike fear and terror into their opponents. Their first victim was the Grand Vizier Nisam al-Mulk, who was stabbed to death in 1092. Exploiting the weakness of the Fatimids, who were being harried in the east by the Seljuks and in the north by Byzantium, the Assassins took possession of several impregnable fortresses in the north of Syria.

The Seljuk Turks tried once again to unite the greater part of their empire by establishing a unified religion. They did this by reorganizing the education system which had previously been directed by Shiite Ismailis. To this end they built the first *madrasas*, where administrative personnel and clerics loyal to the government all received a standard education in religion and the law.

Baghdad Gate, Raqqa

This gate was built in the mid 12th century in the southeastern corner of the Abbasid fortress wall.

The ground plan of the *madrasa* called for four large vaulted *iwane* around an internal courtyard. Though it was first used in Isfahan, this layout was soon being applied throughout the empire. Buildings from the Seljuk era are mostly found in present-day Iran; little of their architecture has survived in the western regions of their empire.

The minaret of the Great Mosque of Aleppo, built from 1090 to 1095, is the first example of a nascent Syrian architectural style in Islamic times. The tower, 150 feet (45 m) high and of a square design, is located to the north outside the mosque. The four registers of its facade form a harmonious whole, despite their different patterns; a Kufic inscription appears between these registers. Above the final row, which is decorated with niches known as *muqarna*, is the wooden-roofed gallery of the muezzin (who calls the faithful to prayer).

Architectural and archaeological investigations have shown that many of the Crusaders' buildings were erected on much older structures. In Damascus parts of the citadel have been dated back to the Seljuk era. The ground plan of this building more or less corresponded to the form visible today but must have been smaller, since original citadel from the Ayyubid epoch was surrounded by a new structure twice as large. Between the two outer walls – which date from different periods – was a type of passageway. The south gate, which was later incorporated into the Ayyubid masonry, was framed by two half-towers.

In general, few buildings from this era have been found in the Levant. More recent archaeological research, though, has demonstrated that the entire region had already been settled in Abbasid times – knowledge for which we are indebted to recent progress in the dating of pottery. At the beginning of the 1990s a number of workshops for glazed ceramics were discovered in Syria, such as those at el-Mina (near Antioch), Raqqa, and Qalat el-Rahba. New decorative techniques had been employed here which were taken up in Egypt and Persia.

Iwan of the Qasr el-Banat, Raqqa

The *iwan* pictured here is located to the rear of the 12th-century courtyard of the Qasr el-Banat.

Arab castle, Marat el-Noman

The Arab castle at Marat el-Noman was captured following a siege during the First Crusade. After massacring the inhabitants, the starving troops of the Crusaders are said to have eaten the corpses of the dead.

Citadel, Jerusalem

The citadel of Jerusalem was remodeled by the Crusaders in the 11th century and then destroyed and rebuilt several times in the course of the 12th century. Its present shape is largely derived from the Mameluke era (1310). Along with the minaret, other buildings were added during the Ottoman period.

The establishment of Crusader states

The Crusaders from Christian Europe disembarked on the Levantine coast at a time of political and, to a lesser extent, religious turmoil. The Crusades were to lead to far-reaching changes in the region and to the mobilization of Islamic forces in Bilad el-Sham – historical Syria – and from as far away as Baghdad.

The Crusades – there were a total of seven – were the result of changes in Christian attitudes to the Muslim presence in the Middle East. The founding of the Seljuk empire in Asia Minor and that of the Almoravids in Spain alarmed Christendom. At the synod of Clermont on 27 November 1095, Pope Urban II's call for a holy war, with the aim of reconquering Jerusalem and the tomb of Christ, acted as a signal for the organization of the First Crusade. The pope's message enabled him to direct to a common cause the energies of the knights, and to bring a degree of order to a feudal world torn apart by constant quarreling.

The First Crusade was led by four great knights of Europe: Raymond of Saint Gilles, Count of Toulouse; Godfrey of Bouillon, Duke of Lower Lotharingia; Hugo of Vermandois, brother of the French king Philip I and Duke of the Ile de France and Champagne; and Bohemond of Tarentum, ruler of Southern Italy and Sicily, who was accompanied by his nephew Tancred. Vast numbers of the poor, spurred on by religious fanaticism, set off with these knights in 1096. In Asia Minor the Crusaders found themselves confronted by the Orthodox Byzantines, whom they regarded as heretics, as well as the Turkish Seljuks and the Christian Armenians in Cilicia. The princely crusaders were permitted to assemble in Byzantium, but the masses in this "popular crusade" were denied entry because the emperor feared for the safety of his city. After helping the emperor defeat the Turks in 1097 in Dorylaion they swore an oath of loyalty to him, promising to return to him all those lands they conquered from the Turks which had previously belonged to the Byzantine Empire.

Just a year later Baldwin of Boulogne, who supported the Armenians against the Turks, named himself Count of Edessa. The Franks, used as a generic term for the Crusaders, continued on their way to Antioch, which they captured following a seven-month siege after the town was betrayed to them. This city – a massive fortress with walls 6 miles (10km) long punctuated by 150 towers – went to Bohemond. The second of the Crusader states therefore was centered on Antioch, which was bound in the east by the emirate of Aleppo and in the north by Byzantium. All previous assurances of returning Antioch to Byzantium were quickly forgotten. At the end of the year the Crusaders captured the small town of Marat el-Noman. Contrary to promises given

City walls, Jerusalem

The city walls of Jerusalem (here to the south of the citadel) were rebuilt during the Ottoman period.

Ahmad-Djazzar mosque, Akko

Underneath the Ahmad-Djazzar mosque (built in 1871) lie great vaults which are today used as cisterns. They once belonged to the church of St. John of the Knights Hospitaller.

by Bohemond the inhabitants were massacred, and the fanatical hordes who followed in the knights' train were sent into a cannibalistic frenzy.

In 1099 the Crusaders reached Jerusalem and, fortified by prayers and fasting, they began to lay siege to the city. Jerusalem finally fell on 15 July and here, too, the Crusaders carried out a massacre of the Jewish and Muslim inhabitants that appalled the entire Middle East. The Christian populace of Jerusalem, who had been a majority in the town, had been expelled by the Muslim defenders before the siege, since they feared collaborators within their ranks. Godfrey of Bouillon was named "Protector of the Holy Sepulchre." After his death he was succeeded by Baldwin, Count of Edessa who became Baldwin I, King of Jerusalem.

The Franks, however, controlled only a small piece of territory between Syria and Egypt, and most of the knights returned to Europe after fulfilling their mission – the conquest of the Holy City. With the aid of fleets from the Italian maritime cities and the constant influx of Christian pilgrims wanting to settle in the Holy Land, they were nonetheless gradually able to expand their territory. Eventually they held most of the coastal cities between Ascalon and Beirut (Sidon, Tyre, Haifa, Caesarea, and Jaffa) and built fortresses to deny Damascus access to the Mediterranean.

The city of Akko, which was Damascus' main port, fell in 1104 and became the Crusaders' most important port under the name of Saint Jean d'Acre; it was here that most pilgrims and Christian soldiers landed. A period of relative prosperity began for the city, which developed into a great trading center, while smaller harbors in towns such as Caesarea were relatively neglected. Part of the Frankish city of Akko has been excavated by archaeologists and its architecture closely scrutinized.

Crusader castle, Shobak

Built by Baldwin I, king of Jerusalem, after 1115, Shobak (Krac de Montréal) was designed to guard the road between Syria and the Red Sea. The visible remains are largely Mameluke buildings which survived the attentions of the Ottomans.

Frankish fortress church, Shobak

Several details from the Frankish fortress church at Shobak (Krac de Montréal) recall churches in Safita, Tartos, and Jerusalem.

The capture of Shobak (Krac de Montréal) in 1115 secured the kingdom in the south as far as the Red Sea and allowed the Crusaders to control communications between Damascus and Cairo as well as the Bedouins of northern Arabia. The location of the fortress was ideal for plundering the caravans of pilgrims on their way to Mecca, and these ventures occasioned the building of fortresses along the Wadi Musa.

One such castle was Wueira, a square-shaped *castrum*. It has survived in its 12th-century form because it was abandoned after being destroyed by Saladin in 1188. The towers, storehouses, soldiers' quarters and chapel can therefore be categorized precisely in terms of their architectural history. The fortress of el-Habis has a completely different ground plan; its walls follow the lie of the land. El-Habis was probably destroyed by an earthquake between 1157 and 1170, and is of inestimable value for researchers studying the architecture of the Crusaders.

Tripolis, which was not conquered until 1109, was promised to Bertrand of Saint Gilles. His lands bordered the Djebel Ansariye, the base of the Assassins, in the northeast. To the east the territories were sheltered by the Lebanon Mountains, while the route from Homs was safeguarded by a tower at Safita (Chastel Blanc) and the Krac des Chevaliers. The Franks were the first to take up quarters in these conquered fortresses, in both the Arab fortress at Hosn el-Akrad, later the Krac des Chevaliers, and the Byzantine *castrum*, whose remains can still be seen today within the walls of the Château de Saône (Qalat Saladin).

Fortress of St. Gilles, Tripolis

This fortress was built on Mont-Pèlerin (Pilgrims' Mount) facing the city during the siege of Tripolis by Raymond of St. Gilles towards the end of the First Crusade (beginning of the 12th century).

Fortress of St. Gilles, Tripolis

The foundations of the Crusader structure were unearthed in the southwestern corner of the Crusader castle built by St. Gilles. At the left can be seen the great *iwan* from the age of the Mamelukes, and at the right is one of the rooms in the curtain wall from Crusader period.

The Crusader states were organized along the lines of European monarchies. The court (*haute cour*), in which all matters concerning the kingdom were discussed, was composed of all the king's vassals. Real power, however, lay in the hands of the barons and the decision of the king had priority. It was he who dispensed the various fiefs to barons and knights. The former were given the cities which slowly grew due to the influx from Europe, while the latter received villages. Little is known about how Crusader towns and villages were administered. Surveys in Israel are expected to show the distribution of Crusader settlements in the countryside. In Caesarea part of a town from this period has been unearthed, and it is known that in Tell Bashir (Turbessel), in the principate of Edessa, a town with ramparts was laid out at the foot of the castle.

Decorated pottery, el-Mina

End 12th/beginning 13th century
Ceramic; diameter 23.7 cm
Victoria and Albert Museum, London

A ceramic plate with a partially etched pattern
and colored glaze (sgraffito) produced in the
workshops of el-Mina, near Antioch.

The Franks left the local administration
unchanged, but abolished the Muslim legal system
with its *qadis*, or judges, replacing them with their
own courts of law. The Crusaders imposed a poll tax
on the entire subject population, which was almost
completely rural, and they did not differentiate
between the Oriental Christians and their own
Muslim countrymen.

The kings of Jerusalem, the Prince of Antioch and
the Counts of Edessa and Tripolis saw power slip
from their grasp, however. Constant waves of
immigration forced them to create ever more fiefs in
a land whose possibilities for expansion were
relatively limited. The mighty barons strengthened
their position through alliances, while the lot of the
knights, who received ever smaller parcels of land,
deteriorated. The king was forced to assert himself
against both an invigorated aristocracy as well as the
newly created chivalric orders.

The Order of the Knights Hospitaller, founded in
the 9th century in Jerusalem, was entrusted with the
protection of the pilgrimage routes outside the
jurisdiction of the cities and forts ruled by the Franks.
The order of the Poor Knights of the Cross, founded
in 1118 by Hugo of Payens, was charged with the
same task. In 1119 its members adopted the name by
which they are best known today – the Knights
Templar – because they resided on the temple mount
in Jerusalem, the site of the former Temple of
Solomon. Members of this order lived according to
the rules of the Cistercians, which required poverty
and simplicity, and they combined the callings of
cleric and knight. The knights wore a white cloak
with a red cross over their armor.

The duties of these orders grew constantly,
and as they formed standing armies they became
indispensable for defending the states' borders.
Well organized and – contrary to their vows –
endowed with great wealth, they took over
responsibility for maintaining and reinforcing the
fortresses which proved too costly for the king or
the princes to operate on their own. In time they
became a potent force, independent of both king
and church. The Order of Teutonic Knights was
formed in 1198, long after the Hospitallers and
Templars; their possessions were restricted to the
citadel of Montfort.

This period was also characterized by the
construction or extension of various fortified sites;
this may have meant the fortification of an entire
village or the building of a single tower. The age of
the Crusades was a time of considerable progress in
the sphere of military architecture. During the siege
of Antioch the Franks faced a stone fortress on a scale
never previously encountered. Their own forts in
Europe were generally built of wood and earth, stone
being reserved for religious buildings. Oriental
fortresses must have seemed impregnable to them
by comparison.

The Crusaders used many of the area's
abandoned buildings as quarries and over time
acquired many local building techniques, such as the
ability to construct round towers and vaulting. Due
to these influences the shape of their fortresses took
on ever more sharply defined forms; in addition
advances in weapons technology led to new forms
of architecture.

The use of pottery to try to determine an
archaeological chronology of the 150 years of
Crusader rule has proved difficult. Investigations at
sites from the 12th and 13th centuries show a pattern
of distribution of varying ceramic products which
runs from the mountain ranges with their citadels in
the north to the steppes in the east. It has also been
shown that no luxury ceramic ware was produced
during the Middle Ages in Palestine itself. Luxury
ceramics were imported from Cyprus, Muslim Syria,
southern Italy, or the region around Antioch.

Crusader castle, Montfort

This Crusader castle was the only property belonging to the Order of Teutonic Knights in the Holy Land; purchased from Jacques de Armigdala in 1127/29, it was renamed by the order and greatly extended. Surrounded by forests and hills, the castle is still difficult to get to today.

Qalat Saladin Fortress

This view of the Château de Saône (Qalat Saladin) shows the phases of construction the fortress went through under its various owners. To the right are the walls of the Byzantine fortress, to the left the Crusader entry tower, while in the center is the mosque of the Mamelukes.

Aqueduct, Caesarea

Ancient ruins were treated as quarries during the construction of both the Byzantine and Crusader cities at Caesarea.

Crusader castle, Musayla

The Crusader castle of Musayla was built on a rocky peak in the 12th century, and served as a watchtower along the road from Beirut to Tripolis. The bridge in the foreground is probably from the same period.

Crusader castle, Musayla

After the battle at Hattin, Saladin is said to have stationed a garrison here.

The mobilization of Islam against the threat from Europe

The expansion of the kingdom of Jerusalem into the Transjordan region cut communications between Syria and Cairo, and forced the Muslim powers to act. In contrast to the Crusaders, their troops had no heavily armored cavalry; instead, they used light weapons which gave them greater mobility in battle. The Muslims resorted to using surprise attacks, and their battles with the Crusaders were invariably murderous struggles.

While the Fatimids waged five campaigns against the kingdom of Jerusalem between 1101 and 1105, the emirs of Mossul, Aleppo, and Damascus were also gathering their forces, and they were able to inflict punishing defeats on the Franks at Harran in 1104 as well as at Edessa in both 1110 and 1111. Al-Ghazi, the emir of Diyarbakir, was tireless in his efforts against the Crusaders and shortly afterwards he crushed the army of Roger, Prince of Antioch, at Atareb.

When Baldwin I of Jerusalem died in 1118 he was succeeded by his cousin, Baldwin II, who had previously governed Edessa. Edessa passed to his vassal, Joscelin de Courtenay, who was captured in 1122 by al-Ghazi. Several months later Baldwin II was also attacked while out hunting with falcons, and promptly joined Joscelin in a dungeon from which, however, they later made a daring escape.

The Muslim side was not able to take advantage of its victories. The emirates were not always prepared to offer each other support, and they were reluctant to ask the Seljuks in Baghdad for help too often for fear of forfeiting their autonomy. Moreover, the Sunni rulers were being destabilized by constant attacks from the Assassins: Maudud, the emir of Mossul, who had been victorious against the Franks, fell victim to them in 1113.

Imad al-Din Zengi won great fame through his attempts to unite the world of Islam by force; he founded the Zengid dynasty, which played a central role in the fate of the Levant until the Ayyubids came to power in 1175. In 1126 Zengi inherited the throne of Mossul, and in 1128 he gained control over Aleppo. A year later he conquered the city of Hama, but failed in his attempt to capture Homs and Damascus. Soon afterwards he drove the Crusaders from their fortress at Atareb, between Aleppo and Antioch, and ordered it to be razed to the ground. In 1137, after unsuccessfully besieging Homs, he decided to attack the fortress of Barin (Montferrand). King Fulk of Jerusalem, the successor to Baldwin II, who hurried to the Crusaders' assistance, was defeated and the besieged army was forced to capitulate. In 1138 Zengi pursued the army of the Byzantine emperor, John II, which was retreating to Antioch after the unsuccessful siege of Sheizar; he took a great number of prisoners and seized valuable booty. The same year Homs surrendered to him and the garrison in Baalbek was destroyed. Another attempt at laying siege to Damascus, however, proved unsuccessful once again, since the city commander supported the Crusaders. Several years later, in 1144, he crushed Edessa; two years later, in 1146, he died during the siege of Qalat Djabar. His possessions were divided among his sons, with Aleppo going to Nur al-Din Mahmud, who displayed great skill in continuing his father's policy of uniting the Muslim Orient.

After the Crusader states in the north had lost half their territory to Zengi, the Franks attempted to strengthen the territory belonging to the kingdom of Jerusalem, building fortresses at Ascalon, in the Transjordan, and in Galilee (1135–1146).

The loss of Edessa – an entire Frankish principate – led to a revival of the crusading ideal. This time not only knights but kings also followed the call of the Cistercian abbot Bernard of Clairvaux. Both the French king, Louis VII, and the German emperor, Conrad III, set off on the Second Crusade which ended in a complete fiasco. In 1148 the German crusading army was almost completely wiped out on its arrival in Syria, with the survivors soon returning home. Louis VII's army had suffered fewer losses and decided to capture Damascus on its way to Jerusalem; this contingent was quickly forced to capitulate to Muslim troops rushing from their bases in Aleppo and Mossul. This group of Crusaders also left the Holy Land shortly afterwards.

Above left

Ottoman mosque, Caesarea

The streets of the Frankish city of Caesarea are paved with Carrara marble from the antique ruins of the surrounding area. In the background can be seen the Ottoman mosque.

Above right, and left

Crusader castle, Musayla

According to local tradition, descendants of Saladin are said to have extended the castle in the 16th century.

By the end of 1150 the borders of Islamic power had moved from the Euphrates to the Orontes river after the conquest of Apamea (Qalat el-Mudiq), Harim, Tell Bashir, and other fortresses. Nur al-Din also tried to seize Damascus a number of times, using several different pretexts. On each occasion the governor of the city called for the assistance of the Franks before finally acknowledging the suzerainty of Nur al-Din in 1151 – although the city was able to retain its autonomy. With his conquest of Tartus in 1152 Nur al-Din was able to render unreliable the land link between the earldom of Tripolis and the princedom of Antioch, while at the same time organizing his own communications by means of carrier pigeons. In the following year he was able to win the confidence of the citizens of Damascus through the skillful use of propaganda, and the city's governor withdrew to Homs. With a strategy which combined diplomacy (armistices were agreed with Antioch, Jerusalem, and Byzantium) and successful military campaigns, he was able to strengthen his position and extend his domains. In 1155 he took Baalbek and in 1157 Banyas, while in the latter year he was forced to reorganize his Syrian fortifications, which had been destroyed in an earthquake.

The following years were marked by his attempts to win back Edessa, which had been seized by his Muslim neighbors, the Seljuks, from Asia Minor. After suffering two defeats, at Harim and Qadesh Nur al-Din, however, he lost confidence in this enterprise.

From now on the battle was conducted with the Koran as well as the sword. Nur al-Din built or extended a whole series of buildings which were to be used to spread the orthodox Sunni creed; these include several mosques, among them the Great Mosque at Aleppo.

The *madrasa*, a type of building developed by the Seljuks, also assumed an important role in these religious and political measures; Nur al-Din built around 40 of these buildings in the Muslim lands under his control. They were used as law schools, while the teachings of the Prophet were conveyed to pupils in the corresponding institution of the *dar al-Hadith*. The Madrasa el-Muqqadamiye in Aleppo, the oldest *madrasa* in the city, is a former church which was converted into a Koranic school in 1168 in response to the Crusaders who were at that time laying siege to the city.

Qalat el-Mudiq, Apamea

The Arab settlement of Qalat el-Mudiq in the Orontes valley formed the border between Arab territories to the east and the possessions of the Crusaders to the west.

Fortress of Qalat Djabar, Edessa

The fortress of Qalat Djabar was incorporated into the principate of Edessa as early as the First Crusade. In 1149 it was reconquered by the Arabs. A large part of the building work was carried out under Nur al-Din (1146–74).

Prayer-hall of the Madrasa Halawiye, Aleppo

The prayer-hall was erected in the 12th century on the site of the cathedral of St. Helen. The columns of the cathedral were retained in the new structure.

Citadel, Rahba

Built at the end of the 12th century, this citadel was the most western of those in Bilad el-Sham. The castle is among the most impressive fortifications in Syria and is situated on one of the important ancient connecting roads between the Levant and Iraq. The city which surrounded the castle has been the subject of excavations by American and Syrian archaeologists for several years; it was one of the most prominent cities on the Euphrates during the Middle Ages.

Opposite

Interior of the Umayyad mosque, Aleppo

The tomb to the left of the *mihrab* is said to contain the head of Zacharias, the father of John the Baptist. This venerated relic and the tomb of John the Baptist in the Umayyad mosque in Damascus show the importance of role played by New Testament figures in Syrian Islam.

The ground plan of the Mabrak mosque in Bosra (1136) represents one of the first instances of the new *madrasa* design from the 12th/13th centuries. According to legend the building was erected on the spot where a camel carrying the first copy of the Koran to Syria once kneeled.

After Amalric ascended to the throne of Jerusalem in 1163 on the death of his brother, Baldwin III, the Franks began to develop a greater interest in Egypt, where the Fatimid caliphate had been weakened by domestic political strife. Egypt witnessed a succession of viziers who fought bitterly for power during the regency of a child caliph. Shawar, who had seized power in 1162, was overthrown by his deputy after just nine months and he fled to Damascus to plead with Nur al-Din for support, providing his host with assurances of his future loyalty. When the Franks exploited the situation and undertook their first attack on Egypt, Nur al-Din dispatched an army led by his capable general Shirkuh, while he stayed to threaten the Crusaders' northern flank. After the successful conquest of Egypt, however, Shawar reneged on his promise and turned to the Franks for help in eliminating the Syrian army occupying his country. After several clashes for supremacy in Egypt the Syrians finally gained the upper hand over the Franks. Shirkuh returned to Syria in 1167 and was given Homs and Rahba as a reward for his service. In the same year the Syrians succeeded in contrtolling Arqa, thus securing the route between Tortosa (Tartus) and Chastel Blanc (Safita). Following successful negotiations in 1168, Nur al-Din received the fortress of Qalat Djabar on the east bank of the Euphrates.

In 1196 Shirkuh assumed the position of vizier in Egypt and when he died after just two months he was succeeded by his nephew Salah al-Din ibn Ayub, more commonly known to the West as Saladin. At the same time Nur al-Din used the fact that the Franks were preoccupied in Egypt to expand his domains as far as Mossul, which he conquered in 1171. It did not take long for divisions to appear between Nur al-Din and Saladin over the direction of the war against the Franks. Saladin, who had been strengthened in his position by the untimely death of the last Fatimid caliph, needed the Franks as a buffer zone between himself and his master in order to retain the independence he had established in Egypt. On two occasions he allowed the siege of Kerak to fail (in 1171 and 1173). Shortly after Nur al-Din decided to invade Egypt and bring Saladin to heel in 1174, his sudden death set the seal on Saladin's power.

The greatest of the Zengids was buried in a *madrasa* tomb in Damascus, which he had built in the southwest of the Great Mosque. The building (Madrasa Nuriye, 1167–1172) still retains parts of its original ground plan. The dome with *muqarnas* over the burial chamber is, along with the entrance to the hospital (Maristan Nur al-Din) which he built in 1154, one of the few examples of a typically Mesopotamian style of architecture in Damascus.

Fortress architecture

The Muslim counteroffensive led to an increase in military construction work on both sides of the border. The Krac des Chevaliers, in the hands of the Crusaders from 1110, is the finest and best-preserved example of a fortress in the Levant. It represents a synthesis of the different styles of military architecture up to that point, and its design integrated the new defensive concepts which had developed in the course of the Crusades. A number of different aspects had to be considered in the construction of this kind of defensive complex. In order to withstand sieges, the entrance to the castle had to be made as inaccessible and difficult to attack as possible. For this reason there was often only one entrance which was usually just big enough to permit horses and carts to pass through. Often, however, there were also gates through which the castle's occupants could escape, and these were sometimes connected to underground passageways. The fortresses were built on rocky ridges or were surrounded by moats which could be crossed by a drawbridge. Supplies of water – so essential in times of crisis – were provided by reservoirs in the interior of the castle.

Glacis of the citadel, Krac des Chevaliers

The flanks of the citadel of the Krac des Chevaliers were laid out as a perfectly stereometric glacis. The reservoir situated between the two walls was fed from the outside by a rainwater aqueduct; it also served as added protection for the keep.

Passage between portal and courtyard, Krac des Chevaliers

The kitchens and living quarters lay at the northwestern wall of the citadel. This hall has a length of 130 yards (120 m).

Opposite

Gallery in the late Gothic style, Krac des Chevaliers

The gallery in late Gothic style in front of the great hall is an architectural modification and dates from the second half of the 13th century.

Fortress, Marqab

The fortress at Marqab lies on a basalt cone which provided its own construction material. It overlooks the main road between Asia Minor and the Holy Land.

Left

Hall of honor, Marqab fortress

The great hall of honor in the fortress at Marqab was built over a cistern which provided the entire complex with water.

Opposite, left

Fortress chapel, Marqab

The fortress chapel dates from the first phase of construction under the Knights of St. John (end of the 12th century). It is a good example of the severe style of the Crusaders, which was influenced in its early stages by French Gothic.

Opposite, right

Moat of the Crusader castle, Qalat Saladin

The moat of the Crusader castle at Château de Saône (Qalat Saladin), with the rocky spur which supported the drawbridge.

At the fortress of Château de Saône, which was built on a rocky spur, and at the castles of Edessa and Qalat el-Rabadh (1185), a pillar was left standing after excavation of the moat to serve as a support for the bridge. The steeply rising glacis forms a transition between the hewn natural rock of the base and the walls of the citadel. The thick and high outer walls were reinforced with towers, and were designed to withstand the salvoes of catapults; their loopholes and battlements meant that the immediate surroundings could be carefully observed. At twin-walled fortresses such as the Krac des Chevaliers or the fort at Marqab the outer walls complex contained a second, completely independent defensive installation – that of the castle proper. Access to this inner set of buildings was provided by broad ramps designed for cavalry and a single gateway with a portcullis and hole through which boiling pitch could be poured onto the enemy. Provisions and animal feed were stored in this inner structure; in the magazines of the Krac des Chevaliers there are to this day massive urns for storing grain. Water – a matter of life and death in the event of a siege – was provided by a gigantic reservoir open at the top (in the Krac des Chevaliers and Kerak), or by equally vast cisterns as at Château de Saône. While the stables and sleeping quarters for the soldiers were built along the outer walls, the chapel, kitchens, refectory and knights' quarters were all in the innermost buildings. In the castle at Kerak, built in 1142, these apartments were built below ground to provide protection from the summer heat. The last line of defense was provided by the keep, the most impregnable building in the complex, and the residence of the lord of the castle. Muslim fortress architecture differed from the Frankish model only in having baths and a mosque, as at Qalat Djabar and the Château de Saône, where they were added later. Religious buildings were often retained in the event of the fortress being taken by an enemy, churches being converted into mosques and vice versa.

Jerusalem

In Jerusalem the Franks attempted to restore a monumental architectural style to the city. They converted mosques into churches or used them for secular purposes. In addition they also used the structures the Byzantines had been allowed to rebuild after the Fatimid caliph al-Hakim had confiscated the property of Jerusalem Christians and destroyed their churches in 1009. The most important of these was, of course, the Church of the Holy Sepulchre – the most holy site in Christendom. It had been partly rebuilt in 1048 at the instigation of Emperor Constantine Monomachus. Though the rotunda of the tomb was given a new upper section, the late antique basilica which adjoined the rotunda to the east was not replaced. From 1144 to 1149 the Crusaders built a new monumental structure which was to be one of the most remarkable pieces of architecture of their era. The Byzantine rotunda remained largely intact,

transformed into a great western apse by the addition of a transept with a further apse to the east. Both apses were provided with platforms which were heightened by adding a choir ambulatory with a cornice featuring arrangements of three capitals. The various relics of Christendom – Christ's tomb, the "navel of the world," the rock of Golgotha, the stone on which the Savior was anointed, and "the prison of Christ" – which had previously been accommodated in various buildings, were now brought together under one roof. In the east, a monastery and buildings for the church canons were built. The bell tower, erected between 1160 and 1180, consisted of vaulted rooms stacked vertically; its walls were pierced by large window arches supported by white marble columns. The three top floors were destroyed by an earthquake in 1719.

Holy Sepulchre, Jerusalem

The Holy Sepulchre rises up in the center of the rotunda in this Frankish church, which originally possessed an ambulatory.

Church of the Holy Sepulchre

The façade of the church dates from the first half of the 12th century. The tower originally had three stories with windows and marble half-columns separated by dome-shaped vaults.

Opposite

Interior of the Church of the Holy Sepulchre, Jerusalem

This complex has been destroyed, rebuilt and extended several times since it was first erected by the emperor Constantine, and now features a church, chapels, and additions from a variety of epochs. This picture shows the basilica, looking towards the choir.

Church of St. Anne, Jerusalem

The church of St. Anne in Jerusalem is the finest example of a Crusader church. The crossing is surmounted by a dome.

The church of St. Anne (first half of the 12th century), with its cross-shaped ground plan, is an excellent example of a Crusader church. Its three aisles end in a transept of three apses and together with the large, central apse they form the cross shape of the church. An egg-shaped dome rises over the crossing. The church was built over a crypt venerated as the place of the Virgin Mary's birth. The simplicity of the architecture and the interior – the barrel vault is influenced by the early Gothic style and features slightly pointed vaults supported by plain capitals – add considerable emphasis to the harmony of the building's Romanesque proportions and lend it a unique beauty.

The fortress chapels of Chastel Blanc (Safita) and Qaryat el-Enab show a similar ground plan. From the outside they have the appearance of massive, thick-walled structures. A roof terrace enabled a watch to be kept on the surrounding area. Chastel Blanc had a subterranean cistern, and there were apartments in the first floor above the church itself. At Qaryat el-Enab the chapel was built over a Roman fort with a spring which was integrated into the cross-shaped church. The crypt over the spring and the interior of the church were decorated with frescos.

Crusader castle, Safita

Only the keep has survived from the Crusader castle of Chastel Blanc (Safita). It was rebuilt after being destroyed by the Knights Templars in the 13th century.

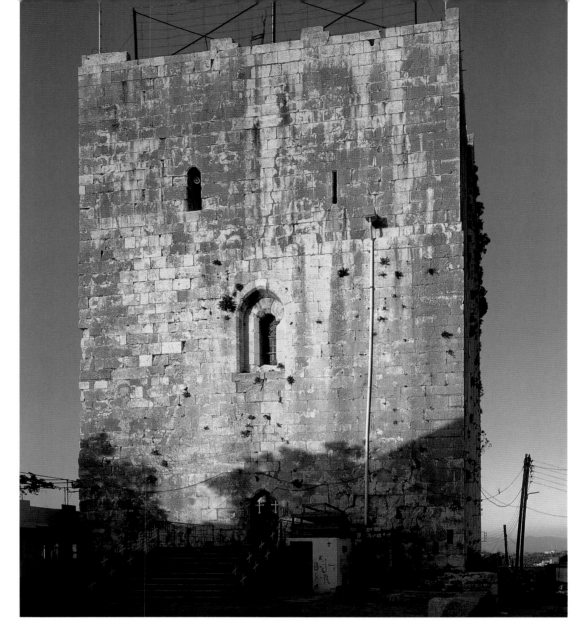

Nave of the church of St. Anne, Jerusalem

The nave and aisles of the interior feature groin vaults. The harmony of the interior is emphasized by light entering from side windows.

Citadel, Masyaf

The citadel of Masyaf is the best-preserved citadel of the Assassins. It lies in the mountainous region between the Orontes valley and the Mediterranean coast.

The triumph of Islam

When Saladin, the founder of the Ayyubid dynasty, came to power (1174–1193), the beginning of the end was signaled for the Crusader states. He too took up the policy of waging the holy war against the Franks which the successors of Nur al-Din had been too weak to continue. Within a short space of time he was able to unite most of the Muslim forces in the region and to form an empire which included Egypt, Muslim Syria and part of the Djesire. It was not just the Franks who attempted to deny his ambitions however; the Zengids in Aleppo, headed by Nur al-Din's son, also saw him as a usurper and were hostile to his intentions. First, though, Saladin had to fend off the radical Shiite Ismailis who were determined to bring down this Sunni successor to the Shiite empire of the Fatimids.

The Assassins had by this time withdrawn into their virtually impregnable mountain fastness, with headquarters located at Qadmus, between Masyaf and Banyas. Under the leadership of the "Old Man of the Mountains" (Rashid al-Din Sinan, 1163–1193), the fortress at Masyaf developed into one of their main centers. Under pressure from the Zengids in Aleppo, the Assassins attempted on several occasions to murder Saladin. After an unsuccessful attempt to beseige Masyaf, Saladin concluded that he had more than enough enemies to deal with; he reached an armistice agreement with the Assassins, who were then able to turn their attentions to the Crusaders. Although the activities of the sect declined after the death of the "Old Man" they continued to carry out their murderous campaigns until the Mongols conquered their headquarters at Alamut in 1256 and destroyed their valuable library.

The Franks, who were conscious of Saladin's strength, tried everything they could to limit his power. Headed by Amalric's son and successor, the leper Baldwin IV, they were at first able to deal a defeat to Saladin's troops. In 1180 Saladin finally reached an armistice with the Crusaders. There was however increasing discord in the camp of the sick Frankish king. Reynald of Châtillon had spent 16 years as a prisoner in the citadel of Aleppo and was obsessed with revenge; he attacked a wealthy caravan on the pilgrims' route to Mecca which he controlled from his fortresses at Montréal and Kerak.

The fortress of Kerak had often been of great strategic significance due to its position on a plateau east of the Dead Sea. In response to this attack Saladin laid waste to Galilee and Samaria. In the following year Reynald of Châtillon decided to attack the holy sites of Islam. Although Saladin was able to crush the Crusaders, Reynald escaped. In 1183 Saladin captured the most important towns in the Djesire region as far as Aleppo, finally uniting Syria and Egypt.

He continued to wage war against the kingdom of Jerusalem, but was thwarted by the efficient defensive system built by the Franks. Not a single Crusader castle fell to him. In 1185 both parties agreed a four-year armistice. Saladin used this time to extend his fortresses (Qalat el-Rabad/Adjilun, 1184–85) and to turn against Mossul, which was finally obliged to provide troops for Saladin's holy war in 1186.

Saladin now had an impressive number of troops at his disposal, even if the contingents provided by the emirs of the various provinces could only be called up at certain times. And Saladin also possessed the secret of "Greek fire," a mixture of petroleum and other substances capable of sparking conflagrations whose flames were virtually impossible to extinguish with water. At this critical juncture the Franks wasted their energies in their struggles over the issues of access to the king and of his succession. After the lingering death of Baldwin IV and the demise of his successor, Baldwin V, the two main rivals for power were Guy of Lusignan and Raymond of Tripolis. To make matters worse, Reynald of Châtillon chose the most inconvenient possible time to break the armistice with the Muslims by attacking a caravan on its return from Mecca in 1187. Saladin called for a holy war; he besieged Reynald's castles at Montréal and Kerak, crossed the Jordan and encircled Tiberias.

Crusader castle, Shobak

The buttresses provide the interior building of the Krac de Montréal (Shobak) with stability and distribute the pressure of the heavy stone vaults. Differences in the style of the masonry indicate that the building was constructed at different times.

Magazine in the interior of the Ayyubid palace, Shobak

Finds from excavations carried out in the 1980s are stored here.

View of the interior of the Crusader castle, Shobak

Archaeological investigations in the 1980s demonstrated that the site had been in almost continuous occupation since the 12th century.

The Franks were at odds over what tactics to pursue. Raymond of Tripolis advised caution, pointing out that there was only one source of water on the route to Tiberias and that temperatures were unbearable at that time of year. Guy of Lusignan refused to wait, however, and gave his army orders to march. Cut off from access to water his army was forced to dig in on a hill at Hattin, where they were surrounded and utterly wiped out by Saladin's numerically superior forces. The Franks had the Cross of Christ torn from their hands and almost all their noblemen were taken prisoner, including Guy of Lusignan. Guy was treated in a manner befitting a sovereign ruler and spared along with the other prisoners. Only Reynald of Châtillon fell victim to Saladin's rage.

The fortresses and cities of the Franks proceeded to surrender one after the other until in 1187, after a siege lasting two years, Jerusalem once again fell into Muslim hands. Saladin was finally able to provide the Al-Aqsa mosque with the *minbar* which Nur al-Din himself had never been able to donate to Jerusalem. The Muslim buildings which had been consecrated as Christian churches were converted back to their original purpose. The Dome of the Rock and the Al-Aqsa mosque were restored. Many Christian buildings were also rededicated to the Muslim faith: the church of St. Anne was converted into a *madrasa* in honor of Saladin (Madrasa Salahiye) in 1189, and the main church of the order of St. John became a hospital in 1192. The Holy Sepulchre remained a Christian shrine, but was only reopened to pilgrims in 1192.

Apart from Tripolis and Antioch only Tyre, under the rule of Conrad of Montferrat, remained in Frankish hands, and it soon became a center for Christian refugees. The shock caused in the West by this defeat led directly to the Third Crusade.

Minbar of the al-Aqsa mosque, Jerusalem (destroyed)

The minbar of the al-Aqsa mosque in Jerusalem was built between 1168 and 1174 in Aleppo by the greatest craftsmen of their day. It was commissioned by Nur al-Din to be presented to the Holy City after he had reconquered it. Until Jerusalem was captured by Saladin the minbar stood in the great mosque at Aleppo. In 1969 it was destroyed in an act of terrorism.
This photograph is from the archive of Max van Berchem (1863–1921), who visited Jerusalem three times (1888, 1893, and 1914). Van Berchem's research into medieval Arabic inscriptions also focused on the places – buildings and countryside – where these texts were discovered.

In 1188 the German emperor Frederick I Barbarossa reached Cilicia by traveling overland; he drowned while crossing a river, however, and his army disintegrated. Two years later Philip Augustus of France and Richard I, "Cœur de Lion" or lionheart, of England set off for the Holy Land by sea. On their way they conquered Cyprus, which now provided a secure naval base and refuge should they need to retreat. The Crusaders supported Guy of Lusignan – who had since been released – in his siege of Akko which fell after two years in 1191. Saint Jean d'Acre became capital of the kingdom of Jerusalem for the next 100 years. In the same year Saladin ordered the destruction of the city of Ascalon so that it could not be used as a base for future incursions by the Crusaders.

Saladin was a poor accountant and no longer had the means necessary to defeat the strong and well-equipped troops of Richard the lionheart, and the Franks were now able to dominate the coast from Tyre to Jaffa. In 1192 Saladin signed a peace treaty with his Christian opponents and died just a few months later. His body was first interred in the citadel of Damascus before being transferred in 1196 to a newly built mausoleum in the Madrasa Aziziye. Today only parts of this *madrasa* in the north of the Umayyad mosque can be seen alongside the burial chamber.

Saladin built a large number of military installations. These included the citadel of Cairo, begun in 1176 but only completed after his death. The rebuilding measures carried out at Montréal (Shobak) were the object of excavations at the start of the 1990s. The most remarkable feature discovered is the Ayyubid palace, whose tripartite reception hall and lateral *iwan* anticipate the style of the great Mameluke palace halls.

After Saladin's death his empire was divided among members of his family. Of his three sons, one received central and southern Syria, the second Egypt, and the third Aleppo. Hama was given to a cousin, Homs to a grandson of Shirkuh, and the Djesire went to Saladin's brother al-Adil Sayf al-Din. As the most important remaining member of the Ayyubid family he took over responsibility for the dynasty. In 1200 he had himself declared sultan in Cairo and compelled the princes to pay him homage.

Peace was welcomed by both sides. The Ayyubids had no desire for any further military activity which might threaten trade and provoke further crusades. The Franks were similarly opposed to new crusades and the arrival of new rulers from Europe, as these would only have interfered with their power and disrupted the trade which was beginning to develop with the Syrian hinterland.

Tomb of Saladin, Damascus

The tomb of Saladin (end of the 12th century) lies near the Umayyad mosque. It was originally integrated into the Madrasa Azizye (partly lost). The faience tiles were added during restoration work under the Ottomans.

Reception chamber of the Ayyubid palace, Shobak

The reception areas of Ayyubid palaces consisted of a central courtyard with – ideally – four *iwans*. In smaller buildings, such as at Shobak, Bosra, or Baalbek, a vaulted central room with flanking *iwans* replaced the courtyard.

A time of peace

In the West, meanwhile, Rome was determined to pursue a fourth crusade. In complete contrast to the original concept of the Crusades, which were directed against the Muslims, this venture led to the conquest of Constantinople in 1204 – the greatest Christian capital of the age – and to the founding of a Latin empire in the East. A further attack was directed against Egypt which, despite isolated successes, ended in failure.

When the Chorasmian riders – Muslims from the east of the Caspian Sea who were fleeing a Mongol invasion – entered first Mesopotamia and then Asia Minor, a temporary alliance was forged between the Ayyubids and the Seljuks in Turkey. The Chorasmians had attempted to settle in the Arab plains of northern Syria. The Fifth Crusade occurred at around this time led by the German emperor Frederick II; he had been so reluctant to respond to the urgings of Pope Honorius to undertake this expedition that he had finally been excommunicated. Al-Adil's son, al-Kamil, who became ruler of Egypt after his father's death, was mainly interested in keeping the peace and allowed the Crusaders to take possession of Jerusalem for a period of ten years. In return, the Crusaders were obliged not to build any further fortifications and to guarantee the Muslims the right to exercise their faith (Treaty of Jaffa, 1229). Though he lacked the support of the clergy, the emperor had himself crowned king of Jerusalem. A genuine friendship then developed between the two rulers, which caused a scandal in both the Christian and Muslim worlds.

Citadel, Aleppo

The citadel of Aleppo was partly built on a tell with a glacis; the history of the city since its founding can therefore be traced due to the archaeological material which in the course of construction was sealed inside. The entrance was rebuilt after the invasion of Tamerlane (Timur-Lenk) in the 15th century.

The half-century which elapsed between the death of Saladin and the death of al-Kamil in 1238 was a period of reorganization for the Ayyubid empire. Peace with the Franks and a strict fiscal policy provided for an intensification of trade with Italy and had a positive effect on the economies of both Egypt and Syria. In the territories under Ayyubid rule, especially in Syria, cultural life flourished. A military strategy largely based on diplomacy was accompanied by the construction of great urban citadels in Cairo, Jerusalem, Bosra (conversion of the Roman amphitheater into a citadel), Damascus (rebuilding of the city walls and citadel by al-Adil 1207), as well as Aleppo.

The citadel of Aleppo was built on a hill over the remains of one of the oldest settlements in the Middle East, referred to in the first chapter of this book. The most striking features of this masterpiece of Arab military architecture are the extremely steep glacis (48°) and moat, which is 71 feet (22 m) deep. The bridge over the moat was protected by an easily defensible, 65 feet (20 m) high tower built in 1211, though it has since been rebuilt several times. The facade of the citadel entrance is representative of Mameluke fortress architecture. A second entry bastion led into the interior of the citadel, where many of the original buildings have been preserved: the palace of Sultan al-Aziz, built in 1230; the great mosque, rebuilt by al-Zahir Ghazi in 1214; and the Abraham mosque, which can be dated from an inscription to 1167 and is attributed to Nur al-Din.

Tower at the southwest of the fortress, Damascus

This tower was reconstructed by the Department of Antiquities according to plans from the Ayyubid period.

Ayubid palace, Aleppo

The Ayyubid palace lies at the highest point of the citadel; the domes of the baths were built at a later date (1367).

The orthodoxy of the Ayyubids can be seen in the more widespread diffusion of the *madrasa* in Syria and Djesire, as well its introduction to Egypt. Under Nur al-Din the *madrasa* type containing the tomb of its donor became more commonplace. The Madrasa al-Zahariye in Aleppo (1217) with its welcoming courtyard and lively fountain contains only a cenotaph of its builder, al-Zahir Ghazi. The tomb of the Sultan al-Adil Sayf al-Din, Saladin's brother, who died in 1218, is located in the Madrasa Adiliye in Damascus; its entrance doorway with a projecting keystone is decorated with *muqarna*. The courtyard has only a single *iwan* on the right-hand side, while the tomb located to the left of the entrance under a dome has *muqarna* pendentives.

The finest *madrasa* in Aleppo is the Mardasa Firdaus (School of Paradise). It was built between 1234 and 1237 by Daifa Khatun, the widow of al-Zahir Ghazi. A great *iwan* opens on to an elegantly proportioned courtyard. The prayer-hall has a vaulted roof provided by three *muqarna* domes. This building can be considered a precursor of the great tomb complexes of the Mameluke era.

The Franks also used this period of relative peace to rebuild some of the structures destroyed by Saladin. In 1228 in the harbor at Sidon they erected a citadel on an island close to the shore. It was during this time that the cathedral at Tartus, begun in 1123, was finally completed; it is considered the finest of the Crusader churches. As with older churches at Beirut, Byblos, and Ramla, the nave features a pointed barrel vault while the aisles have rib vaults. As with the church of St. Anne in Jerusalem, the simplicity of the proportions radiates a sense of great dignity.

Citadel, Sidon

Situated on an island, the citadel at Sidon was designed to protect the harbor. Construction of the fortress by the Crusaders took just a few months (in 1228). It was connected to the shore by a bridge and two easily dismantled wooden causeways.

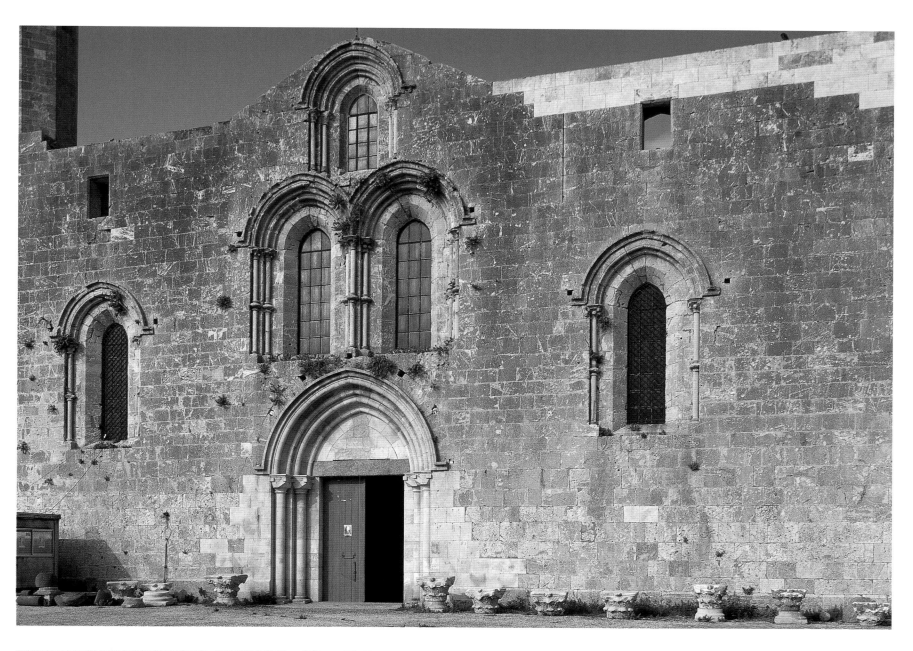

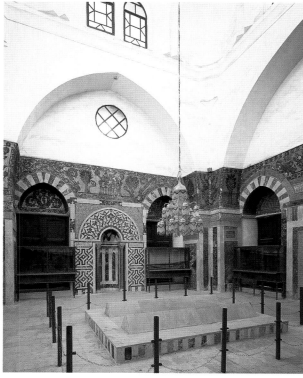

Cathedral of Notre-Dame, Tartus

The façade of the 13th-century cathedral of Notre-Dame in Tartus reflects the division of the interior into three parts.

Below left

Madrasa al-Adiliye, Damascus

The Madrasa al-Adiliye houses the tomb of Saladin's brother (d. 1218). The entrance is an excellent example of a *muqarna* with projecting keystone.

Interior of the Madrasa al-Zahiriye, Damascus

The interior of the Madrasa al-Zahiriye, also known as the Mausoleum of Baybars, continues the tradition of the funerary madrasa from Ayyubid times.

Madrasa Firdaus, Aleppo

The Madrasa Firdaus, one of the finest buildings in Aleppo, was built in the first half of the 13th century by the widow of the sultan al-Zahir Ghazi.

Mameluke tower of the citadel, Jerusalem

The entrance to the citadel was defended to the south by the great Mameluke tower, and to the north by the tower of David. This is the largest structure built to strengthen the curtain wall.

St. Louis and the end of the Crusades

The Ayyubid empire was never a unified entity, and fighting once again broke out over the succession when Kamil died. His eldest son, al-Salih Ayub, was finally able to seize power in Cairo with the support of an army of Turkish slaves – the Mamelukes – and Chorasmian riders. The Syrian Ayyubids promptly formed an alliance with the Crusaders in order to fight their Egyptian cousins. Al-Salih broke the treaties negotiated by his predecessors and in 1214 he took Jerusalem, plundering the city, murdering its inhabitants, and violating the Holy Sepulchre as well as other churches.

With this act al-Salih Ayub unleashed the Sixth Crusade. This campaign, led by the French king Louis IX – who was later canonized – ended quickly in the same year (1250) with the capture of the Crusader army at Mansura. A year earlier the Mamelukes had seized power in Egypt on the death of al-Salih. In exchange for a high ransom and the conquered city of Damiette, the Crusaders were released. Louis remained in the Holy Land to enlarge the fortresses and reestablish cordial relations between the Italian maritime cities and the rulers of the Crusader states. Jerusalem remained in the hands of the Egyptian kings until it was conquered by the Ottomans in 1516. St. Louis was responsible for a series of important buildings. The walls and citadel at Caesarea, for example, were repaired between 1251 and 1252. Excavations at this site in the 1960s unearthed cisterns, the remains of the cathedral and an entire residential quarter. By using methods developed for underwater archaeology the harbor installations were

also examined. In the mid 13th century however, the region was confronted with a danger which compelled Christians and Muslims to put aside their differences temporarily. After their conquest of Baghdad in 1258 the Mongols prepared next to attack Syria. In the face of this threat Franks and Mamelukes ceased hostilities. This enabled the Mamelukes to halt the advance of the Mongols in 1260 at Ayn Djalut – though Aleppo and Damascus had previously been captured.

The Mameluke sultan Baybars then proceeded to capture Ayyubid Syria, the Frankish fortresses of the interior and the coastal towns of Caesarea, Arsuf, Jaffa, and Antioch. Castles which no longer had a function in this new order were systematically destroyed, while others were extended. In Tell Bashir (Turbessel) the curtain walls disappeared, as did the towers and the vaulted ceilings of the palace. On the other hand, the only known Mameluke palace in Transjordan has survived at the fortress of Karak; its forecourt and keep are also from this period. Urban fortifications, such as those at Aleppo and Damascus, were repaired and beautified.

The Seventh Crusade was the Christian response to these Mameluke conquests, but the army never reached its goal, since Louis IX died on his arrival in Tunis. Muslim power in the area had been greatly bolstered, placing the survival of the Crusaders in the Holy Land once again under threat. A faction of the Franks considered entering into an alliance with the Mongols, but this only hastened the collapse of their power. Deciding to end the matter once and for all, the Mameluke sultan, Qalawun, seized Akko from the Templars in 1291 and razed the city to the ground. The last Christian fortresses capitulated and the Templars abandoned Château Pèlerin (Atlit), the last Frankish fortress on the coast, without a fight. The Franks were expelled from the Levant, never to return.

The Crusades were both a military and religious defeat for Europe. They drove a wedge of misunderstanding between Christians and Muslims and led to a consolidation of Sunni Islam; and the conquest of Constantinople in 1204 only deepened the divide between Byzantium and the Christians of the West. The greatest service provided by the Crusades can be seen in the intensification of trade between Europe and the Orient. The Italian maritime cities of Pisa, Genoa, and Venice had been given trading rights in various ports such as Tyre, Sidon, Beirut, Tripolis, and Tartus in return for supporting the Crusaders. After the Franks withdrew they were able to retain these rights and so form a "bridge to the Levant."

Synoptic chronology

Given the state of the sources, any attempt to relate early developments in the Levant to cultural and historical processes in the early cultures of Egypt, Mesopotamia and Iran must inevitably remain provisional. As the various scientific dating methods all harbor potential sources of error, no comparative chronology has yet been accepted by all scientific disciplines. Nonetheless, it appears to us both worthwhile and helpful to the reader to present the history of the Levant side-by-side with the developments of the neighboring major cultures of Egypt, Mesopotamia and Iran, in the form of a synoptic time chart. Besides information provided by the authors, the chronological information is based on the *Cambridge Ancient History* collection. To establish the dates of Egyptian dynasties and select the Egyptian rulers named, Jürgen von Beckenrath's *Egypt. The world of the Pharaohs* (Cologne, 1997) was consulted.

Age: Period Rulers • important events • *cultural achievements* in the **Levant**	in **Egypt**	in **Mesopotamia**	in **Iran**
Bronze Age 310-1200 B.C.			
3100–2000 B.C.: Early Bronze Age			
3100–2900 B.C.: Early Bronze Age I • Semitic peoples appear • *First evidence of writing. Genesis of first towns. Development of metallurgy*	c. **3000–2707**: Early Dynastic Period; 1st Dynasty; development of Egyptian script; southern unification struggles against the north	c. **3000–2000**: Uruk period	Proto-Elamite period based in Susa; Indus Valley culture
2900–2650 B.C.: Early Bronze Age II • *Development of urban cultures*	Early Dynastic Period; 2nd Dynasty; **2707–2170**: Old Kingdom; 3rd Dynasty; beginning of monumental stone architecture	c. **2800–2700** Jemdet Nasr period	Proto-Elamite period, based in Susa; first mention of Elam in a Sumerian source (c. **2680**)
2650–2400 B.C.: Early Bronze Age III • c. **2500**: export of cedarwood from Byblos to Egypt documented • *development of urban cultures*	Old Kingdom, 4th and 5th Dynasties; age of the pyramids: Snofru, Cheops, Khepren and Menkaure, the great pyramid builders	.c. **2600–2340**: Early Dynastic period (Ur I)	**2500–1500**: Old Elamite period; Elam intermittently in control of southern Mesopotamia
2400–2000 B.C.: Early Bronze Age IV **Five rulers of Ebla documented: Igrish Khalam, Irkab-Damu, Ar-Ennum, Ibrium, Ibbi-Sipish. Four rulers of Mari documented: Iku Shamagan, Ebil-il, Enna-Dagan, Shura-Damu** • Egyptian expeditions to Syria; Mesopotamian expeditions to Syria (Sargon of Akkad) c. **2000**: Amorite invasion • c. **2000**: *crisis in old Bronze Age urban culture*	Old Kingdom, 6th–8th Dynasties; sun worship becomes state religion; 1st Intermediate Period: 9th and 10th Dynasties	c. **2340–2150**: Akkadian period; Sargon of Akkad (c. **2340–2284**)	**2500–1500**: Old Elamite period; Sargon of Akkad tries to bring Elam under his control (c. **2325**); his successor succeeds; rulers of the house of Eparti (c. **1850–1500**)
2000–1500 B.C.: Middle Bronze **1775–1761: Zimrilim, king of Mari; between c. 1930 and 1660 nine kings of Aleppo documented** • **1935**: Shamshid-Adad of Assyria conquers Mari; from **1900**: Hurrians (Horites) in the northern Levant; **1757**: Hammurabi of Babylon conquers Mari; c. **1745**: Hittites conquer Aleppo and Babylon; c. **1530**: Mitannian kingdom in northern Syria; c. **1500**: Thutmosis I of Egypt (**1504–1492**) conquers Syria • *Rise of the coastal towns; Phoenician city culture unfolds; c.**1800**: shaft graves in Byblos*	**2119–1794**: Middle Kingdom; unification of kingdom by Mentuhotep I; 11th and 12th Dynasties; **1794–1550**: 2nd Intermediate period; 13th–17th Dynasties; Hyksos rulers (c.**1660–1550**)	c. **2065–1995**: Ur III; c. **1955–1700**: Isin-Larsa period; from c. **1950**: rise of Assyria; c. **1850–1530**: 1st dynasty of Babylon (Hammurabi dynasty); Hammurabi (**1792–1750**)	**2500–1500**: Old Elamite period; Hammurabi subjugates Elam (**1764**); Epartid rulers (until c. **1500**); end of the Indus Valley culture; various peoples on Iranian plateau documented by name; proto-Iranian cultures on the Iranian plateau
Phoenicians 1200–330 B.C.			
1200–800 B.C.: Early Iron Age Local rulers are known by name, especially in Tyre, the most important town, on which other coastal cities were often dependent; **Hiram the Great (970–936)**, contemporary of David and Solomon; **Baal-Utsur (936–918); Abd-Ashtar (918–909); Ethbaal (887–859); Badezor (859–853); Mattan (853–821); Pygmalion (831–785)** • c. **1200**: invasions by the Sea Peoples; **1192**: Rameses III of Egypt defeats the Sea Peoples in the Nile delta; a remnant of the Sea Peoples, the Philistines, settles on the coast of Palestine (named for Philistines); c. **1190–800**: period of relative independence for the coastal cities – the Golden Age of Phoenicia; **1094**: first Assyrian thrust into the coastal regions; from c. **1100**: Phoenician colonies round the Mediterranean in Spain, North Africa, France, Malta, Greece, Cyprus; the Phoenicians sail round Africa and their ships explore the Atlantic; **879**: Assurnasirpal II of Assyria takes Syria and the coastal region; **855**: rebellion of inner Syrian and coastal cities against the Assyrians, which is defeated; **814**: founding of Carthage • c. **1200**: *metalworking under the influence of the Sea Peoples; development of glass and textiles manufacture; Phoenician ivory work widely distributed; an individual (eclectic) Phoenician style in art; crimson dyes; shipbuilding; Phoenician colonies (Carthage **814**); c. **1000**: first lengthy Phoenician inscription from Byblos; c. **970**: construction of the temple in Jerusalem*	**1557–1085**: New Kingdom; 20th Dynasty; Rameses III (**1183–1152**) defeats the Sea Peoples in the Nile delta; Rameses IV–XI (**1152–1064**); decline of the empire	**1380–1160**: Middle Assyrian Kingdom; **1112–1074**: Tiglath-Pileser I: campaigns to the north and Syria, repulse of Arameans; from **1100**: Aramean incursions, weakening of Middle Assyrian Kingdom and fall; Arameans occupy Babylon and reduce Assyria to its heartlands; **909–612**: Neo-Assyrian Kingdom; **883–858**: Assurnasirpal II overcomes the Arameans in Mesopotamia; **858–824**: Shalmaneser III consolidates the kingdom, brings Babylon under Assyrian control, undertakes several campaigns to Syria and conquers the coastal district.	**1205–c. 1100**: Ighehalkid rule in Elam; c. **1200**: Iranian immigration from Central Asia to the Iranian plateau, proto-Iranian groups (Guteans, Lulu-beans, Maneans etc.) on the Iranian plateau: from **900**: mention of new ethnic groups on the Iranian Plateau, including Parsa (Persians) and Medes; c. **900**: Persian immigration from northwest Iran to south Iran (Persis), the southwest part of Iran still named Fars for them today.
800–500 B.C.: Middle Iron Age The coastal towns come under Assyrian, Babylonian, and finally Persian dominance; the role of Egypt becomes secondary and of only episodic importance; c. **722: Hiram II, ruler of Tyre and Sidon** • Weakening of Assyrian control; **732**: Damascus finally taken by the Assyrians; **732–690**: Elu-eli, ruler of Tyre; **722**: Shalmaneser V of Assyria regains the Syrian provinces and coast; **675**: Sidon rebels and is destroyed by Assyrians; **672**: Tyre rebels; during Ashurbanipal's reign (**668–626**) the Assyrians gain control of Egypt as well; **612**: the Babylonians and their allies destroy Nineveh, the end of the Assyrian Empire; **597**: the Babylonians take Syria, Palestine, and the coastal regions; **585–572**: Babylonians besiege Tyre; **539/538**: the Persians capture Babylon and take over the Babylonian conquests in the west; Phoenicia becomes part of the Achaemenid Persian Empire (until **333**) • *spread of Phoenician alphabet; spread of eclectic Phoenician style of art; c. **660** Phoenician seamen sail round Africa*	**1070–730**: 3rd Intermediate Period; 21st–24th Dynasties; **950–730**: Libyan Dynasties; 22nd/23rd Dynasty; **730–715**: Sais rulers in the delta; 24th Dynasty; **730–655**: Late Period; Ethiopian Dynasty; 25th Dynasty in Upper Egypt; **671–663**: Assyrian conquest, destruction of Thebes; **525–404**: 27th Dynasty of the Persians, Egypt becomes a Persian satrapy.	**745–727**: Tiglath-Pileser III (**745–727**) drives the Arameans out of Babylon, becoming king of Assyria and Babylon; **724**: Tiglath-Pileser takes Damascus and Samaria; **680–669**: Esarhaddon conquers Egypt, greatest extent of Assyrian Empire; **668–626**: Ashurbanipal quells revolt in Egypt; **616**: The Medes under Kyaxares conquers the Scythians and prepare to fight the Assyrians; **612**: Medes and Babylonians capture Nineveh; **606**: end of Neo-Assyrian Empire; **625–539**: Neo-Babylonian Empire; **605**: Nebuchadnezzar II drives the Egyptians out of Syria and Palestine; **539**: Cyrus II of Persia conquers Babylon; Persian rule in Mesopotamia; Mesopotamian culture develops independently under benign Persian rule	**760–644**: New Elamite Empire with 11 kings known by name; **673**: the Median prince Kashtaritu sets up an alliance against the Assyrians; c. **665**: Deioches (II) founds the first Median state; **612**: Medes and Babylonians conquer Niniveh and end Assyrian rule; **558–530** Cyrus II (the Great); **553**: Cyrus II defeats the Median king Astiages; **549–539**: Persians conquer Elam, northern Iran, Asian Minor and Central Asia; **539**: Persians conquer Babylon; **538**: Persians conquer Syria and neighboring regions; **530–522**: Cambyses II king of the Persians, conquest of Egypt (**525**); **522–486**: Darius I (the Great) king of the Persians; Persian Empire at zenith of power

Age: Period Rulers • important events • *cultural achievements* in the **Levant**	in Egypt	in Mesopotamia	in Iran
Phoenicians 1200–330 B.C. (cont.)			
500–0: New Iron Age **Client rulers of the Persians, Hellenic kings and Romans** • **349–344**: Phoenician revolt against the Persians; **345**: Artaxerxes recaptures Sidon; **332**: Alexander conquers Tyre in a bloodbath after a long siege; **331**: Alexander defeats the Persians at Nineveh; **330**: Alexander takes Hamadan; Darius III, the last Achaemenid king, is murdered as he flees; **323**: Alexander dies in Babylon on his way back from India; from **305**: Phoenicia a bone of contention between the Ptolemies of Egypt and the Seleucids who rule the east; Phoenician cities enjoy relative autonomy under the Ptolemies and Seleucids; Sidon is the leading city; **64**: Pompey conquers Syria for Rome; **47**: Caesar visits the Phoenician cities; **40–38**: Parthian sortie into Syria and the coast; up to c. **180 A.D.**: heyday of whole Levant • *peaceful development of local culture under Persian rule; recognizable Persian influences in art; from c. 330: Hellenization of the Levant. The cities acquire a Hellenic patina; Syria and the Levant become a spiritual center of the Graeco-Roman world*	**404**: With Amyrtaeus of Sais, the local 28th Dynasty comes to power; several Persian attempts to regain power; **380–343**: last cultural blossoming of Old Egypt under the 30th Dynasty; **343**: Persian reconquest; **332**: Alexander conquers Egypt; **303–30**: The Greek Ptolemies rule Egypt; Alexandria becomes the cultural center of the western world; **51–30**: Cleopatra is last Ptolomaic queen; **30**: Roman conquest of Egypt, which becomes part of Roman Empire.	**331**: Alexander the Great king of Babylon; **312**: Seleucos I (**312–281**) conquers Babylon; start of Seleucid rule in Mesopotamia; **305**: Founding of Seleucia on the Tigris (near Baghdad); **141**: the Parthians make their first thrust into Mesopotamia	**490–448**: Achaemenid–Greek wars; **331**: Alexander defeats the Persians at Gaugamela; **330**: the Greeks take Susa and Persepolis; end of the Achaemenid Empire; **312–305**: the Seleucids consolidate their rule in Iran; **247**: the Arsachids found the Parthian Empire; **171–138**: the Arsachids complete the conquest of Iran; **129**: Parthian victory over the Seleucids; Parthian rule in Iran (until **225 A.D.**)
Greco-Roman Antiquity 330 B.C.–330 A.D.			
Alexander the Great (336–323) • conquests of Alexander • *beginning of Hellenization of the region*		Conquest by Alexander	
Beginning of Seleucid dynasty (c. 305–64 B.C.); Seleucus I (305–281) • Between **323** and **280**: Orient divided, with Seleucids in Syria, Mesopotamia, and Central Asia, Ptolemies in Egypt and southern Syria; Nabataeans first documented in Petra, and display increasing economic and political strength as regional power; Greek attack on Nabataeans under Antigonus I (**312**); the "people of Rabbel" receive a grain shipment from the Hauran (**259**); **275–217**: Four Syrian wars between Seleucids and Ptolemies • *founding of the Tetrapolis in northern Syria (Antioch, Apamea, Laodicea, and Seleucia Pieria; the Nabataeans use "Syrian" characters, i.e. write in Aramaic; as nomadic shepherds, they are already involved in long-distance trade in spices from Arabia Felix; they begin building houses in the lower town in Petra in the 3rd and 2nd centuries*	**323–30 B.C.**: Ptolemaic dynasty; Ptolemy I (**304–285**)	Founding of Seleucia on the Tigris (**305**)	Seleucus I conquers eastern Iran; peace treaty with the king of India (**303**); Antiochus I is viceroy of Mesopotamia and Iran (**292**); Parthians establish Parthian empire in eastern Iran (**250–238**)
Antiochus III the Great (223–187) • fifth Syrian war, reunification of Levant (**205**)			**248**: Beginning of Arsachid rule in Iran (Parthian Empire)
Aretas I, "Tyrant of the Arabs" (c. 168) • Syria under Seleucid hegemony (**198**); Hasmonean Jews reject Hellenization policy of Antiochus IV (**167**); Jason flees; the Nabataeans meet the ringleaders of the Jewish rebellion, Judas and Jonathan Maccabeus, in the Hauran (**163**); Jonathan Maccabeus entrusts his possessions to the Nabataeans (**160**); **152**: independence of Judaea (Hasmoneans) • *Poseidonius of Apamea (135–50/51); construction of Iraq el-Emir by Hyrcanus (end of 2nd cent.)*	Ptolemy VI (**181–145**) regains parts of Syria	Conquest of Mesopotamia by the Parthians (**141–129**); capture of Dura Europus (**135**)	Parthian expansion to the west under Mithridates I (c. **170**); end of Seleucid rule in Iran (**129**)
Aretas II (c. 120/110–96) • Alexander Jannaeus occupies the Nabataean port of Gaza (**100**) • *Strabo (64/63–21)*			Mithridates II is king of the Parthians (**123–87**)
Obodas I (c. 96–85) • Obodas defeats Alexander Jannaeus in battle in Golan (**93**); Alexander Jannaeus returns the regions of Moab and Gilead to the Nabataeans (c. **90**); **87**: Antiochus XII wars against the Nabataeans; death of Antiochus (**88**); Mithridatean wars in Asia Minor and Greece (**88–63**)	Ptolemaic rule	Parthian rule	Parthian rule
Rabbel I (?) (c. 85/84)			
Aretas III Philhellenus (84–62/61) • Aretas rules in Damascus (**84–72**); conflict with Alexander Jannaeus flares up again; Aretas loses 12 cities in Moab and Edom and several Mediterranean ports (**82**); death of Alexander Jannaeus and his widow Alexandra (**76** and **67**); quarrels over succession between his sons Aristobulus II and Hyrcanus II (**76** and **67**); Aretas III embarks on siege of Jerusalem (**65**); establishment of Roman province of Syria (**64**); Aretas defeated in battle by Aristobulus in the Jordan valley (**64**); Roman governor Scaurus campaigns against the Nabataeans (**62**); highpoint of Nabataean territorial expansion, extending from Damascus to Hejas and from the Negev to Wadi Sirhan • *Nicolaus of Damascus (64 B.C.–c. 4 B.C.)*			
Obodas II (62/61–59/58)			Orodes II (**57–37**)
Malchus I (58/57–30) • Successful campaign by the Roman governor Gabinius against the "city of the Nabataeans", undoubtedly Petra (**55**); Malchus I supports Caesar at the battle of Alexandria (**47**) • *first dated inscription in Palmyrene (44)*	Reign of Cleopatra VII, last of the Ptolemies (**51–30**)	Defeat of Crassus by the Parthians at Carrhae (**53 B.C.**)	
Herod the Great king of Judaea (41 B.C.–4 A.D.) • Malchus allies himself with the Parthians against the Romans (**40**)	Egypt annexed by Roman Empire (**31**)	War between Parthians and Romans (**42–39**). Mark Antony's campaign against the Parthians (**37**)	Phraates IV (**38–2**)
Augustus (63 B.C.–14 A.D.) • death of Herod the Great (**4 A.D.**); census by Quirinius reveals population of 117,000 in Apamea (**6–7 A.D.**); Judaea becomes authorized province (**6 A.D.**) • *first dated Syrian inscription in Birecik (now southern Turkey), 6 A.D.*		Peace treaty between Parthians and Romans (**20**)	
Obodas III (30–9 B.C.) • disastrous expedition to southern Arabia by the Prefect of Egypt, Aelius Gallus (**25 B.C.**)			
Aretas IV, "who loves his people" (9 B.C.–40 A.D.) • Apostle Paul flees Damascus, where the city gates are watched by the "ethnarchs of King Aretas" (between **37** and **40/41**) • *cultural heyday of Nabataean kingdom; construction of the great temples in Petra; the Nabataeans settle and build splendid houses.*	The old Egyptian bureaucracy continues under Roman rule	Under Parthian rule	Parthians
Tiberius (14–37 A.D.) • Colonnaded street in Antioch; dedication of temple of Bel in Palmyra (**32**); road-building (**69–96 A.D.**); New Testament written (1st/2nd cents.); Flavius Josephus (**37–100 A.D.**)		Artabanus III (**12–38**) fights the Romans	
Malchus II (40–70)			Vologeses I (**51–80**)
Nero (54–68) • Jewish revolt (**66–70**) • *completion of Temple of Jupiter in Baalbek*			
Rabbel II, "who loves his people and brings them life" (70–106) • Co-regency of Shaqilat, mother of Rabbel II (**70–75**); Bosra becomes a sort of second capital of the empire; final annexation of the areas ruled by the heirs of Herod (**92/93**) • *development of Nabataean agriculture in Hauran and southern Syria; the colonnaded street in Petra takes its present form – paved (c. 100); Babata archives (90–130)*			Artabanus IV (**80–105**)
Trajan (98–117) • Annexation of Nabatea by Cornelius Palma; creation of the Roman province of Arabia (**106**); status of metropolis conferred on Petra (**114**); Trajan's campaign against the Parthians (**115–117**) • *Construction of the "Via Nova Traiana" (111–114); an earthquake destroys part of Apamea (115) – the great colonnaded street is subsequently rebuilt*		Mesopotamia and Dura Europus briefly annexed by Romans (c. **115**); northern Mesopotamia becomes a Roman province	Vologeses II (**105–147**)
Hadrian (117–138) • Petra acquires the status of metropolis and the cognomen *Hadriana* in honor of a visit by Hadrian; second Jewish revolt (**132–135**); oriental campaign by Avidius Cassius (**165**) • *tomb of Roman governor Sextius Florentinus built in Petra (c. 127–129); Lucian of Samosata (119 to around 180); completion of the temple of Bacchus in Baalbek (c. 150) and construction of the shrine of Artemis in Gerasa*	Revolt in Egypt (**153**); devastation of Egypt begins		Vologeses III (**148–192**)

Age: Period Rulers • important events • *cultural achievements*	in the **Levant**	in Egypt	in Mesopotamia	in Iran
Graeco-Roman Antiquity 330 B.C.–330 A.D. (cont.)				
Marcus Aurelius (161–180)				
Commodus (180–192)				
Septimius Severus (193–211) • provinces of Coele Syria and Phoenicia established • Plotinus, Neo-Platonic writer (*205–270*) and Longinus, who belongs to Zenobia's advisers in Palmyra (*213–272*)			Heyday of Hatra; Romans occupy Ctesiphon, the Parthian capital (**197**)	Artabanus V (**213–227**), the last Parthian king
Elagabal (218–222) • Petra given the honorary title of *colonia* (c. **220**); death of Severus Alexander and beginning of the "crisis of empire" (**235**) • *death of Ulpian, the Tyre-born jurist and praefectus praetorio (223); Porphyrius of Tyre (233–305)*				The Sassanids oust the Arsachids in Iran (**225**); Ardashir (**225–239/42**)
Philip the Arab (244–249) • *Philip the Arab celebrates 1,000 years since the founding of Rome*			Destruction of Hatra by the Sassanids (**240**)	Shapur I (**239/42–272**)
Valerian (253–260) • Sassanid attacks (**251–261**), Valerian dies in Sassanid captivity (**261**)			Capture of Dura Europus by the Sassanids (**256**); Manis preeminent (executed **273**)	
Aurelian (270–275) defeats Gallienus, and ends Zenobia's bid for independence • death of Odenathus, prince of Palmyra. His wife Zenobia takes over the regency (**267**); Petra is incorporated into the province of Palestine (**295**)	Decline of Indian trade following the increase in Sassanid power	Sassanids	
Diocletian (284–305) • provinces divided into smaller units • *last persecution of Christians (303–305)*				
Constantine the Great (324–337) • Founding of a second imperial capital called Constantinople (**330**); beginning of Byzantine era; Petra incorporated in the province of Palestina Salutaris (**358**); first documented bishop of Petra, Germanus (**359**); Petra partly destroyed by an earthquake (**363**); second earthquake in Petra (**419**); in the 5th cent. the city becomes a place of exile • *Edict of Milan (313) grants Christians religious freedom; Council of Nicaea (325); Libanius of Antioch (316–393); school of law in Beirut, founded c. 200, flourishing until the 6th century; urn grave in Petra turned into a cathedral by Bishop Jason (446)*				
End of the Roman Empire in the west (476) • third earthquake in Petra				
Early Byzantine Near East 330–640				
Constantine I, sole ruler (324–337) • Edict of Milan (**313**); 1st Council of Nicaea against the Arians (**325**); founding of Constantinople (**330**) • *cathedral of Tyre (**from 314**); Eusebius of Caesarea (d. **339**); churches in the Holy Land (**326–335**): Holy Sepulchre, Mount of Olives, Mamre, cathedral of Antioch (**327–341**)*	Beginning of monasticism with SS. Anthony and Pachomius (**300–346**); Athanasius Bishop of Alexandria, opponent of the Arians (**328–373**)		Sassanid king Shapur II marches into Arabian peninsula c. **330**
Constantius (337–361) • Gallus Caesar rules the Oriens diocese (**351–354**); Jewish rebellion (**352**); edicts against pagan cults (**353–356**); Scythopolis trial (**359**)			Byzantine–Persian wars (**337–350** and **359–363**)	
Julian the Apostate (361–363) • edicts against Christians (**362–363**); abortive attempt to rebuild temple in Jerusalem (**363**) • *Libanius, orator of Antioch, pagan (**314–393**); St. Helena discovers the Holy Cross (**326**)*				
Jovian (363–364)				
Valens (364–378) • *Ephraim of Nisibis (**306–373**), Syrian hymnographer*			Byzantine–Persian wars (**370–378**)	
Theodosius I (379–395) • uproar over the Statutes of Antioch (**387**); ban on all pagan cults (**391–392**) • *pilgrimage of St. Egeria (**381–384**); St. Paula comes to Jerusalem as a pilgrim (**385**); destruction of Temple of Baal in Apamea by Bishop Marcellus (**386**); Ammianus Marcellinus completes his history (**393**)*	Destruction of the temple of Serapis in Alexandria (**393**)		Ardashir II (**379–383**; Shapur III (**383–388**); Bahram IV (**388–399**)
Arcadius (395–408) • final split between empires in east and west (**395**); destruction of the temple of Marnas in Gaza (**402**) • *St. Jerome (c. **348–420**); John Chrysostom, patriarch of Constantinople (**398–404**), exile (**404**)*				Yezdegert I (**399–420**)
Theodosius II (408–450) • pagans banned from public office (**416**); end of Jewish patriarchate (**429**); Council of Ephesus against the Nestorians (**431**); Monophysite Council, called the "Robber Synod of Ephesus" (**449**) • *church of St. Paul and Moses in Dar Qita in northern Syria (**418**); Nestorius, patriarch of Constantinople (**428**); publication of the Theodosian Codex (**438**); Empress Eudocia in Jerusalem (**438–439** and **443–460**)*	Cyril patriarch of Alexandria, opponent of the Nestorians (**412–444**)	Byzantine–Persian wars (**421–422**)	Bahram V (**420–438**); Yezdegert II (**438–457**)
Marcanius (450–457) • Council of Chalcedon against Monophysitism (**451**) • *Juvenal, bishop of Jerusalem (**422–458**) is elevated to patriarch (**451**)*			The Nestorians close the theological school of Edessa (**457**); school of Nisibis founded	
Leo I (457–474) • *death of St. Simeon Stylites the Elder (**459**); death of St. Euthymius, founder of Palestinian monasticism (**473**)*	Timotheus Elurius, Monophysite patriarch of Alexandria (**457–460** and **475–477**)			Ormazd III (**457–459**); Peroz I (**459–484**)
Leo II (474); Zeno, 1st reign (474–475); Basiliscus (475–476)				Balash (**484–488**); Cavad I (**488–531**)
Zeno, 2nd reign (476–491) • Samaritan rebellion (**484**)			Zeno closes the school of Edessa (**489**)	
Anastasius I (491–518) • Destruction of Akko, Carmel, and Tyre by earthquake (**503**) • *school of rhetoric at Gaza (end 5th/early 6th cent.); Severus, Monophysite patriarch of Antioch (**512–518**), in exile (**518**)*			Byzantine–Persian war (**502–506**); founding of Dara-Anastasiopolis (**505**)	
Justin I (518–527) • Olympic games of Antioch annulled (**520**); destruction of Antioch by earthquake (**526**)				
Justinian I (527–565) • abolition of freedom of conscience for pagans (**529**); Samaritan revolt (**529**); Persians plunder Antioch (**540**); Jacobus Baradeus of Edessa founds the Monophysite church of Syria (**542–578**); earthquake in Beirut (**551**); Samaritan uprising (**555**) • *death of St. Saba in Palestine (**532**); Justinian's codification of Roman law (**532–565**); construction of the Nea in Jerusalem (**531–543**); monastery of St. Simeon Stylites the Younger (**541–565**); Sinai monastery (**548–565**); Procopius of Caesar writes his histories (**550–554**); Cyril of Scythopolis, monk and hagiographer (c. **525–558**)*		Byzantine–Persian war (**527–531**); "eternal peace" between Justinian and the Sassanids (**531**); Byzantine–Persian wars (**572–591**)	Khosrow I (**531–579**)
Justin II (565–578) • Apamea plundered by the Persians (**573**) • *pilgrimage of the Pilgrim of Joy (**570**)*	First appearance of bubonic plague (**541**)	Byzantine–Persian wars (**572–591**)	
Tiberius I (578–582) • al-Mundhir given the title of king (**580**)			Ormazd IV (**579–590**)

Age: Period **Rulers** • important events • *cultural achievements* in the **Levant**	in Egypt	in Mesopotamia	in Iran
Early Byzantine Near East 330–640 (cont.)			
Mauricius Tiberius (582–602)			Khosrow II (**590–628**)
Phocas (602–610)		Byzantine–Persian wars (**602–629**)	
Heracleus (610–641) • conquest of Jerusalem by the Persians (**614**); Heracleus enters Jerusalem with the True Cross (**630**); conquest of Syria and Palestine by the Muslims (**634–642**) • *Sophronius, patriarch of Jerusalem (633–638) and writer*		Battle near Niniveh: Heracleus defeats the Persians (**627**); Arabs conquer southern Babylon (**633**)	Cavad II (**628**); Ardashir III (**628–630**); regents (**630–632**); Yezdegert III (**632–651**)
Heraclonas and Constantine III (641)			Arab conquest of Iran (**640–644**)
Constantius II (641–668)			
Islamic Era and Crusades 630–1290			
Birth of the Prophet (c. **570**); beginning of revelation (**610**); "hegira," beginning of the Muslim era (**622**); death of the Prophet (**632**)			
Abu Bakr (632–634) • Occupation of Palestine as far as Caesarea and Jerusalem (**634**); Arabs victorious at Ajnadayn (**635**)			
Omar (634–644) • conquest of Syria; victory by the Yarmuk and final capture of Damascus (**636**)		Battle of Qadisiya; conquest of Iraq (**636**)	Victory at Nihawend. conquest of Iran (**642**)
Uthman (644–656) • capture of Jerusalem (**638**)	Victory over the Byzantines at Ayn Shams (**640**)	Founding of Basra (**637**)	
Ali (656–661) • Caesarea captured (**641**); naval victory over Byzantines (**655**); battle of Siffin on the Euphrates: Muawiya against Ali (**657**) • *Damascus capital of Ommayad empire (661)*	Founding of al-Fustat (old Cairo) (**643**)	Founding of Kufa (**638**)	
Muawiya I Ibn Abi Sufian (661–680) • Ommayad caliphate (**661–750**) • *Dome of the Rock in Jerusalem (691)*		Death of Hussain in Kerbela (**680**)	
Abd al-Malik (685–705) • Fighting among Arabs in Syria (**683**) • *Construction of the Great Mosque of Damascus (708–715)*		Muchtar's revolt (**685–687**)	
al-Walid I (705–715) • Arab conquest of Spain (**711**); battle of Poitiers (or Tours) (**732**) stops further Arab advance into Europe • *Al-Aqsa mosque in Jerusalem (709–717)*		Founding of Wasit (**702–705**)	
Hisham ibn Abd al-Malik (724–743) • Massacre of Ommayads, beginning of Abbasid dynasty (**750**) • *Construction of desert castles (from c. 703); poetry of Abu Nuwas (747–815)*		Abbasid caliphate (**750–1258**)	Abbasid revolt in Khorassan (**746**)
al-Mansur (754–775) • *Construction of Raqqa (772)*		Founding of Baghdad (**762**)	Mukanna revolt in eastern Iran (**778–780**)
Harun al-Rashid (786–809) • *Cisterns of Ramla (789)*			
al-Mamun (813–833) • *Heyday of Arab scholarship*		House of Wisdom (**832**)	**821–873**: Tahirid dynasty
al-Mutasim (833–842) • Break-up into Muslim states begins	Tulinid dynasty (**868–905**)	Founding of Samarra (**836**)	
al-Mutawakkil (847–861) • *al-Farabi, philosopher (874–950); al-Tabari, historian (839–923)*	Ibn Tulun's mosque (**879**)		Samanid dynasty (**875–999**)
Between 900 and 1000: nine Abbasid caliphs • Hamdanid dynasty in Aleppo (**944–1003**); victories of Nicephorus II Phocas, capture of Antioch (**958–969**); Aleppo pays tribute to the Byzantines (**970**); Damascus captured by the Fatimids (**978**) • *Mas'udi, historian (956); al-Muqaddasi, geographer (985)*	**935–969**: Dynasty of Ikhshidid emirs; **969–1171**: Fatimid caliphate; founding of Cairo (**969**); founding of Al-Azhar University in Cairo (**972**); Caliph al-Hakim (**996–1021**)	Hamdanid dynasty in Mosul (**914–978**); dynasty of Buyid emirs in Baghdad (**945–1055**)	Heyday of Nishapur and Bukhara (**904–954**); construction of Ghazna (**999–1020**)
Malik Shah (1072–1092) • Destruction of Holy Sepulchre by al-Hakim (**1009**); Seljuks defeat Byzantines at Manzikert (**1071**); Seljuks take Damascus from Fatimids (**1076**) • *death of Avicenna (Arab. Ibn Sina, 1037); reconstruction of the citadel of Damascus (1076)*	Great conflagration at al-Fustat (**1020**); Badr al-Jamali vizier in Cairo (**1074–1094**)	Seljuks capture Baghdad (**1055**); Seljuk sultanate (**1040–1194**)	Ghaznavid ruler Mas'ud defeated by the Seljuks (**1040**)
Tutush emir of Syria (1087/1078?–1095) • Founding of the counties of Edessa and Antioch (**1098**) by the Crusaders; capture of Jerusalem by the Crusaders (**1099**) and founding of the kingdom of Jerusalem • *minaret of the Great Mosque at Aleppo (1090–1092)*		Nisam al-Mulk murdered by the Assassins (**1092**)	Mosque of Isfahan (**1088**)
Baldwin I, king of Jerusalem (1110–1118) • Capture of Caesarea from the Fatimids (**1102**)			
Nur al-Din Mahmud (1146–1174) • Founding of the county of Tripolis (**1109**); capture of Eilat by Baldwin, breaching the pilgrim route (**1116–1118**); "ager sanguinis", victory of the Seljuks of Aleppo over the Crusaders (**1119**); first attacks by Crusaders on Damascus (**1128**); Second Crusade against Damascus (**1147–1149**); Nur-al-Din defeated at Tiberias (**1158**) • *St. Anne's church; construction of Shobak (1115) death of Omar Khayyam, Persian mathematician, astronomer and poet (1122) construction of Kerak (1142); extension of Holy Sepulchre (1144–1149); Maristan Nur-al-Din in Damascus (1154)*	Egypt occupied for the Zengids by Skirkuh (**1164**)	Zengid dynasty in Mosul (**1127–1175**); reconquest of Edessa by Zengi (**1144**); other successors to Seljuks beside Zengids, viz. the "Atabegs"	Death of Hassan al-Sabbah, leader of the Assassins (**1124**); Seljuks (to **1154**); Chorasmian Atabegs, successors to Seljuks, in Iran (from **1150**)
Saladin (1169–1193) • *Adiliye madrasa in Damascus (1172–1222)*	Saladin in Egypt (**1169**)		
Ayubid dynasty (1169–1260) • Saladin captures Aleppo from the son of Nur al-Din (**1183**); victory at Hattin and reconquest of Jerusalem by Saladin (**1187**); Saladin takes all states from the Franks except Tyre, Tripolis, and Antioch (**1188**); Third Crusade, control of the ports (**1189–1192**) • *Salahiye madrasa in Jerusalem (1189); reconstruction of the citadel of Aleppo by al-Zahir Ghazi (1209)*	Saladin abolishes Fatimid caliphate (**1171**) Citadel of Cairo (**1176**)	Ayyubids control parts of Mesopotamia	
al-Adil (1200–1218) • Fourth Crusade, Latins capture Constantinople (**1202–1204**) • *al-Adil builds fort on Mount Tabor (1210)*	Fifth Crusade (**1217–1221**)		First incursion by Genghis Khan (**1219**)
al-Kamil (1218–1238) • Sixth Crusade, treaty between Frederick II Hohenstaufen and al-Kamil (**1229**); capture of Jerusalem by the Turkic Chorasmians (**1244**) • *construction of the citadel at Sidon (1228); Firdaus madrasa in Aleppo (1234–1237)*	Seventh Crusade (**1248–1254**) Louis IX in captivity in Egypt (**1250**)		Mongols overrun Iran (**1235–1239**)
Mameluke dynasty (1250–1517) • The Mamelukes stop the Mongols at Ayn Jalut (**1260**)	Mamelukes take power (**1250**)	Destruction of Baghdad by Hulegu's Mongols (**1258**)	Hulegu (**1256–1265**)
Baybars (1261–1277) • Eighth Crusade; Louis IX dies in Tunis (**1270**); Baybars captures Krac des Chevaliers (**1271**)			Mongols devastate Alamut (**1260**)
Qalaun (1280–1290) • Capture of Akko and end of Crusades (**1291**)			

Glossary

A

Abbasids: Second dynasty of caliphs. They ruled from 750 to 1258 A.D. from Baghdad, the capital of their empire.

acanthus: A type of thistle commonly found in the Mediterranean region. Stylized patterns based on its leaves were a popular form of decoration, especially on column capitals.

Achaemenians: Ancient Persian dynasty founded around 700 B.C. by the legendary Achaemenes, the son of Perseus. They ruled the whole of Persia, the Near East and Egypt, and died out in 331 B.C., when Darius III was murdered following his defeat by Alexander the Great.

acropolis (Gk. "upper town"): Upper, usually fortified part of an ancient Greek city, where the religious buildings and palaces were generally found.

acroterium (Gk. "outermost piece"): Pedestal for a statue at the ends and summit of a pediment or burial stele.

Actium, Battle of: Battle on the west coast of Greece in 31 B.C., where Octavian (later called Augustus) defeated the combined fleet of Mark Antony and Cleopatra. Actium led to the annexation of Egypt by Rome and finally to Augustus' rule as sole emperor.

adytum (Gk. *adyton*, "not to be entered"): The inner sanctuary of the temple, where only the priest could enter.

ædicula (Lat.): A small temple or inner part of a temple where a cult statue of the deity was installed.

aedicule: The framing of a door, window or niche with a pair of columns or pilasters supporting an entablature and a curved or straight-sided pediment.

agora (Gk.): The central open area in an ancient Greek city where political, religious, and trading activities took place.

Akkadians: Dynasty in central Mesopotamia, founded by Sargon of Akkad c. 2300 B.C. The Akkadians ruled the first territorially large empire in Mesopotamia until c. 2170 B.C.

Akkar: Plain along the north coast of Phoenicia, extending from Tripolis and northern Lebanon in the south to the Tartus region in Syria.

akoimetes (Gk. "sleepless ones"): Term for monks associated with Alexander Akoimetos (350–430). The name derives from the unbroken liturgy that the monks practiced, choirs succeeding each other without a break.

Alexandrian art: Style of classical art centered on Alexandria, which was one of the centers of Hellenistic art in antiquity. Today we are unable to get an overall view or coherent impression of the style, but characteristic features of the sculpture included soft modeling and a uniform flow of folds in robed figures.

Ali: Favorite cousin of the prophet Muhammad, in whose household he grew up. By marrying Muhammad's daughter Fatima he became the father of his only male descendants, Hassan and Hussein. The contested election of Ali as fourth caliph in 656 A.D. led to the split between Shiites and Sunni in the Muslim world.

Almoravids: Islamic community and dynasty in Moorish Spain and north Africa. They ruled in Spain from 1036 to 1147, and in 1062 also conquered Morocco.

Amarna (el-Amarna; Egyptian Akhet-Aten): Capital of Egypt under Amenophis IV / Akhenaten (1350–1334 B.C.). In 1885, the royal archive was discovered here. It contained a great number of clay tablets with texts in cuneiform script. They constituted diplomatic correspondence between the court of the pharaoh and the most important states in the Near East.

ambo: Mostly stone-built pulpit structure in early Christian and Byzantine churches, used for scriptural readings, the singing of graduals and preaching.

Ammon: A district of east Jordan settled by the Ammonites, a Semitic tribe.

Amorites: A nomadic Semitic people that migrated from the Syria region to Mesopotamia in the late 3rd/early 2nd millennium B.C. and founded the first dynasty of Babylon there in 1894 B.C.

anchorites: Term for Christian hermits and reclusive ascetics of the early Christian and Byzantine period who could nonetheless live together in very loose anchorite communities .

Apologists: Members of a group of Greek writers of the 2nd century A.D. who wrote in defense of Christianity.

apse: Semi-circular or polygonal recess, especially at the east end of a church, near which are situated the altar and seats for the clerics.

Aramaeans: A group of Semitic peoples that lived in Syria and Mesopotamia beyond the Euphrates from the end of the 2nd millennium. The "Aramaean states" refers to the kingdoms in north and central Syria annexed by the Assyrians from the 9th century B.C. Even under Assyrian rule, the Aramaeans retained their own traditions.

Arians/Arianism: Arianism is the Christian doctrine preached by Arius of Alexandria, according to which the consubstantiality of Christ with God the Father is incompatible with the belief in a single God and is therefore to be rejected. In this view, Christ was an entity created from nothing by the divine will, but is acknowledged as its "son" to make the concept acceptable. Arianism was condemned by orthodoxy, but became particularly influential in the 4th century.

Arsacids: A dynasty established c. 250 B.C. by Arsaces I, founder of the Parthian kingdom in the Syrio-Mesopotamian plains region. Overthrown in 226 A.D. by the Sassanids.

Assassins: Western term for the Ismailites, an extremist Shiite sect that sprang up towards the end of the 11th century. Their power and influence was sustained by terror and assassination, and lasted until the mid-13th century.

Assyrians: Semitic people settled in the upper reaches of the Tigris. At the height of its power in the 9th century B.C., the Assyrian empire encompassed the whole of the Near East from Babylon to the Mediterranean, including Palestine and Egypt. Overthrown in 612 B.C., with the help of other peoples, by the Babylonians.

Astarte: The goddess Astarte was venerated in every Phoenician city, whether as the goddess of love or of war. In Sidon she was worshipped along with the god Eshmun, in Tyre along with Melcarth. In Byblos she was called Baalat Gebal (the "Lady of Byblos") in line with her paredrus, Baal Gebal.

astragal: A small molding, circular in section, for cornices, doorways and windows.

atabeg (Turk. "father-prince"): Governor of the Seljuk princes. The normal meaning is emir, i.e. a high military or civil dignitary in the administration.

atrium (Lat.): Central room of a Roman house, with a rectangular roof opening.

attic: Low top story or structure above the pediment level of a building, usually adorned with pilasters or reliefs.

autocephaly: In the Orthodox Church, an independent national church that appoints its own head.

Ayyubids: Local Islamic dynasty in Egypt and Syria that ruled there from 1169 to 1250, representing orthodox Sunnite Islam.

B

Baal (Hebrew: "lord"): A deity in the Phoenician pantheon. He is mostly shown as the god of lightning, like the Greek Zeus or the Roman Jupiter.

Baalat Gebal (Hebr.-Phoen. "Lady of Byblos"): A phonetic transcription of the Egyptian title *Nbt Kbn*, which in the 1st millennium B.C. refers to the goddess Astarte of Byblos. The Greeks equated her with Aphrodite.

Babylonians: Population of the lowlands besides the lower Euphrates and Tigris, the heartland of the great Near Eastern empires. Around 1700 B.C., the Old Babylonian kingdom was founded by Hammurabi with Babylon as its capital, but this fell apart soon after his death. After a period of decline and foreign rule, around 612 Nabopolassar established the Neo-Babylonian kingdom. Babylon flourished again and became the most splendid city of antiquity. In 539 B.C., the Neo-Babylonian empire was destroyed by the Persians. However, Babylon continued to play an important role until the conquest by Alexander the Great.

basileus (Gk.): The Byzantine emperor.

basileum (Gk.): Attribute that distinguishes the wearer as ruler, such as the crown of the goddess Isis.

basilica (Gk.–Lat.): In Roman architecture a large rectangular hall, as used in public administration, from which the form of the early Christian church evolved, with a nave and aisles.

bema (Gk. "step"): A raised altar area one or two steps high in front of the apse in early Christian and Byzantine churches.

betyl: Sacred stone that is venerated as the seat of a god and/or identified with him.

Buyids: Shiite dynasty that ruled in Iran and Iraq from 932 to 1055. The Buyids were originally mercenary leaders, and their rule was strongly militaristic, though relatively stable and secure for the Sunni part of the population.

Burids: Seljuk dynasty in Damascus that ruled from 1102 to 1154. Their decline is generally associated with their over-close connections with the Christian Franks.

C

caliph (Arab. "successor"): Muhammad's successor at the head of the Muslim community.

cardo (Lat.): Main street, one of the two main axes of a Roman military camp and city, generally running north to south.

Carmathians (Qarmathians): Secret Ismaili Shiite sect of late 9th century, named after their leader Hamdan Qarmat. First documented in Babylon, whence they spread into Syria, Khorassan, and Arabia, subsequently spreading fear and terror throughout the Levant and Arabia.

cartouche: Oval frame round a king's name in Egyptian hieroglyphic inscriptions, created from the symbols for the globe of the sun and the horizon.

castrum (Lat.): Fortified building with a rectangular ground plan, rounded corner towers and originally four entrances in central positions. This ground plan, from Roman and Byzantine times, originally used for constructing marching or winter quarters for Roman troops, was further developed during the Imperial period for extended fortifications, and influenced the first Muslim fortified structures and desert castles.

cella (Lat.): Main room of a temple, where the figure of the deity resided. Generally reserved for priests. The Greek equivalent of this Latin term is *naos*.

Chalcedonians: Champions of the results of the Council of Chalcedon (451 A.D.) at which Monophysitism was condemned and Dyophysitism was made a compulsory tenet of Christian faith.

chora (Gk.): Land or lands belong to an ancient Greek *polis*. The *chora* included the surrounding villages that were controlled by the polis and provided it with supplies.

colonia (Lat.): Settlement, in Roman times a settlement or city outside Rome and the Roman citizenship area.

Copts: Egyptian Christians, and descendants of the ancient Egyptians. The Coptic Church is one of the independent national churches of eastern Christianity. Coptic art influenced the Mediterranean region up to the Arab conquest of Egypt in 640 A.D.

comes orientis (Lat.): Byzantine civil rank. A top official with jurisdiction over a diocese.

cornice: Projecting horizontal member at the top of an entablature, or subdividing a building and emphasizing certain parts.

council: Assembly of high dignitaries of a church to discuss and decide matters of faith and church.

curia: Council of a city state responsible for administering law and order and taxes, among other things; members of the curia were city notables and membership was hereditory.

D

deambulatorium (Lat.): Ambulatory. The semi-circular or polygonal continuation of the choir aisles round the east end of the church, suitable for processing.

decapolis (Gk.): A group of ten Hellenized cities in southern Syria, designated thus in Roman times and separately administered. The list of the ten varies.

deposition: Archaeological term for the habit of depositing or burying valuable objects in specified sanctified places in order to dedicate them to the gods, or possibly in order not to have to throw away a sanctified object.

diaconicon (Gk.): The room beside the apse in early Christian and Byzantine churches used by the deacons and to keep liturgical equipment and robes.

diocese: Byzantine administrative unit, subdivision of a prefecture. Every prefecture comprised several dioceses, every diocese a number of provinces.

Diodorus: Greek historian of the 1st century B.C. from Sicily, who wrote a comprehensive history of the peoples of antiquity up to 54 B.C. in 40 books, of which volumes 1–5 and 11–20 have survived complete. Substantial fragments of the rest crop up in Byzantine historians.

Diophysitism: The dual nature of Christ. The doctrine of divine and human nature co-existing in Christ, two natures "without confusion, without change, without division, without separation," i.e. Christ is at the same time entirely man and entirely God. The dual nature of Christ was dogmatically made into a compulsory tenet of faith by Christian orthodoxy.

diorite: Very hard plutonic rock, black, dark green or greeny-gray in color, that is often used in sculpture.

dux (Lat.): Byzantine military rank: legionary commander, or commander of the troops of a province.

dynasts: Minor rulers of semi-independent principalities, especially on the frontiers of Roman provinces.

E

Edom: Uplands east and southeast of the Dead Sea which was inhabited by the Edomite people in antiquity. Like the other peoples of Palestine, the Edomites also came under Assyrian, and later under Babylonian rule. Around 126 B.C. they were incorporated into the state of Israel.

emir (Arab.: "commander"): Initially the title of a tribal leader, subsequently military commander or provincial governor.

emporium (Gk./Lat.): Trading place or market place for dealing, especially with foreigners.

engobe: A variety of pottery slip containing a different color clay to cover the natural color of the ware.

ephor (Gk./Lat.): Supervisor, head of a church administrative or supervisory district, who was also in charge of markets.

epigram: Numerous inscriptions on monuments, religious offerings, and buildings take the form of an epigram.

epigraphy: The study of inscriptions.

epitropos (Gk. "plenipotentiary"): The Nabataean kings were primarily priests and spiritual leaders of the people. For secular state affairs the *epitropoi* were responsible, occupying the second rank after the king. (Often translated as first minister, chancellor or grand vizier.)

Eshmun (Phoen. "anointer"): A god of healing who appeared on the scene from the 8th century B.C. Equated by the Greeks with Aesculapius, and also with Apollo. He and Reshef were the leading gods in the pantheon of Sidon.

estrade: Platform one or two steps above floor level inside a room, e.g. to give prominence to a throne.

ethnarch (Gk.): Subordinate local princeling in the Roman empire, esp. in Syria and Palestine.

Etruscans: Ancient people in Etruria, an area in Italy beside the Tyrrhenian Sea between the Tiber, the Apennines, and the Arno, roughly corresponding to modern Tuscany. The Etruscans probably reached Italy by sea from Asia Minor in the 9th century B.C. In the 3rd century B.C. they entered the Roman-dominated areas.

Eulogy (Gk. "blessing".): souvenier from holy site in the form of small devotionals that the pilgrims brought back home. It could have various forms, for example clay or metal medallions or even a bottle filled with holy water.

evangeliary: Texts from all four gospels compiled into a life of Christ.

F

Fatimids: Shiite (Ismaili) dynasty that ruled in Egypt from 909 to 1171 and from there expanded its domain to Palestine and Syria. During Fatimid rule, Islamic Egypt attained a level of material and intellectual culture it never regained. The Fatimids were the only real Shiite caliphs.

favissa (Lat.): Ditch in which the surviving votive gifts of a sanctuary were buried after ritual profanation.

fibula: Clasp or needle with clip for securing a garment.

finial: Ornamentation of an upright structural element such as a tower, pinnacle of bench end. Often took the form of stylized flowers.

foggara/qanat (Arab.): Part of an irrigation system: subterranean conduits that carry the water collected into a central cistern.

G

geomorphology: Branch of geology that deals with the shape and development of the earth's crust.

Ghassanids: Arab ruling family that held power particularly in the 6th century in parts of Syria and Palestine. The Ghassanids were Monophysite Christians and owed feudal allegiance to Byzantium.

glacis: Part of a fortification. Deposit of earth at the outer foot of a wall made from excavation of the moat, though it can also be made of masonry or rock. It is generally the outer defense of the fortifications, protecting the base of a high wall. The glacis is often reinforced with a layer of stone and usually steeply battered. This prevents the wall offering the enemy cover, and allows raking fire more easily.

glyptics (Gk.): The art of carving seals (cylinder seals, stamp seals, scarabs) was an elite occupation in the Near East. Seals were objects of daily use, for sealing documents, signing contracts and closing doors, jars etc. They also served as amulets and were worn around the neck.

graffito: Inscription incised in a wall, or marble tile in which figured representations or ornaments were inlaid in different shades (*sgraffito*).

Gublitic: From the Semitic name for Byblos, i.e. Gublitic culture is the culture of Byblos. In Phoenician, Byblos was called Gebal (modern Jbail).

H

hagiography: Christian literature telling the lives of the saints and the miracles they performed, particularly those effected by their relics and at their shrines after their death.

Hamdanids: Arabian princely family that ruled in Mosul and Aleppo in the 10th century. Politically more of a small local dynasty, they nonetheless achieved fame for their patronage of poets and scholars. They have to this day preserved an aura of brilliance in Arab cultural consciousness.

hammam (Arab.): Bathhouse in the Near East. The Arab world adopted the Romano-Byzantine taste for steam baths, and the tradition still exists in the form of the Turkish bath.

haram (Arab. "the consecrated ones"): Originally the same as a taboo, haram are consecrated places that may normally be entered only by particular people, the consecrated ones. Later, in Islam, *haram* meant sacred places, such as the region of Mecca and Medina, but also the inner area of a mosque.

Hasmoneans/Maccabees: Jewish dynasty that broke the Seleucid yoke over the Jews and succeeded in establishing a Jewish state again in 142 B.C. In 63 A.D., they came under Roman control.

haute cour: (Fr.) Supreme court in the Crusader states, made up of the king and his vassals.

hegira: Muhammad's withdrawal from Mecca to Medina in 622 A.D. This is the date on which the Islamic calendar, introduced by Caliph Omar 17 years later, is based.

hegumen: Abbot of a Byzantine or other Orthodox monastery.

Hellenism: Historical period from the death of Alexander the Great (323 B.C.) to the conquest of the last Hellenistic kingdom by the Romans (in 30 B.C., Egypt became a Roman province), when classical Greek culture was blended with oriental elements to produce a new universal culture.

Herodians: A dynasty of Idumaic origin derived from the name of Herod the Great, who was king of Judea from 37 to 4 B.C.

Hesychius: Byzantine lexicographer from Alexandria, probably from the 5th or 6th century A.D., who wrote an alphabetical dictionary that is a valuable source of our knowledge of Greek poetic diction and dialects.

hippodrome: Horse race-track, usually a double track with a semi-circular end.

Hittites: A people settled in eastern Asia Minor from the 2nd millennium B.C., who established an extensive empire. It was destroyed around 1200 B.C. by the incursion of the Sea Peoples. However, small Hittite kingdoms survived in northern Syria into the 8/9th century B.C.

honorati (Lat.): High-ranking personages in a community. In the Early Byzantine period they were mostly former officials and officers.

Hurrians (Horites)/ Mitannians: a people that migrated from the east to northern Mesopotamia, northern Syria and Palestine in the 16th century. The Mitannian empire was at its greatest extent circa 1450 B.C.

hypæthral: A building part of whose interior (the *hypæthron*) is open to the sky.

I

iconoclast: Destroyer of religious images.

Idumeans: Inhabitants of Idumea, a province created by the Persians west of the Dead Sea in the 4th century B.C.

imam: Prayer leader of Friday prayers in the mosque. Among Shiites, also refers to their religious leader.

Ionic entablature: The *entablature* is the totality of the architrave, frieze and cornice in classical architecture. In the Ionic order, the individual parts are particularly richly ornamented with curved and vegetable forms.

Isis knot: The Egyptian goddess is usually depicted in a robe clasped at her breast. Her priestesses wore the same dress clasped with an Isis knot.

Ismailis: Radical Shiite sect whose doctrine is based principally on the distinction between the outward and inward, such that the outward is the generally recognized meaning of doctrine while the inward things are the real immutable truths that lie concealed within and can be rendered visible by various mystic techniques.

Itureans: Inhabitants of the territory between the Lebanon and Anti-Lebanon mountain ranges, where they founded the tetrarchy of Chalcis, which Pompey made into a client state in 63 B.C.; it was then incorporated into the province of Syria under the Empire.

iwan (Arab.): A hall open on the courtyard side of a building and vaulted with a half-dome or barrel vault. An important component of Islamic architecture.

J

Jacobites: Adherents of the Syrian Monophysite national church.

Jezebel: Daughter of Ethbaal, king of Tyre and Sidon in the 9th century B.C., who married Ahab, the king of Israel. A symbol of paganism and idolatry.

Judea: The name of the southern part of Palestine in antiquity. After the collapse of the kingdom of Judah, Judea became an autonomous Persian province and gathering place for Jews returning from exile in Babylon. Control then fluctuated until in 6 A.D. it came under a Roman provincial governor. Since the Jewish War (66 A.D.), the name of Judea has applied to the whole territory of Palestine.

K

Kharijites: Former followers of Ali who stopped supporting him after the battle of Siffin in 657 A.D. Advocates of a strict, egalitarian doctrine.

Kufic script: Stylized Arabic script

L

Lachmids: Arab princely family in the lower Euphrates region that ruled from the 4th century A.D. to shortly after 602 A.D., when the territory came under Sassanid control.

lapis lazuli: Dark blue, very valuable semi-precious stone, often containing bright, golden yellow particles. Very popular in jewelry in antiquity.

laura (Gk. "narrow alley"): monastic establishment; semi-anchorite form of monastic life in eastern Christianity in which otherwise solitary recluses lived in a loose community, partially sharing a communal existence.

limitanei (Lat.): Frontier troops of the Byzantine Empire who were stationed in camps and forts to safeguard the frontiers.

litholatry: Worship of stones.

loculus (Lat.): An arcosolium or niche tomb, where the deceased were interred. Found in underground cemeteries and catacombs.

M

maabed (Arab. "shrine, temple"): Term for the central building in the shrine at Amrit. It is in the form of an Egyptian chapel and is adorned with an Assyrian frieze.

madrasah (Arab.): A mosque-college with the primary objective of education in the religious law and ancillary disciplines.

magister militum per Orientem (Lat.): Byzantine military rank. Military commander of the troops of a diocese.

Macedonians: Greek people from the northwest fringe of the Aegean who were not considered Hellenes by the other Greeks. Their heyday was under Philip II (359–336 B.C.), whose conquests ranged over the whole Balkan peninsula, and his son Alexander, called the Great (336–323 B.C.), who briefly created a world empire out of Macedonia.

Maccabees: Hasmoneans.

Mamelukes: Dynasty that ruled Egypt and Syria from the 13th century A.D. to the Ottoman conquest in 1516/17. It was established by liberated slaves of Turkish or Circassian origin who had distinguished themselves militarily and administratively in the empire until finally they seized control themselves.

Marcionites: Followers of a Christian sect established in the 2nd century by Marcion that rejected the Old Testament and considered the letters of St. Paul to be forged. They therefore "purified" them and put them together with a tendentiously abridged Gospel of St. Luke to make a new book.

martyrium: Funerary building or memorial church over the grave of a martyr or at the site of his martyrdom.

mazdaism (Zoroastrianism): Old Persian religion founded by Zoroaster.

Medes: People living in northwestern Iran. They arrived in the 9th century B.C. and until the 7th century constituted a major state, which was conquered by the Persians in 550 B.C. Subsequently the Medes and Persians merged and shared a common history.

Medusa: A gorgon. A female monster of Greek legend whose gaze turned the onlooker to stone. She is generally shown winged, with snakes for hair and a face distorted like a mask and with bared teeth.

Melcarth (Phoen. *Mlqrt*, "king of the city"): Patron god of Tyre, recorded from the 9th century B.C. Equated by the Greeks with Hercules.

Mesopotamia: The Land of Two Rivers, i.e. the land between the Tigris and the Euphrates in the Near East. Nowadays most of it falls within Iraq, with a smaller area in the northwest belonging to Syria.

metallurgy: The skill of bringing down metal from ore, refining it and working it. When the technology of forging and copper smelting were added to metalworking in the Bronze Age, this represented not only a further development of metallurgy but also a new age in human development.

metropolis: In antiquity the capital of a country or province, in the Byzantine period, the capital of an ecclesiastical province. The title could also be used of city-states that were not capitals.

metropolitan: A bishop in the Byzantine and Orthodox churches who was head of a metropolis or ecclesiastical province.

mihrab (Arab.): Prayer niche in a mosque that shows the direction of Mecca and is usually very decorative.

millarium (Lat.): Milestone beside Roman roads, set one Roman mile from the next (estimated at 1,618 yards, compared with the US/UK mile of 1,760 yards).

minbar (Arab.): Pulpit in a mosque, mostly with a flight of steps and decorative railings. This is where the Friday sermon is given. The *minbar* is often a moveable wooden structure, but can be made of stone and fixed to a wall.

Mitannians: Hurrians/Horites.

Mithras: Old Persian god of light, giver of fertility, peace, and victory. The cult of Mithras was very popular, especially among Roman soldiers, and spread with the legions throughout Europe and the Near East. The religion was strongly persecuted by early Christendom and suppressed.

Monophysitism: The doctrine of the single (as opposed to dual) nature of Christ, whereby God in Christ and man in Christ are united in a single natural entity. Although condemned by orthodoxy, Monophysitism remained predominant, especially in the eastern provinces of the Byzantine Empire.

motab (Arab.): Podium specially designed for erecting a *betyl*.

muezzin (Arab.): The cleric who summons the faithful to prayer from the minaret.

muqarnas: Decorative element in Islamic architecture, in the form of small honeycomb niches in regular patterns above or beside each other, and mostly decorating a vault or base of a vault. The ends of the small niches look from below like stalactites.

myrrh: aromatic resin of the Arabic *commiphora* shrub that was used as incense because of its scent.

N

naos: Greek equivalent of the Latin *cella*.

nefesh (Arab.): Sacred monument, commemorative stele or monument in the shape of an obelisk or pyramid.

Nestorianism: Christian doctrine according to which humanity and divinity manifest themselves separately from each other in Christ and are bound together only by the bond of love. The Nestorian Church still survives, mainly in the Near East and India.

Neo-Platonic: Further development of Plato's philosophy from 200 A.D. Its most important representative was Plotinus (c. 205–270 A.D.). Besides Plato's own thought, Neo-Platonic writing embraced Aristotelian and Stoic ideas, and concepts drawn from late classical mysticism.

O

Ommayads: First dynasty of caliphs in Damascus, from 661 to 750 A.D.

Ophir: Apparently almost legendary region abounding in gold, whence the expeditions of Solomon and Hiram of Tyre brought back exotic goods to Jerusalem. In antiquity, Ophir was believed to be in India or the middle of Africa.

opus sectile (Lat.): Two-color geometrically arranged floor mosaic.

Ottomans: Turkish dynasty, founders and rulers of the Ottoman Empire. Established c. 1300 on the ruins of the Seljuk state in Asia Minor, the Ottoman Empire expanded very rapidly and at the time of its greatest extent in the 16th century encompassed Mesopotamia, Arabia, the Caucasus, Asia Minor, and Egypt, plus (in a state of semi-dependency) the countries of the north African coast as far as Morocco, and in Europe the whole of the Balkans and a large part of Hungary.

P

paideia (Gk.): Education, breeding, general knowledge acquired from instruction and study, as the purpose of education in classical antiquity.

palmette: Stylized palm-leaf pattern with leaves spread out symmetrically like a fan but with a strong emphasis on the center axis.

panegyrist: A writer of laudatory speeches and poems (*panegyrics*), also the person who recited them.

papyrus: Plant whose stems were used in ancient Egypt and classical antiquity to make material on which to write by cutting the decorticated core into strips, sticking the strips together crossways and then drying them. The finished papyrus was used either as a roll or in individual sheets.

Parthians: Iranian people who conquered Iran and Mesopotamia and ruled them from the mid-3rd century B.C. to the 3rd century A.D. They repeatedly clashed with the Seleucids and later with Rome.

Parthian art: Term for the art of the cities of the Syrio-Mesopotamian steppe (Palmyra, Dura Europus, Hatra) in the first three centuries A.D. Though an eclectic style, Greek elements preponderate over oriental. The style was notable for a certain hieratic character and the principle of frontality. Even when several people are shown, they all appear frontally beside each other, not facing each other dramatically or narratively. The figures are a rigidified version of Greek and Persian forms with a schematic linear treatment of folds.

patera (Lat. "offertory dish"): Circular ornament in friezes shaped like a classical offertory dish (the flat, open vessel, Gk. *phiale*, served for drinking and offering of libations during religious ceremonies).

patriarch: In Byzantium, the patriarch was the head of a group of church provinces. Among the many independent churches of eastern Christendom, it is the title of the current spiritual leader. The patriarchate is his area of competence.

peraia (Gk.): Mainland possessions of an island city in ancient Greece.

Pergamene (art): Art of the Pergamene empire (Attalid dynasty, 283–133 B.C.) based in Pergamon on the Aegean coast of Asia Minor, which was a powerful artistic and cultural center of the Greek Hellene world in the 3rd and 2nd centuries. The features of Pergamene art are a vivid naturalism and a preference for large, well-balanced compositions with large numbers of figures.

peribolus: A wall enclosing the sacred area around a classical temple.

peripteral: A temple whose *cella* is surrounded on all four sides by a simple colonnade.

peristyle: The *periptery* or colonnade surrounding a court.

perpend: A specially shaped stone header used as a cross-piece to bind walls.

Philistines: The Philistines ventured into the Mediterranean region in the wake of the invasion of the Sea Peoples, settling on the coast of Palestine, which was subsequently named for them.

Phoenicia: Here a geographical term, not indicating political extent. The political power of the Phoenicians was broken by the Persians in the Achaemenian period from 539 B.C. The Phoenician coastal cities and Phoenicia as a geographical concept retained their size until 330 B.C.

phylarch: The ruler of a phyle or tribe in ancient Greece. A title that originally described only a duty but in the course of time came to mean the office.

pilaster: Flat decorative wall buttress that otherwise bears the same features as a column (base, fluting, capital etc.) and is often paired with a column (e.g. in a portico) in the same style.

pistikos: Low-ranking Byzantine civil title roughly equivalent to a village headman.

polis (Gk.): Political and administrative structure in Greco-Roman antiquity that survived long into Byzantine times. A *polis* consisted of a city and its *chora*, and governed itself.

Pompeian style: The paintings in Pompeii are mainly classified according to two styles that differ largely in the treatment of the background. The first Pompeian style is notable for highly sculptural imitations of differently colored marbles, with strong color contrasts and a subtle interplay of abstract lines and surfaces. In the second Pompeian style, architecture dominates the paintings, and it is assumed that the compositions are imitative of theater sets.

portico: Covered entrance to a temple or other building, usually carried on columns and open at the sides.

præfectus prætoria (Lat.): The title of a prefect in Byzantium was given for a particular mandate. A praetorian prefect was a top civil administrator whose area of competence was called a prefecture.

prefect: High-ranking civil or military official in the Roman Empire.

presbyterium (Gk.): In early Christian and Byzantine churches a niche for the altar at the end of the choir, where the clergy remained during the liturgy.

proconsul: Former consul who became governor of a province of the Roman Empire on the expiry of his year of office. In Imperial times, effectively all governors of provinces of the Senate were called proconsuls.

procuratorial province: Roman province administered by a procurator or administrator.

prostyle: Type of temple having a row of columns at the front of the portico.

Ptolemies: Dynasty that ruled Egypt from the death of Alexander the Great in 323 B.C. to 30 A.D. All the male rulers were called Ptolemy and were successors of Ptolemy I, son of Lagus, one of Alexander's generals. The most famous queen of the dynasty was Cleopatra (VII.).

pyxis: a little box or casket for jewels, medicine, toilet materials, and so on.

Q

qanat: *foggara*.

qibla (Arab.): The direction of Mecca, towards which all Muslims face during prayer. The *qibla* wall in the mosque is the one showing the direction of *Mecca* and where the *mihrab* is located.

R

Ramessids: The Egyptian pharaohs of the 19th and 20th dynasty (1293–1185 and 1185–1070 B.C.) were named for their founder Rameses I and his numerous successors of the same name.

rapi'uma/rephaim (Arab./Hebr.): Religious site dedicated to the worship of deceased kings.

ravine: In geographical terms, a depression caused by (sometimes seasonal) fast-flowing water.

Re'Harakhty: Egyptian sun god. He emerged from chaos as creator and created the first divine couple, Shu and Tefenet.

Reshef: (west Semitic) God of war equated with Apollo. According to the Greek author Pausanias, who wrote a description of Greece and the surrounding countries between 160 and 180 A.D., he was the father of *Eshmun*, the god of healing.

rhetor (Gk./Lat.): Orator and teacher of rhetoric who had mastered the high art of public speaking. By extension, anyone who had attended courses of rhetoric.

rhetoric: The art of oratory, i.e. effective public speaking, an important part of education in classical antiquity.

rotunda: Central building with a circular ground plan, usually domed.

S

Safaites: Tribe of wandering shepherds who lived in the eastern Hauran. They left behind a large number of *graffiti* (over 20,000 are known) written in a language and alphabet of their own.

Samaritans: Inhabitants of Samaria, a part of central western Palestine. They are the result of the Jews left behind after most Jews were carried off into captivity by the Assyrians in 722 B.C. mixing with the new rulers of the country.

Sanhedrin/Synedrium: The High Council of the Jews in Greek and Roman times.

Saracen bishops/camp bishops: Bishops assigned to Christianized nomadic Arab tribes to monitor their loyalty.

Sassanids: Persian dynasty that ruled from 224 to 642 A.D., when they were overthrown by the Arabs.

satrapy (Persian: *khshatrapa*): Province of the Persian Achaemenians ruled by a satrap.

Shiites: Followers of one of the two principal Islamic confessions. The Shiites look to the 4th caliph Ali and his successors as the sole rightful leaders of the Islamic world and contest the legitimacy of the Ommayad and Abbasid caliphs. Shiites have always been a minority compared with the Sunni Muslims.

School of Antioch: Christian movement of the 4th/5th century that adhered to the dual-nature theory of Christ, which it expanded in argument with other Christian sects.

scriptorium (Lat.): Writing room which in the early Christian period still had the sense of a modern office, but later became a writing workshop where books and documents were set up and copied.

Scylax: Greek seafarer of the 4th century B.C., who wrote a detailed report of his journey to explore the Indus river at the commission of Darius I (521486 B.C.). The descriptions of the Phoenician coast in it are not always credible.

Sea Peoples: Term for a group of peoples that presumably came from the Black Sea region and migrated into the Balkans, the Aegean and Asia Minor. In the 13th and 12th centuries B.C. they attacked Syria, Egypt, and Palestine. In 1177 B.C. they were finally pushed back by the Egyptians into Palestine. The Philistines are included among the Sea Peoples.

Seljuks: Turkic people and dynasty that conquered Baghdad in 1055, took over the protection of the caliphate and thus for more than 150 years were the most influential ruling dynasty in the Near East.

Seleucids: Dynasty that ruled in Syria from the carve-up of Alexander's empire c. 301 B.C.) to 63 B.C. Their name derives from Seleucus I (358–281 B.C.), the founder of the dynasty.

Seth: An Egyptian god, son of Gebt and Nut, husband of Nephthys. Equated in Semitic cultures with the god of thunder and lightning (Baal).

shakkanaku: A Sumerian word meaning "governor." It designates the ruler of Mari, a city in the middle Euphrates, at the end of the 3rd century B.C.

Stephanus Byzantius: 5th- or 6th century lexicographer and grammarian who wrote a comprehensive geographical dictionary, the *Ethnika*, in which he put the main stress of his observations on explaining various forms of name. Unfortunately we only have extracts of the work.

stibadium (Lat.): Banqueting room with benches arranged in a horseshoe.

souk (Arab.): Market or bazaar in the Arab world.

Strabo: Greek historian and geographer (c. 63 B.C. to 20 A.D.). His historical work is lost, but not his observations on geography. He acquired his knowledge of ancient geography on long journeys he made himself and presented in 17 books, which have largely been preserved.

stylites: Pillar saints. A peculiar form of eastern Christian monasticism where an ascetic spent his life on a pillar. The most famous was Simeon Stylites, who spent 37 years on a column, dying in 459 A.D. The ascetic principles of staying in one place (two yards square), of being unhoused, and of renouncing the world were thus taken to excess.

stylobate: Topmost step of the base structure on which an ancient temple or peristyle stood.

Suda: 10th-century Byzantine encyclopedia which contains not only lexical definitions but also many historical comments from partly lost works of antiquity.

Sumerogram: Cuneiform sign representing a Sumerian word.

Sunnites: Followers of the principal (orthodox) confession of Islam, who constitute a majority of Muslims. The name derives from the *Sunna*, the collection of the Prophet Muhammad's words and deeds which serve as a guiding principle of Muslim life.

synthronon: Benches for the clergy along the semicircular wall of the apse of a church, often with an episcopal throne in the middle.

T

talent: Monetary unit in antiquity. Also a weight or money of account of varying size, ranging from nearly 66 lb/31 kg in Babylon to c. half a hundredweight (56 lb/26 kg) in later Attic Greece.

tambour: Cylindrical or octagonal drum inserted beneath a dome to raise it. Often pierced by windows.

tell: Hill with a settlement on it, or artificial mound with several layers of human occupation stratified within it.

temenos (Gk.): Sacred temple precinct in an ancient Greek temple complex, demarcated by a wall or peristyle.

terebinth: Type of pistachio tree from the Mediterranean region which yields turpentine and tanning matter

terra sigillata (Lat. "sealed earth"): Ancient pottery of red clay, so-called from the manufacturer's seal impressed in it. Usually very ornate and furnished with the maker's stamp.

tambour : corps cylindrique ou octogonal installé au-dessous d'une coupole ; il sert à surélever la coupole ; il est souvent pourvu de fenêtres.

tell : colline artificielle, tertre ou tumulus formés par la superposition de plusieurs strates de peuplement.

téménos **:** sanctuaire du temple délimité par un mur ou un portique à colonnes dans le culte de la Grèce antique.

térébinthe : sorte de pistachier ; arbre de la zone méditerranéenne d'où l'on extrait la térébenthine ainsi que des tanins.

terra sigillata **:** terme dérivé du sceau du fabriquant, désignant la vaisselle antique en glaise rouge, en règle générale pourvue d'ornementations artistiques et du tampon du fabricant.

tétraconque : bâtiment (généralement une église), dont le plan montre quatre coquilles, des absides hémisphérique et recouvertes de demi-coupoles.

tétrapole: groupe de quatre villes. Surtout utilisé pour les quatre grandes villes fondées par les Séleucides en Syrie du Nord : Antioche, Séleucie, Apamée et Laodicée.

tétrarchie : ce terme désigne la nouvelle forme de gouvernement introduite par l'empereur romain Dioclétien à la fin du IIIᵉ siècle apr. J.-C : deux empereurs (les Augustes) se partagent l'Empire avec deux souverains subalternes (les Césars).

thalassocratie : terme désignant la culture du règne des Mycéniens en Méditerranée orientale vers la fin du Bronze récent, du XVIᵉ au XIVᵉ siècle av. J.-C.

thiasos **ou thiase :** union religieuse de la Grèce antique qui organisait des fêtes pour un dieu (notamment Dionysos) ou pour les défunts. Les *thiasoï* pouvaient cependant aussi servir des fins économiques. Ce type d'associations religieuses existait aussi chez les Nabatéens, où elles portaient le nom de *marzehâ*.

tholos : forme spécifique de la rotonde antique avec un péristyle concentrique. Temple rond dont la *cella* est entourée par une couronne de colonnes.

thyrse (bâton de) : le bâton couronné d'une pomme de pin etentouré de lierre et de vigne, est un attribut de Dionysos.

Transjordanie : région historique à l'est du Jourdain et dont le territoire correspond, à quelques centaines de kilomètres carrés près, à l'actuelle Jordanie.

triclinium, *triclinos* **:** salle de fêtes, salle de banquet du logement antique, entourée sur trois côtés par des couches (grec, *klinè*). Chez les Nabatéens, on trouve des triclinums dans les sanctuaires ou près des tombes, pour les repas sacrificiels ou funéraires.

tumulus : en règle générale, colline funéraire.

tunique : vêtement de la Rome antique, masculin et féminin ; chemise de laine cardée, au début sans manches, puis à manches courtes, qui descendait jusqu'au-dessous du genou et que l'on portait sans ceinture à la maison, avec une ceinture à l'extérieur.

tyran : homme qui gouverne par la violence ; dans l'Antiquité une forme non légale de la monarchie, contrairement à la royauté. Tandis que les anciens tyrans de l'histoire grecque, aux VIIᵉ et VIᵉ siècles av. J.-C., permirent souvent aux villes de connaître l'épanouissement culturel et économique, les tyrans ultérieurs, aux IVᵉ et au IIIᵉ siècles av. J.-C., utilisaient leur pouvoir sans limite pour satisfaire des objectifs personnels.

V

via maris **:** itinéraire de cabotage qui reliait l'Égypte aux cités-États de la côte phénicienne.

Z

Zangides : dynastie arabe locale dans le nord de l'Irak et en Syrie, dans la première moitié du XIIᵉ siècle apr. J.-C., qui passait pour très pieuse et orthodoxe, et refusait toute espèce d'alliance avec les souverains chrétiens, ce qui leur valait une grande sympathie parmi la population musulmane.

Select bibliography

The Bronze Age

La civilisation phénicienne et punique. Manuel de recherche, Leiden/New York/Cologne 1995

Alexander, D. & P. (eds.): Lion Handbook to the Bible, Oxford 1992

Curtis, A.: Ugarit. Ras Shamra, Cambridge 1985

Garelli, P.: Le Proche-Orient asiatique, des origines aux invasions des Peuples de la Mer, Paris 1969

Huot, J. L., Thalmann, J. P. und Valbelle, D.: Naissance des cités, Paris 1990

Klengel, H.: König Hammurapi und der Alltag Babylons, Düsseldorf/Zürich 1999

Margueron, J. C.: Recherches sur les palais mésopotamiens de l'âge du bronze, Paris 1982

Margueron, J. C. and Pfirsch, L.: Le Proche-Orient et l'Egypte antiques, Paris 1996

Matthiae, P.: Un impero ritrovato, Turin 1989. English version: Ebla, An Empire Rediscovered, tr. C Holme 1980.

Reden, S. von: Ugarit und seine Welt. Die Entdeckung einer der ältesten Handelsmetropolen am Mittelmeer, Bergisch Gladbach 1992

Roaf, M.: Bildatlas der Weltkulturen. Mesopotamien, Augsburg 1998

Saade, G.: Ougarit: métropole cananéenne, Beirut 1979

Yon, M.: La cité d'Ougarit sur le tel de Ras Shamra, Paris 1997

The Phoenicians

Baurain, C. and Bonnet, C.: Les Phéniciens. Marins des trois continents, Paris 1992

Berytus, Beirut 1942

Briquel-Chatonnet, F. and Gubel, E.: Les Phéniciens. Aux origines du Liban, Paris 1998

Bulletin du Musée National de Beyrouth, Beirut 1934 [1995–: Bulletin de l'archéologie et d'architecture du Liban]

Gehrig, U. and Niemeyer, H. G. (eds.): Die Phönizier im Zeitalter Homers, Mainz 1990

Gras, M., Rouillard, J. and Teixidor, J.: L'univers phénicien, Paris 1995

Gubel, E. (ed.): Les Phéniciens et le monde méditerranéen, Brussels 1986

Hachmann, R.: Frühe Phöniker im Libanon. 20 Jahre deutsche Ausgrabungen in Kamid el-Loz, Mainz 1988

Jidejian, N.: Byblos through the Ages. Tyre..., Sidon...Beirut, Beirut 1968–1973 Exhibition catalog:

Liban. L'autre rive, Paris 1998 Exhibition catalog:

Land des Baal. Syrien – Forum der Völker und Kulturen, Mainz 1982.

Lipinski, E. (ed.): Dictionnaire de la civilisation phénicienne et punique, Paris 1992

Markoe, G.: The Phoenicians, London 1999

Martin Ruíz, J. A.: Catálogo documental de los Fenicios en Andalucía, Barcelona 1995

Moscati, S. (ed..): Die Phönizier, Hamburg 1988

Moscati, S.: I Fenici e Cartagine, Turin 1972

Nunn, A.: Der figürliche Motivschatz Phöniziens, Syriens und Transjordaniens vom 6. bis zum 4. Jh. v.Chr., Freiburg 2000

Parrot, A., Chéhab, M. M. und Moscati, S.: Die Phönizier, Munich 1977

Rivista di Studi Fenici, Rome 1973 Studia Phoenicia, Leuven 1983–1995 Exhibition catalog:

Syrie, mémoire et civilisation. Institut du Monde Arabe (IMA), Paris 1993

The Nabataeans

Amadasi-Guzzo, M. G. and Schneider, A. E.: Petra, Munich 1998

Annual Report of the Department of Antiquities of Jordan, Amman 1951

Bignasca, A., Desse-Berest, N., Fellmann Brogli, R., Glutz, R. et al.: Petra. Ez Zantur. Ergebnisse der Schweizerisch-Liechtensteinischen Ausgrabungen 1988–1992, in: Terra Archaeologica 2, Mainz 1996

Bowersock, G. W.: Roman Arabia, Cambridge/London 1983

Browning, I.: Petra, 3rd edn., London 1989 Dossiers d'archéologie (Les), No. 163, Dijon 1991 Freedman, D. N. (ed..): The Anchor Bible Dictionary, New York/London/Toronto/Sydney/Auckland 1992

Hammond, P. C.: The Nabataeans – Their History, Culture and Archaeology, in: Studies in Mediterranean Archaeology 37,

Gothenburg 1973 Exhibition catalog: Jordanie, sur les pas des archéologues. Institut du Monde Arabe (IMA), Paris 1997

Khoury, R. G.: A Guide to the Capital of the Nabataeans, London/New York 1986 Exhibition catalog: Der Königsweg. 9000 Jahre Kunst und Kultur in Jordanien und Palästina. Rautenstrauch-Joest-Museum Köln, Mainz 1987

Laborde L. de, Linant de Bellefonds L.-M.-A.: Petra retrouvée. Voyage de l'Arabie Pétrée, 1828. Précédé de la découverte de Petra de Johann Ludwig Burckhardt et augmenté d'extraits du carnet de voyage inédit de L.-M.-A. Linant de Bellefonds (édition revue et corrigée su la direction de Augé, Chr. et Linant de Bellefonds, P.), Paris 1994

Lindner, M. (ed.): Petra. Neue Ausgrabungen und Entdeckungen, Munich 1986

Lindner, M. (ed.): Petra und das Königreich der Nabatäer, Munich 1989

McKenzie, J. S.: The Architecture of Petra, in: Archaeology 1, Oxford 1990

Meyers, E. M. (ed.), The Oxford Encyclopedia of Archaeology in the Near East, New York 1997

Monde de la Bible (Le), Nos. 14, 1980 and 88, 1994, Paris The Nabataeans. Aram First International Conference, in: Aram 2, Oxford 1990

Sartre, M.: L'Orient romain, Paris 1991

Stern, E. (ed.): The New Encyclopedia of Archaeological Excavations in the Holy Land, Jerusalem 1993

Starcky, J.: Petra et la Nabatène, in: Cazelles, H. und Feuillet, A. (ed.): Dictionnaire de la Bible. Supplementary vol. 7, Paris 1966

Weber, Th. and Wenning, R. (eds.): Petra. Antike Felsstadt zwischen arabischer Tradition und griechischer Norm (special number of Antike Welt), Mainz 1997

Wenning, R.: Die Nabatäer. Denkmäler und Geschichte, in: Novum Testmentum et Orbis Antiquus 3, Freiburg/Göttingen 1987

The Greco-Roman Period

Balty, J. C.: Guide d'Apamée, Brussels 1981

Bowersock, G. W.: Roman Arabia, Cambridge 1983

Dentzer, J.-M. and Orthmann, W. (eds.): Histoire de la Syrie, Vol. II, Saarbrücken 1989

Garnsey, P. and Saller, R.: The Roman Empire, Economy, Society and Culture, London 1987

Gros, P.: L'architecture romaine. 1. Les monuments publics, Paris 1996

Holum, K.G. et al.: King Herod's Dream, Caesarea on the Sea, New York 1988

Krencker, D. and Zschietzschmann, W.: Römische Tempel in Syrien, Berlin 1938

Kuhnen, H. P.: Palästina in griechisch-römischer Zeit, Munich 1990

Lyttelton, M.: Baroque Architecture in Classical Antiquity, London 1974

Millar, F.: The Problem of Hellenistic Syria, in: Kuhrt, A. and Sherwin-White, S. (eds.): Hellenism in the East, London 1984

Millar, F.: The Roman Near East 31 BC–AD 337, Cambridge/London 1993

Netzer, E.: Die Paläste der Hasmonäer und Herodes des Grossen, Mainz 1999

New Encyclopaedia of Archaeological Excavations in the Holy Land, Jerusalem 1993

Sartre, M.: L'Orient romain, Paris 1991

Sartre, M.:
L'Orient sémitique, in: Lepelley, Cl. (ed.): Rome et l'intégration de l'Empire. 2. Approches régionales du Haut-Empire romain, Paris 1998

Schürer, E.:
The History of the Jewish People in the Age of Jesus Christ (revised edn by G. Vermes, F. Millar, and M. Black), Edinburgh 1973–1986

Seyrig, H.:
Antiquités Syriennes, Paris 1931–1970

Seyrig, H.:
Scripta Varia, Paris 1985
Starcky, J. and Gawlikowski, M.:
Palmyre, Paris 1985
Exhibition catalog:
Syrie, Mémoire et Civilisation (1993–1994). Institut du Monde Arabe (IMA), Paris 1993

Will, Ed:
Histoire politique du monde hellénistique (323–30 av. JC), Nancy 1979–1982

Will, Er.:
Les Palmyréniens, la Venise des sables, Paris 1992

Will, Er.:
De l'Euphrate au Rhin, Beirut 1995

The Early Byzantine Near East

Abel, F.-M.:
Géographie de la Palestine, Paris 1967

Abel, F.-M.:
Histoire de la Palestine, depuis la conquête d'Alexandre jusqu'à l'invasion arabe, Paris 1952

Balty, J.:
Mosaïques de Syrie, Brussels 1977

Balty, J.-C.:
Guide d'Apamée, Brussels 1981

Balty, J.:
Mosaïques antiques du Proche-Orient, Paris 1995

Biscop, J.-L.:
Deir Déhés, monastère d'Antiochène, Beirut 1997

Bottini, G. C. et al. (ed.):
Christian Archaeology in the Holy Land, Jerusalem 1990

Brünnow, R. E. and von Domaszewski, A.:
Die Provincia Arabia, Strasbourg 1904–1909

Butler, H. C. et al.:
Publications of an American Archaeological Expedition to Syria in 1899–1900, New York 1903–1930

Butler, H. C. et al.:
Syria, Publications of the Princeton University Archaeological Expeditions to Syria in 1904–1905 and 1909, Leiden 1907–1949

Canivet, M. T. and Canivet, P.:
Huarte, sanctuaire chrétien d'Apamée (IVe–VIe s.), Paris 1987

Canivet, P.:
Le monachisme syrien selon Théodoret de Cyr, Paris 1977

Canivet, P. and Rey-Coquais, J.-P. (eds.):
Actes du colloque "La Syrie de Byzance à l'Islam", Damascus 1992

Dentzer, J.-M. and Orthmann, W. (eds.):
Archéologie et histoire de la Syrie, Saarbrücken 1989
Devreesse, R.:
Le patriarcat d'Antioche depuis la paix de l'église jusqu'à la conquête arabe, Paris 1945

Donceel-Voûte, P.:
Les pavements des églises byzantines de Syrie et du Liban. Décor, archéologie et liturgie, Louvain-La-Neuve 1988

Downey, G.:
A History of Antioch in Syria from Seleucus to the Arab Conquest, Princeton 1961

Dussaud, R.:
Topographie historique de la Syrie antique et médiévale, Paris 1927

Festugière, A. J.:
Antioche païenne et chrétienne. Libanios, Chrysostome et les moines de Syrie, Paris 1959

Festugière, A. J.:
Les moines d'Orient, Paris 1960–1965

Hirschfeld, Y.:
The Judean Desert Monasteries in the Byzantine Period, New Haven/London 1992

Hirschfeld, Y.:
The Palestinian Dwelling in the Roman Byzantine Period, Jerusalem 1995

Honigmann, E.:
Évêques et évêchés monophysites d'Asie antérieure au VIe siècle, Leuven 1951

Humphrey, J. H. (ed.):
The Roman and Byzantine Near East: Some Recent Archaeological Research, in: Journal of the Roman Archaeology, Supplementary Vol.. 14, Ann Arbor 1995

King, G. R. D. and Cameron, A. (eds.):
The Byzantine and Early Islamic Near East, II, Land Use and Settlement Patterns, Princeton 1994

Lauffray, J.:
Halabiyya-Zenobia, place-forte du limes oriental et la Haute-Mésopotamie au VIème siècle, Paris 1983

Maraval, P.:
Lieux saints et pèlerinages d'Orient, Paris 1985

Exhibition catalog:
Mosaïques byzantines de Jordanie. Musée de la Civilisation Gallo-romaine, Lyons 1989

Mouterde, R. and Poidebard, A.:
Le limes de Chalcis, organisation de la steppe en Haute Syrie romaine, Paris 1945

Mundell Mango, M.:
Silver from Early Byzantium. The Kaper Koraon and Related Treasures, Baltimore 1986

New Encyclopaedia of Archaelogical Excavations in the Holy Land, Jerusalem 1993
Piccirillo, M.:
Chiese e mosaici di Madaba, Jerusalem 1989
Piccirillo, M.:
The Mosaics of Jordan, Amman 1993

Ruprechtsberger, E. M. (ed.):
Syrien. Von den Aposteln bis zu den Kalifen, Linz 1993

Sartre, M.:
Trois études sur l'Arabie romaine et byzantine, Brussels 1982

Sartre, M.:
Bostra, des origines à l'Islam, Paris 1985

Tate, G.:
Les campagnes de la Syrie du Nord du IIe au VIIe siècle, Paris 1992

Tchalenko, G.:
Villages antiques de la Syrie du Nord, Paris 1953–1958

Tsafrir, Y.:
Excavations at Rehovot in the Negev, Jerusalem 1988

Tsafrir, Y. (ed.):
Ancient Churches Revealed, Jerusalem 1993

Tsafrir, Y. et al.:
Tabula Imperii Romani, Iudaea Palaestina, Jerusalem 1994

Ulbert, T.:
Basilika des Heiligen Kreuzes in Resafa-Sergiupolis, Mainz 1986

Vööbus, A.:
History of Asceticism in the Syrian Orient, Leuven 1958–1960

Islam and the Crusades

Burlot, J.:
La civilisation islamique, Paris 1990

Burns, R.:
Historical Monuments of Syria, London 1994

Cahen, C.:
Orient et Occident au temps des Croisades, Paris 1983

Creswell, K. A. C.:
Early Muslim Architecture, Oxford 1932–1940

Deschamps, P.:
Le Crac des Chevaliers, B.A.H., Paris 1934

Deschamps, P.:
La défense du royaume de Jérusalem, B.A.H., Paris 1939

Deschamps, P.:
La défense du Comté de Tripoli et de la Principauté d'Antioche, B.A.H., Paris 1973

Dussaud, R.:
Topographie historique de la Syrie antique et médiévale, Paris 1927
Elisseeff, N.:
Nur ad-Din: un grand prince musulman de Syrie au temps des croisades, Damascus 1967

Enlart, C.:
Les monuments des Croisés dans le Royaume de Jérusalem, B.A.H., Vols. VII and VIII, Paris 1925–1928

Eydoux, H. P.:
Les châteaux du soleil, Paris 1982

Lawrence, T. E.:
Crusader Castles, London 1936

Maalouf, A.:
Les croisades vues par les Arabes, Paris 1983

Mazaheri, A.:
La vie quotidienne des Arabes au Moyen-Age, Paris 1951

Oldenbourg, Z.:
Les Croisades, Paris 1965

Pernoud, R.:
Les Templiers, chevaliers du Christ, Paris 1996

Sourdel, D. und Sourdel, J.:
La civilisation de l'Islam classique, Paris 1968

Tate, G.:
L'Orient des croisades, Paris 1991

Indexes

Index of place names

Index of personal names

Index of subjects

About the authors

Pierre-Louis Gatier

is Professor of Archaeology at St. Joseph's University in Beirut and research fellow at the Oriental House in Lyon. His doctoral thesis in 1978 concerned the inscriptions of central Jordan, since when he has participated in several archaeological missions to Cyprus, Syria, and Lebanon. Notable among his numerous publications on the history and archaeology of the Near East in the Roman and Byzantine eras are: *Inscriptions de la Jordanie*, Vol. 2, Paris 1986; *Géographie historique au Proche-Orient* (in collaboration with B. Hély and J.-P. Rey-Coquais), Paris 1988, and *Lettres de Firmus de Césarée* (in collaboration with M.-A. Calvet), Paris 1989.

Eric Gubel

is a curator at the Royal Museums for Art and History in Brussels and lecturer in Art History at Vesalius College, Free University, Brussels. His doctoral thesis in 1983 concerned Phoenician furniture, since when he has done research at the NFWO (Belgian National Foundation for Scientific Research), has advised UNESCO on the reconstruction of cultural treasures in the Lebanon, and has been a consultant to the Louvre for a publication on Phoenician antiquities. Gubel has taken part in excavations at Phoenician settlements in Cyprus, Syria, and the Lebanon, and is co-editor of a dictionary of Phoenician culture (*Dictionnaire de la civilisation phénicienne et punique*, Paris 1992), and co-author of *Les Phéniciens. Aux origines du Liban* (in collaboration with F. Briquel-Chatonnet), Paris 1998.

Philippe Marquis

works as an archaeologist for the city of Paris, where he also studied archaeology. He was a consultant to UNESCO and coordinator of the excavations in the city center of Beirut. Since 1980, he has taken part in numerous excavations in the Near East, the United Arab Emirates, Bahrain, Oman, and Pakistan, the results of which he has made accessible to an international public in a wealth of publications.

Laïla Nehmé

has been a researcher at the CNRS (Centre national de la recherche scientifique) in Paris since 1995. She wrote her doctoral dissertation on the city of Petra, and since then has focused on the two centers of Nabataean culture at Bosra (Syria) and Khirbet el-Darih (Jordan). She is a specialist on Nabataean inscriptions and Safaitic sgraffiti in an old northern Arabian dialect.

Marie-Odile Rousset

has been a member of the IFAO (Institut français d'archéologie orientale) in Cairo since 1997, having previously worked at IFEAD (the French Institute for Islamic Studies in Damascus) for three years. Her doctoral dissertation in 1997 concerned Islamic ceramics. She has taken part in several archaeological excavations in the Islamic world, including Iraq, the United Arab Emirates, Kazakhstan, Syria, and Turkey. Notable among her publications, especially on Islamic ceramics, is her work on Islamic archaeology in Iraq (*L'archéologie Islamique en Iraq*, Damascus 1992).

Jean-Baptiste Yon

is preparing a corpus of work on Greek and Latin inscriptions in Palmyra. His doctoral dissertation in 1999 concerned the *honorati* of Palmyra from the 1st to 3rd centuries A.D. Yon took part in excavations in Dura Europus in Syria and Zeugma in Turkey, and has published various articles on the history of the Near East in the Hellenic period, including *Les conditions de travail de la mission américano-française à Doura-Europos*, in: *Doura-Europos, Études IV, 1991–1993*, Beirut 1997; *Le palais du Stratégie* (in collaboration with P. Leriche et al.), loc. cit.; *Remarques sur une famille caravanière de Palmyre*, in: *Mélanges E. Will, Syrie 73*, 1999; *La présence des notablos dans l'espace urbain à Palmyre*, in: *Actes du Colloque sur les Patriciats urbains*, Tours 1998.

About the photographer

Robert Polidori

specializes in the photography of archaeology and landscapes, always with an eye to the preservation of our cultural heritage. His photographs have appeared in countless international periodicals, including the magazines of the *Frankfurter Allgemeine Zeitung* and *Figaro*, and in *Archaeology*, *Muséart* etc. He exhibits at one-man shows all over the world. In 1990, he received an award for his work from the Direction des Affaires Culturelles de la Ville de Paris, and in 1998 the World Press Award in the category of art. In 1999 he was honoured with the Eisenstadt Award for his work on the architecture of the Cuban capital of Havana. Among his most mportant book publications are *Versailles*, Paris 1991; *Chateaux of the Loire*, Paris/Cologne 1997; *Ancient Libya*, Paris 1998.

Acknowledgments

The photographer wishes to convey his heartfelt gratitude to all those who have contributed to such a far-reaching and complex photographic project as the present volume represents. In the first place, to Olivier Binst, Béatrice Comte and Muriel Tohmé and her family for making the first trip to the Lebanon and Jordan possible; to François Villeneuve of the IFAPO and Ghazi Bisheh of the Antiquities Department of Jordan, also Claudia Vincent of Royal Jordanian Airlines, for their support in the Jordanian part of the project.

Thanks are also due to Mohammed Jammal al Barri for his unflagging daily assistance on the spot. The photographer wishes to thank Pesso and Ronli Avram for their help in Israel and the Palestinian autonomous territories.

Moussa al Houchi introduced the photographer to the beauties of Syria. Osmane Aidi and his team, especially Mme de Chadarevian and Rawa Batbouta, facilitated the journeys in Syria. Thanks are due to them, also to Nabil Redda for the conscientious assistance during the journey.

The photographer is indebted to Guy Bourreau of Kodak France Professional for his generosity – and especially Catherine Balet for her continuous support throughout the duration of the work.

The publishers wish to thank all the scholars who have contributed to the realization of this book. After the authors, we are indebted to Heinz Gaube, of the Orientalisches Seminar of Tübingen, for comprehensive advice, help and corrections in the production of the Synoptic Chronology and matters of transcription; to Astrid Nunn, of the Institut für Vorderasiatische Archäologie, Munich, for advice in the field of early history; to Andreas Schmidt-Colinet, of the Institut für Klassische Archäologie in Vienna for the transcriptions of Arab place names in Syria and Jordan; to Patrick Schollmeyer and Thomas Weber, of the Institut für Klassische Archäologie in Mainz, for help in matters concerning classical archaeology; and to Robert Wenning, of the Seminar für Zeit- und Religionsgeschichte des Alten Testaments in Münster, for advice in matters of Nabataean culture. We owe gratitude to Andreas Fuchs, of the Institut für Altorientalistik in Tübingen, for assistance in the production and correction of maps.

We are also indebted to Hanna Wiemer-Enis for corrections and completion of the glossary, Astrid Roth for extensive research, Kirsten Skacel for correcting the manuscript and producing the indexes, Gerald Behrendt for his assistance with the setting and Annette Ocker for her editorial work.

Frontispiece: View over the Euphrates, Hallabiye
The former city of Zenobia in the Byzantine province of
Euphratensis was built as a fortress by Justinian.
This is a restoration from the Islamic era.

Endpaper: City view of Sidon, 1839
Color lithograph, from a watercolor by David Roberts (1769–1864).
Sidon, present-day Saida, was one of the important Phoenecian
trading cities in the eastern Mediterranean.

© 1999 Könemann Verlagsgesellschaft mbH
Bonnerstr. 126, D-50968 Cologne

Publishing and Art Direction: Peter Feierabend
Project Management: Kirsten E. Lehmann
Project Coordination: Claudia Hammer
Layout: Gerd Türke, Malzkorn Büro für Gestaltung; Bernd Elfeld, e-design
Picture Research: Monika Bergmann, Astrid Schünemann
Cartography: Astrid Fischer-Leitl
Production: Mark Voges
Repro Studio: Niemann and Steggemann, Oldenburg

Original title: *Die Levante. Geschichte und Archäologie im Nahen Osten*

© 2000 for the English edition
Könemann Verlagsgesellschaft mbH

Translation from German: Paul Aston, Peter Barton, Mark Cole, Eileen Martin and Christine Smith
in association with Cambridge Publishing Management
Editing: Philippa Youngman in association with Cambridge Publishing Management
Typesetting: Cambridge Publishing Management
Project Management: Jackie Dobbyne for Cambridge Publishing Management
Project Coordination: Kristin Zeier
Production: Mark Voges
Printing and Binding: Imprimerie Jean Lamour, Maxéville

Printed in France
ISBN 3-8290-0495-8

10 9 8 7 6 5 4 3 2 1

Sidon, April 28th 1839.